The Age of Dimes
and Pulps

ALSO BY JEREMY AGNEW
AND FROM McFARLAND

---

*Crime, Justice and Retribution
in the American West, 1850–1900* (2017)

*Spanish Influence on the Old Southwest:
A Collision of Cultures* (2016)

*The Creation of the Cowboy Hero:
Fiction, Film and Fact* (2015)

*Alcohol and Opium in the Old West:
Use, Abuse and Influence* (2014)

*The Old West in Fact and Film:
History Versus Hollywood* (2012)

*Entertainment in the Old West: Theater, Music,
Circuses, Medicine Shows, Prizefighting and
Other Popular Amusements* (2011)

*Medicine in the Old West:
A History, 1850–1900* (2010)

The Age of Dimes and Pulps

A History of Sensationalist Literature, 1830–1960

Jeremy Agnew

McFarland & Company, Inc., Publishers
Jefferson, North Carolina

All photographs are from the author's personal collection unless otherwise indicated. All pulp images are the trademark and copyright of their respective copyright holders.

LIBRARY OF CONGRESS CATALOGUING-IN-PUBLICATION DATA

Names: Agnew, Jeremy, author.
Title: The age of dimes and pulps : a history of sensationalist literature, 1830–1960 / Jeremy Agnew.
Description: Jefferson, North Carolina : McFarland & Company, Inc., Publishers, 2018. | Includes bibliographical references and index.
Identifiers: LCCN 2018023992 | ISBN 9781476669489 (softcover : acid free paper) ∞
Subjects: LCSH: Pulp literature, American—History and criticism. | Dime novels, American—History and criticism.
Classification: LCC PS374.P63 A36 2018 | DDC 813.009—dc23
LC record available at https://lccn.loc.gov/2018023992

BRITISH LIBRARY CATALOGUING DATA ARE AVAILABLE

ISBN (print) 978-1-4766-6948-9
ISBN (ebook) 978-1-4766-3257-5

© 2018 Jeremy Agnew. All rights reserved

No part of this book may be reproduced or transmitted in any form or by any means, electronic or mechanical, including photocopying or recording, or by any information storage and retrieval system, without permission in writing from the publisher.

Front cover image of stack of books © 2018 Diane Labombarbe/iStock

Printed in the United States of America

*McFarland & Company, Inc., Publishers
Box 611, Jefferson, North Carolina 28640
www.mcfarlandpub.com*

For Dennis,
a lifelong friend who has traveled with me
down the trail of sensationalist literature
over many, many years

Table of Contents

Preface 1

1. A Love of the Lurid — 5
2. Publishing the Sensational — 22
3. Enter the Dime Novel — 33
4. Dime Novel Heroes — 50
5. Glorifying the Outlaws — 64
6. The Rise of the Detective — 79
7. Transition to the Pulps — 91
8. Fantastic Heroes and High Adventure — 105
9. Detectives Become Hard Boiled — 121
10. And Even Harder Boiled — 134
11. Pulp Visions of the Cowboy — 145
12. The Western Pulp Matures — 158
13. Pulps for Everyone — 173
14. Yellow Perils and Weird Menaces — 188
15. The Pulps Fade Away — 204

Postscript 219
Chapter Notes 221
Bibliography 228
Index 231

Preface

Sensationalism
The use of subject matter, style, language, or artistic expression that is intended to shock, startle, excite, or arouse intense interest.—*Webster's New World Dictionary of the American Language*, 1959

Writing in the July 1937 issue of *Harper's* magazine, Margaret MacMullen said, "[S]ensationalism is the age-old need of the uneducated."[1] While this is a valid opinion, it is not a totally accurate one because it should apply to all readers, not just the uneducated. Lurid and sensationalistic writing has fascinated readers of all socio-economic groups for as long as reading has been a form of cultural entertainment. The lure of the lurid, as it might be called, has attracted avid readers to stories of crime, war, pirates, romance, exotic adventures, horror, westerns, detectives, science fiction, mysteries, terror, sea stories, sports, and many others.

Because of their lurid reputation, pulp books and magazines, which are the focus of this book, have been considered by much of the academic world to be inferior literature not worthy of extended interpretation. Not too many years ago researchers looked down on them, believing that the investigation of everyday culture was not suitable for academic study. W.H. Hutchinson, a professor of history at California State University, echoed this view when he said, "The pulp paper magazines [are] looked down upon by any and every right-thinking literary person."[2] A more modern viewpoint, however, is that dime novels and pulp magazines were the forerunners and foundation for much of today's popular fiction. Furthermore, they can serve as invaluable references for researchers looking for information that reflects the popular culture of earlier times.

Although sensationalist and lurid stories have been told and read for hundreds of years, this volume will concentrate on the history of dime novels, pulp magazines, and other sensationalist literature from their start in the nineteenth century to the transition into today's paperback novels in the 1950s. Part of the focus of this book will be on two of the most successful literary creations of American popular reading in dime novels and pulp magazines, the cowboy hero and the hard-boiled detective. Due to the prevalence and popularity of these two iconic figures, the reader will note a corresponding emphasis on them in this book. The western hero arrived in print in the 1820s with James Fenimore Cooper's Hawkeye, was reborn in the dime novels and pulp magazines in the last half of the nineteenth century, was promoted in film starting at the turn of the twentieth century, and persisted into television in the 1950s. The hard-boiled detective (and the crime fighter in general) is considered by many to be the essence of pulp literature. Stories about both of these characters involve an emphasis on violence, chases, criminal activity, the use of guns, beautiful women, and simplistic morals.

When I first started researching and writing this book, I did not quite realize the difficulty of creating an adequate coverage of the field. Rather than not finding enough material, I quickly found that there was too much material. I established early in the project that I would have to be selective in my journey through the main theme. Thus the end result is not an exhaustive study of sensationalist literature in detail, as there are far too many books, magazines, literary characters, and authors within that classification. It is, rather, an overview of the field that presents its background and evolution with, I hope, adequate discussion to place the subject matter in terms of its contemporary culture. I have tried to present as examples a representative selection of dime novels and pulp magazines that are among the most popular and interesting. But I will make apologies in advance to those readers who feel that I have slighted their favorite pulp, character, or author by not including them.

My personal introduction to pulp fiction and sensationalist literature occurred when I was sent by my parents to a boarding school for boys in England and discovered that the school library had books by authors admirably suited to eight- to twelve-year-old boys. Edgar Rice Burroughs, Arthur Conan Doyle, H. Rider Haggard, Leslie Charteris, John Creasey, W.E. Johns, and others from the era of lurid pulp literature kept me entertained for hours, occasionally under the bedcovers by flashlight after "lights out," just as many young readers of dime novels earlier had to do to escape detection. Like other adolescents, I was captivated by stories of lost worlds, Martian princesses, African jungles, fantasy space adventures, and stories of daredevil World War II flying aces piloting their open-cockpit planes across the skies of France looking for the Red Baron. My fascination with this type of literature has remained with me over the years. Though a number of these books and magazines have become somewhat old-fashioned in their themes and use dated prose, many of these authors are still eminently readable and provide rousing entertainment today. Highly appealing to later generations, as well, much of this type of swashbuckling adventure fiction formed the basis for recent popular motion pictures, such as the *Star Wars* and *Indiana Jones* series of movies.

Sensationalist tales can be traced back to scary tales, mythology, and the stories of mythic heroes and their deeds that were recounted around the campfires of primitive man. This type of entertainment was the basis of such classic legends as Jason and the Argonauts and *The Iliad* and *The Odyssey* by the Greek epic poet Homer. I have chosen, however, to start this study at around 1830, with the modern versions of these types of tales. In the early 1800s, few people could read, printing methods were expensive and time-consuming (which made books and magazines costly), and distribution was limited. Tabloid-types of newspapers emerged in the 1830s and dime novels appeared around 1850 as a result of improved printing technology, new concepts in marketing, and improved methods of book and newspaper distribution. The corresponding explosion of sensationalistic popular reading material was created by improved schooling and increased rates of literacy, along with the invention of the rotary steam press and more efficient methods of printing, binding, and typesetting for the mass production of inexpensive books, newspapers, and magazines. At the same time, expansion of the railroads across the country and special mailing rates from the post office allowed timely and cost-effective distribution of printed material.

This new literature was characterized by mass production and low cost, and was aimed at a wide audience of readers, rather than just the elite. It appeared in inexpensive, efficient formats, such as newspapers and story papers at the low price of a penny and dime novels at the price of 10¢, which made reading affordable to everyone. In fact, the name "pulp fiction" was a term originally used to describe the physical characteristics of this literature, as the pages were made from the cheapest grade of pulpwood paper.

Dime novel stories were intended to excite, astonish, and arouse, providing readers sensationalism and escapism. The purpose of this type of literature was to make money for the publisher, so the contents were fashioned for the lowest tastes of the working-class masses. Publishers realized that high profits were dependent on providing readers with a steady supply of thrills, thus much of what they published were stories of melodrama, horror, and crime, with some mild eroticism stirred in. This focus gave sensational literature the alternate name of "Blood and Thunder" novels. American dime novels were so popular that they spread to England and became the "penny dreadful" and the "shilling shocker."

Publishers needed to maintain a high weekly output and sales, so they frequently repeated plots and dramatic situations that had been previously successful, and used recurring popular series characters. In order to maintain publication schedules and a steady stream of novels, stories were produced by writers whose level of output was more important than their quality. Unknown writers were often used, paid as little as possible, and given little or no public recognition. Their work was often published under publishing house pseudonyms, with perhaps two or more writers working on the same series of stories at the same time. Publishers typically didn't want writers to achieve personal fame, as that might encourage them to demand more money.

In the late 1800s and early 1900s, western novels and pulp magazines continued the hero tradition of bravery, chivalry, romance, and excitement that had been found in the earlier dime novels, with lurid tales of daring cowboys, sinister black-clad villains, marauding Indians, and smoke-filled gunfights. Dime novelists helped amplify the cowboy myth over a very short period of time. The formula mass-market western story that continues to appear in paperbacks today has played a great role in keeping alive the traditions of the mythic Old West and continues to spark the imagination of readers.

According to Edward Jay Whetmore, the *cone effect* means that successful stories and novels exaggerate and magnify real life to make it more interesting and entertaining. The results are what he called "constructed mediated reality" (CMR), a process that makes exaggerated stories more intense, violent, and sexy and more colorful than they are in real life.[3] People perceived this exaggerated media construction to be real life and modified their behavior to conform and incorporate it into their own lives. For example, Carey McWilliams remembered that the cowboys on his father's ranch in Colorado read Beadles dime novels about the West and tried to imitate the cowboy heroes described in them.[4] Ironically, life was imitating fiction.

Dime novels eventually faded away and were replaced by pulp magazines. The pulps reached a high point in the 1920s and 1930s but were gradually replaced by comic books, movies, and television as America's primary sources of entertainment after World War II.

Sensationalist literature continued in pulp magazines with titles such as *Argosy, Astounding, Ranch Romances, Popular Detective, Short Stories, Blue Book, Fantastic Story Quarterly, Startling Stories, Amazing, Wonder Stories*, and *Weird Tales*. Though they were considered to be transient literature, their popularity should not be discounted. Estimates from the 1930s maintain that approximately 10,000,000 pulp magazines were purchased every month. Multiplying sales figures by three as a standard practice to estimate circulation, the readership of these magazines would thus have been around 30,000,000 readers each month.[5]

Despite the decreased popularity of dime novels and pulp magazines, sensationalist literature did not and has not disappeared. Pulp tabloids and scandal magazines can still be found at the grocery stores in checkout-lane newsstands. Paperback novels still churn out tough detective and mystery fiction. Westerns are still a very popular niche source of reading material.

One of the difficulties in studying these pulp books and magazines is that they were cheaply printed on highly acidic paper, which made them subject to rapid yellowing and decomposition. They were assumed at the time to be disposable literature. Magazines were either discarded after reading or they soon disintegrated. Because the disposable paper disintegrated easily, many pulps have been lost, and those that have survived are in the hands of private collectors or stored in environmentally controlled conditions that are difficult to access. For example, the study of dime novels is typically concentrated on the period from 1860 to 1910 because that is what is available in major collections, such as the Stanford University collection, the University of Minnesota's George Hess collection of Beadle novels, and the Frank O'Brien collection of Beadle novels at the New York Public Library.

The study of this part of our literary culture can be fascinating in its reflection of the events of the time. I hope that readers will enjoy this look back at the world of caped crusaders, hard-boiled detectives, and romantic western heroes.

1

A Love of the Lurid

As the famous author of fantasy and adventure fiction Edgar Rice Burroughs aptly stated, reading stories of kidnapping and assassination, "is an expression of the normal morbid interest in the horrifying."[1] This morbid interest and ghoulish delight in horrible things produced sensationalist literature that titillated many readers from the 1830s to the 1960s, and still does. This resulted in a circular cause-and-effect. As more people wanted to read sensational stories, publishers eager to cater to the reading public and make more money provided them with expanded and increasingly more sensational lurid stories, which in turn stimulated sales, and the whole cycle started again.

The fear of something horrible happening to one's own person or to someone else functions as a strong stimulus. Fear causes changes in physiological functioning, such as an accelerated heart and breathing rate and increased blood sugar, along with "goose bumps" and "butterflies in the stomach," that can be perceived by some people as pleasurable.[2] The commonest horrors are a fear of death (of oneself or others) and a fear of the unknown. Other common fears are criminal violence against oneself, demons and ghosts, and the existence of evil powers. Though this is a very simplistic statement of a very complex issue, these are the elements of sensationalistic literature.

As a result, readers throughout the ages have been simultaneously scared, revolted, and fascinated by lurid stories of crime, assault, death, thievery, kidnapping, murder, and the associated villains of the worst type. Murder was a favorite topic in Greek and Roman dramas. The use of scary material continued in Elizabethan drama, such as the works of Shakespeare using the ghost in *Hamlet* and the witches in *Macbeth*. Small children have been scared and simultaneously delighted for over 200 years by the horrors of *Grimms' Fairy Tales*.

The Attraction of Real Crime

Sensationalistic popular accounts of criminals and their crimes were prominent in the literature of the seventeenth and eighteenth centuries. By the late eighteenth century criminal cases were being reported with gusto by the press, and Europe and America were flooded with sensational broadsheets and pamphlets about crime. These were "police gazettes" that contained tales of true crime, along with colorful descriptions and lurid accounts of individual criminals, their deeds, and their accounting to justice if they were caught. A particular favorite among readers was a confession narrative by and about a criminal who ended up on the gallows.

Published accounts of crime started to appear in the late 1700s, consisting of descriptions of the crimes of lawbreakers held in custody at the notorious Newgate Prison, which was located at the site of Newgate, an ancient gate into the City of London. For many years the confessions of these criminals were published in broadsheet form, which was a large piece of paper printed on one side and devoted to a single topic.

In 1776, a chaplain at the notorious prison, the Rev. John Villette, who had made a hobby of collecting material on crime, published an account of his contacts with murderers, rapists, thieves, and other criminals, and their often bloody crimes. The book was titled the *Annals of Newgate; or The Malefactor's Register*. It was not widely read at the time as it was published in four volumes, which was an expense beyond the reach of most people. To cater to the common man, the weekly papers started publishing the details of "Newgate Crimes." These were referred to as "penny papers," as they cost a penny. If the papers ran out of factual material, they often invented their own gruesome and sensational accounts of crimes. Though facts were important to reporting, colorful writing was what sold the most newspapers.

This sensationalistic material was also collected for the so-called Newgate Calendars, which published descriptions of crime and criminals, often illustrated with engravings of executions. This type of reading material was very popular as the law at the time was as violent and brutal as the criminals. The prison system was built around punishment and there were no attempts at rehabilitation. Public hangings, which continued in England into the 1860s, were very popular spectacles with huge crowds attending, using them as an excuse for entertainment, drinking, fighting, and general rowdiness.

In 1816 George Wilkinson published *The Newgate Calendar Improved*. Two years later, in 1818, William Jackson published *The New & Complete Newgate Calendar*. The lurid stories inside were accompanied by engraved illustrations of crimes, executions, and the torture of criminals. In the mid–1860s, *The New Newgate Calendar*, which detailed crimes and included fiction as well as fact, was issued weekly. It was quite candid about its focus, as it was sub-titled *Containing the Remarkable Lives and Trials of Notorious Criminals, Past and Present*.[3] The publication sold in large numbers for a penny an issue. Particularly popular also were the so-called "Newgate Novels," which were essentially fictional descriptions of crime and criminals set in and around Newgate.

Nineteenth-century newspapers were typically a large sheet of newsprint folded on itself twice to make a four-page journal intended for the elite reader and dominated by business reports and foreign news. They were sent by mail to subscribers at 6¢ an issue. The introduction of the "penny press" in the 1830s changed journalism and newspapers.

In the early 1800s French newspapers commonly contained inserts describing the worst details of true crime, along with fictional tales and social gossip. In the United States the format progressed from an insert to direct publication of the "story-papers" and "penny press."[4] Weekly serials in the form of a single page of newsprint folded to make a book-like format described crime in a vivid and sensational manner, often using engravings for illustrations. The crime stories were often fictionalized versions of famous crimes, told in the eight pages of each issue. In common with some of the later pulp magazines, the lurid illustrations used by the penny press often had little to do with the stories, but served to make the tales appear more sensational. As these stories were printed in serial form on a predetermined size of paper with a limited space, the story had to reach a suitable stopping point at the end of the last page or be continued. An episode often ended at the last line of available print space, wherever it was in the narrative, and the first line of the next issue might pick up the story with no further explanation.

In the 1830s, the emergence of the penny publications, which mostly published sensational tabloid news and were sold by vendors on the street for only 1¢ an issue, caused the readership of newspapers to soar. The new style of newspaper was aimed at a broad readership and contained dramatic reporting of local events. The articles in the penny press were based on reality, but also contained hefty doses of fiction to increase the drama in their stories.

The first of the penny papers in the United States, four pages long, was Benjamin Day's *New York Sun*, which was established in 1833, shortly after the invention of the steam-powered press. The *New York Sun* was sold on the streets, and was full of local events and stories about everyday people involved in the ongoing daily life of the city. The paper was aimed at the new urban masses, immigrants, and factory workers.[5] To try to capture the interest of people who had recently arrived in the city (and thus stimulate purchase), the *New York Sun* concentrated on stories of crime and violence, along with lurid reports of murders, fires, trials, executions, and other sensational topics. Another popular feature was a daily column that reported on police court activities. This was apparently a successful combination as the paper's circulation rose to 10,000 by the end of the first year. After five years it had soared to over 30,000.[6] Other penny-press newspapers soon followed, including Joseph Pulitzer's *New York World* and Horace Greeley's *New York Tribune*. A similar paper was James Gordon Bennett's *Herald*, established in 1835, which published stories about the ordinary life of ordinary people who lived in the city, and also sold for a penny.

To boost their circulation figures, this new type of newspaper started to publish news of crime, which soon changed into the staple of their reporting. Readers loved stories of the crime and violence that was occurring among the anonymous strangers in their rapidly growing city. These newspapers commonly contained some fictional additions to factual stories as reporters tried to produce the most sensational stories from whatever limited facts they had at hand. Journalism teachers of the time even taught reporters how to make a story more interesting story by fleshing out the facts with lively, imaginative writing. For example, when the *Herald* reported on the story of a young murdered prostitute named Helen Jewett in 1836, the paper serialized a sensationalized version of the story that lingered over several weeks, and embellished the facts by hinting at elements of yet-unsolved mystery.

As a method of boosting circulation, these newspapers often contained stories that were outright hoaxes, such as the story that appeared in 1835 in the *New York Sun*, which reported the discovery of man-like creatures on the moon. It worked, though, as the circulation of the *Sun* rose to 20,000 as a result.[7]

By the early 1840s new periodicals were emerging that published pirated copies of serial novels. During 1840s and 1850s, publishers produced longer stories in stand-alone installments and then eventually printed a collected complete version of the story under one paper cover. Typical topics were crime and justice, scandal, and descriptions of all the sorts of corruption and immorality that could be found in big cities. These small books specialized in lurid tales of violence, crime, and mystery. In England, this type of cheap publication received the nickname of the "penny dreadful" and the "shilling shocker." The terminology came from the name of the English coins, the penny and the shilling, which were used to purchase them. British currency of the time consisted of the pound, which was composed of 20 shillings and each shilling was divided into 12 pennies.[8] Penny dreadfuls were also called "penny bloods," "penny awfuls," or "penny horribles." Publisher Edward Lloyd in London was one of the leading producers of penny dreadfuls.[9] Typical of many of the titles of these cheap publications was *Varney the Vampyre; or, The Feast of Blood* (1847), a lurid tale about vampires.

The British penny dreadfuls often contained romanticized stories about real-life English highwaymen, such as Dick Turpin, Claude Duval, and Jack Sheppard. Dick Turpin was a hero in many of these stories and his fictional exploits were so popular that they were reprinted in American dime novels. The real Dick Turpin was indeed a highwayman and housebreaker, but he was also a notorious vicious and unscrupulous bandit who stole sheep, and robbed and tortured his victims. He was arrested and hanged in 1739. Claude Duval was a highwayman who was born in France, but operated in England. He was supposedly courteous with the ladies, but was eventually hanged in 1670. Another fictionalized and romanticized English thief was Jack Sheppard, who appeared in numerous penny dreadfuls in England. The real Jack Sheppard was hanged in 1724 at the age of 22.

Another version of the English highwayman was the legendary outlaw Robin Hood, who appeared in invented romanticized stories that were published in Britain and reprinted in America. A fictional bandit and road agent who crossed the Atlantic in the opposite direction was Deadwood Dick. He was an American literary invention, but he appeared in reprints in England.

In the 1840s chapbooks, small inexpensive paper-covered booklets of 8 to 24 pages that were sold by street vendors, were the forerunners to novels and contained some of the earliest sensational writing. In an attempt to attract readers, their lurid descriptions often contained narratives about vice and degradation written in the form of self-righteous public disclosures of the seamy side of the city. One such was *The Affecting History of Sally Williams; afterwards Tippling Sally. Shewing how she left her father's house to follow an officer, who seduced her; and how she took to drinking, and at last became a vile prostitute, died in a hospital and was dissected by the surgeons. Tending to show the pernicious effects of dram drinking*.[10] The entire story is almost told in the title.

Victorian Morbid Obsessions of Death

Part of the fascination of gruesome crime stories and violent murders for readers at the time was that Victorians as a society had a morbid obsession with death and disease.[11] A lack of contemporary medical knowledge about the treatment of illness and the diagnosis of death resulted in people being surrounded by both in their daily lives. To further this fixation, popular amusement attractions catered to morbid obsessions about the body with "anatomical museums," which displayed grisly specimens of diseased and malformed organs for public viewing and titillation under the guise of "scientific education." These displays were the source of vicarious entertainment. Anatomical models and displays that dealt with reproductive functions and diseased reproductive organs were particularly popular attractions in these museums, because any open discussion of anything related to sex was a taboo subject in polite Victorian society.

Dying and death were literally close to home. Mortality in Victorian times was high, due to a lack of knowledge of the cause of diseases that were incurable at the time, such as tuberculosis, cholera, typhoid, and diphtheria. Women died frequently as a result of various medical difficulties associated with childbearing. Birth rates were high due to a lack of knowledge about contraception, but infant mortality was high also, and less than 28 percent of women survived to see their last child leave home.[12] Hospitals were rarely used in cases of illness, and child-bearing, recuperation from disease and accidents, and dying, took place in the home. As opposed to modern western funeral customs, until about the 1870s, the bodies of relatives who died remained on display in the parlor until burial for all to see.

One terrifying issue for the living was that doctors at the time were not sure how to accurately determine the finality of death. Collapse and coma from various causes such as diseases, accidents, shocks from the newly developing electricity, and noxious gases were not unknown. Thus, the fear of being buried alive prematurely was widespread.

In 1819 the Doctor Regent of the Paris Faculty of Medicine wrote that one-third or perhaps even one-half of those who died in their beds were not actually dead when they were buried, and the "corpse" had merely been unconscious.[13] Such large numbers seem unlikely, but according to doctors of the nineteenth century this happened with great frequency. Dreadful stories were told of disinterred coffins found with scratch marks on the underside of the lids where the "dead person" had tried to claw his or her way out. Whether true or not, the fears were real, though some experts have theorized that a sealed coffin contained so little air that the occupant would quickly have lost consciousness and died from asphyxiation.

To try to evoke some sort of a response from the newly dead, doctors would stick objects down a body's throat, tickle it with a feather, or blare a trumpet into its ear. Bodies were not commonly embalmed until after the mid-nineteenth century and nothing could equal the fear of the thought of being buried alive. This fear was so great that the Association for the Prevention of Premature Burial was formed in London to combat the problem.

One way to confirm that a person was really dead was to place the body in a special "waiting mortuary." Here the corpse was stored for the period between supposed death and the onset of decomposition. The buildings were manned by watchmen, and had supplies of food and water on hand for any "corpses" that woke up. These mortuaries rapidly gained in popularity and were built in cities all over Europe, some of them even publicly funded. In the 1880s Mark Twain visited one. He reported that each of the fifty corpses stored there had a wire attached to a ring on one of the body's fingers. A simple pull on the wire rang a bell at a monitoring watch station that was manned day and night, with the attendants ready to spring into action if one of the bells rang.[14]

To further combat the fear of premature interment, those with enough money could be buried in special safety coffins. For example, in 1822 Dr. Adolph Gutsmuth designed a "security coffin" that had a long tube connected from the inside of the casket to a monitoring station above the ground. If a prematurely-buried person recovered and figured out what had happened, he or she could raise the alarm. Meanwhile, food and drink could be slid down the tube to relieve hunger and thirst while the coffin was being dug up.[15]

In 1843 Christian Eisenbrandt patented a spring-loaded coffin lid, so that if the deceased woke up on the way to the cemetery, the lid could easily be opened from the inside. This design also contained a hammer for the victim to smash his way out. Another inventor, Adembert Kwiatkowski, developed a spring-loaded flag that could be triggered from inside a coffin to wave above the grave to raise the alarm.

The more advanced later designs of coffins were equipped with bells and some even had telephones buried inside. Another complex scheme used a push-button that was buried inside the casket and connected by wires to an electric bell, so that a "corpse" who woke up could raise the alarm. One simpler scheme to raise the alarm involved a cord placed in the corpse's hand that could be pulled to ring a bell mounted on top of the coffin. The motion picture *The Great Train Robbery* (1979) used one type of such a coffin as part of the plot. As a way to gain access to the express car where the strongbox is stored, a young woman pretends she is accompanying the body of her brother, who has recently died from cholera, to his last resting place. The coffin has a bell mounted on top with a cord going into the "corpse's" hand, where it could be rung if he recovered.

The morbid fear of premature burial inspired stories that catered to and amplified this fear. Feeding on these images were stories such as Edgar Allen Poe's "The Premature Burial," which was originally published in *The Philadelphia Dollar Newspaper* in July of 1844. The story was written in the form of an essay that related several accounts of people being buried alive. As it narrative unfolds, it turns out that the narrator suffers from catalepsy and has a morbid fear of being buried alive. So he designs a tomb that allows him to call for help if he should happen to be buried prematurely. Catalepsy is a medical condition that involves a loss of consciousness and results in an appearance of death. This condition was not unknown to Victorians, as it can occur during epilepsy or schizophrenia, and helped to fuel the fear of being buried alive during a cataleptic trance.

Another example that catered to the morbid interest in horrific stories of people being buried prematurely was "The Bride of the Tomb; or Lancelot Darling's Betrothed" by Mrs. Alex Miller. The story was serialized in *The New York Family Story Paper* from

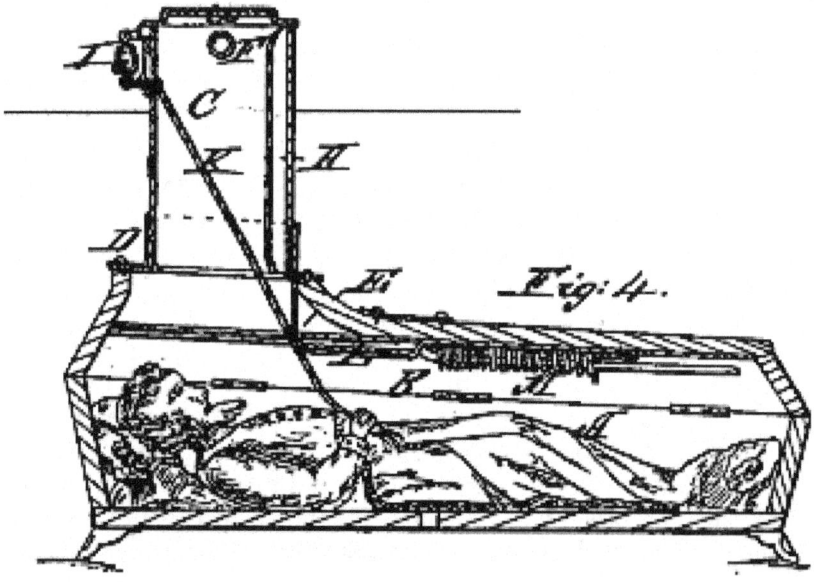

Morbid Victorian fears of premature burial resulted in various models of rescue coffins. This was an 1868 self-saving coffin designed by Franz Vester of Newark, New Jersey. A cord was placed in the deceased's hands and the other end attached to a bell above the ground, so that the interred could ring an alarm if he or she should revive after burial. (United States Patent Office #81,437)

May to August 1881, then republished in 1883 as a full-length dime novel. In the story, the heroine suffers from catalepsy. She falls into a cataleptic trance and is buried before she is dead. A depraved doctor declares her dead so that he can later remove her from her tomb and sell her to another unscrupulous villain. To the Victorians this sort of story was only suspicions confirmed.

Another creepy concern figuring in the Victorian's morbid thoughts about death was an increasing incidence of grave robbing in the early 1830s due to a lack of suitable corpses for dissection in the emerging medical schools. Body snatchers William Burke and William Hare in Edinburgh, Scotland, became notorious by not waiting for nature to take its course, but helping likely victims along by suffocating them. Though the actual number of corpses stolen was small in reality and the practice was outlawed in the 1830s, the thought of this happening to oneself or relatives became another intrusive morbid Victorian thought that continued for a number of years to follow.

Jack the Ripper

Real-life sensationalistic gruesome events reported in the newspapers amplified the insatiable Victorian appetite for reading about murder, mutilation, and all things morbid. The relationship between crime, lurid reporting in the newspaper, and the morbid curiosity of the reading public is well illustrated by the case of Jack the Ripper. From August to November of 1888 an unknown killer stalked London's Whitechapel district and murdered five victims within a quarter square mile of one another. The murders and manner of death created an overwhelming fear among the reading public and was used to create a journalistic sensation. The crime was that five prostitutes, Mary Ann Nichols, Annie Chapman, Catharine Eddowes, Elizabeth Stride, and Mary Jane Kelly, were horribly murdered in London in 1888. Someone cut their throats and used a knife to mutilate four of them. The nature of the crime and dreadful mutilation of the bodies led to the unknown murderer being nicknamed Jack the Ripper.

The first three of the murdered prostitutes were found in Brick Lane, Geirg Yard, and Buck's Row in the parish of Whitechapel in London, which contained some of the worst slums in the city. The murders therefore became known as the Whitechapel Murders, even though the subsequent victims were found in the adjacent parish of Spitalfields.

London's East End at the time was an area of slums inhabited by those living in the most extreme poverty. The poorest families might live in a room furnished perhaps only with a single bed, a table, and a chair. Others lived in common lodging houses, often sharing beds. Sanitation was inadequate or often unavailable. Fresh water came from a common well out in the street that served the surrounding area. The Whitechapel area alone had 233 common lodging houses, which housed 8,530 people. It has been estimated that Whitechapel had 62 houses of prostitution, and an estimated 1,200 prostitutes.[16] As a result, this was the area with the worst of the drinking houses and bordellos that attracted criminals.

Jack the Ripper is remembered because of the time, the place, and the publicity. At the time, London claimed to be the center of the civilized world, so this series of sordid crimes, particularly with its sexual element, attracted unprecedented coverage by the press. The murders were widely, though not necessarily accurately, reported in lurid tones in newspapers, broadsheets, and penny dreadfuls. The reporters drew on the familiar Victorian conventions of popular melodrama and Gothic horror. One headline shouted out, "Horrible Murder by the Monster of the East-End." The fact that the crimes appeared to be lust murders involving women made it even more thrilling to readers. Through this publicity, the Ripper became the original model for a sex murderer, even though he did not rape his victims.

Victorians were nervous yet fascinated with this crime and the penny dreadfuls catered to their morbid fascination. Volume II, Number 15 of *Famous Crimes* magazine (subtitled "Past and Present" in the "Police Budget Edition") contained a description of Jack the Ripper's first murder, complete with a drawing that showed a woman's corpse lying on the ground and a man looking at it, holding his head in horror as he discovers the body. Newspapers were happy to print as many lurid details as they could, though some critics suggested that a few unscrupulous journalists may have planted some of their own evidence in order to produce exclusive reporting and keep the story going.[17]

The sensationalistic newspaper accounts of the time were the reason that the memory of Jack the Ripper and his crimes are still familiar today. Though other dreadful crimes occurred around the same time, a lack of publicity has left them forgotten. For example, in Austin, Texas, between late December 1884 and December 1885, a man nicknamed the Texas Ripper killed nine women in a series of sex murders. These crimes were not as well publicized in the newspapers as Jack the Ripper, thus the murder remains virtually unknown, even in America.

Another Victorian serial killer, who never gained the notoriety of Jack the Ripper because he never received the amount of newsprint publicity that the Ripper did, was Dr. Neill Cream. Cream was a nineteenth century poisoner who practiced medicine in Chicago. After a number of his patients died in mysterious circumstances, he was tried for murder and was sent to prison. After he was released in July of 1891, he left for England. While there, on October 13, 1891, he reverted to his old ways and started to murder prostitutes in the Lambeth area of central London. This eventually gave him the nickname of the Lambeth Poisoner. His technique was to offer a prostitute a capsule that he said was an aphrodisiac, but which in reality was filled with strychnine. He murdered at least four young women in this way. His deadly scheme came to an end after eight months, when he was identified by a woman who had thrown away the capsule he gave to her.

The Jack the Ripper murders occurred at a time when there was an increase in the number of newspapers that were struggling against each other for circulation numbers. It was the intensive newspaper coverage of the crimes that turned them into a national sensation and, ultimately, into an international sensation. Broadsheets that appeared on the streets whipped up the hysteria with sensationalistic headlines such as "Ghastly Murder in the East End. Dreadful Mutilation of a Woman." The cover of *The Penny Illustrated Paper and Illustrated Times* for September 8, 1888, published in London, showed a sketch of a policeman finding the murdered Mary Ann Nichols, with the accompanying text crying out, "East London has a terror that must be stamped out." The cover of another example of the penny press that reported the murders, *The Illustrated Police News* for October 20, 1888, is illustrated with a series of sketches that showed the image of Jack the Ripper as conceived by an artist at the newspaper. One panel shows one of the victims with wounds on her face and neck, another shows the murderer (labeled "The Whitechapel Monster") with his victims, and yet another the dismembered corpse on a mortuary table with doctors trying to identify a missing limb.

Even after the Ripper murders had ended, newspaper reporters filed lengthy "reports" for weeks afterwards that simply rehashed and sensationalized every rumor and theory they could think of about the crimes. Three years after the murders ended, *The Illustrated Police News* for March 7, 1891, was still blared out the headline, "Is the Whitechapel Mystery the work of Jack the Ripper?" in large type, blaming the Ripper for other crimes. Even the methods of the police were brought under close scrutiny and fashioned into the subject of intense debate by reporters who claimed that the public was not happy with the lack of results. As time went on, fueled by these continuing lurid newspaper articles, Jack the Ripper's crimes became more horrifying as they were retold and retold. There were whispered reports of more murders, they became more gruesome, and the number of victims increased. The Ripper was reported to have been seen loose throughout England in the Midlands, the North, and beyond. Some newspaper sightings supposedly placed him in Ireland. The effect was reminiscent of today's "sightings" of Elvis that positively place him all over the country.

The terror instilled by Ripper legends became so great that women were sure they were going to be visited by the fiend. For years afterwards, women living alone locked, bolted, and barred their doors. To capitalize on this fear, Mrs. Belloc Lowndes wrote a sensationalized novel based on the Jack the Ripper murders titled *The Lodger* (1913). In it she captured the fear and horror that surrounded the murders. Spurred on by the book's popularity, she went on to novelize other famous crimes. She also tried her hand at purely fictional tales with books about Milly, a member of the British Parliament and a part-time detective.

The Ripper murders were never solved and the identity of the culprit still remains unknown. But books about the Ripper continue to be published today with each author presenting the "true story" and claiming to prove the real identity of the Ripper.

White Slavery

Another morbid Victorian fear was the horror instilled in women of being abducted into what was called "white slavery." Stories were whispered of how procurers lurked in small towns looking for naive young women. They would promise the women jobs in the big city as maids, seamstresses, actresses, and governesses, or even propose marriage. These unwary girls would supposedly be drugged with opium or plied with liquor until they passed out, only to wake up trapped in a brothel, often without their clothing or shoes. Women felt threatened yet thrilled by these stories, and loved to read about white slavery in sensational publications such as the *Pall Mall Gazette* in London.

The term "white slavery" is attributed to Clifford G. Roe, the Illinois assistant state's attorney. Supposedly Roe was involved in a case where a girl had thrown a note out of the window of a brothel that read, "Help me—I am held captive as a white slave." The term, however, more likely originated from translation of the French *Traite des Blanches*, or "Traffic in Whites," used at a 1902 conference in Paris, France, which discussed the problems of international trade in women and children, to distinguish it from *Traite des Noirs*, or "Traffic in Blacks," the traditional black slaves. The term "white slavery" was originally applied to trafficking in people, not all of whom were slaves. The term was later commonly used for the procuring of women for prostitution.

Lurid tales of white slavery were widely repeated by mothers to frighten their daughters and to impress and horrify young women. Self-proclaimed authorities on the subject knowingly wrote that white slavery was supposedly the work of a powerful international conspiracy that was run by sinister foreigners. Reports with little evidence to back them up declared the existence of a large international traffic in young women who had been kidnapped and moved from country to country for the purposes of prostitution. As will be seen in a later chapter, this was one offshoot of The Yellow Peril fear that was sweeping the country at the time. These tales of women being forcibly kept hostage against their will was also a retelling of the Indian captivity narratives that haunted the first dime novels.

The white slavery hysteria appears to have originated with an article in *McClure's* magazine in 1907. In it, muckraking journalist George Kibbe Turner claimed that women were being kidnapped by an organization of evil immigrants. Clifford Roe took up the hue and cry. He quoted numbers that grew with the hysteria and rose to over 60,000 young women being kidnapped each year, even though no such numbers were being reported to the police or could be verified.[18]

The first American law aimed at white slavery was passed by the Illinois legislature in 1908 and Roe's campaign was largely responsible for federal legislation called the "White Slave Traffic Act," or the "Mann Act," in 1910. This act, introduced by Congressman James Mann of Illinois, provided heavy penalties for the interstate transportation of a woman.

Meanwhile, the paranoia of white slavery was kept at fever-pitch by books such as *Fighting the Traffic in Young Girls: or War on the White Slave Trade* (subtitled *The Greatest Crime in the World's History*), published in 1910 by evangelist Rev. Ernest A. Bell, founder and superintendent of the Midnight Mission in Chicago. The book eventually sold more than 400,000 copies. It warned explicitly of the author's perception of the dangers to young women to be found in ice cream parlors, theatrical agencies, railway stations, and dances. He wrote fervently that such places could lead a young woman to become "immodest, indecent, lawless.... And [a] distributor of vile diseases." Americans, particularly women, became panic stricken. Moral panic ensued and an alarmist mentality linked stories of white slavery to immigration and racial purity in rising impassioned rhetoric.

As grim as these stories sounded, verifiable incidents of white slavery involving respectable American women actually taking place appeared to be very small and, as with all such sensational stories, their incidence and significance was blown out of proportion. white slavery was never the menace to the average woman that it was supposed to have been, and eventually the paranoia and panic faded away. In spite of this, the reading public developed an appetite for tales of white slavery and multiple murders.

These stories, and the fact that they were believed by a gullible section of the reading public, is evidence of the concept of "selective exposure," or that we expose ourselves to information that reinforces, rather than contradicts, our beliefs or opinions. Psychologists know that through this "selective perception," we tend to hear and believe what we want to hear and believe. Thus, in a type of national hysteria, these stories of kidnapping were thought to be real. The overblown stories that appeared in the press were simply looked upon as suspicions confirmed.

Horror and the Supernatural in Literature

Sensationalistic horror stories were another way for Victorian and Edwardian readers to frighten themselves. Horror is the feeling of shock and revulsion brought on by witnessing a scary or nasty event. Terror is the dread that precedes the horrible event. Put another way, Rogers Terrill, the editor of *Dime Mystery Magazine* from Popular Publications, concisely summed up the difference when he said, "Horror is the emotion you feel when you see something awful happening to someone else; terror is what you feel when the something is about to happen to you."[19] Many enjoyed the thrill of a scary story and the resulting sensation of fear and goosebumps.

The origin of tales of horror goes back beyond recorded history to when early man's instincts and emotions were influenced by the environment in which he found himself. He could not understand most of nature's workings and attributed them to the supernatural, worshipping them with sensations of awe and fear. The intensity of the emotion of horror makes it successful for escapist reading, and enjoyment by audiences shows that people enjoy being scared out of their wits. The more intense our response, the more the story takes us away from the humdrum of our everyday existence.

Stories of horror and terror have long been an ingredient of archaic ballads and writings. The Middle Ages produced a dark heritage of folklore associated with ceremonial magic and demons, including witches, werewolves, vampires and other ghouls. Stories were told of satanic worship, black masses, and witches' sabbaths in lonely woods and remote hills. Much of this was based on rites performed by cults of worshippers rooted in fertility beliefs. The result was stories such as *Grimm's Fairy Tales*. Such myths and legends were later combined into the type of stories that appeared in the weird menace pulps that will be discussed later.

Creepy sensationalistic stories, such as Bram Stoker's *Dracula*, titillated Victorian readers at the same time that they frightened them. Stories featured atmospheric settings, such as ruined castles, lonely countryside, foggy British surroundings, and graveyards with trees dripping with rain. To add to the thrill, such places really existed. These are the fog-enshrouded ruins of Whitby Abbey on the coast of Yorkshire where Dracula's ship was supposedly wrecked and set the evil count free to roam England.

The basic form of the novel was developed in the eighteenth century. One of the first science-related fantasy novels was *Frankenstein; or, the Modern Prometheus* (1817) by Mary Wollstonecraft Shelley, the 19-year-old wife of English poet Percy Bysshe Shelley. She wrote the story after she and a group of her friends had been reading eerie stories and four of them decided to each write a ghost story. Her book about the creation of life from inanimate material became the prototype of grotesque horror novels. She subsequently wrote other novels, such as the post-apocalyptic novel *Last Man* (1826) about a plague, but never achieved the same success as her first novel.

An alien being that cannot be explained, such as Frankenstein's monstrous creation, is one of the strangest and most frightening forms of the horror story. Many of such stories revolve around some horrible and terrifying monster and its the ultimate destruction, such as The Thing or Dracula, the vampire count from Transylvania who appears in Bram Stoker's *Dracula* (1897).

Other sensationalistic Gothic romantic novels came from authors such as Joseph Sheridan LeFanu, Wilkie Collins, and Robert Louis Stevenson. Stephenson wrote the classic horror tale the *Strange Case of Dr. Jekyll and Mr. Hyde* (1886). He also wrote the lesser-known *The Black Arrow* (1888), *The Wrong Box* (1889), and other novels and short stories. Washington Irving and Nathaniel Hawthorne wrote stories with eerie themes. *The House of the Seven Gables* (1851) by Hawthorne is about an ancestral curse set against a sinister background. Journalist Gaston Leroux, who had traveled in Europe and Africa before turning to writing fiction, wrote a series of mysteries and thriller full of bizarre sensationalism and frightening thrills. His most famous work was *The Phantom of the Opera* (1911) about a disfigured, masked creature who haunts the Paris Opera House and kidnaps one of the singers and forces her to sing for him. Leroux also wrote *The Man Who Came Back from the Dead* (1916), and *The Mystery of the Yellow Room* (1908), which was one of the first and most ingenious of the murder-in-a-locked-room mystery puzzles.

Many of these stories are about the kidnapping and mistreatment of women, a topic that appealed to Victorian morbid fears. Stories such as this have always been immensely popular. The story of Stoker's *Dracula* (1897), which has been described as "the weirdest of weird tales," is about the power of a vampire over several women. Women readers vicariously enjoyed the thrills in the book as it catered to fears of being captured and seduced by the vampire.[20] Stoker's most famous novel is his story about the horror of vampires, but he also wrote nine other novels with grotesque concepts, such as *The Lair of the White Worm* (1911), about a giant unknown entity that lurks in a vault beneath an ancient castle. He remains best known for his macabre creation of the vampire count and his victims, and Stoker's other novels are all but forgotten today.

Vampires, such as *Dracula* (1897) and *Varney the Vampire* (1847), are described as attacking females in a manner and situation that is the equivalent of vampire rape. Hints of rape and domination are at the core of *The Sheik* (1919), a best-selling novel by British romance writer E.M. (Edith Maud) Hull. This is the sensationalized tale of an Englishwoman in the desert wastes of North Africa, who is taken captive by a handsome Arab tribal leader and becomes his plaything. Despite herself, she at last becomes his willing and adoring lover. This was lurid reading in 1919, with off-stage rape (between chapters two and three), the taboo subject of female desire, and supposed interracial sex. Readers loved it and the story became a star-making vehicle for actor Rudolph Valentino as the menacing desert lover in leather riding boots and a burnoose in the film version of *The Sheik* (1921).

National Police Gazette

One of the newspapers that published the most scandalous, but extremely popular, stories was the *National Police Gazette*. Sensational stories dealing with scandal and sex had been featured in other mid-nineteenth century magazines, but most of them were either fictionalized or were totally fictitious. Stories reported in the *National Police Gazette* were about real crime and real scandal. Americans were fascinated by stories of crime and sex, and wanted to know all the gruesome details. The newspaper created a new type of pornography by describing and hinting at sex, while at the same time sternly moralizing about it.

The *National Police Gazette*, more commonly known simply as the *Police Gazette* was founded in New York in 1845 by two journalists, Enoch Camp and George Wilkes. Its stated mission was to expose and describe the sins of America and then criticize them with a good dose of moral judgment. The newspaper claimed that its articles, editorials, and stories of crime and criminals provided moral guidance to inform and protect the innocent reader. Describing vice and wickedness in detail to titillate the reader, then taking a stance and moralizing against it was one of the popular ways to rationalize lurid and sensationalized newspaper reporting. The moralizing at the end of the story made the preceding lurid descriptions seem acceptable. For example, one newspaper in San Francisco published details of the city's brothels and their locations so that the reader could be sure to know where avoid them. This same hypocritical technique was used later to avoid the Hays Code in lurid movies made in the 1930s. A movie would show each erotic detail of an immoral situation, then the protagonists had to face retribution at the end to make the previous wickedness acceptable.

Camp and Wilkes sold the *Police Gazette* to George Matsell in 1866. After 1877, when the *Police Gazette* blossomed even further as a scandal magazine, it was owned by journalist, editor, and publisher Richard Kyle Fox, a man who showed excellent intuitive judgment for what the public wanted. Fox's formula was the sensational reporting of crime and human interest stories, accompanied by dramatic illustrations. Fox molded the *Police Gazette* into an illustrated tabloid-type of publication that specialized in lurid coverage of the underside of Victorian America, such as murders, lawless happenings in the Wild West, and scandalous events that involved women. The newspaper promised its readers "a most interesting record of horrid murders, outrageous robberies ... hideous rapes, vulgar seductions." Fox also focused on sports and the theater with a sports page and a gossip column.

Typical Wild West stories in the *Gazette* concentrated on the contemporary violence and killing in Texas caused by marauding bands of outlaws, and raids by Comanche and Kiowa warriors after the Civil War. The West was indeed violent in the late nineteenth century, following the Civil War, but the East was just as violent. Fox included lynchings, xenophobic stories about the Chinese, and the scandalous doings of notorious women. The *Police Gazette* reported every crime it could find, whether it was in the North, East, South, or West. By focusing on these types of stories, Fox turned the *Police Gazette* into an immensely popular weekly magazine in the East, with nationwide circulation through subscription.

By the end of the Civil War, his stories were illustrated by woodcuts. Engravings in the *Police Gazette* usually combined the themes of sex, sin, crime, scandal, and moralism in each picture.[21] After 1878, suggestive pictures appeared in the magazine regularly, along

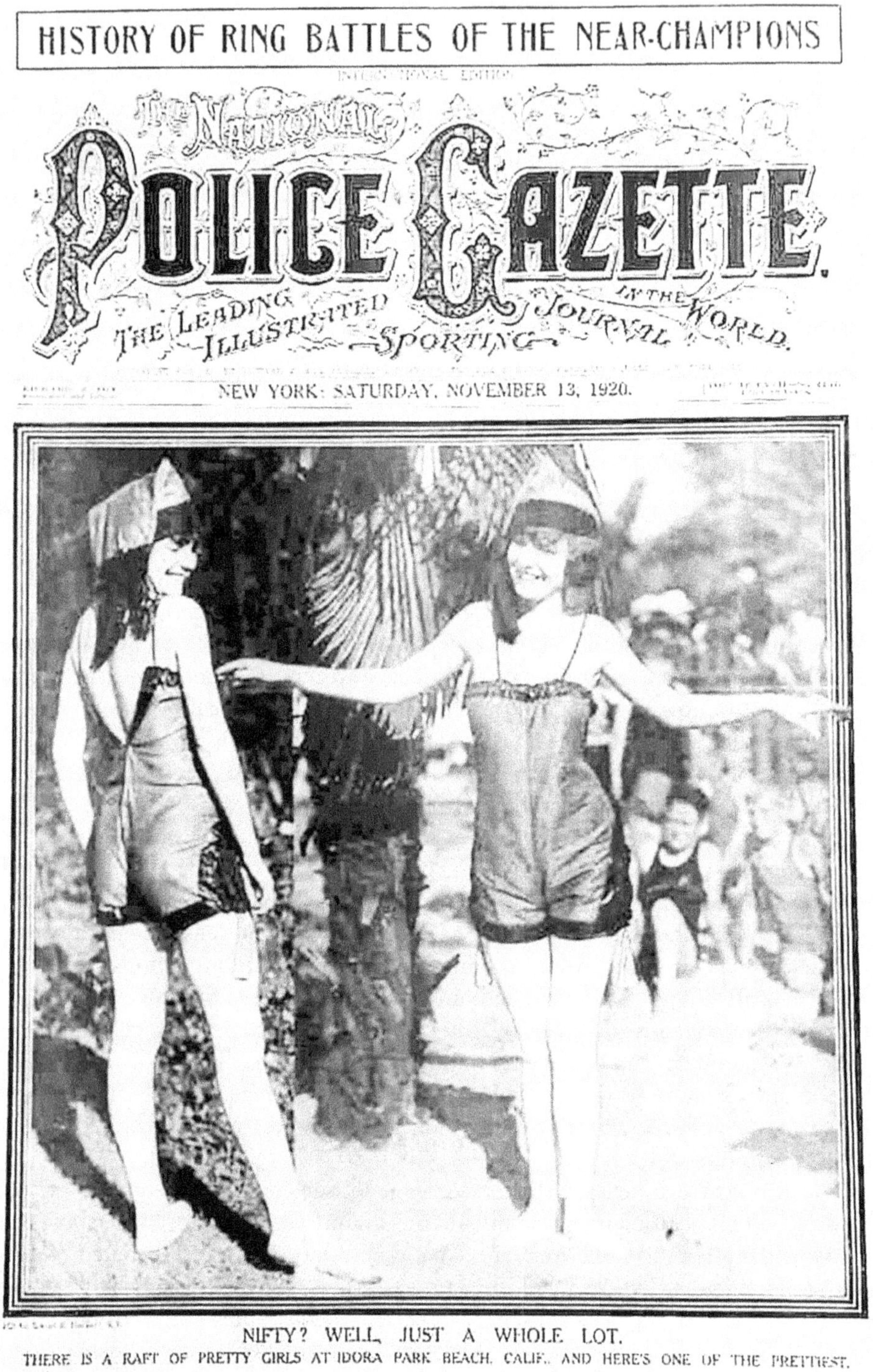

HISTORY OF RING BATTLES OF THE NEAR-CHAMPIONS

The National Police Gazette

The Leading Illustrated Sporting Journal in the World.

NEW YORK: SATURDAY, NOVEMBER 13, 1920.

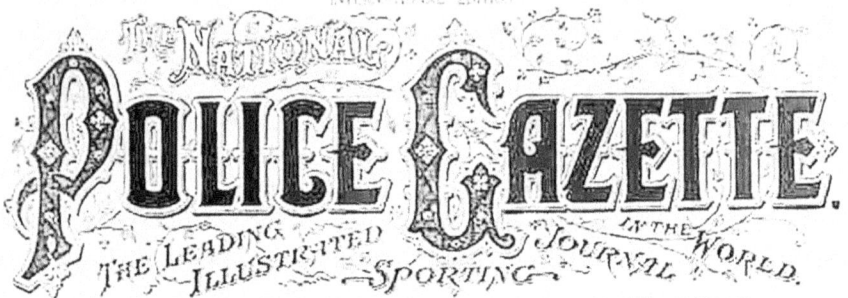

NIFTY? WELL, JUST A WHOLE LOT.

THERE IS A RAFT OF PRETTY GIRLS AT IDORA PARK BEACH, CALIF., AND HERE'S ONE OF THE PRETTIEST.

The *National Police Gazette* was a sensationalistic tabloid newspaper that reported on the most lurid (and at the same time the most popular) stories dealing with real crime and real scandal. The *Police Gazette* specialized in sensational coverage of the seamy side of Victorian America, such as sordid events in the Wild West, murders, and scandalous events that involved women. The paper later added racy (for the day) pictures of burlesque queens in tights and bathing girls in bloomers, such as this cover from 1920.

with exposés of New York's most unsavory brothels. The paper was well known for its racy engravings and photographs of actresses, burlesque dancers, prostitutes, and strippers, along with sports figures, racehorses, and fighting animals.

In 1880 the *Police Gazette* started to report on stories of the New York theater, mostly by featuring popular actresses in tights. In the 1890s, these bawdy pictures and "spicy" stories of burlesque queens and actresses were standard features. In a doubly scandalous illustration, for example, the cover of the *Police Gazette* for November 15, 1879, showed a female tattoo artist creating a design on the leg of a high-class prostitute. The paper even published picture supplements of actresses and athletes. The photographs of women were advertised as the "snappiest of all girl pictures."

This type of "leg art" also appeared in other magazines of the time. *Munsey's* magazine, for example, published similar articles on performers, with some of the articles written by publisher Frank Munsey himself. He described theater activities and used photographs to illustrate articles such as "Plays and Players of the Day," "Stage Favorites," and "Types of Beauties." In the mid–1890s the magazine even featured nude and seminude pictures. Some of the pictures pushed the edge of the contemporary legal limits of obscenity.

Around the turn of the century, *Nickell Magazine* also featured articles on the theater, including gossip about leading actresses and their photographs. This magazine also published nude art and "snappy stories." In the mid–1890s, *Metropolitan Magazine* printed many similar pictures of dancers, artists' models, bathing beauties, and "naughty" French music-hall singers, though in 1898 it changed to become a more respectable literary magazine. In the early 1900s *Broadway Magazine* published pictures of burlesque queens in tights and bathing girls in bloomers. These pictures were widely regarded as shocking, but the size of the magazine's circulation showed that the public was attracted to that type of "art."[22]

In 1878 the *Police Gazette* started printing its issues on lurid pink paper to try to differentiate itself and stand out from the others. The tabloid was widely available in saloons and cheap hotels. Its greatest distribution, though, was in barbershops, where it became known as the "barbershop bible." This lasted until 1922 when women of the roaring twenties started to have their hair bobbed in barbershops. The *Police Gazette* and magazines like it were removed so as not to offend female customers.

The *Police Gazette*'s circulation declined after World War I and Fox died in 1922. By that time newspapers had changed and were trying to increase their circulation figures by intense reporting of crime coverage, which resulted in a more timely and more accurate coverage for readers than the *Police Gazette* could achieve. In response to this loss of one of its major features, the *Police Gazette* turned even more to sensationalism and racy themes, trying to cater to nineteenth-century Americans who were fascinated with any type of lurid vice. For example, the paper commonly printed sensationalized pictures of women in fancy silk dresses supposedly sprawled out helplessly in an opium trance in some Chinatown, with skirts in disarray above their knees revealing their calves and stockings. Men went on tours of opium dens, hoping to see this type of behavior that they had seen in the pages of the popular magazine, but rarely found it.

In the 1920s the moral climate of America changed and sexual themes became more acceptable and more open. Thus the *Police Gazette* became less credible and less shocking. Other "girlie" and "confession" magazines that exposed more of women's bodies became widespread. Accordingly, the tabloid's circulation declined and the magazine went into bankruptcy in 1932. In 1934 the *National Police Gazette* was revived under new management as a monthly magazine. It continued to publish sensational sports features and "hot" girlie pictures, but never recovered its former status as a major magazine. It ceased print publication in 1977.

Many magazines, such as *Day's Doings*, *Last Sensation*, and *Stetson's Dime Illustrated*, imitated the *National Police Gazette* in its early years, but none surpassed its circulation. In 1883 *Fox's Illustrated Week's Doings* claimed to be the "spiciest dramatic and best story paper in America."

Fox's rival for the illustrated newspaper business was *Frank Leslie's Illustrated Newspaper*. It was created by a man named Henry Carter, who had worked as a wood-engraver on the staff of the *Illustrated London News* in England. His father did not approve of his type of work so Henry signed his published drawings as "Frank Leslie."[23] Carter emigrated to New York, changed his legal name to Frank Leslie and launched a ladies fashion magazine.

In 1855 Leslie started *Frank Leslie's Illustrated Newspaper* to compete with *Harper's Weekly*. The magazine's specialty was sensational investigative muckraking reporting with eye-catching illustrations. Leslie eventually became one of most prolific publishers of cheap illustrated books and periodicals with *Frank Leslie's Boys of America*, *Frank Leslie's Boys' and Girls' Weekly*, the spicy *Day's Doings*, and the *New-York Illustrated Times*.

In competition with each other for the market for sensationalism, almost every issue of the *Police Gazette* and *Frank Leslie's Illustrated Weekly* in the late 1870s and early 1880s had some lurid article about cowboys. The reading public delighted in sensational descriptions of their wild and lawless behavior, such as the one in the *Police Gazette* of September 6, 1879, which said, "While in town his home is in the saloons and the dance houses. He soon gets gloriously drunk and then begins to yell like a wild Indian and shoots off his big revolvers promiscuously into the crowd. He is little else than a crazy demon at such times and woe betide the man who crosses his path."

Yellow Journalism

The 1880s and 1890s were the heyday of sensational reporting, with newspapers competing for the attention (and dollars) of the newspaper-reading public. Papers cut their prices in an attempt to appeal to the growing number of factory workers and immigrants of the growing cities of the East.

One innovative technique used to attract readers was the use of female newspaper reporters, called "girl stunt reporters," who deliberately went undercover to expose the undesirable social problems that accompanied increasing urbanization. They investigated stories such as corruption at city hall, poor working conditions in factories, the lack of treatment at public hospitals, the illegal abortion trade, manufacturing sweatshops, and condition in prisons. Reporter Nellie Bly (real name Elizabeth Cochrane) went so far as to have herself committed to the infamous insane asylum at Blackwell's Island in 1887 to be able to investigate and report on the conditions in the notorious mad house for the *New York World*.[24]

In the newspaper world, the years between 1895 and 1900 were known for a type of lurid and scandalous reporting that was nicknamed "yellow journalism." The term was extensively used in the late 1890s to describe the sensational journalism that appeared during the circulation war between Joseph Pulitzer's *New York World* and William Randolph Hearst's *New York Journal* as they fought for the highest circulation. Both papers were accused of sensationalizing the news in order to drive up their circulation figures in a battle that lasted from 1895 to 1898.

Pulitzer purchased the *New York World* in 1883 and filled the paper with crime stories, pictures, games, and contests to attract new readers. The price was 2¢ for an eight to twelve page issue. This approach appealed William Randolph Hearst, who owned the *San Francisco Examiner* and devoted much of his paper to crime, spiced up with lurid stories of adultery and racy pictures. Hearst purchased the *New York Journal* in 1895.

Metropolitan newspapers in the 1890s pursued advertising from department stores, and papers soon discovered that the larger the circulation base, the more they could charge for advertising. So Hearst distributed the *New York Journal* for 1¢ to boost circulation, which jumped up to 150,000. In response, Pulitzer also cut his price to a penny. During the competition, Hearst lured away some of the staff of the *World* to the *New York Journal*, including cartoonist Richard F. Outcault. In 1896 Outcault was drawing a very popular color comic strip titled *Hogan's Alley*, which featured a bald child nicknamed The Yellow Kid who wore a yellow nightshirt. The strip was a major success and is generally acknowledged to be the first newspaper comic strip. Pulitzer continued the strip, thus there were Yellow Kids in both papers.

This piracy of comic artists between competing New York newspapers, in particular for the Yellow Kid, gave rise to the term "yellow journalism."[25] The first to publish the term was Erwin Wardman, the editor of the *New York Press*, referring to the popular comic strip which was published by both Pulitzer and Hearst during the circulation war. The name eventually came to mean a type of journalism that presented news that was not well researched, and instead relied on bold layouts and eye-catching multi-column headlines in huge print to sell more newspapers. In addition, yellow journalism was characterized by the use of sensationalistic illustrations, exaggeration of events, and a scandalous slant to the reporting that included false quotes and misleading information from so-called experts. These journalistic excesses included lurid and sensationalistic headlines, and a focus on stories about crime, sex, and violence. The yellow press newspapers used large illustrations, a heavy reliance on unnamed sources, and unabashed self-promotion. While this type of reporting was known to be of dubious accuracy, the newspaper readers of the late nineteenth century did not expect stories to be pure non-fiction. Historian Michael Robertson has said that "newspaper reporters and readers of the 1890s were much less concerned with distinguishing among fact-based reporting, opinion and literature."[26]

2

Publishing the Sensational

During the latter half of the 1800s, the book and magazine industry was revolutionized by the industrialization, mechanization, and urbanization that brought about major social and cultural changes in the United States. These changes, in turn, created the appropriate conditions for creating the dime novel and the later pulp literature. One of these changes was the introduction of compulsory education, which led to an increased literacy rate.

Rising Literacy

The first half of the 1800s was a time of increasing urbanization in America as employment shifted from primarily rural laboring activities to manufacturing jobs in the cities.

By the 1840s, the Industrial Revolution brought compulsory public education to the masses, and by 1850 the literacy rate was 50 percent. By 1861 America had the highest literacy rate in the world at 58 percent of the total population.[1] By 1880, over half the population lived in cities of over 8,000.[2] The literacy rate grew to 86 percent in 1886 and rose to almost 90 percent by 1890. A similar trend was observed in England after elementary education in Britain was provided by the Education Act of 1870. This promoted learning, even though sometimes meager and elementary, by requiring a village school to be within the reach of every child. In 1880 such schooling became compulsory, which resulted in a rising literacy rate. In 1886 the literacy rate in Britain rose to 97.3 percent.[3]

Newspapers had been in existence since the late seventeenth and early eighteenth centuries, but they were typically read by the educated elite, and not by the general public. The emerging combination of industrialization, public education, and improved literacy rates led to a greater interest in reading newspapers and brought books into the popular culture. However, that said, not all men and women read. The price of most printed material was still too high to create a mass audience. The result was that some working class men and women could not read, some had no time to read, and some had no money for any luxuries, including books. On the other end of the scale, males of the elite class were usually deeply involved in business activities and were not serious readers. Similarly, upper class women did not read very much as they were supposed to spend their days running the household and managing the servants. In England, the number of upper class men and women that did have time to read has been estimated at less than one percent of the population, which was not a large or profitable market for publishers of books.[4]

The largest remaining market for books, therefore, was made up of middle class men and women. Middle class women were traditionally not supposed to work or enter public service, thus they had both the money and the time to be readers. Reading for pleasure had previously been the domain of the upper reaches of American society but in the 1830s, the invention of the steam printing press, expanding postal service and freight transport by railway, and a growing literate working class made fiction affordable and accessible to the masses. As a result, fiction stories published in various cheap formats increased after the 1840s. The likes of Walter Scott, Ralph Waldo Emerson, Homer, Goethe, and Shakespeare were reprinted in cheap books that were available even in the remote silver and gold mining camps of Colorado for as little as 10¢ or 20¢.

Changing Technology

At the dawn of the nineteenth century, printing technology had virtually not changed since around 1440, when it was originally developed by Johannes Gutenberg. The state-of-the art method of the time used separate pieces of type assembled into a frame, letter-by-letter. The frame was installed in a hand-cranked press that forced paper up against the inked type a single sheet at a time. If the press functioned flawlessly, two workers could print around 3,500 pages per day.

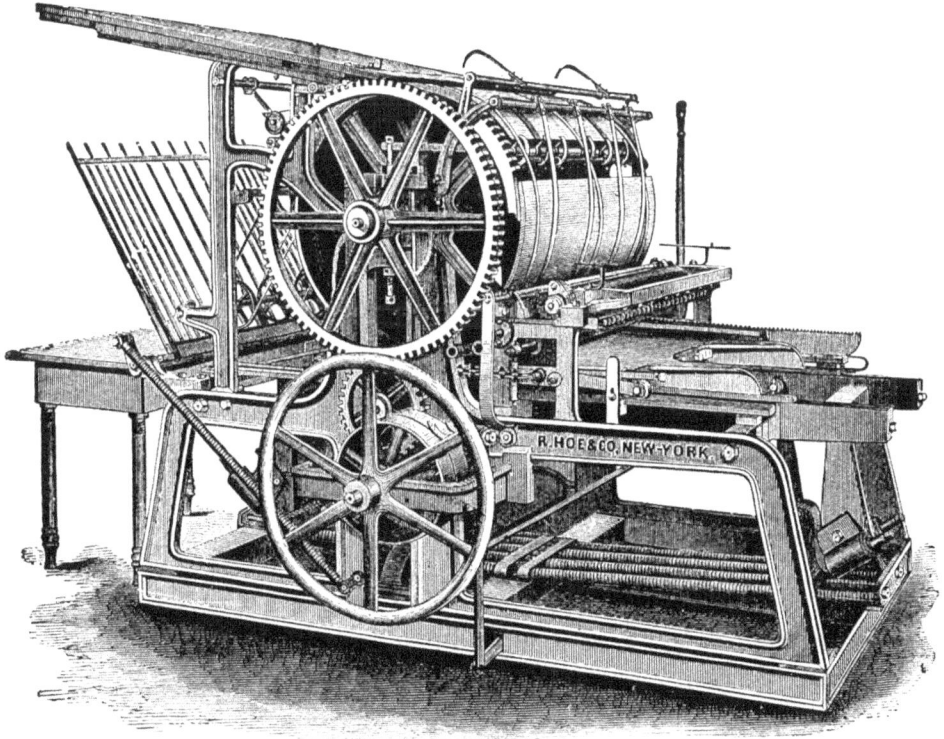

The invention of the steam-powered rotary printing press revolutionized the ability to manufacture cheap reading material. The curved plates on the roller at the center of the machine contained the type to be printed. The cylinder rotated continuously and pressed inked images onto paper that was fed in sheets from the tilted paper-feed rack at the left. Later presses incorporated continuous rolls of paper, instead of single sheets, to speed up the printing process even more. (Library of Congress)

During the mid–1800s a fundamental change took place in publishing. The Industrial Revolution produced a major impact on printing technology with the mechanization of printing presses that were run by steam, then later by electricity. The change started with the development of the high-speed, steam-powered rotary printing press that made it possible to print books, newspapers, and magazines in a shorter period of time than previously. A rotary press is a printing machine that places the type to be printed on curved plates mounted on a cylinder. The cylinder rotates and transfers the ink from the plates to paper that is fed underneath the rotating cylinder. The rotary press used this new technique to print sheets of paper faster, instead of applying them in the slower up-and-down motion that pressed ink onto a single sheet at a time. The entire mechanism was powered more efficiently by steam than it had been by hand.

Printing presses powered by steam had been used in England since 1814, but the first successful steam-powered rotary printing press, capable of printing 8,000 sheets of paper per hour, was patented in New York in 1845.[5] In 1846 a rotary press was developed that could print 290,000 copies of a newspaper each hour.[6]

By 1865, a further important advance occurred when the paper supplied to these high-speed presses during printing was fed from continuous rolls through the rotary part of the press, instead of having a single, cut sheet of paper move under the printing head each time, which improved printing efficiency.

These advances allowed the rapid and inexpensive reproduction of printed material. The time was right for mass-circulation publishing. These inventions, plus reductions in the price of paper, revolutionized printing and allowed the mass production of books at very economical prices, which allowed novels to be published and sold for a dime—or even five cents. Cheap editions of romances, melodramas, and lurid adventure fiction became known as "dime novels," because of their low sales price. This was sometimes also called "steam literature" after the steam presses. A sequence was thus set in motion that led to the creation of the sensationalist dime novels, then to pulp fiction, and eventually to the mass-market paperbacks of today.

Wide distribution of dime novels was encouraged when the post office lowered mailing rates to 2¢ an issue in 1857. Another factor in this publishing expansion was that the transcontinental railroad and its low freight rates made it possible to rapidly distribute books and magazines in as many cities across the country as possible at a low price.

The technological advances in printing and cheaper prices changed the reading public's attitude of how newspapers were perceived. Until around the 1820s, the contents of typical newspapers consisted of political news, business news, shipping reports, essays, and news from abroad that was dated by the time it reached America. This type of newspaper was intended primarily for elite readers. Improved printing technology reduced publishing costs and created a new type of cheap metropolitan newspaper aimed at the common people in the city. Another important change in journalism was that these newspapers started to use the everyday language of the masses to appeal to their lower-class readers, rather than using the stilted style of writing that was previously used for (and presumed to be the preference of) elite readers.

The improved technology that boosted the expansion of cheap newspapers created a related form of family-oriented publication, the inexpensive weekly story magazine. The early story papers, which predated dime novels by a number of years, were printed on high-speed newspaper presses and used cheap newsprint paper. The story papers were initially printed in the format and size of a small weekly newspaper, so that they

This is how the *New York Herald* appeared on October 3, 1846. The cost was 2¢. In contrast to the splashy, lurid headlines, gutter-to-edge typescript, and titillating photographs of the later tabloid-type newspapers, these papers contained no illustrations and tiny headlines, and offered a few densely-packed pages of type reporting news about shipping, business, and politics.

could legally be classified as periodicals. They consisted of a sheet of cheap newsprint paper folded to make a book-like format. According to official postal regulations, a periodical had to be printed with paper covers, issued regularly at least four times a year, stamped with the date of issue, be numbered consecutively, and have a list of subscribers.

These mass-produced, inexpensive paper-covered publications, also referred to as "series" and "weeklies," were about 14.5 inches by 21 inches in size, and usually 16 pages in length. A typical issue featured something to appeal to all the members of a family, including romance stories for the women, western, detective, and adventure yarns for the men, and juvenile stories for the children, including kid success stories. The first page often had a large black-and-white illustration that took up most of the cover in order to catch the potential purchaser's eye and sell the paper. By 1915 the story papers had shrunk to a tabloid size of 11 inches by 16.5 inches.

Approximately 80 story papers were published in the United States between 1830 and 1921. Story weeklies appeared with names like *Uncle Sam*, *The Star-Spangled Banner*, and *The New York Weekly*. Newspapers often printed serialized novels with a new installment appearing each week. The story papers followed this trend and printed only fiction, typically both serialized novels and short stories, along with some poetry and informational fillers.

Specialization in the target audience occurred almost immediately. For example, in the late nineteenth and early twentieth century, some story papers were published that were intended to appeal primarily to American boys, with titles such as *Boys of New York, Young Men of America, Golden Weekly, Golden Hours, Golden Days*, and *Happy Days*. These publications targeted all the types of topics that would appeal to juvenile males, including stories of the circus, travel, exploration, and early forms of science fiction.

Other publishers designed the contents of their story papers for working-class Americans and immigrants. Typical were *The New York Mercury, The New York Ledger, The New York Weekly, The Fireside Companion* and Beadle's *The Saturday Journal*, later called *The Banner Weekly*. Their stories were colorful, full of excitement, and often sentimental. They were escapist literature that was easily read and quickly forgotten. But if one type of story was successful, editors developed endless variations on the same popular theme or character.

A similar trend emerged in Great Britain. The abolition of the newspaper tax, the tax on advertisements, and the tax on paper (all considered to be "taxes on knowledge") led to a dramatic increase in the number of newspapers. In 1846 there were 14 newspapers. By 1880, after the removal of the taxes, there were 158. The most popular newspapers were the penny dailies, including the *Daily Telegraph*, the *Daily News*, the *Daily Chronicle*, and the *Morning Post*.[7]

These papers were intended almost exclusively for upper and middle class male readers. Then in 1880, George Newnes, the branch manager of a fancy goods business, realized that there was no publication catering to the emerging group of lower-class literate readers. To meet what he saw as a need, he launched *Tit-Bits*, a weekly specifically designed to cater to those for whom reading was a new and difficult skill.[8] He also capitalized on sensational stories, as a "titbit" (which is the same as "tidbit") referred to a choice morsel of gossip.[9]

Before 1880, newspapers generally reported the news and left it up to the reader to form his own opinions concerning the facts. The new type of cheap working-class newspaper relied on exciting and sensationalistic stories, and presented the paper's own opinions woven into the story to guide the reader. One of the primary papers of this type was the *Pall Mall Gazette*. The paper was edited from 1883 to 1889 by journalist W.T. Stead, who published many sensational stories that were intentionally written to increase the paper's circulation and revenue. One notable example was an 1885 series of supposedly educational stories titled "The Maiden Tribute of Modern Babylon," which was essentially a lurid recounting and exposé of how English girls were being shipped to Europe to work in brothels on the Continent.[10]

In 1896, a young man named Alfred Harmsworth, who had previously worked for Newnes, founded the *Daily Mail*. When he did so, he changed the direction of British newspapers from the contemporary style of serious political and business reporting to focusing more on entertainment. In this, and another publication named *Answers*, Harmsworth focused on stories that featured crime and death, and on reports of sensational legal cases. His philosophy was that readers would pay to be entertained and "that whatever benefits them [his newspapers] is justifiable, and that it was not his business to consider the effect of their contents on the public mind."[11] The *Daily Mail* was criticized for being sensationalistic, distorting the news, and being in poor taste, but was nevertheless extremely popular.

The Need to Read

It is beyond the scope of this book to delve into the psychology of the reading public's fascination with fear and the vicarious pleasure readers gain from it. People who read, however, have always enjoyed sensationalistic literature and many relish the vivid sensations of being excited, startled, or shocked by stories of crime, scandal, and horror, whether true or not. Most readers of any genre enjoy pursuing the literary excitements of love and death.

This process is called literary escapism, or seeking moments of excitement and interest to escape from the boredom that is common in the secure, routine, and organized lives of most working Americans. Readers like to be confronted by the insecurity, danger, and adventure that accompanies imaginary literary worlds, without being confronted by the same insecurity and danger in real life. Accordingly, to fulfill this desire and need, many literary genres are filled with danger, uncertainty, violence, and sex. Good authors fill their imaginary worlds with extended suspense that involves the temporary creation of fear and uncertainty about characters with whom readers have formed a sympathetic bond. Likewise, cliffhangers are used to create a sense of desperation, suspense, and excitement in the perilous situations that these characters find themselves in. In this way readers can be involved in a believable type of excitement with the knowledge that whatever difficulties confront the protagonist will be resolved successfully by the end. Such stories fulfill our vicarious quest for romance and excitement.

To be able to temporarily forget about our own existence, which may internally be perceived as humdrum, and enter an imaginary world of excitement and romance produces the strongest interest and stimulus. Prominent among this type of escapist literature is the western short story or novel, because it typically relates to an imaginary world that never was. Authors construct exciting adventure stories using cowboys, lawmen, pioneers, outlaws, frontier towns, and saloons, along with familiar cultural themes or myths, such as law and order or the heroic aspirations of the Code of the West, to support the action.[12]

Most readers enjoy literary genres that represent story types in which they have an interest. Genre stories confirm existing interests and attitudes by presenting an imaginary world that is aligned with the reader's interests and attitudes. Some people's desire for escapism and enjoyment is provided by westerns, others by detective stories or spy adventures, and many enjoy a wide range of genres. Many people enjoy mystery thrillers and detective stories for entertainment and relaxation. They let a reader explore in fantasy what is forbidden to him or her in reality, and legitimize actions such as an individual's desire for violent action against criminals in defense of his family and community. Western and hard-boiled detective stories, in particular, present the view that justice depends on the individual rather than the law by showing the helplessness and supposed inefficiency of the machinery of the law.

Between 1850 and 1950, various forms of sensationalistic pulp literature offered this type of intense excitement and gratification for many readers. Whether they were dime novels, the later pulp magazines, or modern paperback thrillers, this type of literature stressed plenty of action and rousing plots, particularly in the pulp magazines, which created a violent type of action involving sex and brutality.[13]

These genres, however, must use characters, settings, and situations that are relevant to the culture that produces them and the reader's interests. For example, it is difficult to write a successful adventure story about a social character that a particular culture or reader does not perceive in heroic terms. Thus, as author John Cawelti only half-humorously put it, there are very few romantic adventure stories about plumbers and janitors.[14]

Slick Magazines Versus the Pulps

At the same time that cheap newspaper were proliferating and competing vigorously for increased circulation figures in the late 1800s, the magazine industry was also expanding. The popular magazines that started to flourish around the same time were the forerunners of modern mass communication. They were a product of the same technological advances in the mechanization of printing and production, wider distribution networks, and mass marketing that were used by newspapers, combined with the growing literacy of the lower and middle classes. The magazine industry grew from 700 publications in 1865 to over 5,000 monthly and weekly periodicals by 1900.[15] Circulation statistics are unclear, but perhaps 50 of them had national distribution. Some of these magazines had circulation figures as high as 100,000.[16]

The American publishing industry in the late nineteenth century went through a period of extremely rapid growth as businessmen took advantage of an opportunity and tried to capitalize on what they saw as an untapped and lucrative market for entertainment. As a result, popular magazines came and went, and the successful ones bred imitators. The number of magazines on the market mushroomed. In 1900 there were 2,369 monthly magazines. By 1920 this number had risen to 3,415, and by 1954 there were 7,429.[17]

Many of the large-circulation pictorial magazines appeared following the American Civil War. *Lippincott's* was founded in 1868 and *Scribner's* appeared in 1870. These magazines published short stories, poems, serialized novels, essays, and commentaries. *Scribner's* and others provided political analysis, editorial cartoons, and humorous and satirical articles.[18] *Harper's Weekly*, sub-titled "A Journal of Civilization," was founded in 1857 to feature foreign and domestic news, fiction, essays, cartoons, and humor. *Harper's Monthly* was founded in 1850, along lines similar to the *Illustrated London News*, mostly publishing established authors, such as Charles Dickens.

The most popular magazines for middle and upper class readers with money and education were *Harper's*, *Scribner's*, *Atlantic*, and *The Century*. They were printed on high-quality, coated, glossy paper made from paper stock that incorporated rags instead of wood pulp. This gave these magazines a shiny, slick appearance, thus they were referred to in slang terms as the "slicks." Newspapers and magazines for the blue-collar masses, on the other hand, such as the *Police Gazette*, were printed on the cheapest possible paper stock made from pulpwood.

The slicks contained fiction and non-fiction, were lavishly illustrated, and contained large amounts of advertising. Another approach, such as that followed by publisher Frank Munsey and his successful pulp *The Golden Argosy*, was to increase the number of copies, lower the cover price, and aim the magazine at the mass market. Sometimes the selling price of these magazines was lowered to below the production cost to increase circulation, and the magazine's primary revenue came from advertising.

Magazines covered a range of intellectual levels. At the bottom of the scale was the weekly, cheaply printed, sensationalistic, lowbrow literature aimed at the masses, such as the *Spirit of the Times* and the *Police Gazette*. Magazines to appeal to middle class readers were *Harper's Weekly* and *Frank Leslie's Illustrated Weekly*. Literary and monthly cultural journals were available for intellectuals and more highbrow tastes in the form of *Atlantic Monthly*, which was founded in 1857, and the *North American Review*, which was the first literary magazine in the United States. These latter magazines were aimed at the upper classes, who were the ones who could afford to purchase them as their cover prices of 25¢ was too expensive for the masses at a time when a worker made $7 a week for laboring six ten to twelve hour days in a factory. The majority of low-income workers, immigrants, and uneducated youngsters read dime novels and lurid paperbacks which cost only 5¢ or 10¢.

During the 1890s, lavishly illustrated magazines such as *Collier's* and *The Saturday Evening Post* started to replace *Harper's* and *Frank Leslie's Illustrated Weekly* as the premier form of reading entertainment. Their pages included adventure and other dramatic tales, and used quality authors, such as Jack London, and the leading illustrators of the day, including Frederic Remington and Howard Pyle.

Magazines contained stories of thrilling action, courtly love, and melodramatic adventure, all illustrated by garish woodcuts or engravings. This included mysteries, swashbuckling adventures, and sensational romances. Along with these fiction pieces were articles, letters to the editor, and the same types of miscellaneous material that makes up today's general circulation magazines. From about 1870 to 1914, many of the popular novels of the time appeared in serial form in magazines, newspapers, and weekly story-papers, rather than in full-length books. The episodes were later collected and reprinted in book form to encourage sales in a new market. Some publishers put out weekly newsletters as advertising and to inform readers of their future releases.

Sensationalistic Victorian Novels

Sensationalistic fiction was not just restricted to magazines and dime literature. After the appearance of the novel in the mid-eighteenth century, middle class women were the major producers and consumers of romantic fiction. Their books and magazines sold dreams, fantasies, adventure, and descriptions of a secretly hoped-for way of life.

The elements of many Victorian romance novels were combined into a steamy mixture of passion, murder, revenge, separation, and mistaken identity. The most popular turn-of-the-century writers filled their plots with action, weapons, and violence. And they included plenty of heaving bosoms and feminine blushing.

Victorian publishers of cheap literature recognized the entertainment value of mayhem and violence, and produced sensationalist literature to cater to this need. To present generations who are exposed to high levels of violence and eroticism on television and in motion pictures, these stories appear to be quite tame and wordy, but they were not considered so at the time.

Women were almost exclusively the authors of certain genres, notably "sensation" fiction. Romances of this type, which started to appear in the 1860s, received their name because of their ability to cause physical sensations and reactions, such as shivers of fright, in the reader. This was considered to be women's literature, as the authors and readers were predominantly female. This type of writing was also categorized as being of low artistic value as it was dependent on flashy plot situations and shock value. Its passionate and unrestrained heroines were condemned as "unnatural" and dangerous by critics, who saw the characters as "depraved" and the genre as "diseased." For example, they complained about the sensation novels *Lady Audley's Secret* (1862) and *Aurora Floyd* (1863), written by Mary Elizabeth Braddon, as the plots of both books involved bigamy, which was a shocking subject at the time. Nevertheless, the books were immensely popular with readers. *Lady Audley's Secret* went through eight editions in its first three months and total sales outnumbered all other novels of the period.[19]

George W. Reynolds was the best-selling author of dozens of racy Victorian romances that featured generously proportioned women with rounded figures and full bosoms. Though considered tame by today's standards, his romances were the sensationalistic fantasy novels of the day. Like many authors of his time, he wrote into his plots a combination of Victorian respectability and a vivid imagination for lurid situations. Women's breasts were an obsession for many Victorian writers and, like other authors, most of Reynold's stories featured "glowing bosoms," "heaving breasts," and "voluptuous fullness."[20] The ideal version of Victorian curvaceous feminine beauty was a tiny waist pinched in by the use of a corset to push up a large bosom and accentuate the hips. Thus well-proportioned, rounded women with full figures were the ideal of feminine attractiveness at the time.[21] It was not until the 1920s that the perception of the ideal shape for women changed and became the slimmed-down, flat-chested, flapper look.

Reynolds edited *Reynold's Miscellany* magazine, subtitled "Of Romance, General Literature, Science, and Art." Most of his readers were young women, many of them single, and most of them worked in factories or shops, or as domestic servants. These women could escape the drudgery and routine of their labors through this type of escapist romantic fiction. As one example, Reynold wrote a novel titled *Wagner: the Wehr-Wolf*, which was similar to *Varney the Vampire* (1847). It was a steamy novel that included flagellation of nuns in a convent. The cover of Chapter 42, serialized in *Reynold's Miscellany* on March 6, 1847, shows the heroine in the coils of a huge anaconda snake, her full bosom almost popping out of the top of her dress to expose far more than Victorian readers would expect to see, and her skirt pulled up on one leg almost to the knee. This was a Victorian shocker when respectable women's legs were supposed to be covered to the ground by floor-length skirts.[22]

Reynolds' plots also played on the morbid fears of Victorian women. He frequently used a stock character, the shapely beautiful heroine—with a heaving full bosom, of course—in constant danger of being abducted into white slavery, seduced, raped, tortured in a dungeon, trapped in a burning building, or threatened by exotic wildlife. By capitalizing on and repeating this formula, he gained a worldwide audience of millions of readers.

Writer of male fiction were just as lurid. Romantic plots featured manly action with heroes wielding and thrusting, with an emphasis on swords, spears, and similar weapons. Pirates used muskets and swordplay. Gallant highwaymen flourished their pistols while they bowed to the ladies. Cowboys fired large revolvers and long rifles. Historian Patricia Anderson has asserted that the firearms, clubs, knives, and swords that were used in these plots were widely known as phallic symbols in humorous writing, in everyday speech, and in the Victorian music hall.[23] As a result, adolescent male readers were fascinated by pistols, swords, fists, and bulging muscles.

Dime novels and popular fiction played a role in portraying the ideals of Victorian masculinity as honorable, nationalistic, and courageous.[24] The hero was supposed to be tall, dark-haired, and handsome, with a strong, well-built body. The ideal of Victorian manhood was a hero with bulging muscles, as hard, bulging biceps implied manly strength and sexual potency. The following idealized description comes from Owen Wister. "Lounging there at ease against the wall was a slim young giant, more beautiful than pictures. His broad, soft hat was pushed back; a loose-knotted, dull-scarlet handkerchief sagged from his throat; and one casual thumb was hooked in the cartridge belt that slanted across his hips…. The weather-beaten bloom of his face shone through it duskily, as the ripe peaches look upon their trees in a dry season."[25]

A well-muscled Victorian hero also implied strength of character, physical toughness, a high capacity for action, and plenty of endurance in the outdoors under adverse conditions. "Plenty of endurance," of course, also implied plenty in the way of romantic prowess. The way to achieve this model of masculinity was considered to be through a boy's school that featured a healthy outdoor life with an abundance of sports and fresh air. The perceived way to masculinity was through athletic activities, such as cricket, rowing, rugby, and soccer. An ability to excel at sports implied superior moral worth and being a Christian gentleman. Strong bodies were equated to strong morals, and a combination of hard work, a hard bed, and plenty of cold baths were supposed to ward off any evil or impure male thoughts. In the late 1850s this concept became known as "muscular Christianity," and stories about it were very popular.

The Victorian romantic heroine, on the other hand, thrived on passion. Victorian novels are full of descriptions of quivering lips and blooming blushes. As the print media was the major source of contemporary mass entertainment, fiction played a major role in men and women's expectations of romantic love and how they should behave with the opposite gender.

In spite of their overwhelming popularity, though, Victorian romantic novels came under attack from nineteenth century physicians and purity writers who were determined that each generation should have higher morals than the previous one. They felt that sensational literature was a need of the uneducated that led to cultural degeneration. They persuaded themselves that romantic novels tended to excite the emotions, thus creating an over-stimulated nervous system in young men and women without allowing sufficient physical activity to compensate for their excited mental state.

Self-proclaimed authorities promoted their attitudes on religion, training, exercise and diet, use of the intellect, amusement, and marriage to try to help to build this national character. Writers of purity manuals projected their own dreams and desires into this portrayal of male youth and the establishment of a world into which they could grow. They felt that if boys could be properly schooled and exercised, then order would triumph over chaos, and progress and morality would become a reality.

Typical of these manual writers was Kate Upson Clark, who wrote *Bringing Up Boys; A Study* (1899), which promoted her concerns over moral integrity. Educator H.M. Burr, who taught instructional courses at the YMCA in Springfield, Massachusetts, favored hero tales, such as Sampson and Hercules; stories of leaders and patriots; and stories of love, altruism, love of women, and love of country and home.[26]

Religious novels, such as *Ben Hur*, were acceptable to moral critics, but, though extremely popular, sensational romance novels were condemned by physicians and reformers. Medical and purity writers blamed the romantic novel for inciting immoral thoughts and activities among boys and young men, and proposed through faulty reasoning, wild claims, and no evidence, that this would lead to insanity. These critics convinced themselves that romantic books "sapped the vital energies of the body and besieged the imagination during its idle hours, tempting the mind from its proper responsibilities." Consequently, purity writers ruled that young men should not be allowed to read a novel until they were at least 25 years of age.[27]

Romance literature was theorized to excite the passions of both sexes and cause disruptive physical effects. Furthermore, the study of books or higher learning were thought to result in harm to a woman's nervous and reproductive systems, and the taxing brain work of reading and education was said to be a danger to their maturation. Women seeking education were considered mannish and therefore objects of suspicion. Medical men even proposed that advanced study was irrelevant or even harmful for women, and put women in danger of many physical ailments, such as sterility, brain damage and nervous collapse. Economic data, anatomical observation, religious doctrine, and social theory were all used with faulty reasoning to justify this viewpoint. Scientists compared animal and human skulls to even "prove" that men were intellectually more advanced than women.[28]

In 1870 social critic Orson Fowler, the inventor of phrenology, wrote: "Reading of a character to stimulate the emotions and rouse the passions may produce or increase a tendency to uterine congestion, which may in turn give rise to a great variety of maladies."[29] His recommended treatment included the avoidance of novels and any intellectual pursuits, and a daily dosing with tonics.

Dr. Mary Wood-Allen, national superintendent of the Purity Department of the Woman's Christian Temperance Union, stated, "I would like to call your attention to the great evil of romance-reading, both in the production of premature development and in the creation of morbid mental states which will tend to the production of physical evils, such as nervous hysteria, and a host of other maladies which depend on disturbed nerves. Romance-reading by young girls will, by this excitement of the bodily organs, tend to create their premature development, and the child becomes physically a woman months, or even, years, before she should."[30]

Purity writers condemned romantic novels and blamed them for creating neurasthenia, hysteria, and general poor health in women.[31] A variety of critics, including most physicians, were opposed to the reading of sentimental novels, claiming that these book created impure passions and excessive emotional stimulation. At the same time, however, it should be noted that other sources of impurity were felt to be drinking tea and coffee before the age of 18, letter writing during early school years, and dancing the waltz. Dr. John Harvey Kellogg, of Kellogg's cornflakes fame and medical director of the Battle Creek Sanitarium, claimed that dancing was the cause of the ruin of three-fourths of the degenerate women in New York.[32] One author even felt that this impurity could be caused by a woman absorbing magnetic emissions from passionate male dancing partners.[33]

3

Enter the Dime Novel

The development of dime novels provided a large increase in sensational material for the general reading public. The firm of Beadle & Adams brought out a first series of simple novels in 1860 in an all-paper format that sold for 10¢, which gave them the name dime novel. Other names for this type of pulp literature were nickel novels, pamphlet novels, novelettes, red-backs, yellow-backs, railroad literature, blood and thunder weeklies, and pulps. These were sensationalist paperbacks, not the traditional sentimental stories of adventure, tragedy, and hope of other contemporary novels, and were not read like the traditional novel with families sitting around the fireplace in the evening while one member read out loud to the others.

The era of the classic dime novel lasted from about 1860 to 1910. However, dime novels were not suddenly invented, but developed out of the previous eighteenth century and early nineteenth century serialized fiction. They were a spin-off in the 1860s from the weekly story papers that were popular in American publishing in the mid-nineteenth century. Story papers were mass-market publications that depended on readers to buy them every week. After 1860 the story weeklies shared the market with dime novels and many of both were written by the same authors to cater to the same readers' tastes. Many dime novels were simply reprints from the story papers.

Dime novels covered every subject. Stories appeared about circuses, railroading, firefighting, sports, mystery, detectives, fantasy, adventure in faraway places, sea stories (polar exploration was a favorite), the Old West, and mining camps. Popular sensationalistic stories were tales of bandits, outlaws, and highwaymen, and their misdeeds. Plots included mistaken identities, disguises and cross-dressing, and women duped, manipulated, seduced, and abandoned. Other popular stories were about gruesome subjects and sensational crimes, such as theft, robbery, arson, and murder. If plot lines, such those in western dime novels, became popular, then other publishers immediately copied them and started their own series. Western dime novels that featured characters that included alliteration were popular. Among the many who had repetitive initial sounds in their names were Deadwood Dick, Rosebud Rob, Denver Doll, Howling Hank, Mustang Merle, Ranger Ralph, Sierra Sam, Solid Sam, Dave Dotson, Canada Chet, Dick Drew, High Hat Harry, Photograph Phil, Omaha Oll, Dash Dare, and the curiously named Nobby Nick of Nevada.

For maximum economy the pulp paper that dime novels were printed on was an even lower grade than newsprint, and was made from the remnants of paper production. The high acid content of this cheap paper made any books printed on them subject to rapid yellowing and decomposition. Few examples of dime novels have survived to today because the paper became fragile and disintegrated with time. These pulp paperbacks were intended to be read quickly, then thrown out rather than saved.

The dime novel business went through cycles of growth and decline in response to fluctuating postal rates and the state of the national economy. For example, postal rates for newspapers increased in 1843 and the rates for books decreased in 1845, which created favorable mailing conditions for dime novels. However, in 1888, the American Library Association supported legislation to exclude libraries of periodicals from low second-class postage rates at 1¢ a pound, and place these paper-covered publications in the third-class category along with books at 8¢ a pound. This included dime novels and works published as inexpensive, numbered, paper-covered publications so that publishers could claim that they were "periodicals" or "libraries." The booksellers' argument was that the postal service was subsidizing cheap publication rates for story papers and dime novels while discriminating against books. The battle over the legislation lasted for twelve years until the bill eventually defeated.[1] This type of setback resulted in periodic re-evaluation by publishers of the production, distribution, and target audience of pulp literature.

Dime novels were the first mass-produced entertainment. However, just as later pulp magazines and paperback books had to compete with television and motion pictures, dime novels had to compete with dime museums, stage plays, vaudeville, circuses, and Wild West shows for the consumer dollar.

The giants of the dime novel industry were Beadle & Adams, Street & Smith, Frank Tousey, George Munro, Norman Munro, and Frank Munsey. Beadle & Adams produced 3,688 issues; Munro 1,362; Tousey 2,154; and Street & Smith 2,802. There were also many smaller publishers.

Beadle & Adams published westerns, along with stories of crime and every type of adventure. The era of the dime novel westerns lasted for such a long time that many people equated the dime novel with the western. Of 1,500 novels from Beadle and Adams, the most prolific of the publishers, 75 percent dealt with frontier subjects, most of them in the West.

Dime novels filled a need for escapist literature as a form of entertainment during the increasing urbanization brought about by the Industrial Revolution. During the American Civil War dime novels were read by little-educated soldiers looking for an escape from boredom between battles until the books fell apart. Publisher Beadle & Adams profited from this need as dime novels were shipped by the millions, packaged in bales like firewood, to army camps by wagon, freight car, and canal boat. By the end of the war Beadle's had sold four million copies. Similar markets for this inexpensive type of reading material were men bored and isolated on ships, working on railroads, and in remote logging and mining camps.

Though Beadle & Adams were the largest publisher, rivals and imitators soon emerged, quick to come out with their own versions of dime novels. Among them were Elliott, Thomes and Talbot, who published *Ten Cent Novelettes*. Another was Robert M. DeWitt, a New York publisher of cheap fiction who produced many classic stories of bandits and highwaymen, publishing twenty-eight different series with over 1,200 titles.[2] DeWitt started *DeWitt's Ten Cent Romances*, and in 1852 published a *Claude Duval* series about the legendary highwayman from England. Richmond and Company of Boston published *Richmond's Novels*. George P. Munro, a former employee of Beadle & Adams, started a series called *Munro's Ten Cent Novels* in 1863. Another competitor was Frank Tousey, who started publishing in 1873. Other publishers of dime novels were M.M. Ballou of Boston, Carey & Hart of Philadelphia, and Fredrick A. Brady of New York.[3]

Books from Beadle & Adams generally sold for 10¢, and the name "dime novel" soon became a generic term for any work of fiction with paper covers, regardless of the selling price. But despite the name, not all dime novels sold for a dime. Some sold for as much as 25¢, others for as little as 5¢, such as the *Nickel Library* and *Beadle's Half-Dime Library*. The latter were intended to be read by boys between eight and sixteen years of age who might not have a dime for reading material each week. The nickel novels cost less, but the stories in them were about half the length of the dime libraries. The early dime novels used lurid black-and-white illustrations, and were sometimes called "black and whites" because of their cover art. By the 1890s the term "library" had been replaced by the name "weekly," and the black-and-white covers were replaced by color. The first publisher to use color printing regularly on their covers was Street & Smith with *Tip Top Weekly* in 1896. As soon as Street and Smith started the trend, other publishers immediately followed.

Early dime novels were intensely patriotic and featured stories from America's history, from the Civil War, and stories about the Wild West. Only a few stories about the Civil War appeared during the war itself, and these were primarily fictional accounts of battles, but such stories became more popular in the 1880s.

Though many people read dime novels, the major audience was schoolboys.[4] Dime novels filled the dreams of young boys with frontier adventures, action stories, and a secret alternate fictional identity provided by an action hero that they could relate to. Popular entertainment that appealed to the youth market had to offer distractions from reality and simplified solutions to problems at a time of life when youngsters were learning their role in the world and questioning their identity. Younger school-aged children liked stories in which the basic struggle was between good and evil, with good winning in the end.

Most dime novels were written very rapidly as publishers required speed and quantity from their authors, at the same time being willing to compromise on quality. This was acceptable as dime novels were not intended to be serious literature, but were written as escapist reading for youths and the everyday man, such as loggers, soldiers, sailors, and other working men. The early books were lightweight and small and could be easily carried in a pocket. If they were printed with two or three columns on each page, with small enough print, a complete book could be printed in only eight pages.[5] The limitation on length due to the format meant that a writer had to be able to tie up loose ends quickly to bring the story to a conclusion within the available number of pages.

Dime novels were small enough that they could be concealed inside a school book or some acceptable magazine for cover. This was satirized in the motion picture *Cat Ballou* (1965). As young schoolteacher Catherine Ballou (Jane Fonda) is traveling out West on a train in 1894, she is pretending to be reading a book of Tennyson poems. In reality, she is using the book to hide a dime novel she is reading titled *Kid Shelleen and the Massacre at Whiskey Slide*. Similarly, to avoid detection, schoolboys and youths read dime novels in the barn or by candlelight late at night in bed as many parent did not approve of them.

Dime novels evolved into a book-sized format that would today be considered a paperback. The size was approximately five inches by seven inches, with 150 to 300 pages. For mailing purposes, each book was part of a series and the collection was known as a library or series. Publisher Street & Smith produced dozens of these over a 40-year period. Some were original works, some were book versions of serials or collections of short stories, and some were collection of three or four previously published novelettes.

The term "library" was used for a series or set of books. It included publications that were 8.5 inches by 11 inches, with at least 16 pages of double and triple-column fine print and issued in regular sequence. Smaller dime novel formats ranged from 6.25 inches by 4 inches to 9 inches by 6 inches with 32 to 100 pages. Larger versions were 9 inches by 12 inches, with more than 60 pages.

Whether a dime novel was considered to be part of a "library" or a "weekly," each issue contained a single story. The frequency of publication, along with the date of the specific issue was printed on the cover in order to qualify for the lower postal rate given to periodicals rather than books. Numbered in sequence, each story was part of a series issued as a new novel at regular intervals, either weekly, monthly, or quarterly. Postal authorities objected to this deceptive practice and so, shortly before World War I, additional material, such as a short story or an installment of a serial, was added to make each number look more like an issue of a periodical.[6]

Many dime novel series were written by individual authors with plots from their own imaginations. Other plots, however, were based on an idea from an editor or publisher. The editor sent the outline of the plot to a professional writer, who would write the story according to the publisher's guidelines for page limits and plot content. Other publishers used a process where women in their offices read daily and weekly newspapers and clipped out exciting stories. Favorite topics were the misconduct of city officials. Editors at the publishers would then select and turn these clippings over to writers who made up a plot to match the story.[7]

Authors were either anonymous writers who churned out dime novels for a living, or were journalists writing dime novels to supplement their income. Some were respectable authors who wrote trashy dime novels under house names or pseudonyms to protect their identity. W. Bert Foster, an author of dime novels and series books, wrote under seven pseudonyms so that his name would not appear too often. Sylvanus Cobb, Jr., who wrote many short stories and novelettes from the 1850s to the 1880s, used the pseudonyms of Austin C. Burdick, Charles Castleton, Col. Walter B. Dunlap, Enoch Fitzwhistler, Symus the Pilgrim, and Amos Winslow, Jr.[8] Pen names came from the most unlikely of sources. Gilbert Patten, for instance, who created many of the Frank Merriwell stories, also wrote dime novels under the name of "Wyoming Bill." He supposedly chose the name because he had once been a passenger on a train that passed through Wyoming.[9] Some authors, particularly those who wrote war, aviation, and Wild West stories under a pseudonym, sometimes included an invented military title for themselves in an attempt to impart more authenticity to their stories. Some novels were credited to a house name and the real author remained anonymous.

Depending on the publisher, some authors might write scenes of implied sex or violence or romance. Even though dime novels contained descriptions of violence and mayhem, the publishers took morality seriously and any outright hint of sex was taboo. Publishers were also careful about the language they allowed. Dime novels were intended for soldiers, sailors, railroad men, loggers, hunters, and other men who led rough lives, but they were also intended for juvenile and teenage readers. As a result, no bad language or anything remotely salacious was allowed. The editors at Street & Smith were particularly careful when they scrutinized manuscripts and removed anything to do with drinking or profanity, or anything else that they felt might offend their readers. Beadle's prohibited any spoken vulgarity or anything that was offensive to good taste, and did not allow any immoral characters. Editors toned down the language of even the roughest characters.

Female characters were usually young, innocent, and beautiful. Some were independent, determined, and tough, though they all knew their place as a daughter, mother, or wife. Others had the tendency to faint or be weak in the face of danger. In line with the moral thinking of the times, even though maidens were captured by Indians and some were tortured or scalped, their "honor" (virginity) was kept intact. These women might be captured and suffer torment or death, but all remained chaste to the end.[10]

Several thousand authors wrote dime novels between 1860 and 1916. Authors could be anyone, including doctors, lawyers, teachers, and journalists. However, they all had to be good storytellers with a good narrative style and precise writing. Some authors made a full-time living from their writing, but others used it to supplement their income.

Dime novel authors typically received no royalties or subsidiary rights, but received a one-time payment either by the piece or by the word. Publishers paid authors anywhere from $75 to $200 for a full-length novel of 35,000 words. An anonymous hack writer might be paid only $50 for a story, while a famous writer who could draw an audience of readers with his name might receive as much as $1,000. The publishers, however, were the ones who made the most money. As they owned the rights to stories, they could reprint them in different dime novel series at no additional cost to them. Most dime novels sold 35,000 to 80,000 copies per title, which was a successful and profitable number for the time for a publisher. A typical initial print run was 60,000.

Both English and American publishers were faced with a high demand for serialized fiction so, before international copyright laws were enacted, they often pirated popular stories that had no copyright protection from each other. Publishers in the United States often plundered European popular fiction without paying a royalty. A popular author, such as French novelist Alexandre Dumas, might have a story plagiarized and printed, and credited to some publisher's house name or the name of a hack writer. Even author Charles Dickens, on an American tour in the 1840s, was horrified to find unauthorized editions of his works for which he received no royalties. By the same token, most dime novels were reprinted in England, and many European publishers plagiarized stories from American publications without attempting to secure permission to do so. Unfortunately, though international copyright legislation (the Chace Act, after Sen. Jonathan Chace) was passed in 1891, this did not always stop the practice.[11]

Eventually editors realized that novels were not only the product of a serious writer, but could be manufactured to a formula by run-of-the-mill authors using standardized plots and characters. To try and maximize profits, dime novel publishers became fiction factories, often repeating the familiar. This was not all bad. Readers found satisfaction and emotional security in a familiar genre and story form, because past experience gave them a sense of what to expect. This worked well, of course, for the publisher. Once a formula was established, a house author could rapidly and efficiently produce a new story based on the same pattern. Formula writers tended to be very prolific because the writer did not have to make as many decisions about plotting and writing as the novelist who had no set structure. In the late 1870s the tales in dime novels became more sensational as more suspense and action were added to the formula.

Dime novel stories were escapist fantasy about heroes, heroines, and successful romance. For that reason, editors and publishers did not want stories that had downbeat or indeterminate endings where the hero and heroine were not reunited and true love did not conquer all.

Dime novels were also promoted by their covers, which commonly attracted buyers by showing some dramatic element from the story inside. The cover might feature the heroine in distress or a lurking villain ready to shoot the hero from ambush. In the 1890s, sometimes the cover was drawn first and the writer had to come up with a story to fit. Speed was essential to artwork and a house artist might have to do several covers each week for different publications. By 1909, writers typically suggested particular scenes for the artist to illustrate.

In spite of their popularity with readers, dime novels were not pleasing to everybody. Some critics correctly claimed that the low cost and dubious literary merit of these lurid stories targeted them at people from the lower classes. Publishers, however, were smart businessmen who wanted to reach the widest possible audience, so they aimed their stories at readers of all ages and economic status. Stories were intentionally written in a "popular" style to appeal to a wide range of readers and the low cost made them available to even those with little money.

Many intellectuals and contemporary critics, who tended to be more educated, conservative, and religious than most readers, considered that dime novels were a sinister threat to American youth. They judged that what they saw as dreadful language, violence, and questionable values was dangerous to the minds (mostly of others), especially those of the young and the working class. They worried about a decline in morals, an increased rate of crime, and even deviant behavior in youth. Fiery preachers condemned them from the pulpit as immoral. They felt that sensationalist prose, and violent characters and plots, along with convoluted moral messages in the stories, changing identities and clothing of some of the characters, and confusion of right and wrong sent an improper message to impressionable young people.

Beadle & Adams

In the mid–1800s, most sentimental novels and romance books sold for from $1 to $2 and a paper-covered novel cost from 50¢ to 75¢. Working men typically made $1 day and women only 25¢ for most jobs that involved labor, thus making the price of books out of reach for most working people. Hoping to create a new business opportunity, printer and publisher Erastus Flavel Beadle had the idea of publishing novels of 25,000 to 35,000 words in length and selling them for only 10¢. He felt the time was right for cheap novels, as more people could read and write, and compulsory education laws had created a high demand for reading material.

Beadle was not the first publisher of paper-covered novels and he did not invent a new genre. Paper novels that were somewhat larger in size and sold for 25¢ had been published as early as the 1830s. One early version of the dime novel was a novelette of the war between Mexico and the United States, Charles Averiall's *The Secret Service Ship; or, the Fall of San Juan D'Ulloa*. This story contained many of same ingredients as the later dime novels: a stalwart hero who saves the heroine from almost certain rape, a "death-couch," from which the hero narrowly escapes, a cross-dressing heroine who is a freedom fighter (similar to the later Zorro plots), scenes of violence, and other sensationalized plot elements.[12]

Erastus Beadle started as a publisher in Buffalo, New York, where he founded a magazine titled *The Home Monthly*. In 1858 Erastus joined forces with his younger brother, Irwin P. Beadle, who had been publishing songs, and the two moved from Buffalo to New York City, where they founded the firm of Beadle & Adams. The Adams name was originally business associate Robert Adams, and later his younger brothers William and David.

The largest of the dime novels publishers was the firm of Irwin and Erastus Beadle, who mass-produced inexpensive pulp publications. Beadle was not the first publisher of paper-covered novels, but it was one of the most successful. Between 1860 and 1865 Beadle sold more than four million dime novels. They were issued on regular basis as *Beadle's Dime Novels* from 1860 to 1874, with a new title appearing every two weeks or so.

The company started to publish cheap children's books, joke books, and various handbooks, all priced at 10¢. Among them were *Beadle's Dime Book of Dreams*, *Beadle's Dime Song Book*, *Beadle's Dime Cook Book*, and *Beadle's Dime Book of Beauty*. These were the first of the dime publications. More were issued under the umbrella designation of *Beadle's Dime Novels* from 1860 to 1874, with a new title every two weeks or so. Beadle intended these books to be read by poor and working class people at home, in public places, and during travel. The stories were lurid fiction, with scenes of violence, cross-dressing (mostly women as men), miscegenation, crime, implied sex, and other lurid plot elements. This type of sensationalized fiction was a radical departure from the previous genteel type of popular sentimental novel. In 1877 Beadle introduced the concept of a recurring hero who appeared in a series of dime novel stories at regular intervals.

During the first four years of publication, Beadle's sold more than five million copies of these dime novels.[13] The original series lasted for 321 issues. These early Beadle's books were often referred to as "yellowbacks," as they had covers of a distinctive orange color.[14] The books measured about 4 inches by 6 inches and sold for 10¢. Each contained a short novel of 30,000 words with a sensational and melodramatic plot. In 1874 Beadle's changed the name of the series to *Beadle's New Dime Novels*. The category continued for another 309 issues, until 1885. All of them were reprints of earlier numbers with the covers changed. By this time Beadle's was using hand-colored covers, with the color applied individually with stencils.

In 1877 Beadle's launched a new format in quarto size, which was a standard sheet of printing paper folded to make a 16 page pamphlet that measured approximately 8.5 inches by 12.5 inches. This was followed in 1884 by an octavo size, which measured approximately 7 inches by 10 inches and contained 32 pages. Different series sold for either 5¢ or 10¢.

Today the name "dime novel" is used as a general, all-encompassing term for cheap sensationalist literature, but originally "dime novel" was a brand name used by Beadle & Adams for their series of cheap, paper-cover works of sensationalist fiction. The firm also published novels as Beadle & Company, I.P. Beadle & Company, and Beadle & Adams. Beadle & Adams also published several newspapers and periodicals.

To fuel their immense publishing output, Beadle's used an estimated 250 authors. Many of them had various pseudonyms, often writing under several pen names at the same time. Some of the more prolific authors could produce a thousand words an hour, or about three double-spaced typewritten pages. A fast writer could complete a 70,000-word novel in less than a week. Author Albert W. Aiken, for example, whose specialty was western stories, cranked out novels at a furious rate and Beadles received a new manuscript from him every Saturday night.

The Beadle & Adams group published various series of books under different titles that were very similar. Among Beadle's publications were *Beadle's Dime Library*, *Beadle's Half-Dime Library*, *Beadle's American Library*, *Beadle & Adams' Twenty Cent Novels*, *Beadle's Pocket Library*, *Beadle's Pocket Novels*, *Beadle's Dime Fiction*, *Beadle's Dime Tales*, *Beadle's Weekly*, *Beadle's Boys Library of Sport and Adventure*, *Beadle's Fifteen Cent Novels*, *The New Dime Novels*, *Beadle's Popular Library*, *Beadle's Half-Dime Novelettes*, and *Beadle's Sixpenny Tales* published by their London Branch. It is difficult to categorize their many publications because stories and series were reprinted under different titles at different times in different series with very similar titles.

Erastus Beadle dominated the cutthroat dime novel business until he retired in 1889 after making a fortune. Erastus died in 1894 and his current partner William Adams in

1896. By then, competition from Street & Smith and Tousey was too intense. Beadle & Adams went out of business in 1898 and the assets were sold to M.J. Ivers & Co., who continued to publish reprints of the Beadle's series, as well as their own, until they went out of business at the end of 1905. Arthur Westbrook Company subsequently bought out Ivers and continued to reprint some of the Beadle stories until the 1930s.[15]

Street & Smith

One of the most important competitors of Beadle & Adams was the publishing firm of Street & Smith, one of the five major dime novel publishers in New York. The firm was founded when Francis Scott Street and Francis Schubael Smith became partners and purchased Amor Williamson's *New York Weekly Dispatch*. Street was the business manager and Smith wrote much of the material. In 1858 the paper became the long-running Street & Smith's *New York Weekly*, billed at the masthead as "A Journal of Useful Knowledge, Romance, Amusement, etc."

New York Weekly was one of the magazines that published successful western fiction. The longer stories were often serialized and ran over several issues, each installment frequently ending with a cliff-hanger to entice readers to buy the next issue.

In the late 1880s Street & Smith began publishing paperback books in series in order to keep their stories in print. This was the beginning of the dime novel paperback or the "thick book" to distinguish them from the fiction pamphlets that were also being published. They published *Log Cabin Library* and *The Nugget Library*, then added other dime novel series. *Log Cabin Library* lasted from 1889 to 1897, *The Nugget Library* from 1889 to 1892, and *New York Five Cent Library* from 1892 to 1896. Their *Nick Carter Library* lasted from 1891 to 1896, though the Nick Carter stories appeared from 1886 to 1990.

Street & Smith were diversified in their publishing program. They changed series, characters, genres, and formats to match changing times in order to keep attracting purchasers. They published detective stories in the *Secret Service* series, adventure and sea stories in *Sea and Shore*, and romance in the *Select Series*. Among other varied publications and genres, Street & Smith published *Diamond Dick, Jr. Weekly*, *Young Broadbrim*, *Tip Top Weekly*, *Mammoth Monthly Reader*, *Brave and Bold Series*, *Sea and Shore Series*, *Boys of Liberty Library*, and *Log Cabin Library*. Other offerings were Buffalo Bill stories, Jesse James stories, and the *Red, White and Blue Library*. Street & Smith actually competed with themselves as they had so many different publications flooding the market at the same time.

Street & Smith were ingenious in their reuse of stories, frequently reprinting previously-published stories at the same time they were adding new ones. One technique they used was to change the name of a series and reprint it as a different series. They also collected stories from three or four issues, such as from *Tip Top Weekly*, and reprinted them as a separate dime novel.[16]

Street & Smith added *Popular Magazine* in 1903, at first to appeal to juveniles, and then in altered form to be like Frank Munsey's successful *Argosy* magazine with stories of action, adventure, and the outdoors. In 1910 they followed with *Top-Notch*, another general fiction magazine. When the market changed again to niche topics, Street & Smith quickly responded with specialized genre magazines such as *Detective Story*, *Western Story*, *Sea Stories*, *Sport Story*, and *Love Story*.

Early in the twentieth century Street & Smith published five major dime novel publications: *Brave and Bold* featuring adventure, *Tip Top Weekly* with sports and adventure, *Nick Carter Weekly* featuring detective stories, *Diamond Dick, Jr.*, a western hero in a modern western setting, and *Buffalo Bill Stories* about the legendary hunter and showman. They later published a series of pulp novels about the James Brothers and various western outlaw bandits. The firm continued to be a major publisher of pulp novels into the 1930s. Among others they published *Mammoth Monthly Reader* and the *Sea and Shore* series.

Some of the Street & Smith series featured recurring characters, such as Frank Merriwell, one of the most famous characters in dime novel literature and certainly one of the most popular sports figures of all times. Merriwell was an all-American youth, handsome, brilliant, athletic, healthy, and clean living—just the type of wholesome masculine image admired by the purity crusaders. He was a hero of school tales and sports whose life was filled with adventure and athletics. Over the course of the series he grew from a boy to manhood. He went to college at Yale and his adventures continued to involve athletic and sports events, such as football and baseball. In time he graduated from Yale and became a coach there. To keep the series going he went out West to investigate the death of his father, and became involved in western adventures.

Frank Merriwell made his debut in *Tip Top Weekly* and was joined by his brother Dick both there and in *New Tip Top Weekly* in 850 issues between 1896 and 1915. Frank, Jr., went on for another 136 weeks in *New Tip Top Weekly*. In 1896 Street & Smith started a trend in dime novel publishing with the use of colored pictures on the cover of *Tip Top Weekly*. Within a year most dime novels were being published with colored covers.

The Merriwell character was developed by Gilbert Patten, a dime novel writer, but under the house name of Burt L. Standish. Patten had not attended college, but was resourceful enough to be able to create believable stories.[17] The stories were reprinted and issued many times in various formats and as collections.

The original Street & Smith firm lasted until Street died in 1883 and Smith retired 1887. The firm continued on under Francis' son Ormond until his death in 1933. Over the years the firm produced over 80 dime novel series, story papers, and libraries, and published 2,802 titles. The publishing firm was eventually absorbed in 1959 by Condé Nast Publications, the publisher of *Vogue* and other fashion magazines.

George Munro

George P. Munro published dime novels and reprinted fiction, producing 39 different series of paper-covered books and periodicals between 1863 and 1905. He published one of the first dime novel detective stories, *The Bowery Detective* by Kenward Phillips, in 1870 in the *Fireside Companion* and reprinted it in the *Old Sleuth Library* (1885–1905) of detective stories.

Munro's knowledge of printing and publishing came from working at the *Pictou Observer*, with American News Company, and as foreman of the Beadle printing plant.[18] He left Beadle's in 1863 to branch out on his own, and formed a partnership with Irwin Beadle to publish dime novels. The first number of *Irwin P. Beadle's Ten Cent Novels* appeared on November 11, 1863. Beadle left the firm after five issues and filed an injunction against Munro, so the title of the series was changed to *Munro's Ten Cent Novels*, which were published from 1863 to 1877. Munro published frontier and western stories, and a popular story paper titled *Fireside Companion*. In 1877 he started his most significant series, *The Seaside Library*, which reprinted classic English and American novels. He published over 2,000 separate issues in various editions. In 1886 alone, Munro printed five-and-a-half million books.[19] George Munro retired in 1893, but his sons carried on the business until 1906.[20]

Norman Munro

One of George Munro's fiercest business competitors was his younger brother Norman L. Munro. Norman had gone to work in 1869 for his brother George, who was 19 years older, to learn the publishing business. He started with *Ten Cent Popular Novels*, which he published from 1870 to 1875. In 1873 he went into partnership with Frank Tousey to publish the *New York Family Story Paper*. He left the business in 1878 to form his own company, Ornum & Co., which was Munro spelled backwards. Among others, Ornum published *The Black Highwayman Novels* about traditional bandits, highwayman, and outlaws.

From 1883 to 1899, Norman Munro published the *Old Cap Collier Library*, one of the first periodicals devoted to detective fiction. Norman's publications were not as prolific as leading publisher Beadle, but his stories were certainly as sensational as ex-partner Frank Tousey's. Norman Munro produced at least 25 paperback series, weekly story papers, and other periodicals. He frequently sued his competitors, including his brother, over proprietary rights. Munro's printing plates and rights to his stories from older libraries and weeklies were sold in 1902 to Street & Smith. Munro continued to publish the *New York Family Story Paper* until 1921.[21]

Frank Tousey

Frank Tousey was a New York publisher who was active from the 1870s to 1917. His firm was one of five major publishers of dime novels.

Tousey started his publishing career as a partner of publisher Norman L. Munro from 1873 to 1876, then founded Tousey & Small with George G. Small. In 1879 they went their own ways and Tousey founded a new company named Frank Tousey, Publisher. The firm continued until 1929.

Around 1910, Tousey experimented with changing the format of his publications, and added short stories, news items, editorial material, and even some advertising in an attempt to outsell his rivals. His publications featured dramatic, lurid, and sensational stories. His cover illustrations were also vivid and dramatic in an attempt to help sell the series with the promise of equally dramatic stories inside. Tousey's ideas made him the most successful dime novel publisher after Street & Smith. He also had inside help as his uncle was Sinclair Tousey, the president of American News Company, the leading distributor of dime novels in the country.[22] American News Company had a standing order of 60,000 copies for each new dime novel as it appeared. Sometimes they could sell more than that and a second edition of a popular novel might appear within a week. Some went through 10 to 12 editions.[23]

A yell escaped the man as he felt the blade go through his thigh, and another as Joe drew it out in such a way as to cut a terrible gash. Quick as a flash Joe gave him another stab in the calf of the other leg, almost ham stringing him. Without another blow the bully bounded out of the room with Joe right on his heels.

Frank Tousey was a New York publisher of pulp literature who was active from the 1870s to 1917. One of the five major publishers of dime novels, his firm cranked out hundreds of books for a total count of 2,154 titles. This example was from the *Wide Awake Library*, which was published from 1878 to 1898, and was priced at a mere 5¢.

Other success followed with Tousey publications such as *Wide Awake Weekly*, *The Boy's Star Library*, *Frank Tousey's Boys Weekly*, *New York Detective Library*, *Pluck and Luck*, and *Wild West Weekly*.

Tousey's company published what dime novels collectors call "the big six." *Pluck and Luck* published adventure stories (1898–1929), *Work and Win* published the sports adventures of Fred Fearnot (1898 to 1925), *Secret Service* recounted the adventures of the Brady detectives (1899 to 1928), *Liberty Boys of '76* was about a group of 100 young men who fought the war against Britain for independence (1901–1925), *Wild West Weekly* contained adventures of the heroic Young Wild West (his first name was Wild) from 1902 to 1927, and *Fame and Fortune* told the stories of boys who made money (1905 to 1928).[24]

Frank Tousey's answer to the youthful Frank Merriwell series from Street & Smith was Fred Fearnot. Fred Fearnot was an author's pseudonym used on westerns and adventure stories with boy heroes who captured kidnappers, bank robbers, and rustlers, solved mysteries, and had similar juvenile adventures. The series ran for 732 stories over 14 years in *Work and Win*. Most of the stories—at least the first 380—were written by Harvey K. Shackleford using the pen name of Hal Standish. Other stories in the series were written by George W. Goode and Francis W. Doughty, also using Hal Standish as a pseudonym.[25] Other similar youthful literary boy-hero competitors were Phil Rushington, Jack Lightfoot, Dick Daresome, and Jack Standfast.

Both Tousey and Street & Smith published many short-lived series and often their stories were recycled into other libraries and series. British publications at the time were publishing popular fictionalized stories about historical highwaymen, such as Claude Duval, Dick Turpin, and Jack Sheppard. Both Frank Tousey and Norman Munro reprinted them in America and added the American equivalents in the form of Jesse James and Billy the Kid.

From the late 1890s until 1915, when the last original dime novels were published, Street & Smith and Tousey dominated the field. In the end Street & Smith bought out Tousey, but continued to use the name in the pulp field.

Frank Munsey

Frank Munsey was originally a grocery clerk and telegraph operator from Augusta, Maine, who moved to New York in 1882 when he was in his late twenties, hoping to start a cheap fiction weekly of inspirational stories for children. On December 2, 1882, he released a small book of eight pages intended as a story paper for juveniles, titled *The Golden Argosy, Freighted with Treasures for Boys and Girls*. It was an example of the early transition between the story paper and the dime novel format. The first issue contained the opening of the serial "Nick and Nellie, or God Helps Them That Help Themselves," by popular dime novel author Edward S. Ellis. Inside was a serial by Horatio Alger, Jr., titled "Do and Dare, or a Brave Boy's Fight for a Fortune."

Weekly story papers had been offering cheap stories like this for almost fifty years, so *The Golden Argosy* did not do particularly well and started to fail amidst all the competition. As the market for this type of periodical fiction was limited, Munsey changed the magazine into a weekly and renamed it *Argosy*. This became one of the most popular and long-running magazines of the twentieth century. The story of *Argosy* will be discussed in further detail in Chapter 7 with the pulp magazines.

Munsey was versatile, acting as editor, journalist, writer, and publisher. Munsey's firm became one of the leading publishers, primarily cranking out westerns and stories about the frontier, sea and sports, and travel and exploration. If one of his magazines didn't do well, he shut it down and started another. Between 1891 and 1925 he owned fourteen newspapers, but he is mostly remembered for magazine publishing. He published various periodicals and even had own distribution company, Red Star News Co.[26]

Improbable Stories

The dime novel was a type of sensationalist literature that was more lurid and affordable than contemporary sentimental novels. They presented cheap, paper-covered fiction featuring outlaws, bandits, villains, detectives, lost love, and damsels in distress. Many contained melodramatic stories about the trials and tribulations of innocent virginal heroines (often described as "only a working girl"), including abduction, false marriage, sexual harassment by an employer or other powerful figure, compromising situations, passion, threatened rape, and a good dose of sensuality. Many were written with cliffhangers in the plots to end each chapter to stimulate purchase of the next issue. Adults scorned them, but read them in secret, so the pressure was on the publishers to supply what the readers wanted and to retain that audience.

Plots often included a brave hero who for one reason or another appeared in disguise as a simpleton, or a young woman who masqueraded in boys clothing to be near her lover and follow him to war or danger. One popular theme was the rise to fame of a poor-but-honest lad. These types of plots appealed to the working class and sold thousands of copies. The long-winded story titles that were in style at the time often ended up almost being a synopsis of the action of the plot. For example, *The Banner Weekly* serialized a story between July 6 and September 28, 1889, with a title that was a mouthful: *The Wild Steer Riders; or, The Red Revolver Rangers, A Story of Lawless Lives, Love, and Adventure in the Lone Star State*. The story was later reprinted in *Beadle's Dime Library* in 1894 with the more concise title of *The Wild Steer Riders; or Texas Jack's Terrors*.[27]

Aimed at adult readers, the first dime novels were stories of the early American frontier, often imitations of James Fenimore Cooper's stories. Plots focused on historical fiction, biographies, novels of the contemporary West, colonists at war with Indians, and western frontier romances with an emphasis on Indian fighting. Many claimed to be about "The Indian War," but exactly which one was never specified. In spite of this, frenzied dime novel plots killed off faceless and nameless Indians in droves.

Dime novels provided something for everyone and offered frontier and western stories, circus stories, school stories, success stories, detective and mystery stories, sea stories, love stories, historical fiction, stories about pirates, and stories about travel, adventure, and exploration. Other topics were sports, railroads, fire fighters, smuggling, science fiction, war, the American Civil War, and bandits. Some dime novels featured the army or the navy in, as one library series put it, "stories of heroism, suffering, and adventures of American soldiers and sailors."[28] There were even stories set in the Klondike after the gold rush. If a plot line or character type became popular in one dime novel, then it was instantly copied by other competitive publishers. For example, sea stories based on the success of Yankee traders became very popular and spread to all the publishers in the 1870s and 1880s.

Publishers shaped many of their dime novels to appeal directly to young boys with topics such as pirates, school and sports stories, and adventure and sea stories using every imaginable hero that a juvenile male might admire. Typical of these libraries were *The Boy's Own*, *The Boy's Own Novels*, *The Boy's Star Library*, *The Boy's World*, and *Boy's Best Weekly*. When weeklies for boys became popular in the 1890s and early 1900s, Frank Tousey responded with *Work and Win* with hero Fred Fearnot, *Pluck and Luck*, and *Frank Reade Weekly* with Frank's electrified inventions. Another popular category, aimed also primarily at young boys, was circus and carnival stories, which featured young boys who ran away from home to join the circus and become performers. *Fame and Fortune Weekly* published popular inspirational success stories of boys who made money and rose to fame.

Sea stories were about shipwrecks, mutinies, castaways, and treasure hunts. Pirate stories were about pirates. *The Red Raven Library* consisted of stories about three boys on the trail of Captain Kidd and other pirates in their ship The Red Raven. The similar pirate and sea stories in *The Red Wolf Series* were taken directly from the English penny dreadfuls. Railroad stories appealed to boys who wanted to become firemen and brakemen, or even hobos. School and sports stories were mostly set in boarding schools, colleges, or universities, and focused on amateur athletes and school sports. A typical story involved how the hero was kidnapped or discredited by the villain or otherwise disqualified from playing with the team, but got back into the game at the last moment and won a victory for the school, in spite of his adversaries.

A few publications were aimed directly at young girls, but they were not particularly successful. Beadle's *Belles and Beaux* lasted for only 13 issues.[29]

Horatio Alger, Jr., was the author of a popular series of 119 stories about poor orphan boys whose honesty was rewarded in the end. His stories about poor-born Americans who reached success were considered inspirational. At the end of "Adrift in New York; or, Dodger and Florence Braving the World" in *Brave and Bold* for October 31, 1903, is a publishing blurb that says, "The next issue, No. 46, will contain 'A Lad of Steel; or, Running Down the Tiger,' by Matt Royal. This is a most marvelous story of a brave, clever boy, whom nothing can down. Almost unassisted, he performs remarkable deeds of valor. Surprise follows surprise, and the reader is led on in breathless suspense from one scene of excitement to another. It is a tale you cannot afford to miss."

Publishers employed all sorts of techniques to make the most out of their libraries. Most stories in dime novels depended on lots of action and were not dated so that they could be reprinted in another series or reissued with the title changed or a new cover. At one time Street & Smith cleaned out their old unsold stock simply by putting new covers on them and selling them as new. A new cover made the novel appear to be new. Publishers also reissued original stories in a different series of dime novels or later in the same series. Some of the Deadwood Dick stories were reprinted 14 times. Occasionally the weeklies even reprinted earlier issues in their entirety. Unlike today's novels, dime novels did not allow much growth for the characters, because the hero had to be the same no matter where the reader started the series. The typical lack of growth of the hero in these stories also allowed reprints in any sequence or series without readers noticing, because the character essentially stayed the same.

The heroes of the dime novels could be anyone. Frontiersmen, cowboys, American Indians, bandits, detectives, fire fighters, inventors, and schoolboys all appeared in dime novels. Popular recurring characters were detectives like Nick Carter, Old King Brady, and Old Sleuth, and western heroes such as Buffalo Bill, Diamond Dick, Deadwood Dick, and Jesse James. Many of these heroes returned in story after story.

The fiction of the dime novels was overblown and full of melodramatic style as each dime novel tried to outdo the others. Stories focused on action and fast-paced conversation. Stories kicked the plot into action with the first few words in order to grab the reader's attention. Author Eugene Sawyer started one story in the Nick Carter detective series, *Ramon Aranda, the California Detective*, with the tantalizing words, "We will have the money, or she shall die."[30]

Fiction set on the frontier or in the West was among the most popular, with heroes who were frontiersmen, cowboys, and bandits. They incorporated stock plots and characters, often repeating themselves frequently. Two of these typical lurid western titles were *Jack Long; or, Shot in the Eye, a True Story of Texas Border Life*, and *Pacific Pete, Prince of the Revolver* by Joseph Badger. The West was mostly considered to be one of two places, either collectively the high plains and prairies of eastern Colorado, Nebraska, and eastern Montana, or the mountain West with dense forests, cascading streams, and fast-running rivers. Also popular for a while were stories about the brave and stalwart Royal Northwest Mounted Police tracking down renegades on the British Northwest frontier.

Most dime novel writers were from the East and had never visited the West when they started churning out highly-imaginary Wild West tales. The heroes of the earliest dime novels were mostly hunters and scouts with flintlock rifles and coonskin caps. The stories authors wrote were what they assumed the West was like, and usually included outrageous manners of speech and dress. Part of the dime novelist's perception of the West was to attribute the most peculiar language to some of the characters. One example of the bizarre language that dime novelists thought was used by mountain men was this one from *The Luckless Trapper; or, The Haunted Hunter* by William Reynolds Eyster (Lew James). At one point the trapper Bill Blaze exclaims, "Minks and mushrats! Blam'd if she ain't Dick Martin's gal! A trump, by mitey! She's cleaned out the hull b'iling; stampeded ther corral, an's bringin' the pick o' the lot into camp! Bill Blaze an' her'll move inter Black Load camp rejoicin.' Waugh!"[31]

Another only semi-comprehensible speech came from the main character in *Giant George, the Ang'l of the Range. A Tale of Sardine-Box City, Arizona,* by James M. Cain. At one point in the story George draws a huge Bowie knife and yells out, "I kin carve ther nose offen ther galoot that laffs at me er Don Diablo. I kin shoot ther eyelids offen the cuss what smiles. I kin dissect ther in'ards o' ther pilgrim or tender-hoof what looks crossways or puckers a lip at me or my outfit, fer I'm plum full an' b'ilin over with hydrophobic."[32]

Not all of the dime novel literature was detective stories and western adventure oriented towards male readers. Women made up a large part of the reading public and their preference for fiction was romantic stories aimed at women. Plots included love, success, moral temptation, friends becoming enemies and vice versa, marriage, divorce, and any romantic situation that determined the heroine's fate. Also popular were boys' and girls' series books, which were aimed at younger readers.

Dime novels even contained some primitive juvenile science fiction stories that featured a boy who used some type of invention in his adventures. The technology described was typically close to that which existed at the time, thus flying machines and underwater sailing ships used to find sunken cities were powered by steam or the new electricity.

One example is *The Huge Hunter; or, The Steam Man of the Prairies* by Edward S. Ellis, which appeared in *Beadle's Half Dime Library*. The story is about a boy named Johnny who invents a gigantic ten-foot-tall steam-powered mechanical man that pulls a wagon at high speed across the prairie during Johnny's adventures among the Indians.

Another early science fiction dime novel was *Electric Bob's Big Black Ostrich; or, Lost on the Desert* by Robert Toombs, which appeared in Street & Smith's *New York Five Cent Library* on August 26, 1893. The cover shows a mechanical machine that looks like a giant ostrich striding through a jungle river with the occupants shooting at a group of men in a rowboat. The caption reads, "Bang! Bang! Bang! Every report from Electric Bob's machine gun was followed by a yell or a splash from the enemy." Many similar adventures followed, with the machines becoming stranger and stranger.

4

Dime Novel Heroes

By the early 1900s America's cities had mushroomed as the county became an industrial giant generating enormous wealth. Between the end of the Civil War in 1865 and the turn of the century in 1900, America's population increased two-and-a-half times, absorbing over 11 million immigrants, with much of the growth occurring in the Eastern cities. In 1900, 10 million people lived west of the Mississippi with 66 million to the east of it.[1]

The American West in which western stories were set was a vast uncharted lawless territory that Easterners were not familiar with, but envied. In the literary world of the first half of the nineteenth century, the American frontier was perceived as some vague borderland to the west of the East Coast, in a land of uncharted wilderness that was characterized by lawlessness and danger. All the land to the west of civilization was seen as a dark, forbidding place, and the vast and gloomy forests of the settlers' frontier was supposedly full of all sorts of terrors. Early tales placed the western frontier at the Allegheny Mountains and only later did "The Frontier" move westwards with advancing civilization towards the American West and Southwest of the cowboy. When President Jefferson purchased the unknown, uncharted, and unexplored Louisiana Territory from France in 1803, "The West" was considered to be all of the land beyond the Mississippi.

The western "frontier" has always been the furthermost edge of settlement towards the west. Over time the perception of the location of this frontier shifted. This started when seventeenth century colonists pushed into the interior from the East Coast. At end of the eighteenth century they advanced beyond the Appalachians. In post–Civil War years, the trans-Mississippi West was the new frontier imagined to be the land of opportunity and individual enterprise where large fortunes could be made in mining and cattle ranching.

Many of the plots of the early dime novels were set in this unknown world. The frontier hero stood as a barrier between civilization and the savagery that was presumed to exist just beyond the boundary of the western frontier—wherever it happened to be at the time. Civilization, which was promoted as the American ideal state of affairs, was equated with progress and the frontier hero was the man who tamed the wilderness and made it safe for the civilization that was advancing westwards.

Before the cowboys of the Wild West appeared in pulp literature, dime novels featured rugged hunters and scouts outfitted with flintlock rifles and coonskin caps. They were bigger-than-life men with outrageous manners, speech, and dress. These were strong-willed, self-motivated individuals who relied on their own skills for survival, because part of the myth of the dime novel frontier was that the white hero could think and fight better than anyone. After the real West became settled, the western hero changed from the woodsman into the cowboy of fiction.

Frontier and western dime novel stories were a continuation of the earlier costume dramas that portrayed the protagonist as a form of knight-errant. The heroes of this overblown style of fiction, whether real like Kit Carson or fictional like Deadwood Dick, took on whatever characteristics the writer thought the hero should have. The plots were whatever the writer thought would make a rousing story and whatever he thought met the public's preconceived notions of the West. Sensationalism was the key to commercial success and the pressure was on authors and publishers to supply what readers wanted and to repeat it to retain their audience.

To be successful, the plots revolved around action. Western dime novels were written with cliff-hanging elements that fed popular fantasies and romantic mythology about outlaws and Indians. To persuade buyers, the cover usually depicted some dramatic element of the tale, such as the heroine in distress, Indian attacks, or the villain lurking behind a bush to shoot the hero.

The Captivity Narratives

One of the early popular plotlines of the dime novels was that of a white woman captured and mistreated by evil Indians, and her rescue by a hero or hunter or woodsman (or a combination of all three), who tracks her through the forests. This type of book was popularly known as a "captivity narrative."[2]

One of the first sensationalized tales of a white woman captured by Indians was not fiction. Mary Rowlandson, the wife of a minister, was captured during King Philip's war against New England settlers when a band of Indians raided the village of Lancaster, Massachusetts, in 1676, killing 35 colonists and kidnapping her and 23 other women.[3] Mrs. Rowlandson became the slave of Indian warrior Metacom (King Philip), chief of the Wampanoag, and spent 11 weeks with the Indians until she was finally set free after a ransom was paid.

In Rowlandson's popular book, *The Sovereignty and Goodness of God*, first published in 1682, she wrote a sensational account of being taken deep into the woods and witnessing Indian ceremonies. The book was a best seller and went through at least fifteen editions. The title tells most of the plot with "*A Narrative of the Captivity, Sufferings and Removes of Mrs. Mary Rowlandson, who was taken prisoner by the Indians with several others, and treated in the most barbarous and cruel manner by those vile savages.*"[4]

A fundamental element of this type of frontier narrative that guaranteed publishing success was the struggle between white men and Indians over the body of a woman. This made for sensational reading, due to the prevailing concept of the time that races should not mix. Though Mrs. Rowlandson's tale of captivity and subsequent ordeal among the Indians symbolized the capture of Christianity and civilization, the story was a strongly moral one. She described how she resisted physical and spiritual temptations while with the Indians, thus vindicating the strength of her values and her moral character as a white woman. The final triumph was her rescue and return to civilization after being held captive. Mrs. Rowlandson's book stimulated the publication of other similar stories, most of them incorporating as many lurid details about the captivity as possible.

In the early decades of the 1700s, the real-life captivity narrative was expanded into fictional versions. These tales recounted the stirring deeds of daring backwoodsmen battling Indians and the wilderness. The typical story featured a heroic white hunter who was completely at ease in the deep forests on the boundary of civilization. The plot thickened when a white woman or young girl was captured from her home by Indians, who were portrayed as barbaric, ruthless, and villainous. She was dragged away into the dark sinister woods where there was danger at every turn and Indians lurked behind every tree. Rescue by the gallant hero comes, of course, by the end of the book. This rescue-in-the-nick-of-time concept commonly carried on into later cavalry stories and other western plots.

The fear of kidnap and rape was promoted by books such as Mary Rowlandson's, which provided ready villains in the form of Indians who abducted white women. Part of the allure for readers was a plot fueled by a fear of the unknown elements of the West. Women readers, in particular, had a morbid fascination that capture and rape by Indians could happen to them.

James Fenimore Cooper and Leatherstocking

The creator of the original western hero in American sensational literature was James Fenimore Cooper. Cooper wrote historical romances with plots formed around variations of the core characters of a hunter, a captive, and a savage Indian opponent. Cooper's first novel, titled *Precaution: A Novel* (1820), had an indifferent reception. He persisted and the next year wrote *The Spy: A Tale of Neutral Ground* (1821), which did succeed and launched his career as a novelist. Cooper's subsequent books were highly successful, were translated into dozens of languages, and sold millions of copies. Cooper's writing was also sentimental and romanticized the Indians.

The hero of these novels was often dressed in a buckskin outfit to authenticate the image of the experienced woodsman. In spite of his seemingly humble appearance, the man underneath was often an aristocratic or upper class character. His background might be that of a British nobleman, such as in *The Pioneers: or, The Sources of the Susquehanna* (1823), or a Virginia planter in *The Last of the Mohicans* (1826).

Cooper's major literary achievement was a series of five historical romances known as the Leatherstocking Tales. The books were centered around the adventures of the fictional woodsman Natty Bumppo and his interaction with the lives of settlers on the western frontier. Bumppo was also known variously as Hawkeye, Leatherstocking, Pathfinder, and Deerslayer. During the nineteenth century and the later dime novels, Cooper's hero as a character was borrowed, imitated, plagiarized, and parodied. His heroic persona served as the protagonist for serious novels and was the prototype for the hero of countless stage melodramas and dime novels. Later pulp writers and novelists further developed and expanded the basic formula initiated by Cooper.

The most enduring of Cooper's books has been *The Last of the Mohicans* (1826), which was possibly based on the real-life kidnapping by Indians and rescue of Daniel Boone's daughter, Jemima, and two of her companions in 1776.[5] The book was written in the style of the time, which is a little difficult to read today. Bumppo tends to be long-winded and the Indians in the stories are very talkative, in contrast to the writing style of the cowboy authors of the later pulp novels, who were all action and not much talk. Nevertheless, the book has remained extremely popular and sold millions of copies. It has been claimed that this was the most widely-read American novel of the nineteenth century.

James Fenimore Cooper's novel *The Last of the Mohicans* (1826) is part of a series of iconic stories of a frontier hero battling savage Indians in the wilderness, in the process taming the frontier and making it safe for civilization. This book was part of the popular "captivity narrative" in which white women were captured and spirited away by Indians, only to be rescued from a "fate-worse-than-death" by the hero-woodsman.

Although Cooper created frontier romances and the first western hero, he was also responsible for much of the generic hero myth. Cooper's version of the myth included a wide variety of white and Indian social and racial stereotypes who showed extreme good and evil, as well as a mix of characteristics in between.

Graphic violence was often a part of these early Indian-versus-whites novels. In the fierce fight between the protagonists and the Huron Indians in *Last of the Mohicans*,

Uncas is described as "leaping on an enemy, with a single, well-directed blow of his tomahawk, cleft him to the brain."[6] Cooper also used the American idea that it is acceptable for the hero to take action outside the law to serve the course of justice. Leatherstocking is a man who stands outside civilization and retaliates against the agents of savagery with death and violence of his own because of his moral superiority. He has little compunction about the morality of his actions and takes no responsibility for them. His violence is used to end their violence. The notion was that good always triumphed over evil if the good had high-civilized moral values. This concept was exploited in later dime novels, such as the adventures of Deadwood Dick, and in the hard-boiled detective pulps of the 1920s and 1930s.

Malaeska

On June 7, 1860, an advertisement that appeared in the *New York Tribune* boldly proclaimed "Books for the Million! A Dollar Book for a Dime!! 123 Pages complete, only Ten Cents!!! Beadle's Dime Novels No. 1, Malaeska; the Indian Wife of the White Hunter."

This was an advertisement for what is considered to be the first dime novel, *Malaeska: The Indian Wife of the White Hunter*. The author was Ann Sophia Winterbotham Stephens, who had previously written a number of romance novels that appeared as hardback books. The novel was extremely popular and sold more than 300,000 copies, an impressive number when the population of the country was about 30 million people.

Malaeska started out literally with a bang to gain the reader's attention and start the plot rolling. The first few lines included:

> "Bang!
> Bang!
> Bang!
> Three shots rang out on the midnight air!
> 'Touch but a hair of her head, and by the Lord that made me, I will bespatter that tree with your brains!'"

The reader could not help but be drawn into a plot that started like this.

It is interesting to consider why the publication of this particular dime novel was a turning point. From the late 1830s through the 1850s other sensationalist literary works that were not traditional novels had appeared, and so had pulp reprints of earlier serialized fiction. Many previous pulp books had been based on exciting and shocking newspaper stories of the day, and *Malaeska* simply continued the trend. And even though it is considered to be the first of the true dime novels, it was actually not a new story, but was a reprint. It originated with a short story titled "The Jockey Cap," published in April 1836 in *Portland Magazine*. The tale was expanded and serialized during February, March, and April 1839 in a magazine called *Ladies' Companion*. Irwin and Erastus Beadle simply paid author Ann Stephens $250 for the rights to reprint the story.[7] It was not even a particularly sensational story. It was also not the first inexpensive book. There had been earlier series of books, such as those published by Ballou's, that could be considered to be dime novels.

What made this book stand out and start a whole new trend in publishing was the cheap cover price, its widespread availability, and the superior marketing used to promote it. Another other factor was that it came at a time when tens of thousands of young men were settling into army camps and needed inexpensive reading entertainment.

Seth Jones

Imaginative advertising and promotion were partly responsible for creating the next huge dime novel success. In October of 1860, residents of the New York area were blanketed with posters and handbills that asked, "Who Is Seth Jones?" These were followed by lithographs of a stalwart heroic-looking hunter with an inscription that said, "I am Seth Jones."

This was the clever campaign used by Beadle & Adams to promote their mass market sensational adventure *Seth Jones; or, The Captives of the Frontier* by Edward Ellis. This was the eighth in their series of dime novels and appeared on October 2, 1860. *Seth Jones* was considered to be one the most successful of the early dime novels. It rivaled *Malaeska* for sales and went on to become one of the bestsellers of its time. The book sold 60,000 copies almost immediately and Beadles eventually claimed that it had sold over 500,000 copies.[8]

Edward Sylvester Ellis was an educator, novelist, poet, editor, and historian who primarily wrote juvenile fiction about frontier adventures of a rousing, hair-raising sort. He was a teacher and administrator in various New Jersey school systems and wrote numerous textbooks for school use. He was one of most prolific writers at Beadle & Adams and wrote for all the major dime novel publishers. One of his series of books featured Deerfoot, the Shawanoe Indian. His output was so prolific that he wrote under thirty-one pseudonyms, including Capt. Bruin Adams, Capt. James Fenimore Cooper Adams, P.T. Barnum, Oscar Gwynne, Capt. R.M. Hawthorne, Lt. R.H. Jayne, Rollo Robins, and a host of others. He liked military titles and at one time promoted himself to Col. H.R. Gordon.[9]

Seth Jones was the story of a backwoods Leatherstocking-type of hero who behaved in a manner similar to James Fenimore Cooper's hero, and the plot imitated the character types, class roles, and settings used by Cooper. The basic plot involves the rescue of a damsel in distress from the Mohawks. It included one of the common plot themes in dime novels of the time that the characters were not always who they seemed to be. The hero was often given an aristocratic or upper class background that was hidden from the reader for most of the book. Ellis used this concept to the fullest. Seth Jones, for example, is presented as an elderly backwoodsman, but in a surprise twist at the end, he is revealed to be the heroine's long-lost young suitor in the disguise of an old man. Seth is revealed to be Eugene Morton, a Revolutionary War hero and a son of a distinguished New England family.[10]

Malaeska had presented a tragic view of life on the American frontier, with themes of war and captivity. *Seth Jones*, on the other hand, was the story of a successful rescue from immoral kidnappers, with a white masculine hero emerging triumphant at the end. The Ellis type of dime novel, using the wilderness as a background and glorified plots of white men rescuing white women from the clutches of the dreaded Indians, became the model for hundreds of other dime novels.

Ellis wrote *Seth Jones* while he was a 19-year-old school teacher at Red Bank, New Jersey. Ellis became a regular contributor of novels and stories, and continued to write hundreds of dime novels until his death in 1916. He wrote in several genres, including popular serial tales about the London underworld titled *Rook the Robber; or, London Fifty Years Ago*, and the exciting *The Boy Detective; or, The Crimes of London*, published in 1860, about a young man who hunted down villains and brought them to justice.

Adding a little spice to the series, in *The Boy Detective*, the youthful hero rescues a scantily clad girl from a burning house. She becomes his girlfriend and they capture a cunning master criminal. Ellis wrote so many stories under so many different names that even experts are not totally certain what should be credited to him.

The Real Heroes of the Wild West

Dime novels made readers in the East believe that the West was a place of romantic adventure, financial independence, and potential fame. With Manifest Destiny a popular concept at the time, the emerging nation was hungry for heroes and wanted to read more tales about adventurous and courageous white men advancing into the threatening wilderness to fight Indians.[11] Searching for more and different frontier heroes for their stories, authors turned to real-life woodsmen who were skilled hunters and Indian fighters. Two of them were Daniel Boone and Davy Crockett. Their images helped to create and propagate the legendary West and the people who lived there.

Backwoodsman Daniel Boone was a legitimate explorer, woodsmen, expert trailblazer, and daring scout. He was skilled at Indian warfare and had a vast knowledge of his opponents. He may have even been part of the inspiration for the hunter-heroes of James Fenimore Cooper's romantic adventure novels.

Davy Crockett was another real outdoorsman and woodsman who became an important literary property. In 1831, a play by James Kirke Paulding titled *The Lion of the West*, based on the real-life Davy Crockett, became very popular. Two years later an unknown author wrote *Life and Adventures of Colonel David Crockett of West Tennessee*. Noting the popularity of the play and the book, Crockett quickly wrote his own sensationalist biography. The book, published in 1833, was titled *Narrative of the Life of David Crockett of the State of Tennessee*. Crockett was already an adept storyteller, so he became the author of his own legend and was one of the first to create his own literary persona. The book became very popular and sold between 5,000 and 10,000 copies, which was a large number at the time. The demand for more of his stories led to another book in 1834 titled *Sketches and Eccentricities of Col. David Crockett of West Tennessee*, ghost-written by James S. French.

Though both Boone and Crockett were important historical figures in their own right on the frontier, they were elevated to almost legendary status after being discovered by dime-novelists. Later real-life westerners who received similar treatment were mountain man Christopher "Kit" Carson and showman William F. "Buffalo Bill" Cody. Men like Carson, Cody, Jim Bridger, and Wild Bill Hickok became better known as dime-novel heroes than for their historical deeds in real life. Overblown novels about these real-life westerners were published before their trustworthy biographies, so the readers of dime novels believed that the exploits and details they read were authentic. Readers formed their own conceptions of these real life heroes solely from the written word.

By the mid–1800s, interest by readers in the frontiersman fighting Indians in the forests of the East started to fade. Tomahawks, muskets, and heroes dressed in coonskin caps and moccasins were seen as out-of-date. The reading public wanted a new, fresh, more contemporary hero. In response, writers of sensationalist stories looked again for someone different to promote. The new fictional model became Kit Carson, plainsman, trapper, Indian fighter, and frontiersman.

Western dime novels remained superb escapist literature. Boys and young men who read them dreamed of going out West to be a cowboy, ride the range, meet a pretty cowgirl, and settle down without a care. This image of a cowboy and his horse personified these dreams and desires, as he sits and gazes out in quiet contemplation at a herd of horses grazing peacefully on the prairie. (Library of Congress)

The real Christopher "Kit" Carson was an authentic westerner and mountain man, born in 1809 in Kentucky. He ran away to the West at age 16, arriving in New Mexico in 1826. He made his life as a trapper and mountain man, later had a military career, and was a guide for several exploratory expeditions into the West.

Even before Carson's death, the dime novel legend makers were hard at work exaggerating the man and his exploits. They gave Carson the literary attributes of strong virile heroes that the reading public demanded. Dime novels boosted the new fictional Carson into a fearless champion and defender of virtue. He was perceived as the new hero of the wilderness of the West.

The first fictional version of Carson appeared in *Kit Carson: The Prince of the Gold Hunters*, written by Charles Averill and published in 1849. Averill's version of Carson was a giant man of action who never lost a battle. The real Carson, however, was not tall. He was a small, stoop-shouldered man who did not look the part of a hero. He was about five-foot four-inches tall, but appeared shorter, as he was bow-legged from years spent riding a horse. In spite of Carson's small build in real life, Averill gave his fictional hero a "mighty frame," "massive arms," and "prodigious strength." The heroic version was at least six inches taller than Carson's real height and was a big man with rippling muscles.

Averill claimed that his story was based on facts, but apparently did not take the time to learn much about the real Carson and did not even obtain permission to use Carson's name as his fictional hero.[12] Carson's literary persona was loosely based on a minimal amount of facts and expanded by myth. In this first improbable yarn, the literary

Carson killed scores of Indians and rescued a young girl kidnapped by Indians. The fictional story contained a prairie fire, a treasure cave, and a perilous escape from the Indians. The plot moved along at a brisk pace and was full of cliffhangers. One of the false "facts" in the book was that Carson was the discoverer of the original California gold strike of 1848.

The real Carson was so unlike his literary persona that people he met did not think they were meeting the real man. One time when he was on the Oregon Trail, Carson met an Arkansas man who had heard that the famous scout was close by. "I say, stranger, are you Kit Carson?" Carson admitted he was. The man looked at him closely and said, "Look here, you ain't the kind of Kit Carson I'm looking for."[13]

The cover of one overblown lurid dime novel showed Carson holding a beautiful woman he has just rescued, with both of them surrounded by dead Indians. The writer described a headlong charge during which Carson killed one assailant with a knife and another with a tomahawk. Carson later said he didn't remember the incident and commented, "Gentlemen, that thar may be true, but I hain't got no recollection of it."[14]

In 1849 the real Carson accompanied an army expedition that was trying to find and rescue a white woman named Ann White, who had been captured by Jicarilla Apaches in New Mexico. Unfortunately, only a few minutes before the troops found the camp, one of the Indians killed her. Searching the camp afterwards, Carson found a copy of Averill's pulp novel that had probably belonged to Mrs. White. Carson was always disturbed by this find and wondered if the book had given her false hope that he was coming to rescue her in the nick of time, just like in the dime novel.[15]

The adventures that Carson supposedly engaged in became so outlandish that even Carson was surprised. A biography published De Witt Peters in 1859, titled *The Life and Adventures of Kit Carson, the Nestor of the Rocky Mountains, From Facts Narrated by Himself*, fueled the legend. But even Carson commented that "Peters laid it on a little thick."[16]

Eventually over seventy books were written by different authors with Carson as a hero, an avenger of Indian depredations, rescuer of captured women, and a superb outdoorsman. Typical of the Carson pulps were *Rocky Mountain Kit's Last Scalp Hunt*, *The Fighting Trapper: Kit Carson to the Rescue*, and *Kit Carson's Last Bride: The Flower of the Apaches*.

Depending on the particular literary market, Carson was described differently for different classes of readers. The Carson of the dime novels intended for mass circulation among the lower and middle classes was a hero of adventure and violent exploits. He was portrayed as a wild hunter who battled Indians and evil renegades in standard types of rescue plots. The Carson that appeared in the novels published in hard cover for a more "respectable" reading audience was a more genteel character with refined ways and manners, though still a man of violence, and a hunter, avenger, and rescuer of women.

By 1900 some of Carson's popularity as a subject for pulp novels had faded, though his fictional self would be revived in the 1940s and 1950s for comic books and television.

"Buffalo Bill" Cody

Another real-life frontiersmen whose fame was exaggerated by dime novels was William F. "Buffalo Bill" Cody. Dime novels helped to establish his mythic persona and expanded both his personal legend and that of the West. Cody quickly grew from a minor historical character on the frontier to a prominent show business personality.

4. Dime Novel Heroes

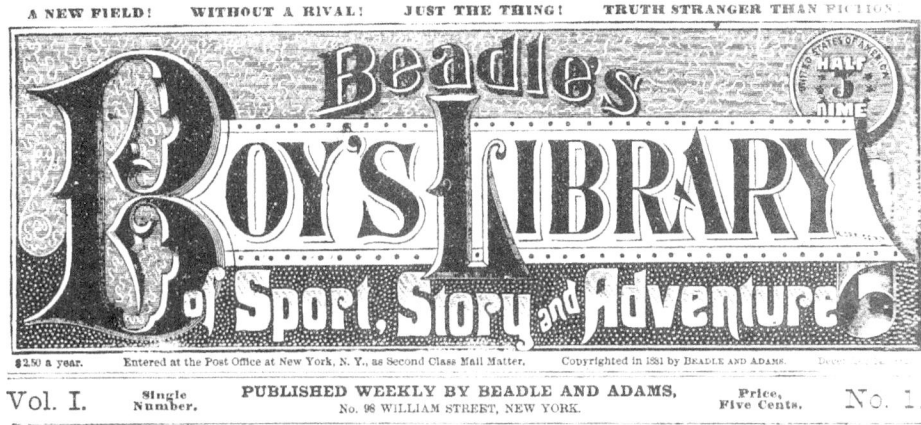

MADDENED WITH FRIGHT, THE BULL BOUNDED INTO THE AIR, SNORTED WILDLY, GORED THOSE IN ADVANCE, AND SOON LED THE HERD.

Though he was an army scout and authentic frontiersman of the West, William F. "Buffalo Bill" Cody was also reinvented as a manufactured literary hero of the dime novels. His outlandish literary persona was the subject of stories by authors such as Ned Buntline, Col. Prentiss Ingraham, and many others. This book, which appeared on December 14, 1881, was partly biographical, based on Cody's autobiography, but was mostly pure dime novel entertainment, including a tall tale shown here of Cody as a lad riding a wild buffalo.

The real Buffalo Bill Cody was a scout for the army, an Indian fighter, a teamster, a drover, a trapper, a Civil War soldier, a stagecoach driver, and a buffalo hunter for the railroad. Cody also claimed in his autobiography to have been a Pony Express rider.[17] Though Cody was indeed a genuine product of the Old West, his inflated fictional exploits in novels and his later *Wild West* show eventually became the perceived reality of the West for many of his fans. The public clamored for violence and fights with Indians, so Cody's publicity men shaped the *Wild West* around what experience had taught them that public wanted.[18] Buffalo Bill and the other Wild West shows catered to escapist needs of urban men with humdrum jobs who wanted to retreat from their daily routine by going west and marrying a pretty ranch girl.

Cody's initial literary fame started with dime novels written by Ned Buntline, one of the pen names of Edward Carroll Zane Judson. Judson was a pulp novelist who wrote about adventure, the sea, sports, and the Mexican War in an estimated 400 or more dime novels and stories, many of them under various pseudonyms, including Capt. Hal Decker, Scout Jack Ford, and Edward Minturn.[19] Buntline was writing lurid fiction even before his Buffalo Bill stories. As far back as 1848, he had written *The Mysteries and Miseries of New York*. One of Buntline's favorite topics was pirate stories, such as *The Black Avenger of the Spanish Main; or, The Fiend of Blood* and *The Red Revenger; or, The Pirate King of the Floridas*. He is best remembered, however, for his Buffalo Bill stories in Street & Smith's *New York Weekly*.

Judson was a bit of a character himself and had a varied background before becoming a full-time professional writer. His own accounts of his life blended reality with myth, as did his later writings, thus many of the details of his early days are not clear. As a boy, Judson ran away from home to serve on a ship in the navy. In the late 1830s he wrote for *Knickerbocker* magazine and in the 1840s, he started a sensationalist weekly magazine called *Ned Buntline's Own*. Judson took part in the Seminole Wars in Florida during the 1830s, and served in the Union Army for a short time during the Civil War. At age 23 in Nashville he shot and killed a man who had accused Judson of having an affair with his wife. As a result, an angry mob grabbed Judson from jail in order to lynch him. The unruly mob started to hang him, but luckily a bystander cut the rope just in time (other accounts say that the rope broke) before he choked to death.[20]

Judson's later career focused on being a journalist, publisher, novelist, editor, writer, temperance lecturer, and social reformer. As a link to his days at sea, Judson wrote stories under a variety of pseudonyms with a definite nautical flavor, such as Charlie Bowline, Frank Clewline, and Jack Brace, as well as his most famous, Ned Buntline. On a ship, a buntline is one of the ropes attached to the bottom of a square sail.

On July 24, 1869, Buntline stopped at Fort McPherson, Nebraska, to interview Maj. Frank North about an Indian skirmish called the Battle of Summit Springs, which had taken place in Colorado in May of 1869 after a battalion of the Fifth Cavalry had marched out to search for two women captured by a band of Cheyenne Indians. Buntline wanted to use this true story as the basis for a dime novel and hoped to promote a heroic character in Maj. North. North was not interested and supposedly told Buntline that Cody, asleep under a nearby wagon, could be the hero of Buntline's adventure story. Cody turned out to be perfect for the heroic image of the western frontier. He was 23 years old, tall and muscular, with long curly hair, and looked the part of a hero in his scout's buckskin clothing. So Buntline changed his story to feature Buffalo Bill.

Buntline's first story about Cody was *Buffalo Bill, the King of the Border Men*, subtitled

The Wildest and Truest Story I Ever Wrote, which was serialized in Smith & Street's *New York Weekly* from December 23, 1869, to March 10, 1870. Though Cody received his nickname of "Buffalo Bill" from his earlier days as a buffalo hunter, this name does not seem to have been commonly used before Buntline called him that in this dime novel.[21] Buntline's story included a liberal amount of imagination and fiction, including using Wild Bill Hickok (whom Cody had not yet met) as a character and having Cody's mother (who was already dead) give him sterling character endorsements.

The story was not what would now be considered a western. Instead it was a lurid fictional story of adventure and revenge from Kansas in the Civil War, with Buffalo Bill and Wild Bill Hickok teaming up to defeat a gang of "border ruffians," as these outlaws were called. Buntline portrayed Cody as a skilled frontiersman and Indian fighter with humility, bravery, perfect grammar, and courage. He was portrayed with a full beard, and was splendidly dressed in an outfit like Leatherstocking. He was heroic, gentle with women, and yet capable of violence against Indians and villains.

Buntline's story was an immediate bestseller, though it used the often overblown Victorian prose that was popular at the time. For example, when Buntline described Bill's family, he said, "A noble-looking, white-haired man sits by a rough table, reading the Bible aloud. On stools by his feet sit two beautiful little girls—his twin daughters—not more than 10 years of age, while a noble boy, 12 or 13, stands by the back of the chair where sits the handsome, yet matronly-looking mother." The villain is introduced with the following convoluted rhetoric: "Hark! The sound of horse galloping with mad speed towards his house falls upon his ear."[22]

Buntline penned Cody's fictional exploits in fourteen more lurid dime novels with titles such as *Buffalo Bill's Last Victory; or, Dove Eye, the Lodge Queen* and *Buffalo Bill's Best Shot; or, The Heart of Spotted Tail*, followed by *Hazel Eye, the Girl Trapper: A Tale of Strange Young Life*. Buntline's last dime novel about Buffalo Bill was titled *Buffalo Bill's First Trail; or, Will Cody, the Pony Express Rider*, published in 1885.

Buntline wasn't the only pulp-novel writer who latched onto Buffalo Bill and helped to propel him to fame. Though Buntline started a trend in the dime novels, he wrote only 25 "western" novels. However, *Buffalo Bill, the King of the Border Men* was the first and most influential of this type of story and was important in shaping the persona of the western hero.

The Cody legend was also promoted by the prolific Col. Prentiss Ingraham, who wrote at least 131 sensationalized stories about Buffalo Bill and may have produced more under various pen names. Ingraham was the son of a minister and had been a Confederate soldier in the Civil War. He started writing in 1870 and churned out two dime novels a month until his death in 1904. Ingraham's first story about Buffalo Bill, written in 1876, was titled *The Crimson Trail; or, On Custer's Last Warpath*. Over the next twenty years he wrote dozens of Buffalo Bill dime novels.

Ingraham was one of Beadle's most prolific authors. Depending on the source, his estimated total output over a period of 34 years was between 500 and 1,000 titles, with a likely number of over 600 novels—all written in longhand. Precise numbers are uncertain as most dime novelists wrote under multiple pen names, making it hard to attribute stories to the correct author.

Ingraham reputedly wrote one entire 35,000-word dime novel in a 24-hour period. Afterwards, he is reported to have modestly remarked: "I was both tired and hungry when I finished, for I had had only a sandwich or two, eaten as I worked."[23]

Ingraham is best know for his Buffalo Bill novels and his other stories of the West. As well as writing extensively about Buffalo Bill, Ingraham also wrote several novels very loosely based on the life of William Levi "Buck" Taylor, a real-life shooting and trick-riding show star who had excellent skills with horses and cattle. He was an authentic westerner and real cowboy, born in Texas and raised on a ranch where he learned to lasso steers and ride wild horses. Taylor was an original member of Buffalo Bill's *Wild West* troupe, but was a lesser-known cast member, even though he was a featured performer in the show for 10 years and worked on Cody's ranch in Nebraska. The first Buck Taylor novel was ostensibly written as a biography with the title, *Buck Taylor, King of the Cowboys, or, the Raiders and the Rangers: a Story of the Wild and Thrilling Life of William L. Taylor*. This book, which appeared in *Beadle's Half-Dime Library* on February 1, 1887, featured Taylor as the first of the real cowboy heroes.

Taylor's adventure was a sensationalized and fictionalized story, as Ingraham had done earlier with Buffalo Bill. The plot moved along at a rapid pace, including Taylor killing Indians, outwitting a band of renegades, fighting a group of Mexicans, and having a narrow escape after being buried alive. To promote the books, Ingraham gave Taylor the title of the "King of the Cowboys," long before movie star Roy Rogers was given the same name by Republic Studios.

Ingraham also wrote several more Buck Taylor stories for *Beadle's Dime Library* and *Beadle's Half-Dime Library*. Titles were *Buck Taylor, the Saddle King; or, The Lasso Rangers' League*; *The Cowboy Clan; or, The Tigress of Texas*; *Buck Taylor, The Comanche Captive*; and *Buck Taylor's Boys; or, The Red Riders of the Rio Grande*. After these, Taylor stories faded from the dime novels. Though Taylor appeared in only a few dime novels, his fictional exploits added to the romance of the literary cowboy. Trying to find another real-life western hero to promote, Ingraham seized on scout, hunter, and occasional stage actor John Burwell "Texas Jack" Omohundro, and wrote a similar fictionalized account of his life titled *Texas Jack, The Mustang King*.

Ingraham also wrote sea stories and detective stories. Some of the many pseudonyms he used were Alden F. Bradshaw, Dangerfield Burr, Dr. Noel Dunbar, Lt. Preston Graham, Midshipman Tom W. Hall, Harry Hart, T.W. King, Col. Leon Lafitte, Lt. Lionel Lounsberry, Harry Dennies Perry, Frank Powell, and Henry B. Stoddard. Ingraham's heroes sometimes showed a clear sense of justice as they stepped outside the law to carry out a punishment that society had failed to bring, a concept that foreshadowed Deadwood Dick stories, and the later cowboy and hard-boiled detective heroes.

Buffalo Bill was probably the hero of more dime novels than any other real or fictional character. Starting with Buntline's first effort in 1869, frontier fact and fiction were mixed in stories about Buffalo Bill that eventually resulted in 557 dime novels by 20 different authors.[24] Many of them were written by Prentiss Ingraham and some were written by others using Ingraham's name. To add to the confusion, some of the Buffalo Bill stories were written by Cody himself with editorial help and some were written by various authors under Buffalo Bill's name. Ingraham himself started ghost writing under Cody's name around 1880. This profusion of names makes it difficult to accurately determine which Cody titles Ingraham actually wrote, which used other names, and which were written under his own name.

Cody's fictional persona appeared in many publications from different publishers. He was found first in *Beadle's Dime Library*, *Beadle's Half-Dime Library*, and *Beadle's Weekly*. He also appeared in Frank Tousey's *Wide Awake Library*. In 1902 Street & Smith started *Buffalo Bill Stories*, which lasted until 1912. It was succeeded by *New Buffalo Bill Weekly* from 1912 to 1919, then was transformed into *Western Story Magazine*, which appeared first in a dime novel format then as a pulp magazine. *Far West Library* reprinted Buffalo Bill stories from 1907 to 1915, as *Buffalo Bill Border Stories* from 1917 to 1925, and finally as *Great Western Library* from 1927 to 1932. The *New Buffalo Bill Weekly* used many authors to write about Buffalo Bill, including O.H. Booth, Stephen Chalmers, William Wallace Cook, W. Bert Foster, William H. Manning, Leander P. Richardson, Maro A. Rolfe, Robert Russell, Eugene T. Sawyer, William Thorpe, Alfred B. Tozer, John H. Whitson, and Ernest Avon Young.[25]

"Wild Bill" Hickok

Another real-life frontier figure that writers felt they could embellish and use for the image of a western hero was James Butler "Wild Bill" Hickok, a gambler and part-time lawman. Hickok had the imposing figure of a hero, over six feet tall with broad shoulders. Like Buffalo Bill, Hickok was an authentic frontiersman, but he later adopted the flamboyant style of clothing and accessories that were described in the dime novels. He grew his hair long, wore buckskin clothing like the frontier scouts, and carried a brace of revolvers in a sash. This theatrical type of appearance was considered to be symbolic of the frontier of the dime novels and in the eyes of fans made him a "real" westerner. This image supposedly connected him to untamed nature, fierce animals, and the western wilderness. Unfortunately, this style of clothing was already outdated when he appeared in Kansas after the Civil War.

Wild Bill Hickok became a minor celebrity after he was interviewed in 1865 by Col. George Ward Nichols, a journalist looking for colorful western characters. Nichols published an account in *Harper's New Monthly Magazine* of Hickok's real-life fight with Dave McCanles at the Rock Creek stage depot in Nebraska on July 12, 1861. Nichols' retelling was a vivid, but mostly exaggerated and inaccurate, account of the real fight.[26]

The first dime novel story about Wild Bill, titled "Wild Bill, the Indian Slayer," appeared in *DeWitt's Ten Cent Romances*, a monthly magazine of action stories. The cover showed Hickok surrounded by opponents with knives, with the bodies of those he had overcome spread around him on the ground. A later issue, which featured "Wild Bill's First Trail," showed him in fierce hand-to-hand combat with an Indian who was aiming a tomahawk at Hickok at the same time that the scout was preparing to knife him.

5

Glorifying the Outlaws

In the latter part of the nineteenth century a new social problem emerged in America due to major changes brought about by industrialization and urbanization. This period in history was characterized by increasing class polarization, antagonism between labor and capital, and the rise of new social ideas that threatened traditional morality. The rise of big business resulted in a distrust of the managing classes by the common working man and created a feeling of being exploited. These particular issues surfaced in the 1890s partly as a result of the uncontrolled economic expansion (particularly into the West) that had occurred over the previous 40 years.

Industrialization used new machines in factories, innovations in design, and new production methods developed by large corporations that took over much of the work of the laboring classes, thus limiting opportunity and eliminating many of the skilled jobs that had previously been performed by hand. As one example, the introduction of pneumatic power machinery in the West in the 1880s allowed the drilling of dynamite holes in rock in less time and with greater ease for blasting in underground mines than when skilled miners used hammers and hand-operated steel bits.

Corporate growth brought wealth to big businesses and monopolies, but did not create universal prosperity. Wealth became concentrated in the hands of business owners and investors in the East, with the working man pushed to the bottom end of the economic scale. The average individual also felt that unscrupulous capitalist members of the upper classes were exploiting his labor through their domination of the political system. This resulted in bitter and violent conflicts between workers and employers.[1] Under these conditions, the average individual felt that he was powerless to make any real change in his life. He saw his lifestyle and freedoms threatened by social and economic forces beyond his control, backed by a political system he perceived as inefficient, unresponsive, and corrupt.

To help combat feelings of frustration, the common man escaped into an imaginary world in the pages of dime novels where writers used the earlier model of Robin Hood to create romanticized crime fighters who fought against tyranny and oppression on behalf of the average person. In this way the working man could fantasize himself to be a self-reliant hero in a fictional story where his problems received a clear-cut resolution. Dime novels invented noble outlaws who provided a way that the working man could temporarily live in a world where the hero could resolve in fantasy the otherwise unsolvable cultural conflicts of the time.

One issue that played a role in the popularity of these outlaw heroes was that many people felt that the law and legal system were not responsive to the needs of the average individual. The intricacies and often-slow workings of the judicial system appeared to them to confirm this idea. This led to a feeling that there was a difference between what was legal and what was morally just. Earlier in the real West, settlers had experienced the same sort of problem and resorted to vigilante action when they felt that the conventional system of law was not serving their needs fast enough.

Exploiting this perceived difference between legality and morality, dime novel writers developed fictional characters who took what they claimed was justifiable revenge against the wrongs done to them. They were criminals, but in heroic roles that made them out to be victims and rebels against an unjust and corrupt society. In these revenge tales, a good man is unjustly persecuted by one or more evil individuals, and finds that the legal system cannot protect him or punish his oppressors due to the villain's wealth and influence in manipulating the law or corrupting those in the judicial process. So the outlaw hero takes individual action to avenge social wrongs, even though to do so he breaks the law and becomes a social outcast. Eventually his hatred of the evil manipulators of big business turns into a hatred of society in general, and the story often concludes with some violent deed against the community.

This type of dime novel outlaw character was virtuous, but rebellious. He was a man who possessed superior powers of moral perception. He took it upon himself to protect the community by acting swiftly, even if he had to come into conflict with the conventional moral and legal codes of the time. The public in these plots often remained unaware of the need for his prompt and decisive action, and inevitably misinterpreted his violation of the law.

One problem for authors was how to reconcile this idea of the hero breaking the law yet still have him retain the virtuous image of a traditional hero. Given the prevailing Victorian morality of the time it was not possible to make an out-and-out criminal the hero of a popular dime novel. The public wanted a hero who would reject artificial restraints, such as the law, to fight villainy, but who would be guided by an unerring sense of right and wrong as he led the forces of good against evil exploiters. One way dime novel writers solved this dilemma of making the outlaw's actions acceptable to readers was to give him a background of respectability. Thus these new outlaws had a veneer of social polish, with courtly manners and chivalrous conduct towards others, particularly women.

Writers also had to invent a proper background and reason for the outlaw hero's misconduct. The commonest justification for his illegal behavior was that he had been unjustly oppressed and driven outside the law. Thus many of the plots revolved around persecution and justifiable reprisal. This new type of hero was supposedly a good man who was driven by circumstances beyond his control, which made him embittered and solely out for revenge.

Noting the popularity among readers who identified frontier heroes with romantic bandits such as Robin Hood and Dick Turpin, writers looking for sensational material to satisfy readers' demands turned to writing outlaw tales. These new protagonists were not only violent, but they offered a different set of moral values than the earlier heroes. Readers liked these bandit characters who were martyrs supposedly responding to injustice done to them by corrupt officials who represented the powerful rich classes.

Unlike the earlier backwoodsman tales, Indians were not the villains of these stories. The villains rather were the wealthy class, such as Eastern industrial capitalists, stockbrokers, and local managers or representatives of big businesses. These types of men were considered by working-class readers to be the privileged class and the elite rich, and represented wealth gained by corrupt means. Behind all this, the real villain was portrayed as the corrupt institutions and artificial business conventions of the East.

The noble outlaw or bandit who has withdrawn from urban society to strike out against unjust tyrants and oppressors of the poor had appeared throughout previous literature. The best example is the legend of Robin Hood. In the dime novels the noble Robin-Hood type of brigand became a western outlaw. The rationale was almost always the same. This was a good man, usually with aristocratic origins, whose rightful position had been usurped by evil and treacherous enemies using unjust laws to legitimize their actions.

This had great appeal for the working public in America and Europe in the late nineteenth and early twentieth centuries, and both the character and situation of exploitation became stock items in Victorian melodrama and fiction. They were also the favorite characters of burlesque and parody.

Not everybody, however, was in favor of the concept of righting wrongs forced on innocent men through further crime. Protests were made to the postal service about the ethics of these characters, and the Postmaster General threatened to take away cheap second-class mailing privileges to try to control what was seen as a decadent trend in literature. However, by then it was too late as the heroic outlaw was already entrenched as a major part of western dime-novel literature.

Deadwood Dick

The first of the fictional noble western outlaws was Deadwood Dick, who appeared in thirty-three Beadle and Adams dime novels between 1877 and 1885. Deadwood Dick was created by Edward Lytton Wheeler, one of the most prolific writers for Beadle and Adams. Like other noble outlaws, Deadwood Dick was forced outside the law to gain revenge on those who wronged him, because the law and the courts failed to punish the evildoers.

Wheeler's first story in the series was *Deadwood Dick, the Prince of the Road; or, the Black Rider of the Black Hills*, which appeared on October 15, 1877, in three columns of small print in the first volume of *Beadle and Adams Half-Dime Library*. This particular issue had no cover date, except for a copyright date of 1877. This first Deadwood Dick book had a heavily dramatic structure, with strong persecution and revenge elements in the plot. It also used the dime novel convention of multiple identities.

The justification for Deadwood Dick's bandit career was the death of his foster parents and the looting of their estate by the villainous Filmore Brothers. Dick pursued them legally, but without success. He finally resorted to taking the law into his own hands and eventually lynched them at the end of the book. The essence of the plot was that Dick had been wronged by powerful villains who were supported by the law, so his later actions of revenge were justified. This was the familiar theme of the little guy fighting back against the establishment.

Throughout the series, Deadwood Dick spouted social criticism with tirades of righteous indignation. One example was that he complained bitterly of citizens who could not distinguish between good and evil, and through their inaction effectively furthered the spread of wrong-doing. He further complained about a social system that condoned the exploitation of the common man by an unscrupulous wealthy class, and the injustice

5. Glorifying the Outlaws

Deadwood Dick, a fictional character of the Wild West, was the first of the literary "noble outlaws." He was the creation of Edward Wheeler, one of the prolific writers for Beadle and Adams. Dick appeared in 1877 and lasted through 33 novels until 1885. He flourished during the transition of the dime novels from western heroes to the new detectives and ended up being a combined character who acted as a detective in the West in over half his stories.

of a legal system that permitted those of wealth and influence to commit dreadful crimes, but punished the common man for the least departure from the law.[2]

Before he became Deadwood Dick, the hero's real name was Edward Harris, a young, intelligent, handsome, and chivalrous man. The essence of the first plot is that Edward and his sister Anita have been adopted by a New England farm family. They are driven from their home by the persecutions of Alexander Filmore and his son Clarence and go West to make a new home. Harris eventually becomes the outlaw Deadwood Dick, who dresses all in black and rides on a black horse at the head of a gang of road agents. Dick seeks to avenge the wrongs done to him by rich white men by robbing stagecoaches, even though this would see to be a somewhat dubious justification. His obsession in life becomes revenge on the Filmores. To maintain the previous popular white-woman-in-distress rescue theme from the frontier stories, this first story also included a character named Fearless Frank, who rescues 17-year-old Alice Terry from captivity by Sioux Indian chief Sitting Bull.

Towards the end of the first novel, Alexander Filmore stabs Deadwood Dick in the neck with a knife, creating a painful, though not fatal wound. After Dick recovers, he explains what the Filmores have done and passes his judgment. "Seeing that nothing could be accomplished through aids, my enemies have at last come out to superintend my butchery in person; and but for the timely interference of Calamity Jane and Justin McKenzie, a short time since, I should have ere this been numbered with the dead. Now, I am inclined to be merciful to only those who have been merciful to me; therefore, I have decided that Alexander and Clarence Filmore shall pay the penalty of hanging, for their attempted crimes. Boys, *string 'em up!*" And then, "...at last the terrible shout of, 'Heave 'o! up they go!' which signaled the commencement of the victims' journey into mid-air."[3] The story ended with "And grim and uncommunicative, there roams through the country of gold a youth in black, at the head of a bold lawless gang of road-riders, who, from his unequaled daring, has won and rightly deserves the name—Deadwood Dick, Prince of the Road."

Wheeler may have loosely based the character of Deadwood Dick on a real Deadwood stage-coach driver named Richard "Little Dick" Cole, who drove the first stagecoach into Deadwood, though four other men have also claimed to be the authentic Deadwood Dick.[4] In 1927 a local 82-year-old Deadwood character named Richard W. Clark (sometimes spelled Clarke) was asked to portray Deadwood Dick in Deadwood's *Days of '76* parade, and he continued to so until his death in 1930.[5]

The fictional Deadwood Dick went on to 32 other adventures. Recurring characters in the stories were an Indian fighter named Old Avalanche, a guide named Alva Hogg, and Calamity Jane, who is variously Dick's friend, enemy, and love interest. Wheeler wrote several other unrelated novels, but generally followed his Deadwood Dick legacy and concentrated on the same persecution and revenge theme. In *Solid Sam, The Boy Road-Agent; or, the Branded Brows, A Tale of Wild Wyoming*, which appeared in *Beadles Half Dime Library* on April 6, 1880, the hero Sam turns to a life of crime because outlaws took over his gold mine.

Wheeler was himself reported to be a bit of a character. His letterhead had *Studio of Edward L. Wheeler, Sensational Novelist* printed at the top. In reality, Wheeler was a flamboyant Philadelphian who spent most of his life in Pennsylvania. Though he adopted the life of a westerner, wore a large Stetson hat, and called most people "pard," he never traveled west of Illinois.[6]

5. Glorifying the Outlaws

A good example of the convoluted plots used in dime novels appears in Wheeler's *Deadwood Dick on Deck; or, Calamity Jane, the Heroine of Whoop-Up* (1878). Several entwined strands of plot intersect at various points, including miners escaping from the clutches of absentee mine-owners, which was a very touchy and real topic in the West. The plot emphasizes the use of disguises and contains an elaborate interplay of gender roles. Almost all the main characters are in disguises. The hero, Earl Beverly, for example, is disguised as Sandy the Miner. Beverly has come West to make a new life, believing he is guilty of murder. Sandy becomes friends with a girl who has (unknown to him) disguised herself as a man, Dusty Dick. She is escaping from villain Cecil Grosvenor who wants to destroy her and has tricked her into a loveless marriage before she realized his true character. Another character in disguise is a detective who tells Sandy that he is innocent of murder and, in the best dime novel tradition of saving the heroine's virtue, that her marriage is invalid. Even Deadwood Dick is disguised as Old Bullwhacker. Other characters play peripheral roles in other wandering plot lines, including Calamity Jane, Arkansas Alf, and Madame Minnie Majilton. At one point Calamity Jane is disguised as Deadwood Dick, who is disguised as an old man unmasked by Deadwood Dick in his disguise. This must all have become very confusing for the reader. In another part of the plot, Madam Minnie loves Sandy who loves Dusty Dick. The plot, of course, involves perilous scrapes, flights, captures, and battles. In spite of all this role-playing and confusion, everyone is pure, including the hero and heroine.

The boyish young woman or girl who disguises herself in a man's role before changing into the hero's love interest played an important role in dime novels and in later western pulps. For adolescent readers just discovering girls in sexual terms (which was most of the audience), the idea of a girl disguising herself as Dusty Dick makes her both a boyish companion and a sexual fantasy. This was part of the Wild West as an adolescent dream society without the complex social restrictions associated with the East. This plotline of innocent transvestite disguise was carried on later by other authors, such as Zane Grey in his novel *Riders of the Purple Sage* (1912).

Deadwood Dick stories, and many other dime novels for that matter, usually contained a cliffhanger written into the end of each chapter of the serial that placed the hero in a life-threatening situation. This was to hook the reader into buying the next issue to see how the hero escaped, a concept carried on into later serial westerns which were shown to adolescents at local movie theaters on Saturday mornings during the 1930s and 1940s.

In one Deadwood Dick story that ended in a major cliff-hanger, villain Piute Dave captures Dick, hangs him, shoots him full of holes, places his body in a sack full of stones, and throws the bag off a cliff into a roaring river hundreds of feet below. That would seem to be the end of Deadwood Dick. However, in the next chapter, Dick reappears in disguise, rounds up the entire gang, turns them over to the sheriff, then removes his disguise and is revealed as himself. Though this rapid recovery and re-appearance rather stretches the bounds of credibility, the explanation was that he had only been unconscious inside the sack and, when he was thrown into the river, the cold water revived him.

One Deadwood Dick novel actually concluded with a cliffhanger. In *Deadwood Dick in Leadville; or, A Strange Stroke for Liberty*, that appeared in June 24, 1879, Dick is hanged at the end, but Calamity Jane cuts him down immediately and tries to resuscitate him. He bounced back apparently none the worse for wear in the next novel, *Deadwood Dick's Device; or, The Sign of the Double Cross*, where he was back to his old calling of persecution and revenge.

Like many other dime novel series, the Deadwood Dick stories were intentionally written to be read at any point in the sequence. In fact, most of them were later reprinted out of sequence in other magazines. In some of the stories Dick is seemingly killed off, but he either comes back later in the same story or in the first chapter of the next story, often without any explanation.

Wheeler originally conceived Deadwood Dick as an outlaw but, over time, he transformed his hero into more of a detective as Deadwood Dick fought for the causes of contemporary miners. He upheld the little guys in their fight for their rights as free Americans against rich Eastern mine owners bent on enslaving them. Following this theme, the outlaw stories of Deadwood Dick were often set in mining towns in the West. Mining camps, such as Deadwood in the Black Hills of South Dakota and Leadville in Colorado, were booming western towns at the time and the Deadwood Dick stories were very appropriate and topical. Labor problems were rampant at western mining camps and clashes often occurred between strikers and strikebreakers hired by mine owners.

Poor working conditions in the mines of the West led to the organization of unions, such as the western Federation of Miners in 1893. Major strikes took place in Colorado from Cripple Creek to Telluride between 1903 and 1914 in the struggle between mine owners and organized labor. The main issues were wages, hours, safe working conditions, health laws, and recognition of the unions. Tactics on both sides included intimidation, violence, and violations of civil rights. These social conditions made it logical for Deadwood Dick to appear as the fictional hero of stories of miners versus mine owners.

Deadwood Dick fought fictional labor wars at the same time real labor wars were wracking the West in mining towns such as Leadville and Cripple Creek in Colorado and Butte in Montana, resulting in unrest and outright warfare between mining unions and the men appointed to keep the peace. Here the Colorado state militia mans an armored Gatling gun in downtown Cripple Creek, during labor disputes in 1903. (Glenn Kinnaman Colorado and Western History Collection)

One of the bitterest and most violent of the real western mining conflicts occurred at the gold mining town of Cripple Creek in Colorado, where the Western Federation of Miners had unionized most of the miners. In 1903, the union tried to organize the processing mills in nearby Colorado City and 3,500 miners went on strike. Colorado Governor James Peabody called out the militia and declared martial law, but the unrest continued with incidents of intimidation and violence. The climax occurred when professional labor assassin Harry Orchard (who also murdered Idaho governor Frank Steunenberg during a labor dispute) blew up the railroad station at Independence, Colorado, on June 6, 1904, killing 13 people and wounding many more.[7]

One of the worst of these mining tragedies started with a strike at the coal camp of Ludlow, a small mining camp southwest of Walsenburg, Colorado. The issues that led to unrest among the miners were those common to mining camps, consisting of bad company housing, poor living conditions, long working hours, low wages, and payment in scrip that could only be redeemed at the company-owned store. On top of that, the working conditions were extremely hazardous. The life span of a coal miner was typically only about 45 years due to constant smog and coal dust in the air.

In 1913, more than 10,000 coal miners, aided by union organizers, went on strike across the West. At Ludlow, the mine owner, Colorado Fuel and Iron, evicted workers from company-owned housing and about 800 to 1,000 people had to set up a tent city near the Ludlow railway station. On April 20, 1914, the state militia and mine guards fired on the tent city, then set it on fire. During the shooting, one militiaman was killed, along with five strikers, one bystander, and a child. The worst was yet to come. Afterwards it was found that two women and eleven more children had hidden in an underground cellar to try to escape the shooting, and had suffocated to death during the fire.

As Deadwood Dick sought revenge and justice through his series of dime novels, he became popular with working-class readers, like these miners, who felt that nineteenth century industrialists and bosses, such as absentee mine owners from back East, oppressed them and ruled their lives. Dick constantly brooded over unjust treatment and his desire for revenge. In Wheeler's later novels the theme of persecution and retribution was expanded to make society in general the oppressor and Deadwood Dick the misunderstood defender of justice. He defied the law to defend the downtrodden from corrupt business empires, where wealth was everything.

Though Dick was a bandit/detective who often "sorted out wickedness in mining camps," he also foiled stage robberies and kidnappers. Dick was a deadly shot, a skilled horseman, and a master of disguise. He was virile, violent, and invincible in combat, able to defeat all his enemies and prevail in every situation as he tracked down villains. He was independently wealthy from his own gold mine. One of his distinguishing characteristics was that he liked to utter "a wild sardonic laugh." He and others like him were so well portrayed in the dime novels that many readers believed that they were real people.

The Deadwood Dick series introduced a new variation and fresh approach to the traditional frontier hero, as Dick was the first dime novel hero who was an outlaw in disguise. However, even though Dick was a bandit hero, the publisher was careful not to promote any bad behavior in the character that might influence youth in a bad way and bring criticism to the series.

Wheeler added some romance to the stories in the form of a fictionalized and romanticized version of the real-life Calamity Jane, who first appeared in Wheeler's introductory

Deadwood Dick story. Calamity Jane was a difficult character to portray. Though Deadwood Dick was a fictional character, Jane was a real person whose name was Martha Jane Canary. In the mid–1870s, the real Calamity Jane became nationally famous after her real and fictional exploits were publicized in a series of dime novels and a small autobiography. Indeed, one of the forces that helped to create a glamorized perception of westerners among the general public in the latter half of the nineteenth century was the publication of dime novels about real-life westerners contained in fictional stories. This type of relentless promotion was parodied in the motion picture *Cat Ballou* (1965), where gunman Kid Shelleen (Lee Marvin) has been made famous by dime novels, whereas the real Shelleen is a boozy, washed-up old ex-gunfighter.

The real Calamity Jane was six-feet tall, smoked cigars, and liked to carouse with the boys. She was a heavy drinker and in her younger days usually dressed in men's clothing. She worked for a while as an army teamster and reportedly swore like one. She had a reputation as an alcoholic at an early age and was linked to occasional prostitution. She was one of the pioneers of Deadwood, South Dakota, and tended bar in the seamier part of the town.

Martha Jane Canary never denied any of the Calamity Jane stories about her, and she even invented some tall tales of her own to go with them in her semi-fictional, ghost-written biography. She was featured in a series of fanciful adventures in almost twenty dime novels in the early 1880s. She was characterized in the earlier novels as drinking, smoking, carousing, and swearing, though the later novels toned down these aspects and made her character more respectable.

Wheeler's fictionalized version of Calamity Jane, on the other hand, was described as having a "trim boyish figure" (unlike the real Martha Jane Canary) and "a wonderful wealth of long glossy hair." In the early novels, Dick tried to persuade Jane to marry him, but she kept refusing. The two did, however, eventually marry in June 28, 1881, four years after the first story appeared, in *Deadwood Dick's Doom; or, Calamity Jane's Last Adventure*. In the next installment they had a small son, Deadwood Dick, Jr. The boy eventually disappeared, and was replaced by an adopted son, Rex. Apparently unsatisfied with the way that the plots were going, Wheeler killed off both characters in *Deadwood Dick's Dust; or, The Chained Hand. A Strange Story of the Mines, Being the 35th and Ending Number of the Great 'Deadwood Dick' Series*. He is killed while successfully destroying a town whose citizens have appropriated his tract of land and lynched Calamity Jane. The story appeared in *Beadles Half Dime Library* for October 20, 1885.[8]

Wheeler died in 1885, but Beadle & Adams realized how popular the character was and continued the series under a series of pen-names with Deadwood Dick, Jr. Junior was indistinguishable from his namesake and continued through another 97 novels. Curiously this was not the son of the original Deadwood Dick, but was another character with the same name. His original name was Richard Bristol. He simply adopted the name of his hero Deadwood Dick and embarked on a similar course of revenge against his stepfather and uncle.

Deadwood Dick, Jr., was so like the original Deadwood Dick that the two were essentially the same character. The junior version also investigated many of the contemporary problems that concerned the working man of the time. In one story, for example, Deadwood Dick, Jr., led the miners in Leadville, Colorado, to win a fair wage for union members. He appeared on January 19, 1886, in *Deadwood Dick, Jr.; or, The Sign of the Crimson Crescent*. In this first story he was assisted by Kittie Kenyon, a female boxer from San Francisco, also known as "California Kit."⁹ By this time, however, dime-novel detectives were becoming popular so Dick, Jr., acted more as a detective than an outlaw.

The credited author of Deadwood Dick, Jr., was Edward L. Wheeler; however, as Wheeler had died in 1885 before the Junior series started, most of the stories were probably written by Jesse C. Cowdrick, another prolific and imaginative writer for Beadle & Adams.¹⁰ The Junior series was not as popular as the original Deadwood Dick.

The Imitators

The dime-novel outlaw heroes appealed to readers because their cultural values catered to the psychological and social needs of the public. The theme of a hero being both good and bad at same time, such as Deadwood Dick who is basically a good man who has been driven to do what he does by circumstances, rapidly became very popular among readers. In response, every dime novel publishers had to have their own dashing lawbreaker heroes who were driven to a life of crime by their situations. The concept succeeded. Street & Smith's *Log Cabin Library*, for example, which contained many outlaw stories like this had a weekly circulation of 25,000 to 30,000 copies by the 1890s.¹¹ The concept of the good-badman character later portrayed with immense success by film actor William S. Hart in the 1910s originated with these dime novels.¹²

In response to the popularity of Deadwood Dick, Street & Smith produced several hundred novels about a frontier lawman named Diamond Dick. He was the creation of William Wallace Cook under the pen name of W.B. Lawson, a house name used on various stories by Street & Smith. Diamond Dick stories were written by William Cook, George Waldo Browne, Austyn Granville, Walter L. Hawley, J.E. Lempfert, Richard McCann, St. George Rathborne, Eugene T. Sawyer, W.B. Schwartz, Alfred B. Tozer, Nathan D. Urner, and others.¹³ Diamond Dick, whose real name was Richard Wade, was a flamboyant dresser who wore a Spanish-style costume with diamonds on it and had the long hair that was the fashion for frontier heroes of the day. He not only roamed the West, but some of his later adventures were set from Central and South America to the Frozen North. The character of Diamond Dick may have been based on real-life Richard Tanner, a scout for Gen. George Armstrong Custer and later a trick shot performer in a Wild West show.¹⁴ Like Deadwood Dick, Diamond Dick was later succeeded by Diamond Dick, Jr., who appeared in his own magazine from 1896 to 1911.

Other similar imitators were Hurricane Bill, Mustang Sam, and Pacific Pete. Panther Paul came from the pen of author Joseph Badger, and Daredeath Smith was written by Leon Lewis. Others were Gentleman Joe, Dead Shot Dave, Denver Dan, and Dakota Dan.

Denver Dan was a vigilante who dressed in buckskin clothes and a broad cowboy hat, and wore a mask over his lower face to conceal his features. Another key part of his outfit was a silver whistle that he used to summon his gang. Dan had been a bank clerk falsely accused of theft, and his mission was to right the wrongs done to others.

Women were typically not used as main characters in these western stories. One of the few was Denver Doll, nicknamed "The Detective Queen," who appeared in 1882 and 1883 in *Beadle's Half-Dime Library*. Dressed in a gray suit, a white cowboy hat, and leather boots, she battled road agents in Colorado. This was very relevant to the time as the rich silver mining town of Leadville, Colorado, was plagued with stage holdups. Four of the Denver Doll stories were written by Edward L. Wheeler.¹⁵

Though women were rarely the main characters in these stories, they appeared frequently as secondary characters. Many of the heroes had a "girl pard," such as Calamity Jane in the Deadwood Dick stories. For example Diamond Dick's girl pard (pardner/partner) was Belle Bellair. These women formed part of the plots as friends and assistants to the hero, though they were usually not a love interest. Some of these girl pards were "sports," a contemporary name for a gambler.

Transforming Real Outlaws

When dime novelists ran out of outlaw characters to invent, they fictionalized and sensationalized the exploits of real historical western outlaws and criminals, such as Frank and Jesse James, the Younger Brothers, Butch Cassidy, Joaquin Murieta, Billy the Kid, and the Daltons, and used them in fictional stories. Bandits and dangerous outlaws in real life were turned by writers into the nineteenth century American equivalents of gallant European highwayman. Writers researched a few facts, altered or invented the rest, and made these criminals out to be further victims of an oppressive social system.

The theme of persecution and revenge in stories about these western "heroes" was applied by authors to popularize legends about these real western badmen. In the fictional stories about Jesse James, Jesse and his brother Frank were supposedly unjustly persecuted and driven outside the law, so they sought revenge against those who had wronged them.

Popular legend and pulp novels transformed Billy the Kid and Jesse James into figures of romantic rebellion, driven to a life of crime by oppressive land barons, grasping railroad tycoons, and crooked greedy politicians. Later, similar legends were created around bank robbers, kidnappers and murderers of the 1920s and 1930s, such as John Dillinger, Al Capone, and Bonnie and Clyde.

Jesse James

In the 1880s, Jesse James and others rose to the level of folk-hero status. The real Jesse James was a robber, outlaw, and cold-blooded killer who rode with Quantrill's Raiders during the Civil War. After the Civil War ended, Jesse and brother Frank continued looting and stealing, using the tactics they had learned as guerrillas. By 1869 the James boys and their gang had turned to robbery. They were different than most common criminals because they were supported by the press and by local civic leaders who had been displaced by the war. Jesse's post-war deeds were seen as championing their lost cause.

Newspaper editors and local landowners mythologized Jesse's exploits. Supporters even tried to gain amnesty for him from the state legislature. By the end of the 1870s publishers were cranking out a series of lurid dime novels that celebrated the "heroic" deeds of the James gang. Part of the myth made Jesse a "guerrilla" rather than a common criminal, even though Civil War guerrillas were actually far worse than ordinary soldiers and were subject to summary execution upon capture, unlike regular army soldiers.

The legend of Jesse James, as told in romanticized stories by dime novelists, presented him as the prince of bandits, a misunderstood knight-errant, and America's version of Robin Hood. Journalists and dime novel writers portrayed the activities of James and his gang as avenging the wrongs and oppression of greedy bankers and scheming railroads.

5. Glorifying the Outlaws

A wild cheer broke over the death-scene, and a dozen men, well-armed and mounted, appeared upon the spot.

The title of this series tells it all. Frank and Jesse James were real western criminals who were romanticized and fictionalized for the dime novels. The real James Brothers continued the guerrilla tactics they learned riding with Quantrill's Raiders during the Civil War and continued in a civilian life of crime, robbing trains and banks. The real Jesse James was eventually shot dead by his cousin for a reward. Frank James was brought to trial, but was acquitted and died thirty years later in obscurity at the family farm in Missouri.

They characterized Jesse as having the moral values of the white hero. He was portrayed as a man of the wilderness, a natural leader, and a noble character with a tendency towards savage violence and merciless revenge when he was wronged. However, there is no evidence that he robbed the rich to give to the poor, rather he kept it all for himself.

The glamorization of Jesse Woodson James started with newspaperman Maj. John Newman Edwards. Edwards was a major influence in transforming the image of Jesse James from the reality of a ruthless robber and murderer into a modern prince of bandits. Edwards started his campaign with an inflammatory editorial titled "The Chivalry of Crime" in the *Kansas City Times* on September 27, 1872, after a robbery by the James gang at the Kansas State Fair during which a child was shot and injured. In spite of this, editor Edwards denied their guilt, justified their crimes, and praised their bravery and valor.

Edwards continued to champion the cause of the James boys in a book titled *Noted Guerillas, or the Warfare of the Border* (1877). In it Edwards called Jesse a Southern version of the frontier hero of folk legends. He was attributed with characteristics such as superb horsemanship, a love of his horse, a fondness for revolvers, and skill with a pistol, all the same attributes that were later given to cowboy movie heroes. In spite of the brutal reality of the actions of the James gang, Edwards continued to glorify and defend them until his death in 1889.

Another author who championed the cause of the James boys was Frank Triplett, who penned a book titled *The Life, Times and Treacherous Death of Jesse James* (1882), in which Jesse was portrayed as an aristocratic hero. The rich capitalists that forced him into outlawry were described as "white trash." This book became part of the foundation of the outlaw's literary mythology as an avenger of the wrongs unjustly forced on his family.

The James gang received national attention when they switched from robbing local banks to robbing trains, which at the time was a federal offense. Jesse was characterized as being persecuted and driven into outlawry by the railroads and holding up trains was considered to be his way of avenging himself. Thus the James legend was essentially rewritten in 1880 to become a conflict with oppressive railroads.[16]

The first series of dime novels about the James brothers was *The Trainrobbers, or a Story of the James Boys* by R.W. Stevens (John R. Musick) in the *Wide Awake Library* published in 1881 by Frank Tousey. Stories also appeared in Tousey's *James Boys Weekly* and *New York Detective Library*. In 1881 Street & Smith also started publishing stories about James in the *New York Weekly*, then followed with *Jesse James Stories* and *The James Boys Weekly*. The Tousey stories used some factual background, but the Street & Smith stories were nearly total fiction and had nothing to do with the historical exploits of the gang. In *Jesse James's Diamond Deal; or, Robbing the Red Hands*, for example, Jesse destroys a criminal secret society and hijacks their loot.

In Tousey's version of James, he was driven to become a guerrilla and into a life of crime by the supposed whipping of his father. Street & Smith published James Boys stories as part of their *Log Cabin Library*, with stories featuring the James gang alternating with detective stories. Some James stories were blended into crime fiction as Eastern dime-novel detective heroes went west to hunt James, and the dime-novel James gang went East and appeared in New York adventures. Publishers presented these stories as authentic by crediting them to detectives who supposedly worked on the cases. Street & Smith claimed that their authority was Capt. Jake Shackleform, a western detective who had actually hunted Jesse James. Tousey's source was supposedly an unnamed "New York detective."[17]

Not everybody, however, was amused by the James gang's popularity and there were complaints from the public that these novels were unnecessarily glorifying crime. The Postmaster-General threatened Tousey, one of the most active publishers of these lurid and sensational books, with canceling second-class mailing privileges if his company did not tone down some of the inflammatory stories. Public clamor became so great by 1903 that the government brought pressure to bear against Tousey and Street & Smith and they stopped publication of the stories. The Jesse James dime novels from Frank Tousey and Street & Smith numbered 227 from 1881 until they ceased publication in 1903.[18]

Billy the Kid

Another minor western outlaw who was elevated to the status of folk-hero by dime novelists was Billy the Kid. Billy the Kid was a small-time local outlaw who had been involved in the bloody Lincoln County cattle war in New Mexico before authors of dime novels grabbed his story with both hands. In real life, Billy was tracked down and killed by sheriff Pat Garrett in 1881 at Pete Maxwell's ranch near Fort Sumner, New Mexico. One dime novel written before the Kid's death was *Billy the Kid, the New Mexico Outlaw; or, The Bold Bandit of the West* by Edmund Fable. After his death, dime novelists amplified the myth in a very short time.

Contributing to Billy's wronged-outlaw legend were fictional dime novels such as *Old King Brady and "Billy the Kid"; or, The Great Detective's Chase* by Francis W. Doughty. Brady was a fictional detective, thus the author was attempting to authenticate Billy the Kid's story by blending the real and the fictional. More accurate was Barton W. Currie, who wrote more realistically about Billy the Kid in *Harper's Weekly* in September 1908.

Authors of dime novels seized on any characters, real or imaginary, that they could develop into dime novel heroes. One of them was the real-life Billy the Kid, an outlaw and killer in New Mexico who was involved in the Lincoln County cattle war in the late 1870s. The volume shown here, written in 1882, was one of the lurid books that helped to fictionalize and sensationalize the life of Billy the Kid as a literary persona. The book was credited to sheriff Pat Garrett, who finally killed him, but was ghostwritten by Marshall Ashmun Upson, who later admitted that he spiced up the story to make the book sell.

Currie said "With the band of desperadoes he led, he raided ranches, 'shot up' towns, killed, burned houses and committed outrage after outrage with the blind recklessness of a maniac."

Another book that contributed to the legend was *An Authentic Life of Billy the Kid*, written in 1882 and credited to Pat Garrett. It was really the product of Marshall Ashmun Upson, a former reporter for the *New York Herald* who was a friend of Garrett's and lived in nearby Roswell, New Mexico. The original long and windy title was *The Authentic Life of Billy, the Kid, the Noted Desperado of the Southwest, Whose Deeds of Daring and Blood Made His Name a Terror in New Mexico, Arizona, and Northern Mexico*, a mouthful that set the tone of the rather overblown account inside. The book publicized Billy the Kid and made Pat Garrett out to be a hero, and in the process helped to manufacture the legend. Upson claimed that he ghost-wrote the book to make it sell.[19] Another boost to the legend came when newspaperman Walter Noble Burns wrote *The Saga of Billy the Kid* (1926), which also made Billy out to be a hero.

6

The Rise of the Detective

Cowboys and noble outlaws in the dime novels had a flourishing but relatively short life, then western plots started to disappear and were replaced by detective stories. When crime and detective stories took over in popularity from the westerns, however, cowboys did not disappear. Western stories continued to be reprinted and sold in large quantities. The western genre flourished again in the 1920s and 1930s when pulp magazines became a dominant force in reading entertainment.

Cowboys Yield to Detectives

Detectives appeared occasionally in stories as early as the 1840s and 1850s, but the detective as a main character in the dime novels did not become prominent until the 1880s. By this time many dime novel stories were being written with added elements of mystery, thus the detective story gradually and naturally replaced the earlier frontier story as the dominant genre. With the appearance of detective fiction in the dime novels, authors immediately turned to the more sensational aspects of crime.

In the late 1800s, lurid dime novels excited readers with scandalous tales of crime, villains, and fictional detectives, such as Nick Carter. As crime and detection stories took over from the westerns in the 1880s and 1890s, they moved to urban settings. Culturally this transition reflected the shift that was taking place in reality as America moved from a rural frontier society to an industrialized urban civilization.

The plots of the detective stories that appeared in the 1870s and early 1880s were often no different than the frontier and western stories that were appearing at the same time, and sometimes both used the same characters and locations. In an attempt to maintain a smooth transition from the western story to detectives, some of these stories were set directly in the West. Author Albert Aiken, for example, located his police spy hero Joe Phoenix in the West for several adventures. Edward Wheeler's western bandit Deadwood Dick acted as a detective in over half of his stories. In a similar vein, Wheeler created Denver Doll, the Detective Queen, and in 1886 St. George Rathbone created Sombrero Sam, the Cowboy Detective. Some of these western detectives even used their skills as outdoorsmen to track culprits.

The first series devoted specifically to detectives was the *Old Cap Collier Library* from Norman Munro's publishing house. The library originally consisted mostly of reprints of translated versions of stories by Emile Gaboriau, a French writer, who created Monsieur Lecoq, a detective for the *Sûreté*, the French National Police.[1]

The first important detective was Old Cap Collier himself, who generated possibly the most print of any detective in the dime novels. He appeared in more than 700 titles in Munro's series. A title was issued every week at a cost of 5¢ each. The first issues were 6 inch by 10 inch pamphlets with green covers and no illustrations. The author of the first series of novels was listed as W.I. James, which was probably a house pseudonym for a group of writers, a favorite tactic of Munro's.[2]

The Cap Collier series consisted of rousing adventures that proceeded at a fast pace. At various times the detective was involved in fights, attacked with knives, poisoned, and buried alive. Collier's favorite tactic was to fling his opponents through the air for as far as thirty feet. Collier made use of elaborate disguises in his adventures, including those of a Dutchman, an organ grinder, a tramp, a cab driver, and a cavalier at a masked ball.[3]

Each publisher was fiercely competitive and each noted the successes and failures of the others. For example, whenever Beadle's initiated a new format or character, the others quickly followed suit. Therefore, when Norman Munro's Old Cap Collier detective stories became popular, all the others came up with their own competitive detectives. Old King Brady appeared in Tousey's *New York Detective Library, Secret Service*, and other series. Beadles had Broadway Billy, a bootblack detective, and Deadwood Dick, the road agent turned detective.

George Munro developed a detective series around Old Sleuth, who appeared in *New York Fireside Companion* in 1872. The character of Old Sleuth was followed by Young Sleuth, Old King Brady and Young King Brady, and various others. Many detectives in dime novels were given the name "Old" or "Young." The name "Old," such as Old Sleuth, Old Search, or Old Broadbrim (which featured a hero with a broad-brimmed hat), suggested maturity, wisdom, and respect. The name "Young" was given to someone less experienced at the start of his detective career.

Dime novel detective and mystery stories followed a set pattern. The author first introduced a mysterious situation, then made startling revelations that led to the resolution of the mystery. The stories were written in a fixed format where some incident grabs the reader's attention in the first scene, then the mystery is revealed in more detail as the plot races along. Thoughtful analytical deductive skills, such as those used by Sherlock Holmes, were not the standard method of the dime novel detective.

The dime novel detective story had several stock situations. The detective was usually a master of disguise and often altered his appearance so that he could eavesdrop on suspicious characters. During his investigations, the detective was frequently kidnapped, knocked unconscious, or even buried alive—but somehow survives. Supporting characters routinely have secrets that are not revealed until near the end of the story, such as the surprise appearance of long-lost siblings. Stories were usually serialized over a dozen weeks, and used a cliffhanger at the end of each chapter to create suspense and promote purchase of the next issue.

Sometimes detectives worked together. In *The Bradys and the Girl Smuggler; or, Working for the Custom House*, that appeared in Frank Tousey's *Secret Service* on July 27, 1900, Old and Young King Brady are called in by customs inspectors to solve a diamond smuggling case that the inspectors cannot. Authorship was credited as "by a New York Detective." This particular story contains a good example of a cliff-hanger at the end of Chapter 3, where the two detectives appear to be doomed. "Bang! went the keen blade upon the cable again where it crossed the wheel. The weight of the car caused the wire rope to part where he cut it, and the elevator's ascent was checked. It began to fall with

6. The Rise of the Detective

After the popularity of western heroes started to fade, detectives took over and became the new dime novel fad. Detectives Old and Young King Brady starred in a very popular series of stories published by Frank Tousey starting in 1899. In this tale, written supposedly "by a New York Detective," the Bradys are called in by customs inspectors to solve a diamond smuggling case that the authorized law cannot.

the detectives in it." As Chapter 4 begins, Old King Brady exclaims, "The safety clutch may save us, Harry." "'No! It don't work,' groaned the boy as the car shot down." Of course at the last minute the safety clutches do work correctly and the two are saved.

As detectives proliferated, some authors went to extremes of characterization to differentiate their stories from the others. Some of the short-lived efforts were Old Opium, the Mongolian Detective; Velvet Foot, the Indian Detective; Zeb Taylor, the Puritan Detective; Old Sledge, the Blacksmith Detective; and Bert Adams, the Fireman Detective. Perhaps two of the stranger ones were Deadwood Dick's Dog Detective and Old Humpey, the Dwarf Detective.

Crossdressing was not restricted to the heroines, as in the earlier dime novels, but was used by detectives for disguise. Though most of the dime novel detectives were described as being masters of disguise, Young Sleuth took disguise one step further with a few unusual characteristics. He was described as having a feminine appearance with slender hands and, as Randolph Cox has put it in *The Dime Novel Companion*, he "delights in dressing up as a girl and flirting with his own father." This odd mannerism was dropped in later stories.[4] Detective stories appeared in dime novels until about 1915, then survived and continued in a different format when dime novels were replaced by pulp magazines.

Nick Carter

Nick Carter was another popular dime novel detective hero. Carter first appeared in the fall of 1886 in a novelette created by John Coryell in Street & Smith's *New York Weekly* for September 18, 1886, titled *The Old Detective's Pupil; or, The Mysterious Crime of Madison Square*. The pupil was Nick Carter, a clean-living, world-renowned detective based in New York, who did not drink, smoke, or swear. Like most dime novel detectives, Carter was also a master of disguise. This particular incarnation of Carter was such a master of disguises that even his associates usually did not recognize him. He worked with various assistants, including the unrelated Chick Carter (who, confusingly, was also used as a pseudonym for the author of some of the stories) and Ida Jones, who was described as the best woman detective in the country.

Coryell wrote the first three Nick Carter adventures, then his other duties for Street & Smith, writing stories under the house name of Bertha M. Clay, made him too busy to continue the series. The name Bertha M. Clay was also used as house name by Street & Smith in the 1870s as the "author" of various pirated stories. Coryell turned to writing love stories for the pulps, so the Nick Carter series needed a new author. Other writers took up the character, and by the end of the series Street & Smith had used 30 different authors.

Many of the subsequent hundreds of Nick Carter stories were written by Frederick Marmaduke Van Rensselaer Dey and by Eugene Sawyer. Dey took over as author for Nick Carter in 1889 and wrote hundreds of adventures. He was another prolific author who could write a 30,000 word novel in only four or five days and wrote a Nick Carter story each week for 17 years. In order to complete a story in seven days, Dey wrote 4,000 to 5,000 words every day. Dey wrote under his own name as well as various pen names, including Varick Vanardy, Marion Gilmore, and the ubiquitous Bertha M. Clay. In spite of his prolific writing, Dey lived in poverty. Eventually unable to cope in his private life, Dey shot himself in his room at the Hotel Broztell in New York in April of 1922.[5]

Nick Carter was a popular dime novel detective who first appeared in the fall of 1886 in a serial in Street & Smith's *New York Weekly* titled *The Old Detective's Pupil; or, The Mysterious Crime of Madison Square*. Between the late 1880s and 1920s, Carter's character appeared in more than 1,000 titles in the *Nick Carter Detective Library*, the *Nick Carter Library*, the *New Nick Carter Weekly*, and *Nick Carter Stories*.

Eugene Sawyer also cranked out many Nick Carter adventures. He received $50 for each story of about 25,000 words. One time he wrote a 60,000 word novel in a little over two days because another writer had missed a publishing deadline. This was before the era of the typewriter, so he wrote the stories in longhand. He remembered, "I locked myself into my room and began, writing in lead pencil, while my wife copied my work in ink. I didn't eat or sleep, living on coffee alone, till the novel was completed, in about sixty hours. In order to have the manuscript reach the publishers in time, I had to have it in the post-office at noon, and I caught that mail with something less than a minute to spare."[6]

Carter's character became so popular that in 1891 Street & Smith started a separate series of his exploits titled the *Nick Carter Detective Library*. The title was later shortened to the *Nick Carter Library*. The character continued in the *New Nick Carter Weekly* through 1912, and in *Nick Carter Stories* from 1912 to 1915.

Nick Carter's adventures alternated between either routine criminal tales or fantastic adventures. A few of the Nick Carter stories crossed over into what would now be called science fantasy. He visited lost cities in the Amazon and a hidden valley in Nepal. He met strange criminals and their inventions, such as Zanabayah, who could give someone an electric shock simply by touching them. *Nick Carter and the Professor; or, Solving a Scientific Problem*, from 1902, involved grave robbers and a mad scientist who employed a secret chemical formula in attempts to restore life to the dead. He failed and Carter stepped in just as the madman was about to continue his experiments on an 18-year-old girl. As a forerunner to the shudder pulps (discussed further in Chapter 14), one Nick Carter story from 1891 featured a villain named Dr. Quartz, a madman who had a passion for dissecting beautiful girls.

When the dime novels faded away, Carter made the transition to pulp magazines when he appeared in the premier issue of Street & Smith's *Detective Story Magazine* in 1915. Nick Carter stories survived in reprints in *Magnet Library* and *New Magnet Library* until 1933. He appeared in his own magazine, *Nick Carter Magazine*, in 1933, as a single character pulp, but the series ran for only three years and seventeen issues until June 1936, when it closed down. Written by Richard Wormser, this was a different vision of Nick Carter who tackled big gangsters and kidnappers. This new Carter was a tough private investigator, but his exploits were so outlandish that there was not much interest among readers. By then the Carter character was outdated and could not compete with the more modern Doc Savage and The Shadow from the same publisher.

The Carter character appeared in a popular radio show called *Nick Carter: Master Detective* from 1943 to 1955. The character also appeared on the stage, in comic books, in several movies, a newspaper strip, and an unsold television series starring Robert Conrad as Carter.

It is difficult to accurately determine precisely how many Nick Carter stories were written as many authors were involved and the original stories were often reprinted, sometimes under different titles. In addition, the use of the Nick Carter name can be confusing. It was used as a pseudonym for Frederick Dey and John Coryell for the early Nick Carter detective stories in the *Shield Series* and *Secret Service Series* detective stories from Street & Smith. Then it was used to name one of the characters in the best-known and most popular detective dime novels in a series of weekly adventures that started in 1891 in the *Nick Carter Library*. A reasonable guess is that Carter appeared in more than a thousand titles between the late 1880s and the 1920s.[7]

The Thinking Man's Detective

Detectives formed a popular part of sensationalist literature, whether the stories involved real life detectives who investigated real crime, or whether they were fictional sleuths who solved fictional crimes in dime novels. By the turn of the nineteenth century, the classical detective story, such as the literary exploits of Sherlock Holmes and the later Hercule Poirot, was the most popular way of reading about crime and detective fiction. The detective story treated crime as entertainment, and in this way, crime and punishment became a way of providing pleasing intellectual and emotional stimulation for many readers.

The most popular form of detective story in the late nineteenth and early twentieth century was the classical mystery story that involved solving a crime through rational thinking and scientific inquiry. The classic mystery story involves an investigation and discovery of secrets hidden from the reader. The "whodunit," as originally conceived by Edgar Allan Poe and further developed in Great Britain, focused on a detective reconstructing events after the fact that led to the crime, instead of tracking and capturing the criminal, as was the later trend. The classical story starts with an unsolved crime and moves logically towards its rational solution. Typically a murder has taken place or something valuable has been stolen, and the detective seeks a solution to explain what has happened.

The term "detective story" is a wide category. Its elements of detection and discovery can even be used as the basis of a western, a horror story, or a ghost story. Variations include the hard-boiled detective, the secret agent, the crime thriller, or the pure mystery, such as the popular "locked room" type of mystery where a dead body is found in a room locked from the inside and no obvious way in which the murder could be committed. No matter how complex or improbable, though, the criminal methodology was always plausible at the end.

The formula of the classical detective story involves introduction of the detective, a crime that seems insoluble to the local authorities, the clues surrounding it, the course of the investigation, and ends with the announcement of the solution by the detective, along with a rational explanation for the crime. The final revelation may include the apprehension of the criminal and his or her confession to legitimize the detective's solution of the crime. In the end, no matter how bizarre the crime, its solution had to be plausible and there was always a criminal motive.

Several main characters appear in the classical detective story. There is a victim, a criminal, and the detective trying to solve the case. Other characters may be those with an interest in the crime, such as characters threatened by a possible repeat of the crime unless it is solved, and those who are unable to solve it. Members of the local police force are often portrayed as inefficient bunglers who require the help of the brilliant amateur detective.

The classical detective often has no real personal interest in the crime he is investigating. He is an amateur, often with a middle or upper class British background and, though intelligent, is often a little eccentric. The story itself may be narrated by the detective's colleague, such as Dr. Watson in the Sherlock Holmes adventures, Dr. Petrie in the Fu Manchu adventures, or Poe's unnamed narrator.

Puzzle, clues, and solution. This type of detective story was very popular in America, England, France, and Germany, and appeared throughout much of the rest of Europe.

Edgar Allan Poe

American author Edgar Allan Poe is considered to have written the first detective story, in which he introduced the classical type of detective. This was "The Murders in the Rue Morgue," which appeared in *Graham's Magazine* in April 1841. Poe followed this with "The Mystery of Marie Rogêt" in 1842 and "The Purloined Letter" in 1844. All three stories featured the logical reasoning and rational explanations of his protagonist Auguste Dupin. This type of amateur detective as a man of reason dominated detective and mystery fiction until about 1920.

Two individuals unwittingly had a major influence on the creation of the detective story. They were a French detective named Eugéne Vidocq and the American detective Allan Pinkerton. Later in their careers both Vidocq and Pinkerton wrote books about their work and their cases, and these writings had a large influence on the later writers of fictional detective stories. Poe, for example, was influenced by Vidocq's memoirs, which were published in 1828 when Poe was a young man.

Eugéne François Vidocq is generally considered to be the world's first private detective. He had a striking career in France. He was born in 1775, joined the military as a member of Bourbon Regiment at age 15 where he killed two men in a duel, and even had a short-lived stint as a pirate. He drifted in and out of jail periodically and felt that he knew the criminal element well, so he offered himself to the Paris police as a secret informant. As a result, in 1812, Vidocq set up a specialized plainclothes security department known as *La Sûreté Nationale*, that eventually became the French National Police. Part of his methodology was to employ reformed criminals as investigators, with the idea that they would be the best people to catch fellow-criminals. In 1833, aged 58, he established the first known detective agency, a mixture of detective agency and private police force in France named *Le Bureau des Renseignements* (The Information Office).

The first American detective to start his own agency was Allan Pinkerton, who set up Pinkerton and Company (later Pinkerton's National Detective Agency) in 1850 or 1852 (Pinkerton mentioned both dates at different times). Pinkerton did not have formal training in the detection of crime, but he had good powers of observation and a natural talent for solving cases. Pinkerton had a broad background in tracking down criminal activities. He had been a Special United States Mail Agent investigating thefts of mail and the activities of dishonest employees in post offices. He organized and became the head of the secret service for the army and was a personal bodyguard for President Abraham Lincoln. He was involved in counterespionage and exposure of government corruption, which helped him to devise techniques of surveillance, infiltration, and crime fighting that are still in use today.

Pinkerton's was the first organization of its kind in the western hemisphere. The agency investigated criminal cases of all kinds, from murder and arson to insurance fraud. Pinkerton's original vision for his agency was to cover the entire nation with operatives who were free to cross jurisdictional lines to investigate crime, and indeed his operatives could, and did, operate across state and county boundaries as a type of national police force. Pinkerton did not like the name "detective" and preferred to call his agents "operatives." Pinkerton operatives didn't directly arrest outlaws and criminals, but gathered information about them and their gangs, then used local law enforcement officers to make the actual arrest. Pinkerton's trademark symbol was an open, unblinking eye with the motto "We Never Sleep" underneath it. This symbol eventually led to the name "private eye" being used as a name for a private detective.

Pinkerton believed in covert surveillance. One of his favorite techniques was to have his operatives go under cover and infiltrate the gangs they were pursuing. The operatives used disguises and assumed names, which allowed them to work from the inside. Pinkerton preferred that his detectives worked undercover or in secrecy, and stipulated that there was to be no mention of his company or his men by the client during the investigation.

The Nick Carter character developed by Frederick Dey owed much to Pinkerton, plus his stories were influenced by Vidocq's earlier writings.[8]

Wilkie Collins

The first full-length (and perhaps the longest) English detective novel was *The Moonstone*, written in 1868 by Wilkie Collins. The novel was an instant success in England, America, and Europe. The landmark story appeared as a serial in the weekly journal *All the Year Round*, edited by no less than his close friend author Charles Dickens. It is generally thought that Dickens wrote *The Mystery of Edwin Drood* in an attempt to show his friend that he also could write a mystery novel. Collins' had previously written one of the first mystery stories, *The Woman in White*, published in 1859.

The Moonstone is the story of a huge, beautiful yellow diamond that is stolen from the forehead of a Hindu idol in India. The stone goes through many hands and finally ends up in England as a gift to attractive Rachel Verinder, the daughter of a cruel British soldier, for her eighteenth birthday. The priceless jewel disappears on the night of her birthday party and the rest of the story revolves around the mystery of who stole it, why, and how it is eventually recovered. Similar to *Dracula* (1897), the story is told from the viewpoints of several of the characters, including Betteredge, the family servant; Sergeant Cuff, the police investigator; Rosanna Spearman, a family maid with a shady past; and Franklin Blake, a would-be suitor to Rachel. Additional plot twists include three mysterious Hindu jugglers, the disappearance of Rosanna, and the use of opium to solve the case. Author Collins was addicted to opium in the form of laudanum (a tincture of opium dissolved in alcohol) for relief from the severe pain of rheumatic gout, thus he knew what he was talking about when he included it as a plot device. Collins' pain became so bad from time to time that he had to dictate part of the story from his sickbed.

Though considered to be an innovative literary detective, Sergeant Cuff was not made from what later writers would consider to be the heroic mold. He is described as "a grizzled, elderly man, so miserably lean that he looked as if he had not got an ounce of flesh on his bones in any part of him.... His face was as sharp as a hatchet, and the skin of it was as yellow and dry and withered as an autumn leaf."[9] In spite of this unprepossessing appearance, Cuff had a keen analytical mind and was able to deduce what had happened after the crime was committed with little effort.

Sherlock Holmes

The ultimate detective who solved crime through logical analysis and deductive reasoning was Sherlock Holmes, created by Arthur Conan Doyle. In the late 1880s and early 1890s, the stories of Holmes were a sensational literary triumph that spawned many imitators. Readers loved Conan Doyle's descriptions of the picturesque, fog-bound streets and the criminal underworld of late Victorian gas-lit London.

Sir Arthur Ignatius Conan Doyle studied medicine at Edinburgh University, where one of Conan Doyle's instructors, Dr. Joseph Bell, provided the model for the later Sherlock Holmes. Bell had exceptional powers of observation and reasoning, which resulted in medical diagnostic skills that amazed his students.

After receiving his degree, Conan Doyle served for a short time as a ship's surgeon on an Arctic whaling ship. He found the conditions too harsh and the pay too poor, so he returned to London, where he roamed the city at night, soaking up the atmosphere of fog-enshrouded streets, dark alleyways, dank buildings, and Hansom cabs.[10] The gas-lit streets with muffled figures of people going about their business later became the atmospheric background for his stories.

Conan Doyle started in practice as an ophthalmologist; however, only a trickle of patients came to his surgery, so he used the time while he was waiting to write. His first manuscript about the master detective Sherlock Holmes and his friend and companion Dr. John Watson, titled *A Study in Scarlet*, was rejected by several publishers. Just as Conan Doyle was ready to throw the story out, it was finally accepted on October 31, 1886, by Ward, Lock & Company, a publisher that specialized in cheap, sensational literature. They paid Conan Doyle £25 pounds outright for the story, with no further payments or royalties.[11] The publishers held onto the story for over a year, then it finally appeared in *Beeton's Christmas Annual* in November 1887. The story was only moderately successful, but it chanced to be read by the editor of the American magazine *Lippincott's Monthly Magazine*, who asked Conan Doyle to write another story. The result was *The Sign of Four*, which appeared in *Lippincott's* in 1890.

In 1891, Greenhough Smith, the editor of the English magazine *The Strand*, asked Conan Doyle for six more Holmes stories. Conan Doyle ended up writing 20 stories for *The Strand* between 1891 and 1893. These stories were later re-published in book form as *The Adventures of Sherlock Holmes* and *The Memoirs of Sherlock Holmes*. Conan Doyle had finally found success and Sherlock Holmes became the most celebrated detective in fiction. His capacity to solve seemingly insoluble puzzles has made him a favorite around the world. Many more stories appeared in *The Strand*, and Sherlock Holmes adventures have appeared on the stage, in motion pictures, and as television adaptations. Unfortunately, also, many of Conan Doyle's early stories were pirated by dime novel publishers.

The typical format of the stories starts as Holmes and Watson are in their flat at 221B Baker Street, often sitting by their fireside to ward off the cold London winters while they discuss local events. Someone brings to them an obscure problem, interrupting their conversation. Holmes listens to the events that have driven the puzzled person to him, ponders them, and then accepts the case. He goes to the scene of the crime or the strange occurrence and studies it, makes some shrewd deductions, and reveals the solution to the mystery. This sequence followed the Victorian perception that most problems could be solved through reason and common sense. Watson was Holmes' quiet companion, used as a counterpoint to narrate Holmes' exploits and join in where needed.

In 1912 Conan Doyle wrote *The Lost World* featuring Professor Challenger, a story in which prehistory is still alive and well on a remote South American plateau. Challenger also appeared in later adventures. Another Conan Doyle series was *The Adventures of Gerard* about a pompous, conceited hussar, written in a very engaging humorous style. The versatile Conan Doyle also wrote horror stories, such as *The Mystery of Cloomber* (1889) and *The*

Parasite (1894). Conan Doyle also wrote serious historical romances, including *Micah Clarke* (1889), and *The Refugees* (1893). Though Conan Doyle preferred his historical writings to Holmes, they were not as popular with readers and are generally forgotten today.

Holmes and Watson, however, endured. Conan Doyle wrote fifty-six short stories and four full-length novels featuring Holmes, a body of work that is known to enthusiasts as the Sherlock Holmes Canon. Though Conan Doyle continued to write other short stories and novels, the detective stories of Holmes and Watson have remained the most popular. The novel *The Hound of the Baskervilles* was even translated to comic book form in *Classics Illustrated* in January 1947. *A Study in Scarlet* appeared in *Classics Illustrated* in 1953. Holmes appeared again in comic book form, battling The Joker (from the later Batman comic series), when Marvel Comics reprinted *The Hound of the Baskervilles* in an April 1976 issue. Sherlock stories, as adaptations for the twenty-first century, are seeing a resurgence on television even today with the modern series *Sherlock* starring Benedict Cumberbach, and *Elementary* with actress Lucy Liu cast as a female Dr. Joan Watson.

Not as well known as Sherlock Holmes was the detective Sexton Blake. He, however, appeared in probably more stories than any other detective. He was created in 1893 by Harry Blyth and appeared until 1963 in over 4,000 stories and books by

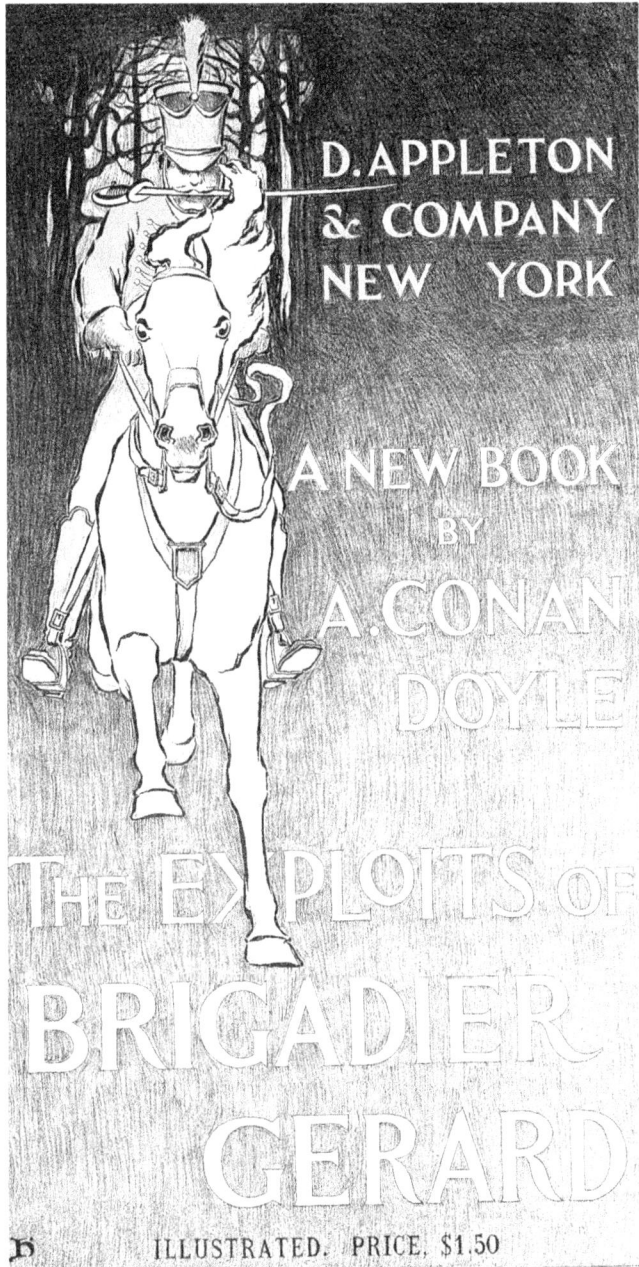

Though Sherlock Holmes, the most famous consulting private detective in the world, was the most popular literary invention of Arthur Conan Doyle, Conan Doyle wrote other stories and novels in different genres. Conan Doyle's boastful Brigadier Etienne Gerard, who served as a Hussar during the Napoleonic Wars, was a pompous blowhard. Nevertheless, the satirical, tongue-in-cheek recounting of his fictional adventures through Conan Doyle's definitive comic touch, still makes delightful reading. (Library of Congress)

200 writers.[12] Blake appeared in the English magazine *The Union Jack* and *Detective Weekly* until he had his own magazine, *Sexton Blake Library*.

Sherlock Holmes paved the way. But, by the early 1900s, a variety of detectives who reasoned their way to the solution of a crime had appeared, such as G.K. Chesterton's Father Brown, the amiable Roman Catholic cleric, and Agatha Christie's Hercule Poirot and Miss Marple. Christie started writing in 1926 with *The Murder of Roger Ackroyd* and continued writing at a rate of one book a year until 1976. Her sales are estimated to be over 400 million. Other popular detective authors were A.A. Milne and Ngaio Marsh. Dorothy Sayers created the amiable aristocratic detective Lord Peter Whimsey. Sayers also wrote stories about Montague Egg, a wine and spirit salesman.

A.J. Raffles, the master cracksman created by E. W. Hornung, was not exactly a detective, but was on the other side of the law. The adventures of Raffles were serialized in *Scribner's* in 1901 and collected as *The Amateur Cracksman* by Scribner's in 1902. Hornung was married to Arthur Conan Doyle's sister and *The Amateur Cracksman* was dedicated to "A.C.D." Hornung, who lived for a while in Australia, went on to create other characters, such as Stingaree, a mysterious highwayman from the Australian bush, and wrote other mysteries, such *The Crime Doctor* about a detective who solved crimes with psychology. Another popular masked gentleman cracksman was Blackshirt, who appeared in over a dozen stories by creator Bruce Graeme.

The dime novels and early pulp magazines delighted readers with lurid stories about urban crime and gangsters, but by the 1920s, the reading public was starting to tire of the solution to a mystery story based on rational cause and effect. Finally the sheer number of all these brilliant and introspective detectives created an overload. Somehow the concept and stories started to seem less exciting. So, to spice up sales, authors developed the hard-boiled detectives and started to create more action and violence, and add erotic themes.

7

Transition to the Pulps

Dime novels were popular from about 1865 to 1910, with their peak in sales occurring in the 1880s. By the early 1900s, the reading public was losing interest in dime novels. Part of the reason was that many of the literary heroes had become unbelievable. One observer summed this up when he said, "Readers undoubtedly were dissatisfied with a continuous line of heroes who fought off 20 Indians and rescued the heroine, even with one arm badly wounded. They wanted a gallant and strong protagonist, but one that was, nonetheless, believable."[1]

In the world of mass entertainment, one medium inevitably takes over from another. Television took over from radio. Talking motion pictures took over from the silent films. And, in the same manner, pulp magazines were an outgrowth of the dime novel and eventually took over the literary market from them and the fiction weeklies. Though dime novels struggled on into the early twentieth century, they had essentially faded away by 1920 when the rise in popularity of the new moving pictures finished them off. Another factor was that boys growing up in the 1910s, 1920s, and 1930s had different tastes and problems than the boys of the 1880s.

One of the final problems for the waning dime novel was that book publishers and moralists had been complaining for a number of years that postal rates for these libraries were essentially being subsidized by the government, thus creating a large post office deficit. After many years of lobbying, in 1901 the postal service finally disallowed second-class periodical rates for dime novel libraries, thus severely reducing their profit margin.[2]

The decline of the dime novel, however, coincided with the rise of the pulp magazine. Pulp magazines were published in their place by the same conglomerates, such as Street & Smith, who had been publishing dime novels. Many of the characters, writing styles, and action-oriented plots of the dime novels were simply transferred to the pulps, and many were direct descendants of the dime novel. Characters like Nick Carter and Frank Merriwell appeared in pulp magazines. Boys and girls series books, which were oriented towards younger readers, also made the transition to pulp magazines.

Between about 1920 and 1950 pulp magazines were the most popular type of fiction in the United States. The pulp form was perfected just prior to World War I, reached maturity in the early 1920s, was the most popular form of reading between World War I and World War II, and started to fade away directly after World War II.

What made the pulps different from the story papers and dime novels was that they were true magazines in size and content. They still sported lurid covers and contained breathless fiction, but they also included novels, short stories, various editorial departments, and letters from readers. Another difference was that the pulps included better artwork on the inside pages as well as the cover.

By the early 1920s dime novels were gone and pulp magazines were the dominant format for adventure and romantic fiction. One study estimated the circulation of pulp magazines to be over 3,000,000 readers in the early 1930s.[3] At the close of World War I there were only two dozen pulps, but by the middle of the Depression years, there were over 200. During the Depression, profits per issue were low, so publishers would bring out a new title and then wait to see if it was successful. If it was not, the magazine was dropped and another was started to replace it.[4]

Like the dime novels, so many pulp magazines were published and changed names as they came and went that it is difficult even for experts to keep track of them. For example, in 1912 the *New Nick Carter Weekly* became *Nick Carter Stories* and the issues were re-numbered at No. 1. *Tip Top Weekly* became *New Tip Top Weekly*. *Buffalo Bill Stories* became *New Buffalo Bill Weekly*, and was later published as *Western Story Magazine*.

Though the pulp magazines pioneered modern methods of book marketing and distribution, they repeated many of the publishing practices of the dime novels, such as continuing series characters, hack writers, house names, an emphasis on action and sensationalism, and exploitation of popular reading trends. Production costs were kept as low as possible, so if only part of the print run sold a profit could still be made.

The forerunners of the pulp magazines were the story weeklies and the paper-covered dime novels. Like the dime novels, pulp magazines were mass-produced reading material intended to provide cheap reading thrills for the common masses. One example was *The Golden Book*, a popular reprint magazine that flourished throughout the 1920s. In 1925 it had a monthly distribution of 175,000 copies and a circulation of over half a million.[5]

Like dime novels, pulp magazines were an inexpensive form of literature. They were printed on cheap, rough pulp paper made from a wood fiber base, referred to as "newsprint." This pulp paper had short-fibers that were fragile and difficult to preserve, which is why very few exist today, even with good conservation techniques. The paper was thick and porous and had a characteristic smell. Pages turned yellow and deteriorated within months. The so-called "slick" magazines, by contrast, were printed on smooth, higher-quality paper. Pulp magazines measured about 7 inches by 10 inches, and were stapled together through the cover, close to the spine. Normally they contained 128 pages of entertainment and escapist fare, with the text in double columns, and about 120,000 words of fiction. They had lurid, colorful covers designed to catch the reader's eye as he passed a newsstand. The covers were printed in four colors on better stock to make the magazine seem like it was of better quality, but the pulps were still only half the price of a typical slick.

Like the quality of the paper, the quality of the writing in the pulps was generally low. Authors worked fast with little or no rewriting, and the cost of production was kept to a minimum. The pulps initially sold for a nickel or a dime, rising later to a quarter. This was acceptable to purchasers when the average wage of a factory worker was $7 for a 10 to 12 hour day.

In the early 1920s these magazines were called "all-fiction magazines" or "wood-pulp paper magazines." The name "pulp" for these magazines came into common use in the 1930s. Though the name originally referred to the cheap, rough, wood-pulp paper that the magazines were printed on, the term was later used generically to refer to magazines that were sensational, mass-produced, affordable, on the sleazy side, and were aimed at an urban, working-class readership. By the mid–1920s "pulp" had entered American slang as a term for nonsense and excess.[6]

The usual meaning of the word was given to poorly written genre writing, such as crime, mystery, romance, or science fiction. However, the importance of the pulps for emerging authors should not be discounted. Many writers who later achieved fame started out in the pulps. For example, Thomas Lanier "Tennessee" Williams was 16 when his first short story was published in *Weird Tales* in August 1928. He was paid $35 for "The Vengeance of Nitocris," a short story about vengeance in ancient Egypt. Pulp magazines also launched the careers of such notables as Raymond Chandler, Dashiell Hammett, and H.P. Lovecraft. One of the first of the swashbuckling sea heroes, Captain Blood, came from the imagination of historical novelist Rafael Sabatini, who wrote about pirates, cutlasses, fighting, pieces of eight, and white sandy Caribbean beaches in the pulps. The first of his adventure stories about buccaneers, *The Sea Hawk*, appeared in 1915, followed by the first of his popular swashbuckling series about the pirate Captain Peter Blood in 1922.

Armchair Escape

In the 1930s, the American public was suffering from the economic hardship of the Great Depression and stressing over the threat of another World War, so readers wanted distraction, entertainment, and amusement. Pulp magazines met that need, and became the rulers of printed entertainment by providing all-fiction periodicals that cost from 5¢ to 25¢.

Pulps were weekly and monthly publications intended primarily for the working class. They published fiction that could be read by adults as well as by boys. Prior to World War II, 25 million readers purchased and read 200 million pulps every month. In any given month in the mid–1930s, at the height of the pulp's popularity, more than 200 of these magazines appeared on the newsstands, written by more than 1,300 pulp writers.[7] Some of the readers with more education considered the stories to be cheap, sensationalistic, and poorly put together. Indeed, much of the pulp fiction that was published was weak in quality and hastily written. It was intended for those who liked to read, but didn't have the money for hardback books. The stories were not great literature, but they offered adventure, excitement, and romance in heart-stopping situations, with relentless suspense and frantic action—all for a dime. Lurid cover art that was eye-catching and entertaining jumped out at the reader passing racks placed in newsstands, drugstores, train stations, and hotel lobbies. The genres published were many and varied sources of romance, fantasy, and escapism, and there was something to appeal to all readers. Pulp magazines were devoted to aviation stories, hard-boiled detectives, mystery, adventure, war, the Old West, romance, African adventures, horror, science fiction and fantasy, and any other topic the reader wanted. The conquest of distant lands and their savage inhabitants was the subject of pulp adventure stories for many years. The westerns, science fiction and fantasy, and the hard-boiled detectives endured and continued on into paperbacks, movies, and television.

In 1951 editor Michael Tilden of Popular Publications stated that their typical reader was a young man in his middle twenties with a couple of years of high school, and was typically employed doing manual labor in a large organization. Most were married, had children, some savings, a used car, and were trying to buy their own homes.[8]

The fiction in the early pulps was relatively mild. Then the editors realized that what made sales thrive was the larger-than-life story that was plot driven, had strong characters, and lots of action—preferably violent action. At the pulps matured, their stories became shorter and moved faster, and were characterized by livelier writing than the dime novels. The pulps enticed the reader into a world of entertainment, excitement, danger, glory, and romance, and provided a temporary escape from everyday reality through exciting stories of fantasy. Pulp magazines gained a reputation for being exploitative, unsophisticated, violent, and sexist, but nevertheless they were the primary source of original popular fiction from about the 1920s until arrival of mass-market paperbacks in the 1940s.

Most pulp magazines contained several stories and possibly a continuing serial, thus offering a greater variety of subject matter than the single focus of a dime novel. The male reading audience wanted adventure, western, and crime magazines that contained stories of action without their pulp heroes bothering with introspection and character development, or having to read much descriptive material. Characters, though, had to be strong, with no reluctant heroes or anti-heroes. The stories had to have a good beginning and middle, and the conclusion of the plot had to be a satisfactory one. For that reason, stories in pulp magazines didn't have downbeat, frustrated, or indeterminate endings. Things had to work out for the hero.

There was something for every reader's tastes and interests, no matter how obscure or narrow, in pulps such as *Fight Stories, Jungle Stories, Wall Street Stories, Weird Stories, Astounding Science-Fiction, Spicy Detective, Romantic Detective, Ranch Romances, Underworld Romances, Gun Molls, Gay Love, Pocket Love, RAF Aces, Ozark Stories, Courtroom Stories, Oriental Stories, Railroad Stories,* and *Zeppelin Stories.* Pulp stories included science fiction, sword-and-sorcery, erotic cowboys stories, weird menace, gangsters, spies, superheroes, and masked avengers, starring heroes such as Conan the Barbarian, Dr. Kildare, The Spider, The Shadow, and Doc Savage.

Magazines with specific themes were founded and sometimes faded away quickly as publishers tried to cater to the reading audience's tastes, fads, and fancies. The scope of some of these magazines was so narrow that they found no readers at all and immediately failed.

Pulp magazines came and went, and merged frequently. For example, Frank Munsey incorporated *The Live Wire* into *The Scrap Book* in 1908. In 1912 *The Cavalier* was absorbed by *The Scrap Book.* In 1914 *The Scrap Book* was combined with *All-Story Weekly,* and the resulting combination became *All-Story Cavalier Weekly.* Similarly, the dime novel series *The Buffalo Bill Weekly* became *The New Buffalo Bill Weekly* (though it featured reprints of old Buffalo Bill stories), then turned into *The New Buffalo Bill Weekly/Western Story Library* and finally *Western Story Magazine.* Some of the logic behind these changes was that this was one way to kill off a magazine with a declining readership that was not succeeding and yet retain and transfer the readership to a new magazine.

No matter how much critics looked down on the literary values of pulp stories, these magazines were obviously popular as they sold in very large quantities. In 1923 Street & Smith's *Sport Story* magazine had circulation of 150,000 a month.[9] In 1921 *Western Story Magazine* had a circulation of 500,000, compared to a circulation for *Vogue* and *Vanity Fair* combined which was less than 200,000. In 1924 the circulation of *Vanity Fair* was 81,856 and *Scribner's* was 71,414.[10] This trend has not necessarily changed. In 1999 the scholarly journal *Western Historical Quarterly* published 2,500 copies of each issue. By contrast, at the same time, the pulp magazine *Wild West* sold more than 150,000 copies.[11]

The transition to the pulp magazines started in 1896 when publisher Frank Munsey decided to switch *Golden Argosy* magazine for children to a pulp magazine format. His idea was to use cheap paper and high-speed printing presses to create an inexpensive magazine that could successfully compete with existing dime novels. The magazine eventually became *Argosy*, a thick 200-page all-fiction periodical for adults. It was one of the best and longest running pulp magazines.

Argosy

The era of the pulp magazines started in 1882 when publisher Frank Munsey launched a cheap weekly story paper for children called *The Golden Argosy*. In 1888 Munsey decided to re-format *The Golden Argosy* into a pulp magazine named *The Argosy* that used a low-grade of paper like the dime novels. His concept was to use cheap paper and high-speed printing presses to create an inexpensive magazine that could successfully compete with the dime novels. Munsey felt that the stories his magazine contained were more important than what they was printed on, so he hoped that the lowest grade of paper could be used and readers would not complain.

Munsey speculated that pulp magazines with reduced printing costs could be successful and still make a profit with a cheap cover price, even if they sold far less copies than the slicks. With the added bonus of inexpensive second-class postage for mailing, his strategy allowed pulp magazines to be successfully published for specialized markets, such as for fans of westerns, science fiction, or romance stories, and still make a reasonable profit. This type of low priced magazine would not have been possible before the development of the rotary steam press for economical printing and completion of the railroad for convenient distribution. In the late 1890s *Argosy* consisted of 191 pages, with yellow covers and 30 pages of coated paper stock for advertisements. The magazine included serial stories and novels, self-contained short stories, and some poetry.

The Golden Argosy turned into *The Argosy*, which was reconfigured for an older readership of a general juvenile and adult audience, instead of only for children. It was a thick all-fiction periodical for adults that was one of the best and longest running of the pulp magazines. As a fiction weekly it was popular for almost 60 years until 1932. Most issues contained about 135,000 words of mainstream adventure and mystery fiction, and were printed on the cheapest paper possible.

Argosy became a thick all-fiction magazine with no illustrations, printed on cheap wood-pulp paper. The lack of illustrations allowed Munsey to print it on the cheapest possible paper. *Argosy* became a top seller and the circulation quickly climbed to 80,000 copies per issue. By the early 1900s, it was selling 500,000 copies a month. The magazine was so successful Munsey converted it to a weekly. *Argosy* published six million words of new material each year.[12]

In the 1920s *Argosy* used a successful all-adventure format, and published authors such as Max Brand, Upton Sinclair, Zane Grey, Edgar Rice Burroughs, Luke Short, Johnston McCulley, and other top authors. Zane Grey's *The Rainbow Trail* (1915) was serialized in *Argosy* as *The Desert Crucible*.

Munsey's other very successful magazine was *Munsey's*. It had a circulation of 500,000 in 1895, the second year of its publication. Between 1892 and 1922 the circulation rose from 2,231 to 2,187,024.[13]

Other Pulp Publishers

As a result of the success of *Argosy*, male-oriented action stories became very popular and other publishers followed Munsey's lead. *Argosy* and *All-Story* were followed by *Adventure, Short Stories, Blue Book, Popular, Top-Notch,* and *People's*, all of which presented a mixed selection of heroics in each issue, such as a cowboy, a pirate, a masked avenger, a detective, or a legionnaire. *People's* published adventure and mystery stories along with genre stories.

Four magazines were considered to be at the top of the pulp field, *Argosy*, *Adventure*, *Blue Book*, and *Short Stories*. *Argosy* offered high pay to authors, three or four times what some of the others paid, but the editors insisted on authenticity, quality writing, and good story construction.[14] *Adventure* was one of the earliest and longest-running of the adventure pulp magazines. The magazine published high quality escapist fiction in serial stories, novelettes, short stories, and complete novels. *Adventure* was published by the Ridgeway Company, a subsidiary of the Butterick Company, which published ladies' dress patterns. In 1910 the relatively unknown Butterick organization was the largest publisher of American magazines.[15] *Blue Book* was a general interest publication before turning to masculine stories. *Short Stories* was a literary magazine, but turned to pulp stories in 1910.

The dime novel giant Street & Smith started converting their paper-covered books into pulp magazines as early as 1901 with *The Buffalo Bill Stories*. They followed with *Popular Magazine*. Though Munsey's and Street & Smith continued to dominate the pulp market during the 1920s, other publishers quickly jumped on the bandwagon and the number of pulp titles grew rapidly. One of the significant publishers of the late 1920s and early 1930s was Dell Publishing, founded by George T. Delacorte, Jr., in 1922.

New York was the home to almost all of the pulp publishers. Munsey's was located at 28 Broadway, Street & Smith at 79 Seventh Avenue, Dell at 100 Fifth Avenue, and Popular Publications at 205 East 42nd Street.[16] Others were Clayton Magazines, Popular Publications, Thrilling Publications, and Culture Publications. Aaron A. Wyn built Ace Publishing Company on pulps such as *Eerie Stories*, *Ten Detective Aces*, and *Secret Agent X*. Fiction House, founded by Jack Kelley and Jack Glenister, published no-nonsense masculine magazines, such as flying adventures in *Air Combat Stories* and *Sky Detectives*, and boxing stories in *Fight Stories*. Publisher Harold Hershey started several magazines that were very short lived. Other publishers, such as Doubleday, entered the business with magazines such as *Short Stories*, the cowboy pulp *West*, and the adventure and mystery pulp magazine *Star*.

When American News Company, the largest magazine distributor, lost their biggest client, Street & Smith, they started their own line of pulps named Standard Publications, which they distributed themselves. Their line included *The Phantom Detective*, *Startling Stories*, and *Captain Future*. They also started a series of pulps in various genres with "thrilling" in the title, such as *Thrilling Detective*, *Thrilling Love*, *Thrilling Western*, *Thrilling Mystery*, *Thrilling Adventures*, *Thrilling Spy Stories*, *Thrilling Wonder Stories*, and *Thrilling Ranch Stories*. At its peak in the late 1930s, the Thrilling Group of magazines was publishing 44 different pulp magazine series.

Popular Publications was founded in 1930 by Henry Steeger who had edited pulps at Dell Publishing and Harold Goldsmith who had worked with pulps at Ace Publishing Company. They started with four titles covering the primary popular genres of the time: *Battle Aces*, *Gang World*, *Detective Action Stories*, and *Western Rangers*. They hoped that at least one of them would be a success. And they succeeded beyond their expectations. They went on to create a dime series of pulps, *Dime Detective*, *Dime Western*, *Dime Sports*, *Dime Adventures*, and *Dime Mystery*. By 1940 Popular Publications was the largest all-pulp publisher in the world. Their *Dime Detective* sold 300,000 copies a month. They added series characters to their mystery stories with *The Spider* and *Operator #5*.

As more and more pulps were published, they turned increasingly to specialization. One of the first very narrow interest pulps was *Railroad Stories*, which published railroad fiction, along with true tales of railroad workers and hobos, and photos of locomotives. Other unusual pulps catering to highly specialized audiences were *Strange Suicides*, about people who killed themselves; *Fire Fighters*, containing stories about putting out fires; *Speed Stories*, about fast moving vehicles; and *Railroad Man's Magazine*, also catering to railroad fans. The lack of success of *Medical Horror Stories* may have been an unplanned tactical marketing error, as a large percentage of its sales took place on drugstore newsstands—not a good location as the magazine featured disturbing stories about medical charlatans. As suspected, none of these lasted much more than one issue. *Courtroom Stories* did a little better and lasted for several issues. One of the more peculiar titles was *Twice a Month Love*, which was appropriately issued every two weeks. The first Munsey publication to specialize was *Detective Fiction Weekly*.

The Wizard (subtitled "Adventures in Money-Making") stories from Street & Smith in the early 1940s were the adventures of a financier named "Cash" Gorman, with the plots revolving around corporate finance and takeovers. The magazine didn't create much interest in the reading public and lasted for only four issues.[17]

In the aftermath of World War I, pulp magazines reflected the tensions of contemporary society. The aviation stories came from an obsession with the recently ended war. The Yellow Peril literature came from the rumors of white slavery and political threats against the West. Hard-boiled detective stories originated with Prohibition, the rise of gangsterism, and urban corruption. The science fiction pulps, such as *Wonder Stories*, grew out of a fascination with new technology and were often cautionary tales of science gone wild. Hero pulps grew from the tensions and frustrations of dealing with crime in the urban population. Western pulps continued the nostalgia influenced by the passing of the era of the Wild West and a disappearance of the freedom of the open range.

Advertising and Editorial

Although the pulps depended primarily on newsstand sales for their revenue, some magazines contained limited advertising, mostly on the front and back pages. As the pulps had a reputation for sensationalism and for attracting lower-class readers, the advertising was seldom for high-class, high-priced products. That type of advertising went to the slicks, such as *Cosmopolitan, Colliers*, and *The Saturday Evening Post*.

Instead, the advertisements in the pulps tended to be of a highly personal nature, such as remedies and relief for burning feet, weak bladders, bad breath, and hemorrhoids. To cater to readers wishing to improve themselves and their self image as they tried to emulate the fantasy figures of their pulp heroes, advertising offered fitness courses and muscle building (such as the popular Charles Atlas advertisements to help scrawny men attract women through bodybuilding), sex manuals and aids, false teeth, eyeglasses, and medicine to clear up acne, which was always a worry for adolescents.

On the racier side of the advertisements were "spicy" 16mm movies and photographs to be viewed at home, and "art" courses that taught how to draw pictures of nude women. Other curiosities were a man's handkerchief made like a small pair of women's panties, and a novelty French photo ring "with a large imitation diamond" and a hole in the side where a viewer could look in and see a pinup photo. For those who were not interested in pinups, one option was to have the photo of the girl replaced with a view of a place

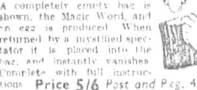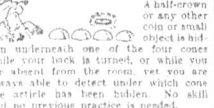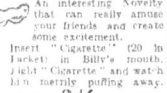

Some of the pulp magazines accepted a limited amount of advertising, mostly on the front and back pages. Here is the back cover of a magazine that would appeal to juveniles, showing novelty items, such as magic tricks, dancing skeletons, dehydrated worms, goofy teeth, exploding pens, sneezing powder, and a multitude of other peculiar novelty items for sale.

of interest in France. As pulps publications were aimed at adolescent boys there is not much question which one most purchasers chose. Along the same lines, fashionable dressers could send away for a striptease tie that glowed in the dark. During the day it sported a picture of a blonde woman on the front, which the advertiser claimed "brings gasps of sheer wonder, thrilling admiration the first time you wear it!" After the sun set at night, the picture turned into a luminescent nude that glowed in the dark.

Other items of apparent interest to readers were a complete telegraph set for 15¢, popular song manuals, a blank cartridge pistol for "protection against burglars, tramps, dogs," and a device that was fitted to the roof of the mouth to throw the user's voice into a trunk or under the bed. For whatever reason the latter was guaranteed to fool policemen and produce high hilarity in bystanders.

The Model 25 nose-shaper promised to reshape the purchaser's nose by "painlessly" reforming the underlying cartilage. The Golden Treatment was recommended for curing drinking problems, with a trial package sent free in a plain wrapper. Other questionable "medicines" promised to treat conditions such as sterility, hernias, epilepsy, "diseases of the blood," and prostate problems. Miscellaneous services included correspondence courses for how to become a private detective, a magician, or an electrician, or how to sell shirts door-to-door. Others promised the secrets of how to get a job as a railway worker, or how to become a government postal clerk.

The editorial material in most pulps consisted of three or four feature stories—up to as many as twelve—along with short fillers, editorials, letters from readers, advice columns, and personal romance columns. A typical pulp might have half-a-dozen short stories, accompanied by one or two longer pieces. Fiction was typeset into two dense columns of imaginative writing.

Similar to some of the dime novels, full novels were frequently serialized over four to six issues of a pulp magazine. The older Munsey pulps had as many as four serials in each issue. Serialization promoted purchase of the next issue as the reader wanted to find out what happened next in the story. In the 1920s, though, changes started to take place. Magazine readers became impatient with serials and preferred the entire story to be in one issue. They did not want to wait for next chapter of serial fiction, so the stories tended to be complete. Serialization as a publishing device continued to some extent through the 1930s, but fell out of favor in the 1940s.

Unlike the one-way transmission of information from the written word to the reader used by literary and dime novels, the pulp magazines promoted interchanges between writers, editors, and readers. Interaction was encouraged by letters to the editor, contests, and prizes. Letter columns in the tough he-man fiction magazines, such as *Manhunt*, *Suspect*, *Accused*, and *Pursuit*, contained congratulatory letters from readers to the magazine, technical questions about the stories, such as how to shoot a gun or a bow, or questions about woodcraft or forestry or taxidermy or ships or sailing or a multitude of other topics that might be of interest to male readers. *Detective Fiction Weekly* had a continuing column on how to break secret codes.

In a further effort to promote interaction and loyalty to a particular magazine, readers could join the magazine's club, such as the Doc Savage club, or the Friends of the Phantom. Interestingly, the American Legion started out as a club for a pulp magazine when the editor of *Adventure*, Arthur Hoffman, created a veteran's "minute man" network in 1914 when World War I seemed unavoidable. The group eventually developed into the national organization now called The American Legion.[18]

The Lone Ranger magazine tried to cajole readers to join its club with what the editors thought to be genuine western speech when they said, "Fill out the coupon an' send it to us, enclose a three-cent stamp an' we'll git your membership cyard out tuh yuh muy pronto, an' welcome yuh around this yere ol' chuck wagon good an' plenty friendly."[19] This type of pseudo-western slang writing was an Eastern conception, intended to impart a tone of authenticity to the writing, but it was often so convoluted that it irritated the readers instead.

Action Stories had a club called the "Brotherhood of He-Men." To be eligible to join, potential members had to have been in the armed services, or merely to have had some grueling experience, such being in a shipwreck. Or the applicant could be a hunter. Just fill out the coupon and send it in. These were the forerunners of fan clubs, fan conventions (such as the later immensely popular *Star Trek* gatherings), and modern internet blogs by celebrities.

Pulp Authors

The pulps, like the dime novels before them, were fiction factories. Dime novel publishers tried to put out as many novels as possible, as cheaply as possible. Likewise, publishers and distributors viewed pulp magazines as the same kind of profitable commodity. Publishers tried to manufacture the most economical product in order to create the most profit. They used the cheapest paper, paid authors as little as possible, and tried to find the magical genre and hero figure that would attract the largest audience of readers. If another publisher seemed to have found a more successful mix of ingredients, the others were quick to copy. Advertisers saw the mass marketing of the pulp magazines as a good medium to transmit their message.

Writers were hired to churn out formularized plots to attract the largest audience, as a form of mass production on an assembly line. Though the pulps had many contributors, the core of the pulp writing was done by a small group of a few hundred men and women who churned out the majority of the fiction. Writers typically stuck with the type of story where they had relevant experience. War heroes wrote war stories, previous cowboys wrote westerns, pilots wrote aviation stories.

Payments to authors became lower as increasing competition among publishers lowered profits. Writers therefore had to crank out pulp fiction on a constant basis to make a decent living. Short stories were typically less than 10,000 words and some authors specialized in writing a 3,000- to 5,000-word story each day. Novelettes mostly averaged around 12,000 words, but could run from 10,000 to 60,000 words in length. Novels told the story in more than 60,000 words. To achieve this, some writers worked at their typewriter for up to 18 hours a day. Authors typically did not spend much time on editing or revision, as there was no time for any second thoughts. The story was put on paper as the author conceived it and wrote it down, and the first draft was usually the last draft. Some pulp authors could crank out 200,000 words a month. Busy writers churned out 500,000 to 1,000,000 words a year. Western author Max Brand and Lester Dent, the inventor of Doc Savage, were reputed to write a million words a year.[20]

The pulp magazines turned authorship into a purely commercial and moneymaking business. Authors earned from one fourth of a cent to 4¢ per word. Thrilling Publications typically paid 1¢ per word. The high-paying markets typically paid 2¢ to 3¢ a word. Top writers in the field, who could draw readers to a magazine, might get 4¢ a word. Lesser writers were paid as little as 1¢ a word, thus making each story worth $30 to $50.[21] Writers, therefore, had to average at least two sales a week to make a decent living. Most of the pulp writers worked on a free-lance basis, so their stories were written on speculation and might take a while to sell—or might not even sell at all. "Salvage markets," where stories went if they would not sell anywhere else, paid from half a cent to 1¢ per word.[22] During the Great Depression the pulps cut even their best rates to an average of 1¢ per word. To make the situation worse, some unscrupulous editors never got around to paying, and some floundering publications paid writers very late or even on an installment basis.

Some authors slaved away, cranked out reams of paper, and were published, but were uncredited. As with the dime novels, the bylines for their stories were often assigned to a house name that was owned by the publisher. Pen names were also used to create a more appropriate personality for the author. For example a sentimental story about an orphan that was actually written by a man might be credited by a pseudonym to a poor orphan girl.

Most authors wrote for more than one pulp. To earn increased income, a good writer might crank out hundreds of thousands of words a year under an assortment of pen names and house names. Richard Sale, for example, wrote for *Detective Fiction Weekly*, *Dime Detective*, *Argosy*, *Bluebook*, *Thrilling Mystery*, and *Double Detective*. In the space of ten years he sold 500 stories at the rate of about one a week. He was one of the authors who could write 3,000 words a day. But his first draft was also his last draft.

The Importance of Cover Art

In the 1920s most publishers reduced the size of their standard pulp magazines from 200 pages or more to a typical 128 pages of dense type on cheap paper with the unbound side untrimmed and uneven. Black-and-white illustrations on the inside pages were drawn in simple bold strokes so that the ink did not bleed into the cheap pulp paper or smudge into unrecognizable blurs.

Cover illustrations, however, were printed on more expensive coated paper, and used three or four colors of ink. The cover paintings of the early pulps tended towards muted colors and restrained illustrations, but in the 1920s and 1930s, the publishers of pulps developed a new type of sales strategy and produced cover illustrations that used bright primary colors and depicted lurid images of sex and violence. The technique was not new, as the publishers of the cheap story papers of the late nineteenth century had previously used brightly colored cover illustrations to capture the attention of potential purchasers. The use of bold primary colors was also important because the printing presses of the 1920s and 1930s were still relatively crude and required hard lines in the illustrations to produce the best reproduction.

Even the cheapest pulp magazine publishers paid careful attention to cover art. While traditional slick magazines were sold mostly by subscription, the pulps had few subscriptions and were sold primarily at newsstands and on racks in hundreds of drugstores and similar place. This type of display made them ideal for spontaneous purchases. The cover was essentially an advertisement for the contents of the magazine, so the front cover had to have eye-catching artwork and high visual appeal to stimulate impulse sales. The artwork on the cover had to be effective at this, because there was intense competition

Pulp magazines were sold primarily on magazine racks in newsstands, drugstores, and similar places. As there was intense competition on the racks, the covers had to be eye-catching and have high visual appeal to stimulate impulse sales by spontaneous buyers. Each magazine had only a few seconds to catch the eye and stimulate a purchase. The front cover had to present striking and compelling images, such as this intriguing cover from *Strange Stories*. A casual glance would stimulate a potential purchaser to wonder who these ghoulish men were, what they were doing to this woman, and how.

on the magazine racks. Illustrations were kept relatively simple as they had to tell the story to the potential purchaser in only a few moments. Each magazine had only a few seconds to catch the eye and stimulate a purchase as the buyer scanned the rack. Colors were bright and tantalizing, and illustrations showed intense titillating action that was exciting, lurid, or bloody. Successful artists used vivid imaginations and clever perspectives to create striking and compelling images.

Artists were typically paid from $50 to $100 for a cover painting, though top artists might be paid twice that. The good ones could complete one in a day. Some writers had to make up a story based on a lurid cover illustration that had been commissioned and completed before a writer had come up with a plot.

In order to try and maintain consistently high sales, Popular Publications conducted research and analyzed the color schemes used on their magazine covers. They found that red, yellow, and black were best for drawing the eye for men's magazines, and blue and green for women's magazines. One artist remembered being told by his publisher that the covers for a particular pulp had to be predominantly yellow, because the color yellow drew the eye and sold well.[23]

Along with bright colors, a vital part of the sales appeal of the cover was flamboyant action. By the late 1920s and 1930s covers were generally well painted and artistically composed. Whether they illustrated the contents of the magazine or not—and they often did not—the covers had to be appealing, vivid, and alluring. Foreground figures were bright and bold, set in close-up, and the backgrounds were often dark and ominous, and faded into blackness to set the mood for menace. Popular covers depicted brawny men and half-dressed women, their action frozen at a moment of maximum dramatic literary impact, such as a knife about to plunge into flesh, a gun exploding, or a half-dressed young woman with a terrified look on her face, frozen in mid-scream. Human female figures were carefully drawn with luxuriant flesh tones, lushly draped with clinging fabric. Backgrounds were usually not fully formed, in order to focus on the foreground action.

The 1930s were the heyday of illustrations for the western pulp magazines. Their cover art reflected many of the myths of the Old West, with dramatic titles splashed across the top and lurid illustrations in vivid colors beneath. These covers were intended to evoke images of action, bravery, chivalry, romance, and excitement. The typical cover art matched the written action, with guns being pulled, horses rearing while the rider was firing a gun, or the hero grabbing the villain in one hand while shooting at his gang with the other, with perhaps poker tables being knocked over in the background.

Detective stories generally had sensationalist color covers that featured half-clad women or some act of mayhem or violence, or preferably both. The stories inside were melodramatic and the covers were richly illustrated, gaudy and lurid, to match. The horror pulps popularly featured grisly illustrations of women being tortured by ghoulish monsters and mad scientists.

Cover paintings for the pulps were not considered to be respectable art at the time. After publication, artists and publishers routinely put them into storage, frequently threw them out, or the artist painted over them in an economy move to reuse the canvas. Today this type of art, even though it is often racist, sadistic, or sexist, has been rediscovered and the few remaining pulp cover paintings (possibly 700 out of about an estimated original 60,000) bring large figures at art auctions.

8

Fantastic Heroes and High Adventure

Heroes drew male readers to pulp adventure stories by making the average working man imagine that he too could be an explorer of new worlds in lost jungles in strange countries. These escapist fantasy projections catered to the needs and desires of a primarily male audience, both young and old.

In the 1920s and 1930s, specialized adventure pulps focused on stories featuring exotic locales, such as Egypt, Russia, Death Valley, and the Himalayas. *Jungle Stories* and *Thrills of the Jungle* told tales of darkest Africa. *Far East Stories* were about the mysteries of Asia. *Pirate Stories* were naturally about pirates. *Foreign Legion Adventures* told stories of the men in the French Foreign Legion. *South Seas Stories* were specialized stories about beachcombers or unshaven heroes in pith helmets and rumpled white linen suits in equatorial climates, who frequented booze-soaked bars where the locals hung out. Tropical adventure stories took place on exotic islands, and involved mysterious maps, sunken ships, buried treasure, crocodiles, and lost islands inhabited by fierce cannibals. Also obligatory were a beautiful girl, a villain, and a sinister gang of lascars (East Indian sailors) wreathed in tobacco and opium smoke.

Pulp adventure stories typically opened with a mysterious or bizarre situation that involved the hero in immediate action, then provided a roller-coaster plot ride for the next eighty or ninety pages. This type of thrilling fiction opener is known as "the hook," as it hooks the reader into the action and makes him want to continue reading.

An example of this is the first few lines of the "Attack of the Blizzard Men," that appeared in the pulp magazine *Operator #5* and started with a wonderful hook to the story. "It was a sultry day in August when the ghastly cold first came. Snow began to fall; ice formed, and in a brief hour, New York City was paralyzed." Readers immediately want to know why it was snowing on a hot day in August and what happened when the city was paralyzed.[1]

Edgar Rice Burroughs

One of the greatest and most influential of the fantasy adventure writers was Edgar Rice Burroughs. His stories are worth considering in some detail as they contain most of the elements of successful fantasy-adventure pulp writing. He was also the most widely-read American author during the first half of the 1900s, more popular even than Hemingway or Faulkner.

Burroughs was born on September 1, 1875, in Chicago to a father who had been a Union Cavalry officer in the Civil War, then became a successful businessman. In 1891 Burroughs was sent to his older brother's ranch in Idaho to escape an influenza epidemic at home. He spent the summer living the cowboy life, and experienced the waning days of the Old West. Burroughs wasn't a particularly good student, but did attend Michigan Military Academy in 1892. He graduated in 1895 and planned to go on to West Point, but he failed the entrance exam. In 1896 he enlisted in the army and was assigned to the Seventh Cavalry (earlier commanded by Lt. Col. George Armstrong Custer) at Fort Grant in the Arizona Territory. Burroughs didn't particularly care for the boring life of a soldier, and didn't see the action he had hoped for. He was discharged after ten months due to health problems. He tried several different jobs, as a clerk, a railroad patrolman, a gold miner, a salesman, an office manager, and a construction supervisor, none of which were particularly successful.

In 1911, at age 35, as Burroughs was thumbing through a pulp magazine, he decided that he could write pulp fantasy just as well (or badly, depending on the viewpoint) as those authors. The result was a novel about an ex-cavalry officer, a Virginia gentleman named John Carter, who is mysteriously transported to Mars, called Barsoom by the planet's inhabitants. Here he encounters fierce giant green men, called Tharks, who are 15 feet tall and have 4 arms. He also rescues the beautiful Dejah Thoris, Princess of Helium, and wins her hand. Burrough's limitless imagination created an entire culture for the vast, dying planet of Mars. He invented races of green, red, white, and black men and their Martian histories, strange creatures, stranger vegetation, and ancient deserted cities. The story starts in a cave in Arizona, using Burroughs' experiences from serving there in the army. He titled the fantasy *Dejah Thoris, Martian Princess* and used the pen name of Norman Bean.

Burroughs sent his story to Frank Munsey's publishing company. Perhaps to his surprise, the story was accepted and he received a payment of $400. The novel was retitled *Under the Moons of Mars* and was published as a serial in *All Story* magazine from February to July 1912. The serial was later collected for book publication and renamed under its more common title of *A Princess of Mars*. The novel brought him writing success and spawned 10 books in the Martian series.

The initial Martian story was a great success with readers and Munsey's asked for more stories. Burroughs wrote a second novel, *The Outlaw of Torn* (1927), as a romantic medieval adventure at the editor's suggestion; however, the editor didn't like the final story and asked for a sequel to the Martian book. Burroughs decided to write a third novel, but not a Martian one. The story was *Tarzan of the Apes*. *All Story* bought Tarzan for $700 and ran the complete novel in the October 1912 magazine. They billed it on the cover as "A Romance of the Jungle." The plot line is so well known that it will not be repeated in detail here. Essentially Lord and Lady Greystoke are abandoned on an uninhabited section of the coast of Africa when the crew of the boat they are on mutinies. The parents die of fever, leaving their baby boy to be adopted and raised by a female ape who has lost her own young one. The tribe of apes names him "Tarzan," which means "White Skin."[2]

The tale was a typical pulp story of adventure and romance. It was even more successful than Burrough's Martian novel and led to *The Beasts of Tarzan* (1916), *Jungle Tales of Tarzan* (1919), *The Return of Tarzan* (1925), and 20 other Tarzan sequels. It is worth noting that the Tarzan tales as written by Burroughs were intended for adults. The original story contained elements of cannibalism, revenge, murder, and other lurid stapes of the genre in the plot.[3] Burroughs knew nothing about Africa, but with his fertile imagination he based his Tarzan stories on what he visualized Africa to be and what he had read in similar romance novels. He obviously succeeded. The hardcover version of *Tarzan of the Apes* was published two years later and sold over a million copies.[4]

Meanwhile, *Under the Moons of Mars* had been so well received that six months later Burroughs wrote a sequel titled *The Gods of Mars*. He followed with *The Warlord of Mars*, which was serialized in *All-Story* magazine from December 1913 to March 1914.

The first three Martian novels, *A Princess of Mars* (1912), *The Gods of Mars* (1918), and *The Warlord of Mars* (1919) form a trilogy that revolves around John Carter, describing his adventures and how he eventually wins the hand of the copper-colored princess Dejah Thoris of Helium in marriage. The stories include plenty of daring adventures and swordplay, intermixed with hair-raising escapes, strange creatures, airships, fierce battles, bloodshed, and plenty of cliffhangers.

In this cliffhanger from *The Warlord of Mars*, Carter is climbing up the almost vertical wall on the outside of a tower in pursuit of the villains, who have captured the heroine. "Dejah Thoris must have seen me at the same instant, for she screamed a useless warning just as Thurid's foot, swinging in a mighty kick, landed full on my face. Like a felled ox, I reeled and tumbled backwards over the tower's side." This was the end of the installment, leaving the reader in suspense. Plunging on to the next part, the reader finds out how Carter escaped the fate of being dashed to death on the ground far below. The next chapter started with "Ten feet only I fell, and then a loop of my tough, leathern harness caught upon one of the cylindrical stone projections in the tower's surface—and held."[5] The hero survived to fight again.

The first two novels, *A Princess of Mars* (1912) and *The Gods of Mars* (1918) both end with tense cliffhangers. *A Princess of Mars* ends with Carter racing across the planet to restart the atmosphere plant that provides the Martian planet with air. At stake are the lives of his princess, the egg containing his unborn son, and the inhabitants of the entire planet.[6] He is mysteriously transported back to Earth again without knowing if his efforts have been successful.

The second book, *The Gods of Mars*, starts with Carter being transported back to Mars, and ends with Dejah Thoris trapped in a subterranean chamber with two other women. The entrance to the chamber is designed so that it will remain closed for a Martian year before anyone can enter again. Carter sees one of the women raising a dagger above his wife, hears a single shriek, and then the passageway into the chamber closes before he finds out who has been stabbed. Another serious cliffhanger. At the beginning of *The Warlord of Mars*, the reader finds that Dejah Thoris is unharmed, but has been kidnapped. Further adventures await until the two are reunited at the end of the book and Carter is given the supreme Martian fighting man's title, The Warlord of Mars.

As Carter and Dejah Thoris were already married and finally reunited after the third novel, Burroughs had the dilemma that is common to writers of stories from pulps to films. Once the hero and heroine are united in marriage, their relationship and situation change. The hero settles down to domestic life with the heroine, thus there can be no more stories of single adventurous heroes fighting for and winning the girl he loves. Burroughs solved this problem by continuing the Martian series using some of the characters that appeared in the previous novels, with Carter playing only a minor role. The fourth book in the series, *Thuvia, Maid of Mars* (1920) featured Thuvia, who had been previously introduced in *The Gods of Mars*, and related how Carter's son Carthoris pursues her through adventures similar to his father and wins her hand. *The Chessmen of Mars* (1922) is about the adventures of Tara, Carter's daughter, and how she is wooed and won by an adventurer from a neighboring kingdom. *The Mastermind of Mars* (1928) introduces another Earthman, Ulysses Paxton, who is transported to Mars in the same inexplicable manner as Carter. Paxton, of course falls in love with a Martian woman and continues the tradition of adventure and sword fighting to win her hand. *A Fighting Man of Mars* (1931) introduced a new character, Hadron of Hastor, and his adventures and efforts to find his own princess, which of course he does at the end of the book. So these books all follow the same basic theme. The hero falls in love, is initially rejected or misunderstood by the heroine, or is blocked by circumstance, has adventures involving strange beings and places, overcomes the hurdles to being reunited with the girl, and all ends happily with the two marrying. This is the same basic plot that had been used in dime novels, Victorian stage melodramas, and indeed continues today in many novels.

As part of his fantasy writing, Burroughs transferred western plots of action and adventure into outer space. Though mostly set on Mars, with some on Venus, his space fantasy novels contained all the elements of a successful western melodrama. The highlights were adventure, action, improbable plots, and a beautiful princess (or several princesses as the series progressed) to be wooed, fought for, and won.

Burroughs' adventure stories appealed strongly to adolescent fantasies. The fantastic world that forms the background of red princesses, false gods, green giants, and strange creatures is described by Burroughs in loving detail. An example of the animals is contained in Burroughs' description of Woola, a Martian animal called a *calot* that acts like his faithful hound. The animal is the size of a Shetland pony, with a head like a frog, and jaws lined with three rows of long sharp tusks. "Imagine, if you can, a huge grizzly with ten legs armed with mighty talons and

The limitless imagination of Edgar Rice Burroughs poured out a series of fantastic adventures. This is the cover page of the novelized version of the second book in Burrough's Martian series, *The Gods of Mars* (1918), which appeared first as a serial in *All Story* magazine. Here, the hero, John Carter from Virginia, disguised with a blonde wig, fights his way onto the airship of one of the fighting men of Mars, as he battles his way across the dying planet to rescue his kidnapped love, Dejah Thoris.

an enormous froglike mouth splitting his head from ear to ear, exposing three rows of long, white tusks. Then endow this creature of your imagination with the agility and ferocity of a half-starved Bengal tiger and the strength of a span of bulls, and you will have some faint conception of Woola in action."[7]

Burroughs was influenced by the Victorian era in which he grew up. As part of this upbringing, he placed great faith in the honor and chastity of women. The heroines are always threatened with "a fate worse than death" (i.e., rape), but are rescued in the nick of time. He also showed his sadness at the loss of the quieter and more ordered Victorian world that was disrupted by the rapid changes of World War I when he penned the following description of dancing on Mars in one of the later Martian books. In it Burroughs offers a subtle rebuke at the flapper-style dances that were in vogue when he wrote *The Chessmen of Mars* (1922). "All Barsoomian dances are stately and beautiful, but The Dance of Barsoom is a wondrous epic of motion and harmony—there is no grotesque posturing, no vulgar or suggestive movements. It has been described as the interpretation of the highest ideals of a world that aspired to grace and beauty and chastity in woman, and strength and dignity and loyalty in man."[8]

Writing until his death in 1950 (marred only by a non-productive period during wartime service as a correspondent in the Pacific during World War II), Burroughs published 74 novels in several genres, including westerns, spy stories, fantasy, and Oriental adventures, selling over 100 million copies in countries around the world. He churned out dozens of Tarzan stories that took place in exotic locations, lost cities, and forgotten African empires, along with ten novels and two novelettes about Mars and John Carter, plus westerns and other fantasies. Another otherworld series by Burroughs featured Carson Napier in *Pirates of Venus* (1934) and three related novels about a fantasy world with Venus as their setting. Like John Carter, the hero meets with strange animals and plants during his fantastic adventures. Burroughs also wrote a series of novels about Pellucidar, starting with *At the Earth's Core* (1922) and *Pellucidar* (1923), that were set in a world beneath the earth's crust. Other prehistoric novels were *The Land that Time Forgot* (1924) and *The Eternal Lover* (1925). The latter linked a prehistoric hero, who has been mysteriously preserved and reawakens after a hundred thousand years, with a modern heroine. The story even included Tarzan, who has now become the new Lord Greystoke.

Burroughs western writing had an authentic background to it as he had his summer on his brother's Idaho cattle ranch and his short western military experience to call on. Two of his westerns were *The War Chief* (1927) and *Apache Devil* (1933), which used his earlier experiences with the cavalry in Arizona. He also wrote *The Bandits of Hell's Bend* (1925), a conventional western, and *Deputy Sheriff of Comanche County* (1940), set on a New Mexico dude ranch.

A few critics have complained that Burrough's prose was ragged, his plots loose and formulaic, and that the stories had too many coincidences.[9] Whether this was true or not is debatable, but he also had a wonderful imagination and a gift for describing breathtaking action that is still very readable today.

Jungle Pulps and Tales of Lost Races

When Tarzan appeared in *All-Story* magazine in October 1912, he opened the door for a flood of what became known as the Jungle Pulps. The success of the Tarzan character meant that others tried to imitate him by inventing similar jungle men. Some of them were Tam, Son of the Tiger; Jongor; Morgo the Mighty, who lived in a cavern deep under the Himalayas; Ozar the Aztec; Kioga, the Snow Hawk, who lived in a strange land north of the Arctic Circle; Sangroo the Sun God, who lived in the jungles of Malaya; and Kwa of the Jungle, who returned the reader to Africa again. There was also Ki-Gor, The white Jungle Lord, who was very similar to Tarzan. The fall 1950 cover of *Jungle Stories* highlighted a story inside with "Ki-Gor—Jungle Lord tracks zombie spoor to the Congo's Dungeon of Despair in *Voodoo Slaves for the Devil's Daughter*." Ka-Zar, who lived in the Congo, was another Tarzan clone, but was saved by a lion instead of a gorilla. Ka-Zar lasted for only three issues in the pulp magazines, but survived for a while in comic books.[10]

The Tarzan-clone adventure pulps were primarily about daring expeditions and adventures in dense jungles. Most of them took place in Africa, but authors tried to differentiate themselves from the others by placing their stories in South America, Borneo, New Guinea, and similar steamy remote wilderness environments. Typical magazines devoted to jungle stories were *Jungle Stories* and *Thrills of the Jungle*. Neither of these particular pulps was successful.

It was not necessary for a writer to have actually experienced the deepest darkest jungle to write these stories. Carl Jacobi, who also wrote weird fiction, wrote exotic adventure stories about contemporary Borneo and New Guinea, such as "Home Life of a Borneo Headhunter," without leaving his hometown of Minneapolis.[11] He was good at research and used the local library to fill in details. He also corresponded with real sweat-soaked colonials in exotic locales and used their replies to add color to his stories. Other writers who did not have this luxury simply made up the details that they thought fitted the story and locale.

A genre that was closely allied to the Jungle Pulps was the Lost Race Tales, also called Lost World Tales. This was a type of fiction that featured stories about a race or tribe of undiscovered people hidden from the modern world by inaccessible jungles, wide and fast-flowing rivers, towering mountain ranges, remote plateaus, or other natural geographic barriers. These natives lived in primitive but barbaric splendor, isolated by their remoteness. The stories were the adventures of explorers following ancient legends and hidden knowledge to seek the fabulous wealth in gold or treasure supposedly guarded by these hostile natives. Adventure stories describing the conquest of distant lands and their savage inhabitants had been around for years, and this was merely an adaptation of the genre.

One of the first and most influential of the Lost World Tales was *King Solomon's Mines* (1885) by H. Rider Haggard, a superb writer of adventure and fantasy stories. This is a romantic adventure that follows a hunt for treasure in deepest exotic Africa. The great white hunter Allan Quartermain leads two Englishmen, Sir Henry Curtis and Captain John Good, into darkest Africa to look for Curtis' brother, who has gone missing while searching for the fabled lost treasure mine of King Solomon. The story has all the ingredient for pulp adventure—a mysterious setting, tribal conflict, and fabulous lost treasure. The story was so popular that it was pirated and printed in the United States before the authorized version was released in England.

Henry Rider Haggard was born in Norfolk, England, to a wealthy family. He started to pursue a law degree, but abandoned it and went instead to South Africa to fill an administrative post, where he remained for five years. He returned to England and his legal studies, but decided he didn't want a career in law and turned to writing instead.

8. *Fantastic Heroes and High Adventure* 111

Comic books were quick to capitalize on the selling techniques of the pulp magazines. This cover for one of the jungle-adventure comics is a small boy's dream. It features a jungle setting with a woman in abbreviated tight shorts showing a lot of leg, holding a machine gun ready to spray the natives in the boats on the other shore with bullets. Nyoka also starred in a movie serial, *Perils of Nyoka* (1943), with Kay Aldridge.

The premise of this type of story, about an unknown race of African natives far beyond the reaches of civilization, was quite plausible at the time, because much of the world in the late 1800s was still unexplored. Readers had no reason to doubt that there could easily be a lost civilization isolated in some hidden pocket of the world. To help convince them, real lost worlds were being discovered at the same time, such as Machu Picchu in Peru, which was unknown until 1911, Angkor Wat in Cambodia, and other remote lost cities in the jungles of Africa and Central America. Thus it seemed certainly possible that Africa could have an unknown tribe of fierce warriors guarding a fabulously rich diamond mine. This type of fantasy and adventure story appealed to readers of all ages.

Haggard became closely linked to exotic adventure stories set in Africa as he followed the popular *King Solomon's Mines* with *Allan Quartermain* (1887). Quartermain eventually became the hero of 14 books and several short stories in follow-ups, sequels, and similar African adventure stories.

Another related lost-race romance novel by Haggard was *She* (1887), which was followed by several sequels. The premise is that Quartermain finds a mysterious kingdom and a remote lost tribe in Africa ruled by a beautiful, but tyrannical, ageless white goddess named Ayesha. This queen has achieved immortality by bathing in the magical "fire of life" in a hidden cavern in a remote mountainside. The result is that she is beautiful, perpetually young, and infinitely desirable. At the climax of story, she bathes in the column of fire again, but this time the process is reversed and she ages 2,000 years instantly and dissolves into an ancient hag.

Masked Avengers and Swashbuckling Heroes

Another category of popular hero that was common in the pulps was not a fantasy adventurer in space or an explorer of lost or unknown worlds, but was an imaginative crime-fighting superhero here on earth. Pulp novels were full of fantasy plots featuring heroic champions in masks and capes, such as the Purple Menace and the Green Menace, battling secret societies bent on world domination. Other similar crime fighters soon joined the line-up including The Shadow, The Spider, The Gray Seal, The Ghost, The Whisperer, The Avenger, and Captain Satan. Pulp literature of the 1930s was bursting with disguised avengers with capes, cowls, and masks. Characters such as The Shadow and The Phantom Detective were forerunners of the later comic book superheroes, such as Batman and Superman.

These costumed crime fighters had dual-identities, with the guise of a mild-mannered socialite or playboy by day, and a masked avenger fighting crime by night. This type of hero was fresh in the 1930s when crime fiction was dominated by hard-boiled detectives. Though this was a new approach for the pulps, masked avengers bent on revenge and retribution had previously appeared in penny dreadfuls, nickel weeklies, and dime novels throughout most of the 1800s. The earlier ones were highwaymen, such as Dick Turpin or other bandits, and the later ones were exemplified by Deadwood Dick in the Wild West. Readers fantasized that they too could secretly be the unpublicized protectors of the weak and avengers of wrong.

The first of the popular new masked avengers was Zorro, created by Johnston McCulley. Zorro first appeared in the serial "The Curse of Capistrano" in five issues of *All-Story Weekly* between August 9 and September 6, 1919. McCulley was a veteran reporter who had worked for *The Police Gazette* and other popular journals, and wanted to write successful adventure stories.

Zorro was a true swashbuckling hero, a skilled swordsman who dressed all in black for his crusade for justice. The dictionary definition of a "swashbuckler" is a blustering, swaggering fighting man, combining the words *swash* meaning swaggering, and *buckler*, a shield. Zorro (which is Spanish for fox) was all of that as a masked swordsman and defender of the defenseless, in a story of high adventure during the Spanish colonial era of early California. The essence of the story is that Don Diego de la Vega returns from Spain to find that his father has been ousted by the tyrannical Alvarado and his henchmen, making life miserable for the peasants under an oppressive regime. By night Vega becomes Zorro, the masked avenger, a mysterious figure in black who avenges wrongs and delivers justice with the blade of a sword. Zorro's other identity during the day as that of Don Diego is a landowner and effeminate dandy who reads poetry and seemingly hates violence. As Zorro, Don Diego eventually leads a revolution, overthrows the wicked governor, and wins the love of Lolita, who spurned him as Diego, but loves him as Zorro.

The story has been criticized as having no originality, a bland and functional style, and characters who were transparent and unbelievable.[12] In spite of this, the story was made into a successful film titled *The Mark of Zorro*, starring Douglas Fairbanks, Sr., in 1920. Though the Zorro novel didn't make a great stir among readers, the motion picture did. The popularity of the swordfights, daredevil action, exciting chases, and typical Douglas Fairbanks acrobatics that involved swinging from balconies, leaping over walls and roofs, and stunts with wagons, started a cycle of similar swashbuckling films. Like many other successful pulp stories, the Zorro story was re-filmed in 1940 as *The Mark of Zorro* starring Tyrone Power, in 1974 starring Frank Langella, and in 1998 as *The Mask of Zorro*, starring Anthony Hopkins and Antonio Banderas.

After the success of the movie, the serial story was republished as a novel from Grosset and Dunlap. The popularity of the first story was followed by *The Further Adventures of Zorro*, which appeared in *All-Story Weekly* from May to June of 1922. Various other sequels appeared over the next 30 years.

The Zorro story was a vague version of the legend of Joaquín Murieta, the most famous of the Spanish social bandits, who terrorized the Anglo community in California in the early 1850s. The real Joaquín (or Joachim) Murrieta (or Murieta) was a semi-fictional hero who was locally famous for his exploits against supposed tyranny imposed on Mexican immigrants. Reportedly his family had been attacked by a group of Yankees who tied him up, beat him, and raped his wife. He escaped and vowed revenge in a manner similar to the fictional Zorro.

Much of the story of Zorro is the same as the Scarlet Pimpernel, a fictional character created by Baroness Emmuska Orczy in 1905. The Pimpernel (a plant from the primrose family) protected the French aristocracy and Zorro (the fox) protected the California peasants. McCulley created several other similar dual-identity characters. For one of them he even reversed the good and bad roles, creating a hooded villain called Black Star. The concept of a masked man riding around the countryside righting wrongs was later carried on by the Lone Ranger.

Zorro was the first, but certainly not the last. Many superhero pulps of the 1930s featured masked avengers, such as Thunderbolt, The Whirlwind, The Man in Purple, and The Crimson Clown. The Thunderbolt, like many of the other masked avengers was from an old and respected family. He had inherited a large family fortune that assured him the financial freedom to prowl around avenging crime, dressed in a black hood and a black costume with peculiar black rubber gloves. Just to be different, The Man in Purple dressed from head to foot in purple clothing, including purple gloves and a purple hood over his face. And of the course the Crimson Clown dressed up in a crimson circus clown outfit.

This trend was part of the group represented by The Shadow, The Spider, and The Phantom. The Phantom solved cases such as "The Jewels of Doom," "The Death-Skull Murders," and "The Corpse Parade." The Patent Leather Kid was given his name because he wore glossy shoes made of leather, and later took to wearing a mask made of shiny patent leather.[13]

People's included the Gray Seal among its adventure and mystery stories. The masked Gray Seal was in reality Jimmie Dale, a crimefighter who left a grey sticker or seal on his victims. Like the other masker avengers, he lurked around town in various disguises that helped him to fight crime.

The Shadow

The first and most successful of the pulp superheroes was The Shadow, who sprang into action to fictionally battle the organized crime that was rampant in America in the 1930s. When *The Shadow* magazine debuted in 1931, the average man was ready for retribution and action against criminals. The Shadow was a champion who could (at least on paper) solve problems and restore order during this felonious crime wave.

The character of The Shadow had an unusual origin. It started with the *Detective Story Hour*, which was a continuing radio mystery program designed as a promotional vehicle for Street & Smith's *Detective Story* magazine, a top-selling pulp that contained stories about private detectives and other mystery tales. Each week, the anonymous narrator, played by voice actor James La Curto, read a story from the current issue of *Detective Story*. La Curto took a Broadway role four months later and was replaced by actor Frank Readick. One of Readick's features was that he started the program with a sinister melodramatic laugh accompanied by the words, "Who knows what evil lurks in the hearts of men? The Shadow knows!"

Readick's creepy cackle became very popular with listeners. The audience liked this new twist and wanted to know more about The Shadow, a character that of course didn't yet exist. So Street & Smith tried to figure out how to exploit this opportunity. In response, circulation chief Henry Ralston created a new series of mystery adventures that were based around a single character named The Shadow. *The Shadow* magazine debuted in April 1931, with the byline of Maxwell Grant. It was a repackaging of the old dime novel formula, somewhat like the masked and caped crime-fighter Zorro, but was targeted towards a younger male urban audience. The Shadow was described as the "scourge of the underworld" and the "nemesis of crime," as he roamed the city at night. He was portrayed as a tall figure who fought crime with his twin blazing .45 Colt automatics and could literally pounce on villains from his autogyro (a type of one-man helicopter).

The Shadow would have been right at home in the nineteenth-century penny dreadfuls because he dressed in a black cloak and a black broad-brimmed felt hat that was bent downwards to obscure his features. The cover illustrations of the magazine showed him with a long, sharp nose. The apocryphal story of the origin of the nose was that it was copied from one of the assistant art directors at the magazine.[14]

In his daytime life, The Shadow was Kent Allard, a famous aviator. Lamont Cranston, millionaire playboy, was only one of Allard's aliases, though that was the one used in the later radio series that starred actor Orson Welles. Welles' radio show also added several other elements that were not in the printed stories, such as The Shadow's female companion Margot Lane. He also had the ability to cloud men's minds and make himself invisible. Another alias was Fritz, the janitor at police headquarters.

The Shadow typically didn't do all of the crime fighting himself, but employed a small army of assistants and associate crime fighters to do the investigative work, then he appeared at the end with his .45 automatics blazing to bring appropriate justice. The new magazine was a sensation and publication quickly went from quarterly to monthly to weekly.

The magazine lasted for nearly twenty years and made a fortune for Street & Smith in sales and licensing fees. The Shadow appeared in an estimated 283 novel-length stories written under Street & Smith's house name of Maxwell Grant. Maxwell Grant was in reality Walter Gibson, a prodigious writer. By the end of 1946, Gibson had written 270 novels about the Shadow. Gibson could crank out four to five pages of story each hour for twelve to fifteen straight hours, which translated to more than 5,000 words a day. This furious pace allowed him to create two 60,000- to 70,000-word books each month. Gibson had been a magician, so his professional perspective allowed him to create curious twists, plot tricks, and threats of bizarre death to his writing, which added a mysterious atmosphere. The secret of the Maxwell Grant house name remained inside Street & Smith and they continued the series with the house byline. A few of the novels were written by Theodore Tinsley, but they were also published under the Maxwell Grant house name.[15] Like many of the pulp characters, The Shadow appeared in low budget movies, such as the fifteen-part serial *The Shadow* (1940) starring Victor Jory, and then later appeared in comic books.

After the success of *The Shadow* at Street & Smith, rival Popular Publications combined elements from various superheroes and came out with *The Spider* magazine in late 1933. The Spider was the secret identity of Richard Wentworth, a wealthy world traveler, but at the same time a ruthless crime fighter who marked his criminal victims with a blood-red symbol of a spider. Like The Shadow, he dressed in a black cape and a broad-brimmed black hat. When in disguise he also had a hawk-like nose.

Some of *The Spider* stories added sex to the violence to create outlandish tales. Popular Publications had started their notoriously sadistic shudder pulps (discussed further in Chapter 14) at about the same time, and stories in *The Spider* reflected a similar callous approach to violence and sex, and contained lurid descriptions of both. Stories had sinister titles, such as "The Devil's Death Dwarfs," "Satan's Death Blast," and "Wings of the Black Death." The spider character later featured in two 15-part serials titled *The Spider's Web* (1938) and *The Spider Returns* (1941) from Columbia Pictures.

The Spider stories were written by several writers, but the harsher and grittier stories were written by Norvell Page, under the pen name of Grant Stockbridge. Page apparently identified closely with his creation, as he often wore a large black hat and a black cape like The Spider. Page was an intense writer. When he wrote "Wings of the Black Death," where The Spider battles a cruel blackmailer threatening New York with bubonic plague, Page described the results in vivid prose including such disgusting details as, "The purple lips opened, suffocation blackened his face. Blood gushed out."

Various masked avengers blossomed in the 1930s and many imitators appeared in the wake of the success of The Shadow. More and more costumed dual-identity crime fighters donned masks, costumes, and elaborate disguises to fight crime, such as The Ghost, The Whisperer, The Avenger, and Captain Satan. They battled super-villains, such as The Octopus, The Scorpion, Doctor Death, Dr. Yen Sin, and The Mysterious Fu-Wang.

The Moon Man had a black cape, black gloves, and a spherical helmet that was constructed from one-way glass. The Ghost was George Chance, a combination magician and detective who had supposedly learned all his skills from circus performers. During his crime-fighting adventures in *The Ghost* magazine, he used make-up to transform himself into a ghastly, ghost-like character. His partners included a man who was his double, a beautiful girl, and a midget. In spite of the premise, the magazine didn't last long.

Another short-lived avenger was Jim Anthony, modestly named the Super Detective. He appeared in *Super-Detective* magazine in the late 1930s. He was described as the rich son of a world-famous Irish adventurer and a Comanche princess. He did his crime fighting in a peculiar outfit that consisted of yellow swim trunks and a pair of Indian moccasins.

The Green Lama debuted in April 1940, in *Double Detective*. He was in reality wealthy playboy Jethro Dumont, who had inherited 10 million dollars and thus could indulge his hobby of crime fighting. When he went into action, he wore a green hood and green robe, accented with a red scarf that he used as a weapon. He was originally supposed to be The Grey Lama instead of The Green Lama, but green made a more striking color for the magazine cover.[16]

In the early 1940s a character named the Black Hood appeared in a pulp titled *Hooded Detective*. Apparently not very popular, the magazine had only a short life. The main character was a policeman named Kip Burland, who had become impatient with the traditional legal system after he had been framed by a criminal named The Skull. In a tradition that went back to Deadwood Dick and the dime novels, The Black Hood pursued his retribution outside the law, and was not above breaking and entering, kidnapping, extortion, and assault.

The Phantom Detective was Richard Curtis Van Loan, a rich Park Avenue playboy, who first appeared in *Phantom Detective* magazine in February 1933. The Phantom was certainly multi-talented. He was a master of disguise, though his outfit often consisted only of a top hat and a small mask that covered his eyes. He was an expert at judo and savate, was skilled with guns, and was also a master of hypnotism and ventriloquism. His stories, with titles such as "The Island of Sudden Death," were written by a group of writers that were credited under the house names of G. Waymon Jones or Robert Wallace. Because of the variety in style of the different authors, some of the plots and characterization were uneven. Nevertheless, the series was popular and lasted for 20 years, until 1953.

The Whisperer, another justice-seeking crime fighter, appeared in 1936. Like The Shadow, The Whisperer had sinister laugh, but to make him different it was reduced to a low chuckle. The Whisperer was in reality James "Wildcat" Gordon, the youngest police commissioner in New York. One odd characteristic was that he used false dental plates as part of his disguise to change the shape of his lips and jaw, and make him talk in a low weird whisper.

Another man from a law and order background who was impatient with the legal process and took short cuts to avenge crime and bring criminals to justice was Assistant District Attorney Tony Quinn. Like other masked avengers, he disregarded the law, made up his own rules, and lived by his own sense of justice. Criminals had previously blinded him. The crooks believed him to be still blind but, unknown to anyone except the reader, he had undergone a secret eye transplant that allowed him to see even in absolute darkness. This gave him a tremendous advantage when prowling dark streets at night to hunt down criminals.

The Black Bat was an avenger who appeared in *Black Book Detective* magazine from Thrilling Publications. Like several of the other superheroes, he appeared in a totally black outfit, including black shoes, gloves, shirt, mask, and cape. And black wings.

There were only a few masked female phantom crime fighters. One of the few was The Domino Lady who became a crime fighter after her father was assassinated by crooked politicians. Her disguise was a domino mask of black silk.

Looking for something other than "Thrilling" in their titles, editors at Thrilling Publications latched on to the word "Masked." Thus a series of new pulps appeared with names like *Masked Detective* and *Masked Rider Western*. The *Masked Detective* stories were written under the house name of C.K.M. Scanlon. C.K.M. were the initials of the wife of Leo Margulies, the editorial director at Thrilling Publications, and Scanlon was a man who worked in the editorial offices.[17] This particular house name was used by many different authors. The Masked Rider was Wayne Morgan, who had a Yaqui Indian partner named Blue Hawk, in a relationship similar to that of the Lone Ranger and Tonto. The two rode together in stories about a type of outlaw like Robin Hood or Zorro.

One of the last avengers to appear was Captain Zero, who debuted in late 1949. His real name was Lee Allyn. Allyn had the peculiar ability to turn himself invisible every day at midnight, a characteristic that was apparently useful in his fight against crime. The author, however, tried for too much realism and the character turned out to be so short, bland, and uninteresting that he became almost a parody. He was so realistic that he couldn't see without his glasses and nothing seemed to go right for him. He only lasted for three issues then became invisible for good.

Superheroes and Supervillains

During the years of the Great Depression in the 1930s, spies and secret service agents were a popular breed of superhero, many of which had their own magazines. Secret Service Operator #5 was in reality Jimmy Christopher, who acted as an undercover secret service agent of the United States government. Operator #5 worked for a man whose identity was so secret that he was known only as Z-7. The two appeared in *Operator #5* magazine, which was subtitled "America's Secret Service Ace." Operator #5's mission every month was to save the United States from monstrous threats of destruction that included plague germs and Asiatic robots. By 1939, when the threat of World War II seemed inevitable, he appeared in war-related stories that included battling Japanese invaders in South Dakota, led by a fiend named The Yellow Vulture.

Most single character pulps had clubs for juvenile and other readers to join. The idea was to promote loyalty to the magazine, as well as provided additional income for the publisher. *Operator #5* magazine had an organization readers could join called the "Secret Sentinels of America." One advertisement for it modestly said, "Any red-blooded American, man or woman, who wishes to enlist in this powerful, patriotic organization … need only fill out the attached enrollment blank." Readers could also obtain a replica of Operator #5's handsome skull-and-crossbones ring by sending a few coins or stamps to the magazine. The magazine claimed that by wearing it, every member of the Secret Sentinels "will be able to identify his comrades-at-arms." Hopefully it was not exactly like Operator #5's original skull ring, which contained a secret compartment filled with enough explosive to blow up an entire building.

Operator #5's counterpart at Ace Publishing Company was Secret Agent X, who worked with the FBI to solve only the toughest of crimes. His crime-fighting career started in 1934 and ran for the next five years. Among his other accomplishments, Secret Agent X could disguise himself totally and mimic the voice of any man. He appeared in rousing adventures that bordered on horror tales, with gruesome-sounding titles such as "Slaves of the Scorpion," "The Curse of the Crimson Horde," "Satan's Syndicate," "Legion of the Living Dead," and "Claws of the Corpse Cult." As the series progressed, the crimes became more monstrous crimes and the death devices even grimmer.

G-Men Detective featured Dan Fowler, a fearless, muscular man with a brilliant mind for solving crimes. For the sum of only 10¢ a reader could join the Dan Fowler G-Men Club.

There was even a breed of super-villains who had their own magazines, such as *The Octopus*, *The Scorpion*, and *Doctor Death*. Other horrible villains included the Vampire Hag, who led a horde of winged dead; the Death Master, who wanted to blow up the world; Herr Feuer (German for "fire"), who was clothed in asbestos; and the Man in Armor, who was the leader of an army of dead men.

Doc Savage

After the huge success of The Shadow and his imitators, the publishing firm of Street & Smith wanted another masked avenger to add to their lineup. The result was Doc Savage in *Doc Savage Magazine*, featuring a brilliant hero who was muscular, strong, and in superb physical condition. The series lasted for sixteen years and 181 issues.

Clark "Doc" Savage, Jr., to give him his full name, had many skills and capabilities, including being a skilled surgeon (hence the nickname "Doc"), chemist, pilot, engineer, inventor, and archeologist, and being the master of many languages. As the independently-wealthy son of an adventurer father, Doc's exploits were funded by vast sums of gold that came from Doc's secret mine hidden somewhere deep in the jungles of Central America. If he needed money, he simply went to the mine and dug out more gold.

Doc made his headquarters in New York, in a Manhattan skyscraper, and was the leader of a curious band of five other adventurer-sidekicks. They were Col. John "Renny" Renwick, who was over six feet tall, weighed over 200 pounds, and was an expert engineer; Maj. Thomas J. "Long Tom" Roberts, a skinny expert with all electronic equipment; William Harper "Johnny" Littlejohn, a geologist and archeologist; Andrew Blodgett "Monk" Mayfair, a little over five feet tall and 260 pounds, but a genius with anything related to chemistry; and Brig. Gen. Theodore Marley "Ham" Brooks, a Harvard lawyer who carried a sword-cane with a poisoned tip. The group fought crime in a long series of pulp adventure and science fiction plots. They traveled worldwide, helped those who needed it, and punished those who deserved it.

The larger-than-life Doc Savage series was written by Lester Dent under the pen-name of Kenneth Robeson. Dent had previously written for a variety of pulp magazines,

Spies and secret service agents were a popular type of superhero during the years of the Great Depression in the 1930s. Operator #5 acted as an undercover secret agent of the United States government. Operator #5 worked for a man whose identity was so secret that he was known only as Z-7. The two appeared in *Secret Service Operator #5*, subtitled "America's Secret Service Ace." Operator #5's mission every month was to save the United States from destruction from bizarre threats that included plague germs, Asiatic robots, and Japanese invaders in South Dakota.

including *War Aces*, *War Birds*, *Sky Riders*, *All Western*, *Western Romances*, *All Detective*, and *Scotland Yard*. He had a prodigious output and could literally write around the clock. He was also a pilot, an electrician, a plumber, and an architect. Dent liked to search for buried treasure and had a yacht in the Caribbean where he searched for sunken gold. He would dive under the ocean during the day and then write Doc Savage novels at night.

Doc was a brawny superhero, described as looking like a statue sculpted from bronze, because his skin was deeply tanned by the sun from his many outdoor adventures in the tropics. Appropriately, when *Doc Savage Magazine* debuted in March of 1933, the introductory story was a 55,000-word novel titled "The Man of Bronze." Dent wrote it in 15 days.

Lester Dent as Kenneth Robeson churned out a 60,000-word novel about Doc Savage every month for Street & Smith. He eventually wrote more than 150 of them.[18] The series was extremely popular, lasting 16 years. Though Dent wrote the majority of the Doc Savage novels, Street & Smith used the house name of Kenneth Robeson for all of them, even those written by others. The Doc Savage novels were later reprinted in paperback and are estimated to have sold over 12 million copies.

Along with dreadful villains, Dent filled the Doc Savage novels with imaginative plots, fantastic villains, plenty of action and violence, and bizarre inventive gadgets. The plot of *The Lost Oasis* in September 1933 contained, among other oddities, a hijacked zeppelin, a gorgeous aviatrix, trained vampire bats, foreign bad guys, and a desert prison. Plot elements included a helicopter dogfight, vultures, car chases, man-eating plants, a slave revolt, and a lost African diamond mine. Some of Doc's unusual inventions were oxygen pills for breathing underwater, a rifle contained in a banjo that was fired by plucking the strings, and a platinum suit for deflecting death rays.

The popularity of Doc Savage spawned The Avenger, also known as the Man of Steel, who combined many of the traits of other crime-fighting superheroes. In reality he was wealthy Richard Benson, who dedicated his life to smashing crooks and the underworld. Like Doc Savage, The Avenger had a group of fellow crime fighters. To try to boost sales, the series was supposedly credited to Kenneth Robeson, as the writer of the Doc Savage series, but in reality it was written by others under that house name.[19] The series only lasted for a short while due to wartime paper shortages.

9

Detectives Become Hard Boiled

In the 1920s two major figures emerged in pulp crime literature, the hard-boiled detective and the urban gangster. The hard-boiled stories about detectives that emerged in the 1920s were not about Sherlock Holmes or Hercule Poirot and their deductive reasoning powers, but were American thrillers, filled with tough and violent action. These stories contained an exciting and usually convoluted plot, plenty of action and mayhem, and a detective who was tough, quick with a wisecrack, chivalrous to the women he met, and unafraid of crooked cops and killers. During the story he was often injured, both physically and emotionally. He is portrayed as tired, disillusioned, and disappointed with the human race, but he will see the case through to the end regardless of the consequences to himself or others.

These stories evolved from the thinking detectives because America in the 1920s was entering a new era. It was a world of veterans from World War I, flappers, Prohibition, and gangsters. Ordinary working people were disillusioned by recurring scandals, incompetent politicians, and corruption in the political system. In response, the reading public was disenchanted and tired of upper-class English gentleman solving bloodless crimes and wanted tougher detective fiction to match the times. American authors transformed the English amateur detective into the hard-boiled detective.

The traditional respect for law and order was being eaten away by frustration over increasing control of the cities by gangsters and the growing evidence of illicit connections between crime, business, and politics. The unpopular and unenforceable Eighteenth Amendment to the United States Constitution that ushered in Prohibition unleashed a major increase in crime and gangsterism based on illegal alcohol. Criminals and bootleggers catered to the alcoholic wants of ordinary citizens while being protected by the government agencies that were supposed to prevent the sale and consumption of illegal liquor. Criminals bought protection from law enforcement and politicians. Civic leaders publicly condemned citizens' drinking habits while enjoying bootleg liquor and conniving with criminals.[1]

The average citizen was frustrated by the hypocrisy of legislated public morals. A judge with a cellar full of bootleg liquor could send a man to jail for having a pint in his pocket. Corruption extended to the highest levels, and even a group of high government officials freely sold liquor confiscated by the Prohibition Bureau from a base of operations in Georgetown.[2] A law that made criminals out of law-abiding citizens unwilling to give up liquor resulted in a lack of respect for the law.

Crime and gangsterism worsened in the 1920s as the decade progressed. Unemployment and poverty increased. The real world of the 1920s and 1930s included speakeasies, bootleg liquor, prostitution, extortion, and gambling joints. One of the low points was the St. Valentine's Day Massacre of February 14, 1929, when seven gangsters were machine-gunned in a garage on Chicago's North Side. Another occurred on October 24, 1929, so-called "Black Thursday," when the bottom fell out of the stock market and the average person's savings were wiped out. The stock market crash led the country into the Great Depression that lasted through the 1930s. By the early 1930s unemployment figures in various parts of the country had reached between 25 percent and 33 percent. By 1933 the stock market had lost almost 90 percent of its value.

Real crime was prominent in the headlines in the 1930s and the average person had grown cynical about the effectiveness of law and order. Publishers cashed in on this concern with magazines such as *G-Men*, sub-titled "The Federals in Action," which was devoted to supporting the efforts of the Federal Bureau of Investigation. The magazine was endorsed by J. Edgar Hoover, the Director of the FBI, but much of the action was exaggerated and unrealistic. Other pulps featuring tough crime stories were *True Gang Life*, *Underworld*, and *Private Detective Stories*, which was tantalizingly subtitled "Intimate Revelations of Private Investigators."

Several pulp magazines, such as *The Underworld*, *The Dragnet*, *Racketeer Stories*, *True Gang Life*, *Gang World*, *Gun Molls*, and *Gangster Stories* featured crime stories from the criminal perspective. They glorified the success of American big city gangsters and the world of the late 1920s with its bootleggers, speakeasies, gamblers, gangster molls, and hoods dressed in tuxedos with Tommy guns speeding around in black touring cars. These gangster stories chronicled the crime boss's rise and fall, with the gangster driven by a desire to dominate the entire political and social system. Typically the gangster protagonist rose from poverty to great wealth and power, extended himself beyond his capabilities, and then met his destruction at the hands of the law. The Robin Hood type of stories of a poor-boy-turned-bank-robber had a lot of appeal and mirrored the events of the day, and reflected the social imbalance of America during the Great Depression. Even though these stories contained tough crime writing, the morally questionable perspective of the rise and fall of ambitious gangsters met with little success with the reading public. It did, however, meet with considerable opposition from local civic groups. Gangsters as popular protagonists quickly vanished from the newsstands.

Crime fiction continued, however, as a vehicle to reflect protest against a seemingly unjust economic and social system. It featured the hard-boiled detective, who was a tough private eye acting as the instrument of vengeance against those who used corrupt and perverse means to success and riches. The new hard-boiled American literary detectives, such as Race Williams, Sam Spade, and Philip Marlowe, took on some of the characteristics of those who would have previously been considered criminals, such as violence, alienation from society, and rejection of conventional values. They did, however, stick to a personal code of ethics. This combined the detective with the melodramatic figure of the romantic brigand of earlier literature, again very much echoing Robin Hood, Deadwood Dick, and others like him.

These new hard-boiled detectives were not exactly deductive geniuses like Sherlock Holmes, and most of them even admitted that they were not very bright. The crime literature of the 1920s and 1930s followed real life and made the protagonists into lower-class figures characterized by crudeness, aggressive violence, and alienation from the morals of conventional society. Most of them had some of the deductive skills of a conventional detective, but primarily they resolved their cases with violence. Though often

Another intriguing cover to pique a casual browser's interest and induce him to buy the magazine. Why is a man in a car using a Tommy gun to shoot down a man wearing a deep sea diver's helmet and diving suit in what appears to be the middle of a big city? Artists racked their imaginations to come up with eye-catching covers with hints of mystery and intrigue, all portrayed in blatant colors. This painting was done by Rudolph Belarski in 1938.

outwardly cynical about women, the hard-boiled detective was constantly being seduced or was seducing the women he encountered, unlike the classical detective who did not become romantically involved at all. Often the villain of the hard-boiled literature was the protagonist's friend or lover, and she eventually betrayed him.

The fictional hard-boiled private eye first appeared in the pulp magazines of the 1920s and 1930s and was one of the primary ways that masculinity was fantasized in the years between World War I and World War II. He was characterized by a tough shell-like exterior, wisecracking speech, and often amoral actions. He became the contemporary icon of American masculinity and was later projected into the tough guy of *film noir*, in which, as author William Hare put it, "shadowy figures engage in dangerous actions in the darkness of late evening in American cities."[3]

Because the contemporary problems of crime in America were primarily urban, the hard-boiled detective typically worked for a detective agency in a large city, such as New York, Chicago, Los Angeles, or San Francisco. Many of the hard-boiled stories were centered in southern California, and Los Angeles and Hollywood became the new Wild West. This was not cowboys shooting it out with black-hatted villains, but hard-boiled detectives fighting gangsters, gamblers, and crooked cops. Stories were about rich movie people mingling with old money millionaires and corrupt politicians. And, indeed, the real Los Angeles in the 1930s was characterized by entrenched corrupt administrations, where politicians received campaign contributions and payoffs from mobsters. It was plagued with gambling, prostitution, organized crime, and corrupt public officials who were controlled by the moneyed elite. Crime and violence were everywhere. The public became frustrated with a justice system that gave criminals light sentences and a seeming inability of the courts to punish criminals.[4]

The emotional demand for civic action and revenge produced the popularity of the hard-boiled private eye. These men were partly detectives, but were mostly avengers who took the law into their own hands. The hard-boiled detective functioned as both an agent of the law and an outlaw who acted outside the structure of legal authority to carry out his own definition of justice, which was often a personal mission or one of revenge. The hard-boiled private eye novels became vigilante literature in a world of corruption, cruelty, and vicarious violence, in a corrupt and violent American city ruled by a hidden alliance of seemingly respectable businessmen, politicians, and criminals.

The hard-boiled detective of fiction, with his personal sense of order and justice, was viewed as an urban incarnation of the frontiersmen and cowboys who had shown rugged individualism in the dime novels. He was honorable and noble with a protective cover of cynicism and toughness, and believed that the law was too inefficient or corrupt to administer the appropriate justice.

Black Mask *Magazine*

The premier magazine for tough detective fiction was *Black Mask*, a pulp magazine that originally published mystery, detective, and cowboy fiction before becoming the leader in hard-boiled detective stories. It was a cheap periodical aimed predominantly at working class readers and contained literary entertainment characterized by hard-hitting, exciting, violent action. The clipped, hard-driving dialog and gritty narrative of these stories changed the entire genre of detective literature. As the circulation of *Black*

Mask grew, its success of created a flood of similar detective magazines, including *Detective Fiction Weekly, Detective Story, Action Detective, Greater Gangster Stories, Dime Detective, Nickel Detective, Black Aces, Black Book Detective, Triple Detective, Strange Detective, Gang Worlds, Thrilling Detective, Crime Busters*, and *New Detective*. The first issue of *Dime Detective* came out in 1931 at the most popular time for hard-boiled private eyes, when almost 10 percent of the working public was unemployed and the Depression was worsening. By the late 1930s over 50 detective magazines had appeared, though *Black Mask* was still the leader.

Black Mask had an unusual background. Writer H.L. Mencken and drama critic George Jean Nathan were editors of a magazine titled *The Smart Set*, a literary magazine intended for sophisticated readers that published discussion and criticism of American arts and culture. *The Smart Set* also published fiction by such literary notables as F. Scott Fitzgerald, Eugene O'Neill, Sinclair Lewis, and Aldous Huxley. The magazine was owned at the time by Eugene Crowe, a paper manufacturer and the publisher of *Field and Stream*.

By 1918 *The Smart Set* was in financial trouble, so Mencken and Nathan entered the lucrative field of lowbrow pulps with two magazines named *Parisienne* and *Saucy Stories*. Pulp magazines were making money at the time, and the two intended their new magazines to cater to lower class tastes and support the floundering *The Smart Set*. The two suggestive names were chosen to take advantage of the somewhat naughty image of France and the craze for French culture existing in the United States in the early days of World War I. Mencken and Nathan figured that these pulp magazines could be produced cheaply, so if the magazines succeeded they would make money, but if they failed then they were not much of a loss. It turned out that both magazines were successful.

Though *Parisienne* and *Saucy Stories* did well, Mencken and Nathan were still faced with financial problems, so they decided to create another pulp. As they thought about it, they noted the success of Street & Smith's *Detective Story*. This was the only on-going crime pulp and it had steadily increased its circulation since it first appeared in October of 1915.

In response they created *The Black Mask*. The magazine's logo was a thin black pirate's mask with a dirk and a flintlock pistol behind it. The first issue, subtitled "An Illustrated Magazine of Detective, Mystery, Adventure, Romance and Spiritualism," contained a dozen stories and appeared in April 1920. The spiritualism aspect was discarded after the first issue and western fiction was added. Early issues of *The Black Mask* used rejects from Mencken and Nathan's other magazines or from the slush pile of submissions they were continually receiving from writers. In November 1920, eight months after the first issue, Mencken and Nathan sold the magazine to Eltinge Warner and Eugene Crowe, the owner-publishers of *The Smart Set*.[5]

Before 1923, *Black Mask* published a variety of stories, consisting of classical whodunit detective tales, romance, suspense, horror, and supernatural and crime stories. The detective stories often used the slang of the criminal and the streets to add a feeling of authenticity and show that the magazine was keeping up with the gangster age. Thus nitroglycerin was called "soup," a safe to be cracked was a "can," and the resulting loot was referred to as "cheese." One slang name for a burglar or safecracker was a "yegg," supposedly from the name of a famous safecracker.

The magazine was edited at first by George W. Sutton, Jr. The magazine was successful and circulation climbed. By the summer of 1926, however, the circulation numbers had lost some ground. The publisher looked for a new editor and found Joseph Thompson

Shaw. Shaw had been an instructor in World War I with the rank of captain, so he was popularly known as "Cap" Shaw. Shaw was a writer, but was a much better editor and his editorial vision re-shaped the magazine.[6] Before Shaw became editor, *Black Mask* published some dark detective fiction, but under his guidance the magazine promoted hard-boiled detective fiction. In 1927 the title was changed from *The Black Mask* to simply *Black Mask*.

When Shaw took over in 1926 the circulation was 66,000. The magazine was popular in America, Canada, and Great Britain, and Shaw increased the circulation to 80,000 within the first year. The circulation peaked at 103,000 in 1930, and then started to drop again in the early 1930s as America suffered through the worst of the Great Depression. Even a price reduction in 1934 from 20¢ to 15¢ per issue did not help. By 1935 the circulation was back down to 63,000.[7]

Shaw encouraged tough, realistic writing, specializing in action stories, such as adventure, westerns, and gritty crime stories. In 1932 Shaw changed the magazine to an all-crime format. His preference was for stories that featured hard-boiled protagonists caught between criminals, the police, and the victim. The format he wanted was a fast-moving sequence of violent events in which the hero was shot at, slugged, choked, knocked out, and doped, yet he survived and was victorious at the end. In a sense these were the same old familiar plots about outlaws, frontiersmen, and vigilantes, but reset in a gritty urban environment of the 1920s and 1930s. Featured authors were the likes of Frank Gruber, Frederick Nebel, Erle Stanley Gardner, Horace McCoy, Lester Dent (Kenneth Robeson), Carroll John Daly, and Dashiell Hammett.

Black Mask and its dark and violent fiction grew out of the Prohibition era of the late 1920s and early 1930s. The fast-paced, action-packed stories captured the cynicism, bitterness, disillusionment, and anger of the public towards the evils that accompanied Prohibition and the economic hardships of the Great Depression. Plots reflected newspaper headlines that screamed out stories of organized crime, urban violence, bootlegging, gambling, and prostitution. And of gangsters who fired machine guns at each other from limousines, speakeasies that served bathtub gin, rum runners who sneaked booze through coastal waters, and the crooks who prowled the back alleys of New York.

Black Mask encouraged and marketed this new type of crime fiction. Shaw did not want the traditional British deductive mystery stories. No more Sherlock Holmes and Agatha Christie solving intellectual puzzles. The elegant sleuth gave way to the violent wisecracking urban vigilante with his booming .45 Colt automatic. Shaw wanted action to get the story going, and lots of it to follow. But he also wanted the plotting to produce identifiable human characters. The victims of murders had to be real humans made of flesh and blood.

One example of the type of author that appealed to editor Shaw were the stories of author Paul Cain. Cain wrote 17 stories for *Black Mask* between 1932 and 1936, featuring criminal protagonists who were closer to the corruption they were investigating than to the law. In his story "Black," the narrator is a hired gun who has been sent to take revenge on a town. He offers to work for rival factions, proposing to take money from each to kill off the other.[8] His novel *Fast One* (1933) was a savage gangster novel full of betrayals, violence and random deaths.

Shaw's changed attitude towards detective fiction was reflected in the covers of *Black Mask*. The cover for May 1920, when the magazine was in its infancy, shows that the detective was still influenced by Victorian thinking and the Raffles-type of hero of E.W.

Hornung. The man on the cover is pictured in evening dress and a top hat, with a carefully cultivated moustache and carrying a thin mask for his eyes. By 1927, the tone of the covers had changed and the December issue featured an ugly, violent-looking, tattooed, muscled thug with no shirt, carrying a knife and sporting a vicious expression on his face. At this point the magazine was sub-titled "The He-Man's Magazine."[9]

In October of 1936, after Shaw had been at the editorial helm for 10 years, the publisher replaced him over a salary dispute. Shaw's successor was Fanny Ellsworth, who had previously edited the same publisher's *Ranch Romances*. Her approach was to soften much of the hard-boiled detective fiction that had been so popular. After another severe circulation drop, she left in 1940. That same year publisher Eltinge Warner sold *Black Mask* to Henry Steeger's Popular Publications. Changes were already taking place in American culture, however, and the pulps had to compete with other dominant forms of reading entertainment, which were comic books and the emerging mass-market paperbacks.

The downward slide for *Black Mask* continued, and the magazine printed its last issue in July 1951. In its 30 years it had printed 2,500 stories by 640 authors in 340 issues.[10] *Black Mask* finally disappeared when it merged into *Ellery Queen's Mystery Magazine*.

Many of the pulp detective magazines also published non-fiction columns that featured true-crime stories and descriptions of police work. Most were written in the same hard-boiled style as the fiction stories. In the early 1920s *Black Mask* briefly published a fingerprinting column. *Dime Detective* had a column headed "Ready for the Rackets."

Carroll John Daly

Two of the prolific writers for *Black Mask* deserve particular mention as they were the inventors of the hard-boiled detective story. The first was Carroll John Daly. The second, who was writing at about same time and carried on where Daly left off, was Dashiell Hammett.

Carroll John Daly was arguably the creator of the first hard-boiled detective story. He changed the existing model of the detective from an eccentric puzzle-solver into a contemporary, wisecracking, violent protagonist. Daly's tough detective made it into print in *Black Mask* in December 1922 with "The False Burton Combs," three months before Hammett. This was arguably the first American hard-boiled crime story. The story was written from the perspective of an anonymous first person author who was a tough-talking and violent gentleman adventurer, rather than a private detective.

Four months later *Black Mask* published another Daly story, the first detective story to feature a wise-cracking, hard-boiled private investigator, in "Three-Gun Terry," which appeared on May 15, 1923. The protagonist was Terry Mack, a private investigator and the prototype for the other later hard-boiled detectives. Mack existed somewhere between criminals and the police, associating with downtrodden victims and violent criminals. By doing this, Daly moved the genre from the detective whodunit into a world of explicit violence. The story was the origin of almost every detective cliché that was used and re-used for the next 60 years.

Daly made his character lawless, hard talking, fast-shooting, and wise-cracking. An example of his hard-talking style is this quote from "Three Gun Terry." "[O]ne of them held a gat right on his knees, but he never made no move to use it.[11] Not that he got the chance, for I had rapped his knuckles with the barrel of my gun—not the butt but the

This is an artist's conception of tough-guy Race Williams, one of the earliest hard-boiled detectives and the most popular detective hero of the 1920s. Created by Carroll John Daly, Williams was a violent, insubordinate, tough-talking, semi-literate, two-fisted character who fearlessly tackled brutal gangsters and master criminals when he felt that the law was too slow and crooks needed to be fought with their own weapons. He was all for justice and fair play, but he often fought crime outside the law using a perception of right and wrong that came from his own ethical standards.

barrel—and his gun just slid down his feet, to the floor. Of course, it's a bit risky using the barrel for such things; once in every so often the gun goes off, 'specially a light shooter like mine; but then you can't really bother about such little accidents; you can see where it would be his hard luck, not mine." Describing a shoot-out, he says, "Of course the shot is heard, and another bimbo ducks out of a side room, just as I make the landing. He don't do no shooting—he don't even get a look—just a spurt of flame and I get him. He falls pretty, blocking the doorway which someone is trying to close, but having no luck." From another, "A tiny splash of red appeared for a moment between his eyes; he stood so, his great eyes bulging in surprise more than pain—the surprise of death—then without a groan or a cry he pitched his length on the floor."[12]

In the next issue of *Black Mask*, Daly introduced a new detective, Race Williams, who was to become the most popular detective hero of the 1920s. Williams first appeared in "Knights of the Open Palm" on June 1, 1923. Williams was characterized as violent, impatient, aggressive, insubordinate, tough talking and semi-literate, but he provided all-conquering, two-fisted action. Williams did not use clues or a chain of reasoning like the classical detective; in fact he had few talents as a thinking detective. But he tackled brutal gangsters and master criminals fearlessly. The gangsters of the Race Williams stories had their hat brims pulled down low, drove long black cars, and wore .45 automatics in shoulder holsters. Editor Shaw got the kind of action he wanted as Williams was frequently shot at, kidnapped, and tortured.

Daly's lively writing was all the more remarkable because he had no experience with crime or criminals. His background was as a former movie projectionist and movie theater manager. His world of crime was all in his imagination. Daly was an average height at five feet nine inches and had a shy personality, but his detective hero Race Williams was tall, rugged, and hard talking. Daly said he created a character who felt that the law was too cumbersome and who needed to fight crooks with their own weapons. His answer to a gunman was another gunman.[13] Echoing the actions of Deadwood Dick, Race Williams fought crime outside the law. He was all for justice and fair play, but his perception of right and wrong came from his own ethical standards.

Daly took the two-gun American hero from the West and transplanted him to New York. At times Race Williams cooperated with law and at other times he took the law into his own hands. He prowled the corrupt urban landscape with utter faith in his own superior sense of frontier justice. He showed contempt for the police, and saw himself as being outside the law. In these stories, set in a corrupt and violent society where crime was not punished in a timely manner, the boundary between legitimate action and illegitimate force was blurry.

Violence was an integral part of the Race Williams stories and Williams loved to shoot people. Picture this graphic scene from "Super-Devil," which appeared in *Black Mask* in August 1926. "When I fired his right eye disappeared, giving place to a gaping, vacant hole ... his huge body took a nose-dive down the stairs—his soul in hell." But Williams was also very matter-of-fact about what he did, as in this excerpt from "Alias Buttercup" in *Black Mask* for October 1925. "I don't waste my lead—one shot was all I needed. The gold-rimmed glasses snapped right across the bridge of his nose ... and he slipped to his knees, pitching forward." A typical Race Williams story might end with "I sent him crashing through the gates of Hell with my bullet in his brain."[14]

Daly wrote over fifty stories for *Black Mask* and eight novels between June 1923 and November 1934. Williams appeared in seven novel-length adventures and twenty-seven short stories. The first complete Race Williams story in book form was *The Snarl of the Beast*, published in 1927 by Edward J. Clode, Inc.

Author William Nolan has called Daly's writing repetitious and melodramatic, with stilted dialog and poor characterization; however, Race Williams stories remained extremely popular with readers throughout the 1930s.[15] The success of the Race Williams character speaks for itself.

After Daly had a dispute with editor Shaw at *Black Mask*, he started to submit his stories to *Dime Detective*, as well as to *Clues*, *Detective Story*, and *Thrilling Detective*. *Black Mask* had paid him 3¢ per word. *Dime Detective* paid him 4¢.

Daly's eventual downfall as the premier writer of crime was that he was not willing or able to adapt to changes in the detective genre. He stuck with the pulp formula that had succeeded for him and Daly was still writing the same type of fiction into the 1950s. It finally failed him as other authors passed him by, and his stories faded from favor as the pulps vanished. Nevertheless, he pioneered all the story elements of hard-boiled detective fiction.

Dashiell Hammett

Samuel Dashiell Hammett was another of the inventors and founding fathers of the hard-boiled detective crime story. Daly and Hammett couldn't produce stories fast enough for *Black Mask*. Readers loved their descriptions of crime that emphasized the grim aspects of the criminal underworld, surrounded by the urban squalor and corruption of the big city.

The stories and style of Dashiell Hammett helped editor Cap Shaw to shape the magazine into his distinctive style, and Shaw always claimed that Hammett was the yardstick for measuring new authors.[16] At the beginning of "Bodies Piled Up" in *Black Mask*, December 1, 1923, Hammett wrote, "I stepped past the maid and tried the door. It was unlocked. I opened it. Slowly, rigidly, a man pitched out into my arms—pitched out backwards—and there was a six-inch slit down the back of his coat, and the coat was wet and sticky." To keep the action moving, a second corpse suddenly falls out, followed by a third one.

Hammett had a varied career before becoming a writer. He was variously a freight clerk for the railroad, a timekeeper, a stevedore, a laborer, and a nail-machine operator. He also suffered from recurring tuberculosis, known then as "consumption." Before the advent of antibiotics to treat the disease, there was no cure. Treatment consisted of plenty of fresh air and rest, and good food to build up the patient's strength. Hammett met his future wife, nurse Josephine Dolan, while he was in hospital for treatment.

From 1915 to 1922 Hammett worked as an operative for Pinkerton's National Detective Agency in Baltimore. He was on-call 24 hours a day at a weekly wage of $21. He was good at shadowing, interviewing, and with guns. He was involved with counterfeiters, bank swindlers, blackmailers, missing gold shipments, forgers, gangsters, and holdup men. At times he was assigned as a guard, a hotel detective, and a strikebreaker. Among other crimes he investigated were the theft of a Ferris wheel, international gold smuggling, and the Fatty Arbuckle scandal in Hollywood.[17] These experiences provided his writing with a supply of plots and characters from real life.

Hammett loved detective work and was very good at surveillance. In one of his investigations he shared a hospital room for three months with a patient, trying to gain the man's confidence and worm out his secrets. In 1917 Hammett was assigned to Butte, Montana, during the conflict between the militant labor union the Industrial Workers of the World (the Wobblies) and the local copper mining companies.

Hammett eventually left Pinkerton's because of his tuberculosis. He became an advertising copywriter, and then tried his hand at writing fiction. Hammett's first published story was "The Parthian Shot," which was published in Mencken and Nathan's *The Smart Set* magazine in October 1922. Around mid–1923, Hammett started to almost exclusively write crime, adventure, and mystery stories for the pulps. In 1924 he omitted the Samuel and used Dashiell Hammett as his literary name.[18]

When Hammett wrote hard-boiled detective stories, he tried to put onto paper the grim world he knew best, using his Pinkerton experiences as colorful background. Many of his characters were based on people he had encountered during his years as a detective. As part of his stories, Hammett used the criminal dialog of the urban streets and set crimes and chases in dirty back streets and alleys of the city. He liked the feel of the streets and used nighttime San Francisco for settings, adding darkness and fog to create an atmospheric feel.

The classical detective story consisted of an eccentric detective finding clues and using them as inspiration to find the solution to a crime. Hammett knew that in real life detective work and solving crimes did not work that way. In his experience, most investigators came from working class backgrounds, the crimes they investigated were not glamorous but sordid, and the solution was eventually found by patient, slogging footwork. Hammett's firsthand knowledge of the world of detectives allowed him to create a convincing representation of detective work and make his characters authentic. This realism in detective stories, however, was not popular with some readers. Hard-boiled crime stories were seen by many enthusiasts of traditional English mysteries as being too violent, and as a consequence Hammett's books were not particularly popular in England or Europe.[19]

Hammett's recurring protagonist, The Continental Op, was first introduced in *Black Mask* on October 1, 1923.[20] The man was an operative for the Continental Detective Agency in San Francisco. His name was never revealed; he was simply called The Op. The character appeared in 34 stories in *Black Mask* over 7 years.[21]

The Continental Op never tells much about himself. Hammett described him as short, heavyset, balding, middle-aged, hard-boiled, and pig-headed. But The Op was also tough, organized, professional, and dedicated to the job. He saw a case through to its conclusion, regardless of the obstacles. He didn't use deductive reasoning and logic, like the classical detective, but used his experience with criminals. The structure of the stories was usually that The Op inspects the crime scene, interviews suspects, cooperates with the police, and finds not only a single solution, but several levels of explanation for the crime, like peeling back the layers of an onion. He could be ruthless, often resorting to violence and killing if it was required to get the job done. The Op was self-reliant and insisted on a personal sense of order and justice.

The Continental Detective Agency was a thinly veiled version of Pinkerton's National Detective Agency, where Hammett had previously worked. Hammett named his fictional agency after the Continental Building, where Pinkerton's Baltimore branch had their offices.[22] The character of the Continental Op was supposedly based on the assistant manager of the Baltimore office where Hammett worked.[23]

Hammett's first book-length work was based on his earlier experiences as a Pinkerton operative in Butte, Montana. The story was serialized in *Black Mask* in 1927. The first part was titled "The Cleansing of Poisonville," followed by installments over the next few months, concluding with "The 19th Murder." The story did indeed contain an overwhelming number of murders. The plot involves corruption existing in American life in a lawless town named Personville. The town is so lawless that it is called Poisonville by the residents. As the plot proceeds, the book erupts into a frenzy of violence and vengeance. The story was later published in hardcover by Alfred A. Knopf in 1929 as *Red Harvest*. The book was dedicated to Hammett's editor, Joseph Thompson Shaw. In 1930 *Red Harvest* was made into the motion picture *Roadhouse Nights*.

This was a new style of crime literature, consisting of detective fiction that was bitter, tough, unsentimental, realistic, and reflected the violence of the time. The Op was a man of action who used using hard-hitting dialog, made decisions according to his own rigid personal code, and fought by his own rules. In "Fly Paper" (1929) The Op shoots a villain in the kneecaps when he won't surrender. The following quotes from *Red Harvest* will serve to illustrate the characteristics of the hard-boiled Continental Op.

The Continental Op is prone to wisecracking. "'Who shot him?' I asked. The gray man scratched the back of his neck and said: 'Somebody with a gun.'"[24]

The Op is a good shot and the plots involve shooting.

> "I steadied my gun-arm on the floor. Nick's body showed over the front sight. I squeezed the gun. Nick stopped shooting. He crossed his guns on his chest and went down in a pile on the sidewalk."[25]
> "A little red puddle formed under the edge of his chair. I was afraid to touch him. Only the pressure of his arms, and his bent-forward position, were keeping him from falling apart."[26]

Red Harvest included 17 murders by the end of Chapter 21, with several more added before the end of the story.

The Op works in seamy surroundings. "I walked around a few blocks until I came to an unlighted electric sign that said *Hotel Crawford*, climbed a flight of steps to the second-floor office, registered, left a call for ten o'clock, was shown into a shabby room, moved some of the Scotch from my flask to my stomach, and took old Elihu's ten-thousand-dollar check and my gun to bed with me."[27]

He uses tough guy talk and gangster slang to make him appear to be more real. "His real moniker is Kennedy. He was in on the Keystone Trust knock-over in Philly two years ago, when Scissors Haggerty's mob croaked two messengers. Al didn't do the killing but he was in on the caper. He used to scrap around Philly. The rest of them got copped, but he made the sneak. That's why he's sticking out here in the bushes. That's why he won't ever let them put his mug in the papers or on any cards."[28]

The Continental Op is tough. When describing some love letters written by the old man who runs Personville he says, "They're hot. I haven't laughed so much over anything since the hogs ate my kid brother."[29]

At the end of *Red Harvest*, the Op tries to fix up his reports so that they will not read as if he has violated so many of his agency's rules. " I spent most of my week in Ogden trying to fix up my reports so that they would not read as if I had broken as many Agency rules, state laws and human bones as I had."[30] "I might just as well have saved the labor and sweat I had put into trying to make my reports harmless. They didn't fool the Old Man. He gave me merry hell."[31]

Hammett later wrote *The Dain Curse* (1929), *The Maltese Falcon* (1930), and *The Glass Key* (1931) for *Black Mask*. Hammett is best remembered for *The Maltese Falcon*, which first appeared as a five-part serial in *Black Mask* from September 1929 to January

1930. It was full of car chases, shoot-outs, and sexy dames. The story introduced hard-boiled private detective Sam Spade. Spade was an instantly recognizable character. Hammett's Spade was not the short, fat Continental Op. He was tall and lean. Spade was an extension of the Pinkerton detective, ready and able to take care of himself in any situation. He carried a .38 and knew how to use it. Again, the same as Deadwood Dick, Spade worked outside the community for the overall good of society.

The Maltese Falcon was made into a motion picture in 1931 with Ricardo Cortez as Spade, remade in 1936 as *Satan Met a Lady*, and of course, the best-known version in 1941 with Humphrey Bogart as the iconic tough private-eye. In book form, Knopf sold over 10,000 copies of *The Maltese Falcon*.

Hammett, and later Raymond Chandler and other tough-writing authors, used a curious literary device in their stories by including male homosexuals to enhance their hero's masculinity.[32] Using homosexual characters exploited the homophobia of the 1930s and was used as a contrast to the male protagonist to make the hero seem even tougher, more masculine, and enhance his macho image. Hammett's *The Maltese Falcon* contains three homosexual stereotypes. Caspar Gutman is the older drawing-room type of homosexual, ridiculed as a "queen." Joel Cairo is a "perfumed dandy." Gunman Wilmer is a "kept boy." Spade refers to Wilmer as a "gunsel," which was contemporary slang in the homosexual world that referred to a kept male. In an unusually frank touch for the movies of the time, in *The Maltese Falcon* (1941), Sam Spade (Humphrey Bogart) openly calls ruthless gunman Wilmer (Elisha Cook, Jr.) a gunsel. The name "gunsel" (also gonsil, gonzel, guncel, and guntzel) refers to an armed criminal or hoodum. But it also means a sexually vulnerable boy or young man. By the 1930s, it was a slang term for a male homosexual.[33] This made Spade seem even more masculine than simply using his other tough talk and ways. Another literary trick was to make the hero successful with any and all women as a type of super stud to achieve the same amplification of his maleness.

In all Hammett wrote fifty-two stories for *Black Mask* between 1922 and 1930, and derived five novels from them. Hammett worked as a screenwriter and wrote radio plays in Hollywood before he died in 1961.

Hammett's last novel was *The Thin Man*, written in 1934. *The Thin Man*, with Nick Charles, a former detective living on the wealth of his wife Nora, was not his best creation, but it became one of his best known because of the motion pictures and radio programs adapted from it. Nick in the books was not the debonair version played by actor William Powell in the movies, but was a worn-out cynic separated from reality by alcohol. Though witty, the original *The Thin Man* novel was much rougher and darker than the series of six popular movies with Powell and co-star Myrna Loy. The movies were light urbane comedy, part of the "screwball comedies" popular at the time, with the two playing a married, wisecracking, squabbling, romantic pair.

10

And Even Harder Boiled

The hard-boiled detective that emerged in the 1920s and was still popular in the 1930s, always armed with a fast-shooting automatic or revolver, wise-cracking and talking tough, is one of most familiar icons of pulp literature. Violence and the threat of violence, and the ready use of a gun or fists, were the defining features of the hard-boiled detective genre. Courage by the hero when he was on the receiving end of violence while hunting down a criminal only added to his heroic status.

Daly and Hammett created characters that practically became stereotypes. When we see a tall, dark man walking in the fog-bound shadows down a damp, dreary street, wearing a fedora hat and a trench coat, with the bulge of a gun in his pocket, we know immediately who he is. In the black-and-white world of the *film noir* movies of the 1940s, he was accompanied by the sound of his shoes on a wet pavement, cars honking in the distance between skyscrapers, and the lonely wail of a trumpet playing a blues melody.

Tough wise-cracking detectives, curvy blonde secretaries, shabby offices, a bottle of booze in the desk, gangster-run speakeasies, mobsters who own night-clubs, their henchmen, and the detective's beautiful clients make up this world. Only westerns rivaled the success of the private eye in the popular culture of the 1920s and 1930s. Succeeding generations of writers continued the hard-boiled literary style, eventually making detective stories tougher and tougher, culminating in the late 1940s in the sadistic violence of Mike Hammer.

Erle Stanley Gardner

Another of the successful authors who wrote for *Black Mask* was Erle Stanley Gardner. Gardner was a lawyer with a practice in Oxnard, California, when he thought he would try his hand at writing pulp stories. In 1923, under the pen name of Charles M. Green, he submitted a story to *Back Mask* titled "The Shrieking Skeleton." It was rejected, but Gardner persevered. After he revised it, the new version was accepted and published.

Once Gardner developed his own style, he did well and published many stories in different magazines under various pseudonyms. He worked at an exhausting pace. He spent his days as a lawyer, used the law library for his work in the evening, then went home and wrote pulp stories for most of the night. He was able to get by on only three hours of sleep and claimed that he wrote 100,000 words a month for 10 years.

Lawyer Perry Mason appeared first in Gardner's novel *The Case of the Velvet Claws* in March 1933. It sold 28 million copies in its first 15 years. Over the next 37 years Gardner wrote eighty Perry Mason novels. The early novels contained smash-bang action and the antics of the typical *Black Mask* private eyes, rather than Mason being the more sedate court lawyer he later became.

Gardner's stories could be as hard-boiled as the best of them. The following is from "Hell's Kettle," which appeared in *Black Mask* in June 1930. "The girl who looked at me over the blued steel of a heavy-caliber revolver was rather young. Under other circumstances she might have been pretty. Now her face was distorted by various emotions." She says, "Never mind what I want. Keep your mitts in the air or you'll get perforated like a bank check." Later on in the story, when the action was really hot and heavy, Gardner wrote, "I whirled the machine gun, started it into action. Coughing spurts of flame belched from the end of the weapon. I could feel the purr of the explosions. The door leapt into a mass of splinters, dissolving into kindling wood. Lena picked up a hand grenade, slipped the catch, rolled it through the door."

Raymond Chandler and Philip Marlowe

Raymond Chandler and Erle Stanley Gardner were two of *Black Mask*'s most popular authors. For many readers of detective novels, the works of Raymond Chandler represent the ultimate in the hard-boiled detective genre.

In the early 1930s Raymond Thornton Chandler was the vice-president of three small oil companies in California controlled by the Dabney Syndicate.[1] At the height of the Great Depression the oil boom faded, the depression bankrupted businesses, and Chandler was faced with starting a new career. Like many others, he had read detective pulps and considered the writing to be poor, and figured he could write a story just as good as those being published. So, in 1933, at age 45, he started to write. His central theme was a knight errant on an honorable mission.

Los Angeles in the late 1930s was controlled by a powerful crime syndicate that included local police officials, lawyers, and politicians. The city had 600 brothels, 300 gambling houses, and 1,800 bookie establishments, all operating freely.[2] Chandler focused on this corruption in his novels. His intimate knowledge of Los Angeles allowed him to create a vivid backdrop for his stories that included guns, gangsters, and low-life crime. He added crackling dialog, bizarre plot twists, and a cast of strange characters.

Chandler's first short novel was "Blackmailers Don't Shoot," serialized in *Black Mask*. The story is about a private investigator named Philip Marlowe, who works out of a shabby office in Hollywood. His style is sardonic, self-effacing, and witty. Marlowe is hired by a wealthy, dying man with two daughters. As the story unfolds, Marlowe finds intertwined threads of drug addiction, nymphomania, pornography, mob activities, and sadistic hired killers. At the end, Marlowe reflects, "What did it matter where you lay once you were dead? In a dirty sump or in a marble tower on top of a high hill? You were dead, you were sleeping the big sleep, you were not bothered by things like that…. You just slept the big sleep, not caring about the nastiness of how you died or where you fell."[3] The story was successful and was published as a novel, *The Big Sleep*, in 1939 by Alfred A. Knopf. *The Big Sleep* was quickly followed by *Farewell, My Lovely* in 1940, *High Window* in 1942, and *The Lady in the Lake* in 1943.

Raymond Chandler's Marlowe was tough and brutal. In *Farewell, My Lovely* he tells the reader, "I used my knee on his face. It hurt my knee. He didn't tell me whether it hurt his face. While he was still groaning I knocked him cold with the sap."[4]

Unlike other pulp writers who churned out their plots in a hurry, Chandler was a slow writer, but he took great care when crafting his prose. He wrote only 23 short stories, 11 of them for *Black Mask*. When editor Joseph Shaw left *Black Mask*, Chandler wrote for *Dime Detective*. He wrote only six Philip Marlowe novels. The reviews of his books were good, but sales were slow. To help support himself, in the mid–1940s he wrote screenplays in Hollywood. Six of his novels were made into movies, including *The Big Sleep* (1946) with Humphrey Bogart as Philip Marlowe; *Farewell, My Lovely*, filmed as *Murder, My Sweet* (1944) with Dick Powell as Marlowe; and *Lady in the Lake* (1946), with Robert Montgomery playing the detective.

Ross Macdonald and Lew Archer

The successor to Raymond Chandler as a writer of hard-boiled detective fiction was Ross Macdonald. Ross Macdonald was the pen name of Kenneth Millar. Millar started to use the pen name of John MacDonald, but found that he was being confused with the mystery writer John D. MacDonald, so he changed his pen name to Ross Macdonald. Millar was well educated and had a doctorate in English literature from the University of Michigan.

With a style similar to Raymond Chandler, Macdonald's literary territory was the seedy hotels, bars, and side streets of 1940s Los Angeles. Also like Chandler, his plots involved plenty of chases, fistfights, and gunplay.

Macdonald created Lew Archer, a southern California private investigator, as a protagonist in 1949 in *The Moving Target*. Lew Archer appeared in subsequent stories in a series of novels that ran from 1949 to 1973. Macdonald started writing in the original pulp tradition, but as his style progressed his writing became serious fiction. He later introduced psychology into his writing, which added depth to his characters.

Mickey Spillane and Mike Hammer

The combination of romanticism, violence, sexual themes, and the punishment of successful evildoers outside the law has long been part of folklore and the popular literature of nineteenth and twentieth century England and America. Examples discussed previously ranged from Dick Turpin, Robin Hood, the Scarlet Pimpernel, and Deadwood Dick to the Continental Op and Race Williams. This theme continued to be amplified and exaggerated in later private eye novels.

Race Williams introduced the violent, hard-boiled detective. As time progressed, in an effort to entice more readers, publishers and authors made their private eyes more and more hard-boiled. The more extreme the writer, the better the sales. Painful death for the victim was matched with revenge and painful death delivered by the protagonist. Sadism was topped by sadism. The newer private eyes stepped outside the law to deliver personal vengeance and became just as sadistic as the criminals they were opposing.

The most sadistic of them all was arguably Mike Hammer, Mickey Spillane's violent private detective, who first appeared in *I, the Jury* in 1947. Spillane opened the doors for sex and sadism. Spillane admitted that Race Williams was part of the model for Mike Hammer. Twenty novels later Spillane was the largest-selling author in the English language.[5]

10. And Even Harder Boiled

Mickey Spillane was the pen name of Frank Morrison, an ex-army fighter pilot and flight instructor. He started out writing stories for comic books, then turned to writing detective novels. He included sex in a more open manner than the pulp magazines would have dared. A typical Mike Hammer plot mixes sexual provocation with extreme violence, the latter consisting of shootings and beatings. This brutality is made to seem necessary as Hammer moves in the shadowy urban world of gangsters, Communist agents, and dope pushers. In plots reminiscent of the 1930s fantasy pulp novels, with the masked hero battling the Purple Menace or the Green Menace who were attempting world domination, the theme of the late 1940s was Mike Hammer battling the Red Menace of Communism.[6]

Spillane started writing after World War II and his novels reflected the violence that many saw during the war. Hammer was a one-man judge and jury, a unleashed killing machine, savage and melodramatic, adapted to the post–World War II era. Hammer was the rough justice of the streets. He had no special skills in solving crimes, but successfully resolved difficult situations through a combination of courage and bull-headed determination. Hammer solves the crime, then takes the law into his own hands and punishes the criminals with extreme sadistic violence, acting as police, judge, jury, and executioner of those he pursues. The eroticized women in the Hammer novels are either women who need Hammer's male protection, or female cheats and villainesses who lead Hammer into a false sense of security with their beauty and sex appeal before turning on him.

Much of Hammer's motivation often involves personal revenge. In a tradition that extends back to Deadwood Dick and others, the popularity of Mickey Spillane's writing can be attributed to the public's impatience with the due process of the law, so a theme of justice and retribution outside the law runs through his books.

Lew Archer was the creation of Ross Macdonald, the successor to Raymond Chandler as a writer of hard-boiled fiction. Archer was a private investigator in southern California who roamed the seedy hotels, bars, and side streets of 1940s Los Angeles, involved in chases, fist-fights, and gunplay. Archer appeared in a series of novels that ran from 1949 until 1973. Macdonald's early stories were in the pulp tradition, but his later writing became serious fiction with a touch of psychology that added depth to the characters. This particular cover appeared when James Bond was in fashion and reflects the Bond image with dinner jacket, cummerbund, shoulder holster, and a blonde hanging over Archer's shoulder.

For example, *I, The Jury* starts with the murder of Hammer's best friend. This makes the subsequent violence justifiable, or at least somewhat more acceptable, to the reader as Mike avenges his murdered friend. Hammer's subsequent rampage of violence is prompted by his feelings that the law will fail to bring the killer to justice. Like the hard-boiled detectives of the 1930s, Hammer gloomily expresses his feelings about the conventional justice system when he says, "I'm not letting the killer go through the tedious process of the law. You know what happens, damn it. They get the best lawyer there is and screw up the whole thing and wind up a hero!"[7]

The villain of *I, The Jury* is finally unmasked as Hammer's romantic interest, the beautiful, rich, and successful psychiatrist Charlotte Manning. She appears to be innocent throughout most of the story, but is revealed—literally—in the famous final showdown between the two. Facing him, she seductively starts to take off her clothing in a striptease. Hammer is not fooled and knows that she has a gun with a silencer on a table nearby, and is merely trying to distract him until she can use it. But he waits and enjoys the show until she has stripped to her bare nothings. Then he shoots her with his .45 and watches her die.

> "'How c-could you?' she gasped.
> I had only a moment before talking to a corpse, but I got it in.
> 'It was easy,' I said."[8]

In spite of this violence and sadism, or perhaps because of it, Spillane's Mike Hammer books were immensely popular in the 1950s. Mickey Spillane's writing has unkindly been called "atrocious by traditional artistic or literary standards," with a style and dialog that are awkward, stilted, and wooden.[9] Another critic called his writing the "embodiment of cultural degeneration."[10] However, after Signet first published *I, The Jury*, subsequent reprints brought the sales up to several million copies, and Spillane may indeed have been America's most popular novelist, as the publicity blurb on the back of one of his books stated. Spillane had seven best sellers and sold over forty million Hammer books. His books averaged four to five million copies for each title, and sold thirteen million copies in one three year period. By contrast, Chandler's *Farewell, My Lovely* and Hammett's *The Maltese Falcon* sold just over a million copies.

The stories of Hammett and Chandler included violence, but their writing treated it as incidental to the plot. In Hammett's stories, the Continental Op even grew to hate violence. Spillane's Mike Hammer, however, uses violence as a tool of his trade. He is a sadistic avenger who brings extreme violence to criminals as payback for the misery they have inflicted on his friends. His primary technique during an investigation is to beat someone up until they talk or confess. An example of these sadistic impulses appears in *My Gun is Quick* (1950) as Hammer says, "Shorty, maybe just for the hell of it I'll take you apart. You may be a rough apple, but I can make your face look like it's been run through a grinder, and the more I think of the idea the more I like it."

This example is from *Kiss Me, Deadly* (1952): "My knuckles cracked across his jaw so hard he went back over the arm of the chair and spilled in a heap on the floor. He lay

---

Opposite: Author Mickey Spillane exploded onto the scene of hard-boiled detective fiction with the hardest-boiled private eye of them all, Mike Hammer. Hammer was the rough justice of the streets, a one-man judge, jury, and killing machine who was savage and melodramatic. Spillane adapted the hard-boiled detective to the post–World War II era, reflecting the violence that many had seen during the war. *I, the Jury*, first published in 1947, opened the doors for sex and sadism in detective stories.

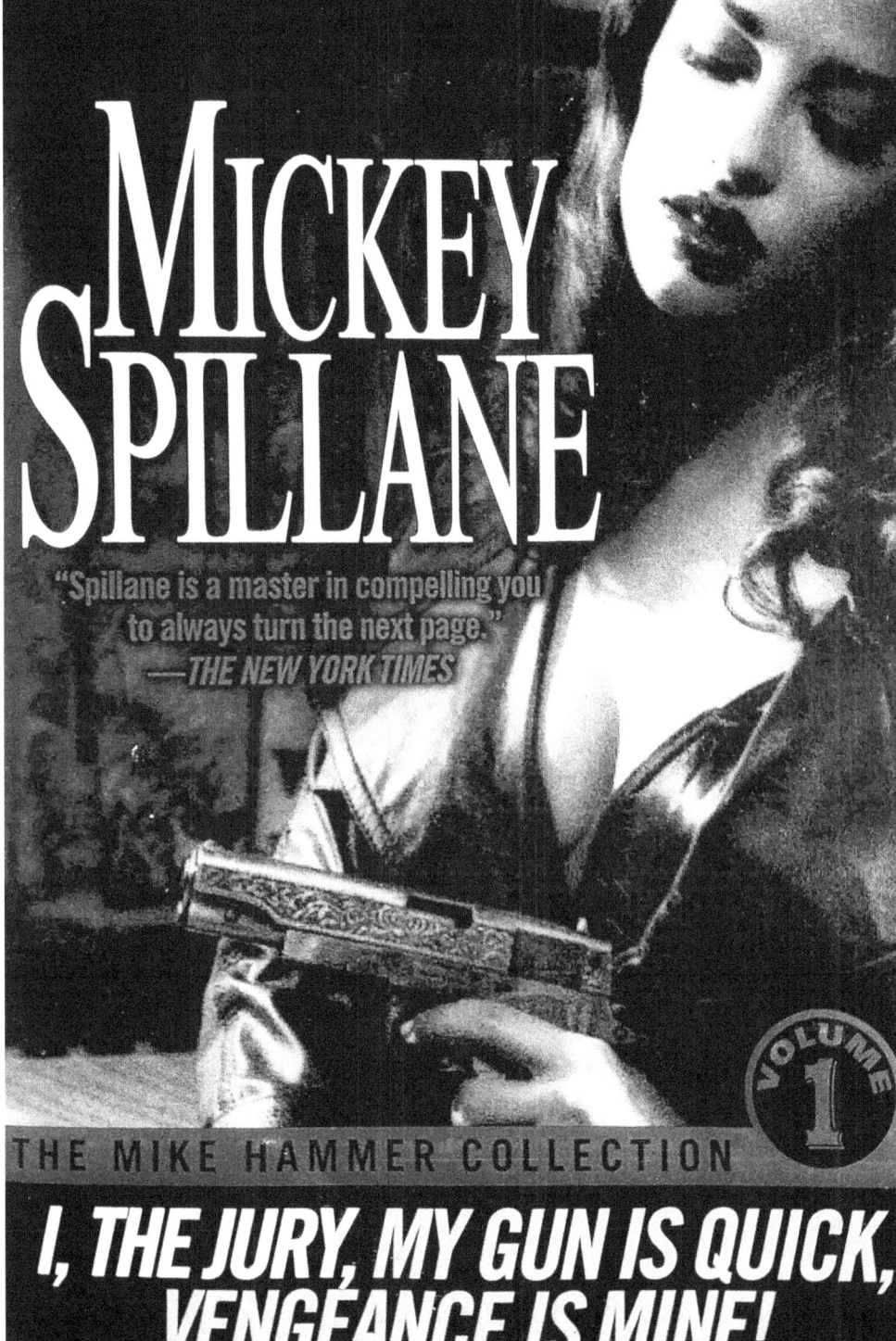

there with his eyes wide open and the spit dribbling out of his open mouth started to turn pink."[11]

Sadism runs rampant in *Body Lovers* (1967), when Hammer's task is to locate the missing sister of a convict. As the novel proceeds, his investigations lead to a group of rich and powerful sadists, mostly made up of United Nations diplomats from the Middle East. He becomes involved with a beautiful woman who turns out to be the procurer for the group. Hammer's dilemma is that these people are performing ritual torture murders for pleasure, but because of their status, they have diplomatic immunity. By the end of the book, Hammer is forced by the circumstances to become his usual judge and executioner.

Mike Hammer, along with Philip Marlowe and Sam Spade, are constantly threatened by a physical violence that was not part of the world of the classical detective. Someone is always trying to shoot them to stop their meddling and get them out of the way. They are constantly being captured, drugged, blackjacked, and beaten up in graphic detail. This example is from *Kiss Me, Deadly*. "But the same incredible pain that had brought the sleep brought the wakening. It was a pain that turned my whole body into a mass of broken nerve ends that shrieked their messages to my brain. I lay there with my mouth open sucking in air, wishing I could die, but knowing at the same time I couldn't yet."[12]

The Mike Hammer novels were popular for their voyeuristic scenes and fantasies of male domination of women. Though much of the fantasy involves striptease and admiration of women's bodies, there is little actual sex. Women are constantly revealing their bodies to Hammer, constantly tempting him, but they typically do not do more than that. A typical Hammer fantasy scene appears in *The Big Kill* (1951). "The soft pink tones of her body softened the metallic glitter of the nylon gown that outlined her in bronze, flowing smoothly up the roundness of her thighs."[13] Often the temptress turns out to be the murderess and so has to be destroyed. The ultimate example, of course, is the ending of *I, The Jury*.

More and More Detective Magazines

Crime literature from the 1920s to the 1950s focused on cynical private eyes in pulp magazines with names such as *Ace-High Detective, Action Detective, Amazing Detective Tales, Best Detective, Black Hood Detective, Clues, Double Detective, Detective Fiction Weekly, Dime Detective, Black Mask, Crack Detective Stories, Gangster Stories, Gun Molls, Hardboiled, Masked Detective, Prison Life Stories, Real Police Story, Red Mask Detective, Strange Detective Stories, Crime Busters, Undercover Detective, Underworld Magazine,* and *Underworld Romances*. And almost 200 other pulp magazines. Along with the racier *Spicy Detective* and *Spicy Mystery Stories*. And for a different approach, *Strange Detective Stories, New Detective Magazine*, and *Thrilling Detective* featured stories that were downright macabre.

The covers of these pulp magazines became shamelessly exploitative. There was no trace of subtlety to cloud their violent and erotic meanings. Women were shown in sheer negligees, frozen in tableaux combining fascination and terror. The covers were created as illustrations that were larger than life, with proportions and dimensions exaggerated and distorted because ordinary photographs would have looked too bland. Artists took ordinary streets, dives, tenements, alleys, cheap hotels, motel rooms, and barrooms with unshaven men leaning over their drinks, and shrouded them in mystery. The cover of *Kiss My Fist* (1939) (British title *Dead Stay Dumb*) by British writer James Hadley Chase (real name Rene Brabazon Raymond) shows a man belting a woman (with a lot of cleavage showing) on the chin. The cover loudly proclaims it as "The saga of a racket 'big shot' who lived, loved and died the hard way!"¹⁴

Other writers sprang up to continue the hard-boiled crime-fighter tradition. Peter Cheney (Reginald Southouse Cheney) in England wrote a shameless imitation of the violent hard-boiled American crime literature of Dashiell Hammett, using slangy, deadpan, wisecracking dialog. Hugh "Bulldog" Drummond, possibly one of the first superheroes to appear early in the twentieth century, was a patriotic, loyal gentleman adventurer created by Sapper, whose real name was H.C. (Herman Cyril) McNeile. A sapper was a slang name for an army engineer, and McNeile chose his pen name after he served in the Royal Engineers.¹⁵ One adventurer-hero patterned after Bulldog Drummond was Tiger Standish created by Sidney Horler.

Other crime fighters were suave, roguish, and debonair. Two of these were The Saint and The Toff. The Saint was the creation of Leslie Charteris, who was born Leslie Yin (he was half-Chinese) in Singapore in 1909. The Saint first appeared in *Meet the Tiger* (1928), later republished to conform to the format of the other titles as

The halo floating above this stick figure reveals it to be the sign of The Saint, a debonair crime fighter and sometime administrator of justice created by Leslie Charteris. This figure was often left for crooks to let them know that The Saint was hot on their trail. The figure also appeared at the end of The Saint books with the legend "Watch for the sign of The Saint. He will be back." This particular version is from the cover of a 1942 hardback version of *The Saint Bids Diamonds*.

The Saint Meets the Tiger. The Saint appeared in the 1930s in magazines such as *The Thriller*, *Popular Detective*, and *Pearson's* magazine, and a series of books chronicling his exploits. Like others, he had his own *Saint* magazine. After some of his adventures he left a calling card that sported a stick figure with a halo. The Saint's real name was Simon Templar, and his initials, ST, created his nickname. Popular Publications had Captain Satan, who had a calling card that looked like a devil with a horned head and a tiny pitchfork. He didn't last long.

The aptly-named Toff was another debonair crime-solving hero who was very similar to The Saint. The Toff was created by John Creasey, who wrote as Gordon Ashe, Ken Ranger, and other pen names. He even wrote as Margaret Cooke and produced 29 westerns as Tex Riley. Creasey had an enormous output, writing 600 full length works over a 40-year career, and averaging a novel every four weeks.[16] Among other books, he wrote a series about a mythical Department Z, a secret branch of the British intelligence service. Like other pulps writers, he produced a prodigious quantity of writing, but unfortunately often at the expense of quality.

Writers and publishers would try any idea, no matter how improbable or outlandish, to come up with a new character or theme that might launch a new series or attract new readership. In attempts to create unique characters, writers came up with many odd individual detectives. There were sinister ones, eccentric ones, fat ones, misers, midgets, acrobats, cracksmen, hypochondriacs, hemophiliacs (the Bleeder), blind men (Peter Quest), and others. There was Speed Dash, who could climb up the outside of any tall building.[17]

Many of the characters were indeed highly improbable. Writer J. Paul Suter invented a hero for *Dime Detective* named Horatio Humberton, who was a combination detective and funeral director. Another curious character, developed by writer Lawrence Treat, was an advertising agency executive who solved crimes. *Dime Detective* also featured Needle Mike, a tattoo artist who was also a detective. Even more confusing, he became a detective because he was bored with his real life as a millionaire playboy.

Clickell Rush, the Gadget Man (created by Lester Dent), was a private detective but also an inventor who used his gadgets to get himself out of trouble. One invention was a container of knockout gas that was attached to his legs and activated by knocking his knees together. A hypodermic needle concealed under his shirt could be used to tranquilize his victims. He also carried tear gas in a secret compartment in the heel of his shoe.[18]

Appearing on the newsstands alongside the fictional detectives were "true crime" magazines such as *Homicide Detective*, *True Detective*, and *World Detective*. Harking back to the early London Newgate broadsheets, these were intentionally sensational publications that described actual crimes in lurid detail in articles that were five to eight pages long. Particularly favored were murders, which were often accompanied by shockingly explicit photographs of the crime scene and murder victims. The stories typically followed a case up to the capture of the criminal. If it was a case of murder, the subsequent trial and execution might be described in detail.

Women Detectives

Almost all the detectives in the pulp magazines were men. Women detectives who starred in their own continuing series were apparently not popular. There were a few, but their stories were written by men. There were no women detectives in hard cover novels until 1939 when Erle Stanley Gardner wrote *The Bigger They Come*.[19]

It should not be assumed from this that women did not appear as major characters in crime fiction. Though the majority were portrayed as helpless females, some women appeared in stories that made them out to be as capable and competent as men. In the July 1935 Street and Smith's *Complete Magazine*, for example, the heroine supports herself by being a world champion pistol shot as she foils a thief and solves a crime. *Gangster Stories* and *Gangland Stories* often featured strong female heroines as women reporters, mob bosses, and detectives.

One of the few women detectives in a series was by writer Cleve Franklin Adams in stories about Violet McDade, who ran her own agency. She was an unlikely heroine, having previously been a fat lady in a circus. She weighed between 300 and 400 pounds, depending on whether or not she was dieting during the story.

Another unlikely heroine was Sarah Watson, who appeared in *Detective Fiction Weekly*. She was middle-aged, heavyset, and always wore practical shoes and dowdy black skirts. She was, however, tough enough to beat up people if she needed information from them.

One of the most successful of the female detectives was Carrie Cashin, the senior partner of Cash and Carry Detective Agency. She first appeared in Street & Smith's *Crime Busters* magazine in November 1937. Her adventures unfolded with breathtaking speed at a high pace. Though Cashin was a very popular character, she never had her own magazine.

At the other end of the spectrum of heroines was undercover policewoman Sally the Sleuth, who was blatantly presented as a sex object. Starting in 1934 in *Spicy Detective* her stories were presented in black-and-white panels in each issue, drawn in comic book style by Adolphe Barreaux. As this was a visual story and the magazine was *Spicy Detective*, Sally usually lost her dress at some point during almost every investigation. Villains were always ordering her to take off her clothes, and her typical working outfit was usually bra and panties. For example, on one page of the May 1938 issue of *Spicy Detective*, in four of the six cartoon panels the skirt of her dress is hoisted up to her waist, revealing her stockings, garters, and frilly panties. Nevertheless, this might not have been the worst of her problems. In the last panel a sinister black-robed figure is threatening to stuff her into a blazing furnace. When *Spicy Detective* was revised into *Speed Detective*, Sally continued on, but her clothing was more modest.

Violence and Mayhem Continue

As readers became desensitized and more jaded towards violence and sadism, the Mike Hammer type of hero evolved into an "enforcer," essentially a repeat of the revenge type of protagonist. An example of this is the successful "Executioner" series of paperback novels featuring tough protagonist Mack Bolan, written in the 1970s by Don Pendleton. In these books, Bolan is an out-and-out killer who goes after the leaders of organized crime that dominate society. A similar example is "The Destroyer" series featuring Remo Williams, by Warren Murphy and Richard Sapir. These series of novels combined extreme violence and illegal activities with combat skills that get the job done. The protagonist performs the assignment to be completed as a bureaucratic assassin. Like the Mike Hammer series, the plots typically revolve around vengeance. Other competing writers were Richard Prather, who wrote the Shell Scott series, and Brett Halliday (Davis Dresser) who wrote the Mike Shayne books, starting with *Dividend on Death* (1939).

The new style of pulp fiction that emerged was gritty and realistic, and often erotic. Fawcett came out with their Gold Medal line of paperback originals with authors such as Edward S. Aarons, who wrote pulp crime and espionage stories. His popular "Assignment" series sold forty novels in 20 years.[20] The stories were mostly formula plots of hard boiled action and brutal violence that tackled issues related to the post–World War II Cold War years, involving looming threats to United States security or world peace, a deadly villain, a beautiful female, and action, action, action.

If anything, some of these later books became even more violent. For example, from *Mafia Wipe-Out* by Frank Scarpetta, "Magellan ripped off Mario's jacket and used it to scoop up more broken shreds of glass lying around them. Then he shoved the jacket hard into Mario's face and held it there. He rubbed the jacket up and down."[21]

In 1960 prolific writer of western and suspense novels Donald Hamilton introduced his super-agent Matt Helm, who featured in a series of tough, gritty thrillers as an undercover agent of an unspecified department of the United States government that specialized in revenge and assassination. The trend of women losing their clothes and the voyeuristic sexual themes from earlier pulps and novels continued with situations such as "She looked kind of silly standing there in her furs, her long white gloves, her blue high-heeled pumps—plus brassiere, pantie-girdle and stockings." Echoing situations in comic strips such as Sally the Sleuth, Hamilton continues, "She looked like one of those leggy pinups you see in bars and garages, that are always getting their skirts snagged on barbed-wire fences in interesting ways."[22] And the sensationalistic sadistic gratuitous violence of Mike Hammer continued with threats such as "One minute a lovely girl is standing there, resisting interrogation bravely, just like you, and the next minute there's just something half human crawling along the floor, something crippled and bloody and whimpering with its nose smashed flat in its face and its mouth full of broken teeth."[23]

As this was the era of the James Bond type of super-spy hero, four of the Matt Helm books were released as motion pictures, *The Silencers* (1966), *Murderers' Row* (1966), *The Ambushers* (1968), and *The Wrecking Crew* (1969). The violence of the books was toned down for the movies, and they were tailored more towards the amiable screen personality of Dean Martin, who starred as Helm, and even included some singing by Martin. But the movies retained as window-dressing the series of beautiful women losing their clothes and fawning over Helm.

11

Pulp Visions of the Cowboy

No nation has taken a time and place from its past and constructed a myth to equal the creation of the American Wild West. Through a process of wishful thinking and romanticization, The West became a fictional idealized place of freedom, individualism, self-reliance, and democracy, where a man could experience comradeship and adventure with few restrictions. The most powerful parts of the myth that the public believed about the West was created by the written word. Western stories were probably the most popular of all pulp fiction stories, and the cowboy has been called America's version of the folk hero. As western writer Frank Dobie once said, "What happened doesn't matter. What people like to believe does."[1] Another astute observer was western movie star Tom Mix, who said in the late 1930s, "The Old West is not a certain place in a certain time, it's a state of mind. It's whatever you want it to be."[2]

The end of the Civil War in 1865, gold and silver strikes in the Mountain States of the West, and the completion of the transcontinental railroad in 1869 focused the country on the West as a land of opportunity. Settlers journeyed west by the thousands to search for gold and claim free land from the government. To match this westward expansion, stories were needed to fill American frontier adventure fiction, but the forests of the East of Leatherstocking had long-since been settled and the time of Boone and Crockett was past. Their stories had become out-of-date and stale, and the reading public was ready for something new.

Dime novels promoted the start of sensationalist western literature, and the image of the "real" Wild West came to be perceived as cowboys, ranchers, lawmen, stagecoach bandits, train robbers, cavalry battling Indians, and wagon trains headed westwards. This vision was created by popular western novels and pulp magazines.

At the same time, entertainers in Wild West shows were promoting the popularity of the cowboy as a western hero by featuring buckskin-clad scouts, Indian braves in war bonnets, and cowboy sharpshooters performing feats of marksmanship and horsemanship. Spectacles such as Buffalo Bill's *Wild West*, *Tiger Bill's Wild West*, and *Thompkins Real Wild West and Frontier Exhibition* toured the United States and Europe, reinforcing the myth of a glorious and romantic American frontier that had never really existed. As one of the prime creators of this image of the West, Buffalo Bill's show focused on only a handful of events and people that eventually became symbols for the West. The fierce Indians, the stagecoach under attack, and the circled wagon train came to represent the real West to millions of attendees in the audience. A standard act in these shows was the Indian attack on the settler's home with cowboys or the cavalry riding to the rescue. The public attending these shows believed that they were watching real history instead of gaudy romanticized entertainment.

The western story is characterized by having the characters wear big hats, ride horses, and shoot guns at each other. Pulp magazines and later paperback novels set the pattern for mass-market westerns that used romance, excitement, and nostalgia for the Old West to create rip-roaring adventure stories. The literary value of these pulp books and magazines was not always high, but the imagery of guns, cowboys, horses, and cattle drives, all set in the wide-open spaces of the Wild West, created a fascination among readers that sold western novels by the millions all over the world.

Before Wild West shows became popular, Americans, particularly those in the East, didn't know much or really care about cowboys until the rise of the dime novel firmly planted the western cowboy hero as a cultural icon. In time, with the help of Wild West shows, the cowboy image was transformed into a romanticized vision of rugged individualism, chivalry, courage, honor, and loyalty. The show cowboys were not the sweat-stained reality of real ranch hands, but wore clean white ten-gallon hats, fashionable furry chaps, and shiny new revolvers. To the readers of dime novels and audiences at Wild West shows, men wearing guns in their daily lives created an image of self-assurance and manliness. This image was promoted in the dime novels, though in reality few westerners wore guns in everyday life unless they were lawmen or outlaws.

In the 1860s and 1870s readers in America became obsessed with stories about frontier and western life. They thrilled to Indian battles, wild animals roaming the Plains, and the exploits of western outlaws and lawmen. Real and fictional heroes, such as Buffalo Bill, Deadwood Dick, Silver Sam, and California Claude, performed superior feats of horsemanship and had incredible shooting skills. Dime novels appeared with exciting titles such as *Redpath, the Avenger; or, The Fair Huntress of the South-West* and *The Ranger's Rifle; or, The Wolf of the War-Path*. Bandits like Jesse James became modern Robin Hoods.

Many of the dime novels borrowed from the plots and concepts of James Fenimore Cooper, and continued his stories and themes of capture, flight, and chase. Eventually the dime novels gradually became darker and contained kidnappers, seducers with false promises, lecherous villains, and would-be rapists. Women in this type of fiction were abducted, bound, gagged, and drugged, and subjected to threats of dishonor, rape, and death.

The new stories moved at a fast pace. This example comes from *Beadle's Pocket Library* for May 28, 1884, which included the adventures of *Roaring Ralph Rockwood, The Reckless Ranger* by Harry St. George. The first chapter was titled "The Prairie Pests." The story starts out with: "The sharp, whip-like crack of a rifle awoke a thousand echoes among the distant foothills, and broke the stilly silence of the night. Following the shot came the shrill neighing of a horse then once more stillness. A person with remarkably keen ears might have caught the low but hearty curse." Readers could not get enough of this type of story.

Western writers started to churn out pulp stories that featured a white male hero challenged by a variety of situations and human opponents. Though the hero was usually a cowboy, he evolved into a generic frontier rider, perhaps a lawman or gunman, rather than a working cowboy. The heroines were young, innocent, and beautiful. Heroes, such as 18-year-old Young Wild West who showed up in *Wild West Weekly* starting in 1902, was featured each week in a 30,000 word novel with titles like *Young Wild West, the Lasso King; or, The Crooked Gang of "Straight" Ranch*.

Western Novels

At the same time that dime novels were flourishing in the 1880s, serious western novels and romances from respectable publishing houses began to appear, so the western novel was already part of popular fiction in the late nineteenth century before *The Virginian* was published in 1902. These books were superior in literary and physical quality to the earlier dime novels and enjoyed fair sales.

One of the first true novels set in the West was *The Colonel's Daughter*, published in 1881 by Capt. Charles King, the creator of the cavalry novel. King was an officer of the Fifth Cavalry during the Indian Wars. He was stationed at military posts in the West, rode in campaigns against the Apache chiefs Cochise and Geronimo, and fought the Sioux before he retired and became an author of military fiction. King wrote sixty-nine novels between 1885 and 1909. Though his many novels were centered around the cavalry, they were nonetheless familiar Victorian sentimental romances characterized by honor, loyalty, and gallantry, though in a western setting. King's plots and characters were generally simplistic, typically involving a romance between a refined young lady and her aristocratic military boyfriend. During the course of the story, the two lovers are separated by obstacles such as status and jealousy, but sometimes by abduction and captivity that results in a daring rescue. Love and virtue, of course, triumph in the end as the two are reunited. Typical of King's books were *Foes in Ambush* (1893), about Indian fighters battling with strikers. A similar novel was *Army Wife* (1896), which used the same general theme as a regiment of Indian fighters battle savage strikers.

The plots of many western novels were run-of-the-mill by today's standards, but the reading public's enthusiasm for the West made them extremely popular. One such novel was *Girl of the Golden West*, which was originally written as a play in 1905 and was later turned into a novel by the author. It has a typical complex plot of the dime novels where no one is who they seem to be. The heroine, the hero, and the villain go through complex machinations where the hero is also a bandit who wants to reform, and the sheriff who is chasing him also wants to marry the heroine so falsely accuses the hero of a robbery and wounds him. The girl finally unmasks the sheriff as the real robber, and the hero and heroine end up together happily.

Very few of these novels, however, had a plot where the hero was a true cowboy or worked with cattle. Any cowboys who appeared in these novels did nothing that a real cowboy would do. The open range and herding cows was not part of the fictional western vision. The closest to a cowboy was an occasional hero like fictional Texas lawman Moccasin Mat, who had a horse that came when he whistled.[3]

Once dime novelists tackled the West with their usual boundless enthusiasm, they characterized the cowboy with a natural nobility the same way as they had the earlier backwoods frontier heroes. Cowboys were turned into romanticized knights-in-armor as the ideal of rugged individualism. Novelists emphasized costume, horse riding, and ranch settings rather than the real and often grubby specifics of cowboy life dealing with cattle. In this way, the real-life cattle drover evolved into the fictional cowboy heroes of Owen Wister and Zane Grey.

In the 1890s young men who were attracted to the cowboy way of life knew what they were supposed to wear. They had read about it in the dime novels and they had seen the costumes of Cody's flamboyant performers. Accordingly, many dressed like show cowboys. As part of the image, professional studio photographs from the period show most young men proudly holding one or more revolvers or rifles.

Buffalo Bill Cody legitimized the cowboy through his *Wild West* show-business extravaganza. Author Owen Wister's novel *The Virginian*, however, marked a substantial advance in the literary image of the mythic cowboy and formed the transition between the dime novel and the modern literary western story. *The Virginian* was written after the real Johnson County Cattle War in Wyoming that occurred in 1889 and Wister incorporated the struggle between cattlemen and settlers into the novel.

Real cowboys read dime novels and often dressed to meet the image that Easterners and other Westerners expected. This young man is decked out in surprisingly clean clothes for a real cowboy. They and his fancy leather chaps look more like an outfit worn for the photographer. He is also wearing a cartridge belt with a revolver stuck loosely in it, an accessory that most cowboys did not wear, and which was usually banned on trail drives and for cowboys working on the larger ranches. (Glenn Kinnaman Colorado and Western History Collection)

The Virginian

Wister's novel, published in 1902, pushed the cowboy into prominence in what is generally considered to be the first serious western novel. The description of The Virginian (he has no other name in the book) echoes show business cowboys like Buck Taylor, and the action sequences in the novel reflect the Wild West shows, filled with plenty of riding, shooting, and fighting. Wister blended the new cowboy hero with the historical West and added romance, action, and good versus evil. Wister's writing was an imaginary artistic treatment of the West based on hero themes. He created a West that was a land of freedom, honesty, and integrity, where the wicked and evildoers received the appropriate punishment. The book was a major transformation of the western formula, and the characters and main ingredients of the plot have been repeated since in countless novels and films.

The public was obviously hungry for a new type of hero and the novel was an instant success. *The Virginian* was on the best-seller list for six months in 1902, its year of publication. It was reprinted fifteen times in its first year. It was the fifth best seller in 1903. By 1904 it had sold 300,000 copies and by 1920 over a million. It continued to sell well and by 1968 had sold two million copies.[4]

Owen Wister was born in Philadelphia in 1860 and graduated from Harvard. He traveled to the West to find a moderate climate to improve his health and to gather material for a novel. He fell in love with the West, feeling that it rejuvenated him both morally and physically, but was distressed that it was disappearing. His vision was that the West was a land of freedom, honesty, and integrity, where the bad guys got what they deserved. The result was that he wrote *The Virginian*, in which he presented his own romantic vision of the West, marked by chivalry, honor, and romance, and championed what he saw as the superiority of western virtues. He invented the nomadic western loner as the chivalrous and romantic hero and made him what he wanted a western hero to be. The Virginian is a genteel Southerner who uses his wits, adds violence if necessary, and shares Wister's nostalgia for the vanishing West. Wister wrote about a West that never was.

The Virginian has an appealing plot of a spirited schoolmarm courted by a handsome cowboy in an exotic western locale. When the hero is introduced in the book, Wister describes him in terms of cowboy worship and admiration, echoing the dime novels that described the hero in sensual terms, such as tall, muscular, sinewy, sunburned, prime of manhood, rugged, slim, lean, and a veritable virile giant.

The Virginian had all the desirable characteristics we associate with movie cowboy heroes of the 1930s. He was honest, healthy, loving, strong, shrewd, gentle, and at the same time daring and gallant. But he was not representative of the cattle frontier or of the real cowboy. This is a cowboy novel without cows. Near the end of the novel the Virginian says he does not want to be associated with the Wild West cowboy, but he and his story have indeed become the legend.

Just as in dime novel plots, The Virginian was portrayed as a diamond in the rough just waiting to be tamed by the heroine. At one point she says, "She looked from her untamed man to the untamed desert of Wyoming," in this way introducing the notion that the western hero is an untamed man that has to be tamed by civilizing influence of a woman.[5] This concept featured prominently in later Zane Grey stories. However, untamed as he was suppose to be, like the outlaw heroes, Wister gave The Virginian the background of a southern gentleman, with eastern respectability underneath his rough cowboy exterior. He created a similar morality and success story as the dime novels of a young man born in poverty who rises to be a success and marry the right girl through his inherent skills and upstanding character. In reality, very few cowboys could marry a cultured Eastern woman and become a prosperous cattleman, but the story provided wish fulfillment for the reader.

Wister is credited with inventing the concluding standoff between the hero and the villain, and the final gunfight between them. Previous novels had included shootings and duels, but not in the way that Wister portrayed the classic showdown. He invented the fictional situation of the gunfighter's walk-down and final shootout where the hero and the villain face each other on the street. In the real West this type of meeting was rare. Most gunfights in the real West tended to be drunken brawls in saloons or ambushes from cover, rather than face-to-face showdowns on the main street. But so strong was this image that Wister's showdown became the standard for pulp fiction and later western films.

Wister's incorporated a type of "Code of the West" in *The Virginian* that was included by other later novelists. Elements included the concepts that the villain has to provoke the final fight, the hero does not shoot anyone in the back, and all the fights have to be fair. This "cowboy code" was Wister's western version of the code of honor and gallantry of the Southern gentleman. At the same time it was a grim code of honor that emphasized the need for a final duel between the two to resolve the conflict. In real life in the Old West most gunfights started over drunken insults. This type of belligerent situation usually turned very rapidly into shots fired with no further warning. The practical code of the real western gunman was self-preservation. Shoot first before the other man shoots you.

Like many other novels, *The Virginian* had its birth in magazines. Wister wrote seven short stories about the Virginian that appeared in *Harper's Weekly* and *The Saturday Evening Post* between 1893 and 1902. Three were written from a first-person point-of-view, and the other four from the point-of-view of an omniscient narrator. The result was that the novel version showed some unevenness, as Wister did not rewrite the collected stories for consistency.

Some critics have claimed that *The Virginian* (1902) by Owen Wister is full of clichés. However, the fact is that Wister transformed the formula of the western story and created a serious romance that formed the template for western novels that followed ever since. This is the famous card game where The Virginian responds to an insult from the villain Trampas with a drawn revolver and the immortal line "When you call me that, *smile*."

After *The Virginian* was published many cowboys started to try to become what the hero was like in the book. One anonymous cowboy has been quoted as saying, "Well, maybe we didn't talk that way before Mr. Wister wrote his book, but we sure all talked that way after the book was published."[6]

The Virginian was the prototype for a new type of hero. His persona was quickly copied by authors and filmmakers, and the general plotting and structure of *The Virginian* were recreated in countless cowboy pulp magazines, movies, and television programs. These novels and magazines stories typically had no theme where the hero was involved with being a cowboy and he typically did nothing that a real cowboy would do. The new heroes fought Indians and bandits, and rescued women from "fates worse than death." The open range and herding cows were not a part of the plot. Thus these were a continuation of the costume dramas and the stories of knights errant. The cowboy represented freedom from society. Readers were looking for a long-lost golden past, and wanted their heroes to return to the old values of individualism, honor, chivalry, nobility of character, self-reliance, democracy, individual action, integrity, and not be under the control of "big business" as was perceived in the real world.[7]

Two Other Authors

One of the major authors of westerns during first half of the 1900s was William MacLeod Raine, who wrote novels as well as short stories and articles. Raine was born in London in 1871, but became an authentic westerner who grew up on a cattle ranch near the Texas-Arkansas border, and knew real lawmen and bandits. He settled in Colorado in the early 1900s and from 1908 to 1954 averaged two books a year, publishing over 80 novels and numerous short stories. Like Tom Mix, quoted earlier, Raine felt that the West was not only a geographical area, but was a state of mind. Dime novels and pulp magazines stimulated thoughts of the freedom of an outdoor life in the saddle and the feeling that each man was an individual.

Another significant author of westerns was Clarence E. Mulford, who was working in a civil service job in New York when he started writing. Mulford had an extensive reference library and research notes on the West, and tried to make his stories authentic. He wrote a series of connected short stories for *Outing Magazine* that were later collected and published as a book titled *Bar 20* (1907). One of the characters in the book was a tough, ornery, hard-drinking, tobacco-chewing, cursing cowboy with red hair, who caroused with his buddies. This rough, yet ethical, cowhand was named Bill Cassidy. More stories and books about him followed and the character eventually appeared in the movie *Hop-Along Cassidy* (also known as *Hopalong Cassidy Enters*) (1935), starring William Boyd as Cassidy.

During the 65 sequels that followed, Boyd's character was not the same as Mulford's original. Cassidy, as interpreted by actor William Boyd, didn't smoke or curse, and as the series progressed, had less shootouts and fights. Boyd is remembered as a clean-living, square-dealing, pleasant, idealistic Cassidy who didn't drink alcohol, but drank sarsaparilla. He also championed "the little guy," which, like Deadwood Dick and the mythic version of Jesse James before him, appealed to Depression-era audiences.

Mulford's original books were rousing action stories, but Boyd's movies became morality plays with simplistic plots. After Boyd became popular in the movie role of Cassidy, Mulford's novels were partially re-written to conform to Boyd's new cleaner image of Cassidy.[8] Thus the hero myth was altered and reflected back into the original creation. Boyd's interpretation of Cassidy, dressed all in black (or dark blue as that photographed better in black-and-white), has lasted, and Mulford's original wild and vice-ridden cowboy has been forgotten.

The Cowboy Continues in the Pulps

The cowboy as adapted to western literature was an invented character that was transformed from actual cowboys who worked with cattle. Real cowboys were itinerant young men with few prospects, who were hired after the Civil War to drive cattle from Texas to the Kansas railheads for shipment to the cattle markets of the East.

The reality of the cowboy was not as glamorous as fiction. As old-time cowboy writer Ramon F. Adams correctly put it, there was little romance "in gettin' up at four o'clock in the mornin,' eatin' dust behind a trail herd, swimmin' muddy and turbulent rivers, nor in doctorin' screw worms, pullin' stupid cows from bog holes, sweatin' in the heat of summer and freezin' in the cold of winter."[9] Cowboys rounded up cattle and branded them, cut and baled hay, and installed and mended fences. They were typically overworked, underfed, and poorly paid. This reality was glamorized in dime novels and pulp magazines by romantic descriptions of riding the open range and the supposed thrill of herding cattle.

The real cowboy wasn't even admired by the popular press. In the late 1870s and early 1880s, almost every issue of the *Police Gazette* and *Frank Leslie's Illustrated Weekly* had some sensational article about cowboys. The two magazines delighted in lurid reports of the cowboy's wild and lawless behavior. The *Police Gazette* of September 6, 1879, said of cowboys, "While in town his home is in the saloons and the dance houses. He soon gets gloriously drunk and then begins to yell like a wild Indian and shoots off his big revolvers promiscuously into the crowd. He is little else than a crazy demon at such times and woe betide the man who crosses his path." Even *The Virginian* (1902) contained notions about cowboys and westerners that had been spread in the East by sensationalistic newspaper reporting. A typically eastern thought for the time was expressed by Molly's aunt when she says about the Virginian, "I suppose there are days when he does not kill people."[10]

Even the original name "cowboy" (spelled as "cow-boy" with a hyphen, or "cow boy" as two words) was derogatory. The name was originally used for bands of guerrilla outlaws who stole cattle and sold them to the British during the American Revolution, and in the 1870s to Texas bandits who rustled Mexican cattle. Cowboys in the Arizona Territory were responsible for the bloodshed in the early 1880s that culminated in the notorious shoot-out at the O.K. Corral.

In spite of the reality, romanticized cowboys began to appear as supporting characters in dime novels in the late 1870s. By the end of the 1880s, the cowboy had completely replaced the frontier woodsman in American popular literature as a new type of western hero. The tomahawk of the early Indian sagas set in the forests of the East was traded for the six-gun, the ten-gallon cowboy hat, and high-heeled boots. As the cowboy's popularity grew, his image was expanded and further fictionalized by journalists from eastern newspapers, dime novelists, and Wild West shows. Aspects of the legend, such as men in high-heeled boots and large Stetson hats carrying loaded guns about their daily business, drinking and carousing all night, and goading each other into gunfights on the main streets of western towns, amazed and fascinated the readers of eastern newspapers and illustrated periodicals. This image was dutifully expanded, fictionalized, and promoted by authors of dime novels and pulp magazines.

The mythmakers were journalists and writers. Dime novelists in particular made little or no attempt to keep fiction separate from fact. Articles that appeared in the eastern newspapers fueled a fascination with the West. The accounts that were the most widely read were the newspapers whose journalists recounted a mix of fact and fiction, trying to please readers' tastes that varied from staid citizens to those who wanted sensational stories. Like the early story papers and tabloid newspapers, these stories became news mixed with indistinguishable colorful editorializing.

By the 1890s, the cowboy was considered to be the primary western fictional hero. In this new romantic myth, the cowboy was a loner who rode the range with no apparent purpose and no visible means of support. When he encountered a town he became involved or trapped in circumstances involving a dangerous situation. He was thrown into conflict with a badman, and usually became involved with a woman. Plots were basically good versus evil, or a variation on that theme. Villains, cheating cowards, land swindlers, and overbearing bullies were added to provide plot conflict. The cowboy hero was allowed to kill selectively and unpunished to right wrongs and deal out justice to the villain.

In reality, the role of the cowboy in opening and settling the West was small and the men themselves were usually vagrants. The story that contained the theme of a cattle drive was popular, because the setting was the rip-roaring cattle towns with their constant shoot-outs and a supporting cast of characters, such as the local marshal, the saloon girl, and the cattle baron. However, the legendary cattle drives that are often the subject of these cowboy stories lasted for only 15 years, from 1866 to about 1881. In spite of this, there was an air of romance about cowboys and "The West" in the late 1800s, and many boys and young men from the East fantasized about becoming a cowboy and participating in cattle drives across the West.

The early heroes were described as frontier figures pushing back the wild and savage frontier as they fought Indian savages. Over time, however, dime novelists realized that though readers wanted heroes with the wilderness skills and the free spirit of the western hero, he also had to have the gentility of the Easterner. The new characters had courage, tenacity, and inner resources, but had Eastern manners, ways, and romantic potential. Early frontier characters were rough, with provincial dialects and backwoods ways, but gradually changed to have respectable English and manners, making them suitable for romantic heroines.[11]

The Thrill of the Western Pulps

Pulp magazines set the pattern for mass-market western stories in the form of rip-roaring adventures that made use of all this romance, excitement, and nostalgia for the Wild West. They created an established formula that sold stories and novels by the millions all over the world. Written by commercial writers who tried for realism and authentic detail, the West and its heroes were nevertheless often distorted, over-dramatized, glorified, sensationalized, and romanticized. But, in spite of a poor literary reputation, the western pulps were probably read in greater numbers than any other popular literature. Millions of people gained their image of the West from reading pulp magazines written by authors who invented much of it. Many stories lacked authenticity and exaggerated the action, because some pulp writers wrote entirely from their own imaginations.

The collective description of "western" meant that a story could be set anywhere from the opening of the frontier in 1830, when the "frontier" was at edge of the original colonies, until after the turn of the century and the final closing of the American western frontier around the turn of the twentieth century. Most pulp westerns, however, were set west of the Mississippi, and took place either during the American Civil War, which lasted from 1860 to 1865, or in what is considered to be the classic age of the West from 1865 to 1900. Many of the undated stories seem to be set in about 1870, though this was not the real 1870 of history.

The location of the fictional Wild West depended on the historical period. Tales placed on the frontier were set in the Alleghenies, the Mississippi, the Northwest, or the American West or Southwest, depending on the date. But it was always a vague "frontier," which could be the Mississippi valley, the fur-trapping country of New Mexico or Wyoming, the Spanish southwest of California or New Mexico, the Texas cattle country, Zane Grey's deserts of Utah and Arizona, the high mountain country of Colorado, or the farming country of the Great Plains. Depending on the location and the time, the hero might be a mountain man, a scout, a cowboy, a soldier, an outlaw, or a gunfighter.

Western pulp stories were mass-entertainment for a mostly unsophisticated audience. They were read primarily by adolescents, the working class, and those without much money to spend on reading. Writer Elmer Kelton grew up on a ranch in West Texas and remembered that most ranch bunkhouses had a stack of pulp western magazines and that the majority of the cowboys loved them.[12] The pulps provided an escape from a depressing world by presenting cheap, instantly-gratifying entertainment. The western, in particular, provided a morality story that offered the masses a temporary escape into the secure fictional world of a West that never existed. One of the appeals of the western for some of the public was that western stories were tough, hard, and fast moving, without many of the gory details and sex scenes that appeared in other genres of the pulps.

Even so, western stories did not differ very much in basic structure from the other popular genres, such as mysteries, spy stories, detective novels, thrillers, science fiction, and even romance adventures. The western, the gangster story, and the spy thriller share the same basic elements of action and adventure. The westerns were simply put into a landscape of the American West. In all fairness, however, this may be a simplistic viewpoint, as some plots could only be resolved in a western environment by using the backdrop of mountains and deserts.

In their quest to differentiate themselves with fresh stories and sensational characters, western pulp authors came up with what many readers came to believe were authentic details. This shaped western novels and films for many years and was summed up succinctly by Franz and Choate, who commented that western authors in the period around 1900, "could lead the reading public, who would be mostly in the East, in almost any direction they chose, for the eastern readers had no actual knowledge of what the West was like, and of what it should be like; but they had imagination, and the writers were learning how to exploit that imagination."[13]

One significance of the western pulps is that so many were published and the size of the public appetite for them. They offered belief in the myth of the western frontier where men and women could begin their lives anew and individuals could be free from the restrictions of eastern society.

The Fictional Cowboy Image

The art of story-telling reflects the society in which the reader and writer live. Over the years changes were made in the hero to reflect the changing values of both contemporary culture and the reader. If the reading public did not accept and keep reading about a literary character, he had to change or fade away.

The hero of the western pulp magazines was like the hero of any other genre, but in a western setting. He was young, handsome, strong, and personable. He was also full of moral courage and character. In addition to his other heroic characteristics, he was an expert shot with a six-gun, an accomplished saloon fighter, and a skilled rider. The mythic image of the cowboy hero became that of a pistol-packing knight of the plains who symbolized rugged individualism. He was a dashing crusader against evil on horseback. He was silent, kind, noble, generous, patriotic, pious, slow to anger, and quick to avenge his (or the heroine's) honor. The hero was also strong, gentle, and handsome—and good to his horse—and though he was often tempted to philander with the saloon girl, he usually didn't do anything about it.

The reality of the cowboy's everyday life was not gunplay and violence, but that of a hired hand on horseback who tended cows and fixed fences. However, the air of romance and glamour associated with the cowboy resulted in the image becoming established in American folklore and their lifestyle stirring the imagination of people around the world.

As author Rita Parks has put it, "The western hero is a subject whose roots are in history, whose image has been transformed into myth, and whose chief function for the contemporary audience is to provide popular entertainment."[14] Editors soon realized that a strong hero-type western character held a greater interest and entertainment value for the reader than an average one. In addition, the use of a popular repetitive character made the reader want to read other stories about that character, rather than just following a particular author. But the story had to include the triumph of good over evil, the preservation of the status quo, and defense of weak and the innocent.

This mythic cowboy lives in a world where men were men. He owns one set of clothes, his horse, and his gun, which are the images of tough, reliable, self-sufficient masculinity. He is a man of leisure and even when he is the town marshal or owns a successful ranch he appears to be unemployed. He spends much of his time in the saloon playing poker in the evening or camping out in the wide open spaces. He is usually a solitary and rugged hero who works alone, though sometimes with a sidekick. This cowboy hero has no past and no particular friends. He never starts a fight but always wins it, and he does not draw first. He shows limited interest in women.

He always seems to have adequate money to eat, gamble, and drink in the saloon, and leads a comfortable life at the local hotel or boarding house. At the end of the story, the hero wins thanks of the community, often the heroine, and sometime a reward.

Cooper's Leatherstocking moved silently around the Eastern forests on foot, but the fictional western cowboy hero has to ride a horse. He loves the wide expanses of land in the West and his horse. The horse is an image of power, authority, and leadership; a cowboy without horse is small and uninspiring, and loses his dignity. The hero's horse is a matter of life and death in the vast open spaces of the West and makes it easier to cover the untracked deserts and mountains, but it is also his companion. The hero becomes one with his horse and will give it his last drop of water. The cowboy hero can ride his horse superbly, draw a gun faster than anyone else, and shoot better than everyone. Several Hollywood characteristics were added to the mythical gunfights—the sinister-looking gunman's crouch, for example, with his hand hovering over the butt of his gun. This serves no practical purpose in a gunfight, but adds to the visual menace during a showdown.

The cowboy hero retaliates only after provoked, as he tracks down, confronts, and defeats the villain in violent physical combat. Like all romantic adventure stories, the pulp western has to have a happy ending for the hero.

The classic climax of the western pulp story or novel is the final gunfight that brings resolution to the plot. The pulp cowboy has to have various guns, including a revolver, rifle, or shotgun, to back up his virility and toughness, to resolve physical conflicts, and to bring order to the frontier. A man without a gun would not be able to defend himself in the supposed dangerous frontier world of dime-novel villains and badmen, so the revolver was an essential accessory. The hero has great skill with it and is faster on the draw than the villain. A gun is used well and wisely by the hero, but not by the badman.

The pulp western story was action-packed drama with plenty of gunplay. The author tried to grab the reader right away with a narrative hook to capture attention and the action had to start in the first sentence or paragraph. Pulps authors joked that if a writer didn't know what to do next, he should have someone come bursting through the door with a gun in his hand. Then continue with the action to keep reader's attention.[15] Authors claimed that action was 95 percent of the story, and that there should be little inner dialog or personal reflection.

The finale of the story had to be a climactic shootout that spells the end of the badman. This was the kind of action men wanted. In the story "Gun Legion" in the February 1942, *Rio Kid Western*, the shootout was described in the following manner:

> His gun flashed from under his coat in a blue blur, but death had struck him before he could cock the hammer. His savage violence sustained a terrific jolt, as Pryor's slug plowed through his check. Blood came to the front of his shirt, widened rapidly, and he looked at it dazedly. All the stiffness drained swiftly from his body then. His head rolled, eyes fading. He swayed off balance, took a long loose step, and then went down to the floor in a crumpled heap.

The heyday of the pulps was also the heyday of illustrations for Western fiction. The lurid cover art of the western pulps helped to enhance and perpetuate the myth of the Wild West and the cowboy-gunfighter image. The covers contained dramatic titles in screaming colored print, overlaying vivid images that maintained the myth of the Wild West, as well as selling magazines. One cover of *Complete Western Book* magazine, for example, showed a man with a bloody bandana around his head blazing away with two guns into an open doorway, while a woman with a baleful glare backwards runs ahead of him, carrying a rifle and cartridge belt. Western *Story* magazine for October 4, 1924, showed a rider threatened by a huge menacing grizzly bear. His horse is slipping sideways to the ground on a hill with a look of terror on its face as the cowboy attempts to shoot backwards at the menace. These were sensationalized images of masculinity at its best.

12

The Western Pulp Matures

The pulp western magazine emerged between about 1900 and 1925. The middle period of western pulp fiction, often called its Golden Age, lasted from about the mid–1920s to the mid–1940s, then pulp westerns declined after World War II. Readers who purchased these western magazines wanted exciting adventure tales. Editors demanded predictable plots and stereotyped characters, and generally did not approve of sex, ambiguous heroes and villains, or unhappy endings.

The western story was differentiated from other pulp fiction by having the characters wear big hats and ride horses. The literary value of these pulp books and magazines was generally not particularly high, but the imagery of smoking guns, cowboys, horses, and cattle drives, all set in the wide-open spaces of the Wild West, created a fascination among many readers. It was escapist literature at its finest. The stories were good-versus-evil, with a white-hatted hero always emerging victorious at the end. The success of the western story was stimulated by a surging interest in frontier life and the legends of America's recent past, and by the popularity of the emerging western movies. Cowboy magazines were the bestselling of the pulps, with characters such as Warwhoop Wilson and Guncat Bodman.

As the dime novels were starting to fade in the 1880s, *Harper's Weekly*, *Scribner's Magazine*, *Knickerbocker,* and *The Atlantic Monthly* started to publish more western fiction and stories of a higher quality than the dime novels. They also printed correspondence from travelers to the West. Visitors to the West who recorded their adventures originally intended their accounts in newspapers and books to be factual, but soon found that the most popular accounts of their adventures were those written in a melodramatic style. During the 1890s, lavishly illustrated magazines such as *Collier's* and *The Saturday Evening Post* started to replace *Harper's Weekly* and *Frank Leslie's Illustrated Weekly* as popular reading material. These magazines featured western and adventure tales by writers such as Jack London, and covers by the premier illustrators of the time, including Frederic Remington and Howard Pyle.

General fiction magazines of the early 1920s featured occasional western stories, then as they became more popular entire magazines were devoted to the western. One of the first of the specialized western pulp magazines was Street & Smith's popular *Western Story* magazine. It was converted in September of 1919 from their dime novel periodical *New Buffalo Bill Weekly*, one of the last of the nineteenth century weeklies. The early issues of *Western Story* were 144 pages long, and included one novel, two serials, and three short stories. This was the prototype of all-western pulp magazines and ran for thirty years, publishing quality stories by premier western authors, such as Max Brand

12. The Western Pulp Matures

Stories of the Wild West have always been steady sellers, whether as dime novels, pulp magazines, or paperback books. Westerns form a genre of adventure story that combine romance and rip-roaring excitement with nostalgia for the Old West. They created an established formula that sold novels by the millions all over the world. Though the West and its heroes were often distorted, over-dramatized, glorified, sensationalized, and romanticized, the western pulps were read in greater numbers than any other popular literature. Millions of people gained their image of the West from reading pulp magazines written by authors who invented much of it from their own imaginations.

and Luke Short. One factual article was usually included, along with various columns and departments, such as *Miner's Potlatch*, which provided advice to those interested in mining, and a column that answered reader's questions on western geography. *Western Story* promoted itself on the front cover as offering readers "Big Clean Stories of Outdoor Life." The magazine was priced at 10¢. It was a huge success, reaching a circulation of 300,000 per issue within a year.[1] Sales grew further in the 1920s when Street & Smith issued the magazine weekly.

To cash in on this success, Street & Smith quickly added *Far West* and *Wild West Weekly* (published by Frank Tousey then continued by Street & Smith). A typical *Wild West Weekly* story was one authored by Guy Maynard that had the following exciting prose, "Crash! Bang! Senor Red Mask's hot guns rocketed lead and flame. El Halcon— The Hawk of the Rio Grande staggered. He was hit. Still he lunged forward. He seemed to bear a charmed life. Snarling bitter oaths, he gripped his guns for a deadly blast at close range."[2]

During the golden years of western pulps, *Wild West Weekly* typically offered three novelettes, supported by four or five short stories. By the mid-1930s, one of the four complete western stories was in comic-strip form. These visual stories would run for multiple episodes and then be dropped to start a new picture story. Originally the pictures had captions underneath them, but later used balloons inside the panels. The magazine used characters such as Dogie Cantwell, Brazos Bell, Slim Harkness, and Omaha Hooker. *Wild West Weekly* became *Wild West* in 1943, but shortly afterwards went out of business.

Other publishers had also cashed in on the western trend. Thrilling Publications came out with *Thrilling Western*, *Thrilling Ranch Stories*, *Popular Western*, and *Texas Rangers*. Popular Publications brought out *Dime Western*. *Nickel Western* appeared in 1932, but failed soon after. Other early all-western pulp magazines were *West* and *Frontier Stories* from Doubleday, *Triple-X Western* from Fawcett, and *Cowboy Stories*, *Ace High*, *Ranch Romances*, and *Western Adventures* from Clayton Magazines. *Frontier Stories* billed itself on the cover as, "A magazine dedicated to the adventures of the dauntless men and women who carved a new empire—The West." There were many western titles and they were among the most financially reliable for a publisher.

Most western pulp fiction was written by men for male readers. An exception was the romance westerns, which primarily had a female readership. About half of them, however, were written by men.

By the end of the 1920s western pulp magazines emphasized adventure, action, and some romance. Publishers wanted writers to use formularized plots and an author's individual style was often overridden by the desires of the editor and the magazine's readers. Everybody copied everybody else. For a while "Kid" heroes were popular and everybody had to have one. Western *Story* had the Polka Dot Kid and the Montana Kid. *Wild West Weekly* had the Silver Kid, Kid Wolf, the Oklahoma Kid, the Sonoma Kid, and the Whistlin' Kid. Others that appeared in the pulps were the Rio Kid, the Arizona Kid, and the Border Kid.

Masked riders like Zorro remained popular. The hero of Thrilling Publications' *Masked Rider Western*, which was written by a number of authors over many years, was outfitted completely in black, including hat, mask, and boots. "To complete the bizarre effect, he wore a long Mexican cloak, which flowed over him in voluminous black folds. It concealed the lines of his figure; and when he rode fast, it usually billowed out behind him fantastically, like the wings of a monstrous bat."[3] Even his stallion (never a mare because of the need to project a masculine image) was black and named Midnight. The Masked Rider was also known as The Black Caballero.

The everyday world of the Depression was dreary and full of economic hardship. In the background were political issues in Europe and the inevitable preparations for World War II. The pulp western offered a temporary escape into a colorful and dramatic world of gunsmoke, rearing horses, and beautiful heroines in distress on horseback. At a time when the ordinary man felt that external events were controlling him, he could enjoy these stories of a lone hero who administered justice and righted wrongs with his fists and six-guns. The resolution of justice was fast and uncomplicated as western heroes simply gunned the villains down. In the 1930s and 1940s the western pulp magazine was selling this escapist reading for 25¢ a copy.

Fans of western magazines wanted action, as seen in the following excerpt from "Lawyer Two-Fist" by Wayne D. Overholser, that appeared in *Western Story* in 1939. "He ducked, came up under Lengel's right, and both his own fists went out in a paralyzing one-two to Lengel's jaw that rocked the big man to his heels.... Lengel's breath went out in a wheezing gurgle and he went down into the dust of the street." With hundreds of pulp western magazines and thousands of writers, even pulp editors found that their stories started to blur together. Nonetheless, western stories became escapist fantasy for adults seeking a temporary release from the routine monotony and issues of daily life.

The early western pulps were very much like the dime novels as they were mostly written by the same authors for the same publishing houses. Over time the language matured and became less stilted—though not entirely. Similar to the dime novels, the editors believed that they were using authentic western speech when they wrote editorials and advice to readers. This excerpt is from the column "Stampede" ("where our reading and writing waddies get together with Powder River Bill"), a column appearing in *Western Trail* that tried to connect readers to those with whom they had lost touch. Here is Powder River Bill's contorted written answer in 1931 to a question from a reader concerning three lost people. "Climb down, hombres an' hombresses, an' rest for a mite. Because as soon as we shake the kinks we gotta fork leather again an' hunt for three missin' hombres." He ended with "S'long pards, see yuh on Dishpan Charlie's trail."[4]

Success, of course, stimulated competition. Action-filled western magazines filled the newsstands with titles such as *Western Story, Ace-High Western, Super Western, Texas Rangers, Masked Rider, All Western, Golden West, Cowboy Stories, Six-Gun, Double Action, Range Riders, .44 Western, New Western, Star Western, Triple-X Western, Dime Western, Western Adventures, Popular Western, Ace Western, Lariat, Quick Trigger, Big-Book Western, Riders of the Range, Thrilling Western, Crack Shot Western, Western Outlaws,* and *Double Action*.[5] Not all were successful, however. Despite fame on radio and television, *The Lone Ranger* magazine lasted for only eight issues, from April to November of 1937.[6]

Two fringe western magazines were *Spicy Western*, which added nudity and eroticism to western plots, and *Ranch Romances*, a romantic love pulp that pioneered the western love story and told it from the heroine's point of view. In 1952, one newsstand in California reported displaying thirty-three western pulps and six western "love" magazines.[7] All were full of vicarious thrills and mythical interpretations of the West. The heroes were red-blooded adventurers who excelled in fighting skills and male attractiveness.

The western formula had more variations than the detective stories; however, it was always bounded by a setting defined by riders, horses, and guns. Most western plots could have been set just as easily to the east of the Mississippi. The difference was the setting.

The location and the land give western novels their unique ambience. The western story took place on the boundary between civilization and the wilderness, between ordered society and lawlessness, wherever that was physically located.

As in the hard-boiled detective stories, the western hero was often knocked out, wounded, beaten up, toppled from his horse, or thrown over a cliff, a type of action that became the staple of later B-western movies. Writers tried for realism and detail but, like the dime novelists, they over-dramatized and romanticized the story. The hero of the West became a romantic and romanticized figure representing those qualities that Americans always wanted to believe were uniquely their own, such as pioneer spirit, initiative, skill, and daring. The hero is portrayed as tall and lean, and wears a tight-fitting outfit. He carries a Colt .45 and Winchester '73. He is independent, self-reliant, expert at what he does, and deadly. The fictional pulp cowboy has no family life and no permanent relationships, but solves the local problems then rides off into the sunset to pursue his lonely destiny.

Women in western stories ranged from the pioneer in a sunbonnet to the sultry dance-hall girl. There were decorative heroines, but they were often linked to schools, churches, families, domestic situations, and all the other characteristics of a civilized life. The heroines were often blonde, which was associated with true love, purity, and lawfulness. The naughty women or saloon girls were often dark-haired and sometimes dark-skinned, traits associated with passion and recklessness. There were also feisty heroines who rode the range and fought back against oppression. They were often red-haired to symbolize the spirit of independence without vice.

Plots had many variations. The pulp hero may have had an unhappy past, such as a wife killed by Indians or a villain, or had been unjustly blamed for a killing. He was sometimes a saddle tramp, who drifted here and there to his next job, a well-known fact that was true of the real cowboy who rarely settled down, but moved on to another ranch when the work ran out.

Zane Grey

The most famous western fiction novelist of his day to produce these types of stories, and probably the most popular and successful of all western authors, was Zane Grey. Grey was the author of pulp-style romance stories in the tradition of some of the classic novels. He specialized in the larger-than-life hero, the young and innocent heroine, the chase, the duel, and the ultimate triumph of good over evil. These elements as he combined them established the form of the western novels for decades afterwards.

Zane Grey was born Pearl Zane Gray in 1872 in Zanesville, Ohio, which was settled by his ancestor Ebenezer Gray. Before becoming a writer, Gray studied to be a dentist, like his father. Dentistry didn't really appeal to him, so he changed the spelling of his last name and started to write short stories and articles. At first his writing didn't sell, but after he married in 1905 his new wife took on the task of being his editor, literary agent, and financial manager. His writing sold slowly at first, then success finally came.

Grey's 89 books sold over 20 million copies and 54 million people are estimated to have read them, more than any other western writer at the time. His stories were influential in the worldwide establishment of the western as the most popular genre in literature and film for most of the 1900s. He created a new version of the myth of a West full of chivalry and romance, and as in the dime novels before him, his protagonists became the agents of retribution in his epic vision of the West. His stories lived on in *Zane Grey's Western Magazine*.

His first three books, *Betty Zane* (1903), *The Spirit of the Border* (1906), and *The Last Trail* (1909), formed a trilogy of the Ohio frontier. Then, after a trip to Arizona in 1907, he discovered the open landscape and breathtaking vistas of the West. He used this western landscape as the background for his subsequent melodramatic novels, which featured heroic men struggling against nature and stereotyped villains. Grey established many of the fictional ideas about the West, such as the mythic Code of the West, in which the heroic held closely to a code of honor, loyalty, and chivalry similar to the heroes of the early dime novels. Grey is credited with introducing the professional gunman to the western and his stories helped to mold the stereotypical western hero as silent, steely-eyed, and fast on the draw. He developed the fictional gunfighter-hero, with two low-slung guns, a mean-looking fighting stance, and a lightning-fast draw. His heroes were brave, uncomplaining, hardworking, soft-spoken, reserved with strangers, hospitable, chivalrous, and kind to women, children, and animals. They had a sense of humor and all dressed the same.

Grey's first successful novel was *The Heritage of the Desert* (1910), which set the tone and theme of most

Zane Grey's *Under the Tonto Rim*, first published in 1926, but updated in this paperback version to what a 1953 cowboy hero should look like, shows the type of action that his readers wanted. This is two-fisted, gut-punching action with brawny cowboys brandishing guns. But, at the same time, Grey created a new version of the western myth that was full of chivalry and romance, though his protagonists became the agents of retribution in his epic vision of the West.

of the later romantic westerns. The main character, like many of Grey's heroes, is an Easterner who has come to the West for health reasons.

One of Grey's best novels, and his most popular book, was *Riders of the Purple Sage* (1912), which sold over a million copies when it first appeared. It helped to define the genre for later authors. In the first few pages Grey introduces Lassiter, a black-clad gunman who is able to frighten away villains merely by his presence and reputation. The novel was important for two elements that affected later writers. One was that Grey established the position of the frontier woman as a civilizing influence who tamed the wilderness. The second was the importance of the fast draw in taming the mythic West.[8]

One of Grey's standard and popular plot devices was to have Mexicans, Mormons, or other contemporary undesirables try to make slaves of white women. Grey was searching for suitable villains for his plots and he disapproved of polygamy, so he reworked the plot of the captivity narrative and replaced the traditional villainous Indians with villainous Mormons and outlaws. He replaced the previous white Slavers (which were still perceived to be a threat to white women) with ruthless Mormons, whom he equated to enforced slavery.

Many of Grey's plots were set in the 1870s in southern Utah where the Mormons were well-established at the time.[9] Grey's elaborate plots, several of which contained abduction and near-rape, usually involved dark secrets and powerful conspiracies that threatened independent-minded innocent heroines. In *Riders of the Purple Sage* (1912), for example, Lassiter has spent 18 years searching for his sister Milly, who has been seduced by a mysterious Mormon, abducted, and chained in a cave. Similarly, attempts are made to force rancher Jane Witherstoon to marry a Mormon against her will. As in most of Grey's novels, the story ends with Jane barely escaping with her virtue and her life.

Meanwhile, rustler Oldring had captured Milly's daughter Bess and forces her to become a masked bandit. The risk of capture and the threat of rape gave an added thrill to the plot by preying on fears of enslavement and the ensuing sexual threat. This type of plot catered to the paranoid fears that there was still a huge network of white Slavers just ready and waiting to capture women and spirit them away to a fate worse than death. Much of this was borrowed from James Fenimore Cooper stories and the unending cycle of pursuit, capture, and escape used in plots in the dime novels.

Some of Grey's stories were "convalescence narratives," in which a large part is played by a man or woman nursing their love interest to back health. This happens in Grey's *Riders of the Purple Sage*, when Venters shoots a mysterious masked rider. When he investigates, he finds that he has shot a woman by mistake. He nurses her back to health and marries her at the end of the book. This convalescence and recuperation theme had been used earlier in *The Virginian*, where Molly finds The Virginian after he is left for dead after an Indian attack and nurses him back to health.

Another very popular novel by Zane Grey was *The Vanishing American* (1925). The plot follows an Indian named Nophaie (the Warrior), who has the heritage of an Indian chieftain. He is "rescued" by well-meaning whites and sent to school in the East where he flourishes as a football star. He goes back to the West and the heroine Marian follows him, planning to stay on his reservation. As in other Grey novels, the heroine Marian does not at first realize that she loves Nophaie, but she finally comes around.

The story was serialized in *Ladies' Home Journal* in 1922, then was published in book form by Harpers in 1925. At the time, the story elements of rape and stealing from the Indians were controversial. In the ending of the original magazine version, Nophaie recovers from influenza, kills off the villains, and marries the white girl. At the time, however, contemporary mores did not allow a white woman to marry an Indian man (though somewhat perversely a white man marrying an Indian woman was acceptable). The ending of the story raised so much controversy that it was changed. In the book version Nophaie suffers a relapse of his influenza and dies.

Grey believed in the simple virtues of western life and his hero is frequently transformed by life in the West. Many of Grey's stories revolve around an Easterner who moves to the West and finally accepts western living. Removed from the oppressive and artificial constraints of the East, he discovers health and happiness in the West. The hero compares the two ways of life and realizes how artificial his previous life in the East has been as he becomes converted to the wholesomeness of western life. Grey was sincere in these concepts and believed that his vision of the West was true.[10]

Grey's string of successes continued. He continued to write novels and many of them were made into films. *The Lone Star Ranger* (1915) was translated into film seven different times under different titles. *The Border Legion* (1916) was filmed five times. In all, 104 films were made from his books, making him the most filmed author in the history of American cinema.[11]

In the period after World War I, when traditional American values were changing, Grey used the western story as a vehicle to promote a traditional view of American life. Even so, his stories dealt with basic conflicts in social roles and values afflicting Americans in the 1920s and 1930s. Two important sources of tension were the relationship between the sexes and the meaning of nature. The early 1900s were a time of controversy about gender roles and determining the appropriate behavior for each. By the 1920s a new morality was emerging. In contemporary American society, women were challenging their traditional roles, but the West of Zane Grey was where men were men and women were women. But, at the same time, Grey's women were strong, proud, and daring. He portrayed their true role in life as being adored by strong, virtuous, and heroic men. For Grey, the West was a place where traditional ideals of male and female roles were still valid and morally proper romance was part of the pattern of heroic virtue.

Part of the paradox of emerging women was played by the role of clothing as women started to dress in what were traditionally male styles of clothing. Women disguised as men and cross-dressing had always been a common theme in the dime novels, and Grey carried it on in his books. In *The Border Legion* (1916), Joan Randle is kidnapped by the villain and forced to cross-dress in a man's black outfit and mask. She dwells on her appearance and how her costume "strangely magnified every curve and swell in her body." But it all works out in the end. When Jim Cleve finds out that the masked rider is actually a women, he marries her. The themes of cross-dressing and slavery also played a part in *Riders of the Purple Sage* (1912). When Venters wounds cross-dressed Bess by mistake, she reacts in the manner that white slaves were expected to as she says, "What-will-you-do-with-me?" when she wakes up.[12]

Though Grey's books contain suggestions of sex and attempted rape, he used no overt sex in his novels. Any successful rape that is part of the plot happens in the background. When an early manuscript version of Grey's *Robber's Roost* (1932) hinted at rape as a motive for part of the plot, he revised the manuscript to take it out. Though he conceded that rape was used in novels, he said he did not want it in his books.[13] Any hint of sexual impropriety was still daring for fiction in the 1920s, though Grey did feature the madam of a bordello in *The U.P. Trail* (1918).

Grey used the development of heroic individual morality and an ideal relationship between men and women as a formula in many of his western novels. Grey's heroes and heroines existed in a timeless and suspended world where romance and heroism was still complete and pure. The hero overcomes the evil and lawless forces that are threatening the heroine and establishes a romantic relationship with her.

Zane Grey wrote wonderfully melodramatic stories that are full of atmosphere. Though they were better plotted than many of the time, critics have been ready to find fault with them, claiming that some of the characters are weakly portrayed and there are too many convenient coincidences. Critic Jim Hitt has said they were "wooden and unbelievable."[14]

Author David Murdoch has claimed that Grey had a rigid formula for his plots, and that his heroes were overly righteous cardboard cut-outs.[15] Buffalo Bill expert Don Russell commented on Grey, "whose writing was atrocious and whose characters were as wooden as a cigar store Indian, but who somehow had a gift for story-telling."[16] Perhaps Grey's novels were overly melodramatic and full of coincidences, and perhaps his prose style was antiquated (somewhat like James Fenimore Cooper, a similarity which was commented on even in Grey's time), but nevertheless Grey indisputably wrote wonderfully entertaining stories. Readers loved them and propelled him to fame and fortune.

Max Brand

Another prolific western author was Frederick Schiller Faust, one of the undisputed kings of the western pulps. He wrote more than 600 stories for magazines and 530 books. His total literary output has been estimated at between 25,000,000 and 30,000,000 words.[17] He wrote under 19 different pseudonyms, including John Frederick, George Challis, Peter Dawson, George Owen Baxter, David Manning, Walter Butler, Martin Dexter, Peter Henry Morland, Evan Evans, Frederick Frost, and his most famous pen name, Max Brand.[18] Many of these pseudonyms (and those of other authors) have a rhythmic sound. Playwright Sophie Treadwell has been quoted as pointing out that pseudonyms with two monosyllables and the same vowel sound in each are the most successful.[19]

Faust's western stories helped to popularize the American West and make cowboy fiction the most popular of all genres. Though he became famous as Max Brand writing about the Old West, he also wrote hundreds of short stories from spies to horse racing, historical novels, detective stories, adventure stories, mysteries, science fiction, and the popular doctor series, Dr. Kildare. By writing so many action and romantic adventures, he became known as the King of the Pulps.

For 12 years Faust lived in a villa on the south bank of the Arno River in Italy near Florence. For about half of the day he worked on poetry, and the rest of the day he churned out pulp stories. Faust originally wanted to make his mark as a poet and spent many hours on his carefully crafted verse, but his poetry did not sell well. It was, however, not without its audience, and his poems were published in small volumes as *The Village Street* (1922) and *Dionysus in Hades* (1931).

To support himself, Faust wrote pulp fiction, usually as fast as he could, sometimes churning out 12,000 words on a weekend and completing an entire novel in three weeks. On occasion he could write as many as 20,000 words a day. He was an even more prolific writer than Zane Grey and, by the 1930s, his books were outselling Grey's.

For sixteen years, between 1918 and 1935, Faust wrote an average of one full-length western novel every month. His nearest competitor was fellow writer Walt Coburn, an authentic Westerner from Montana, who cranked out more than 600,000 words a year in the 1930s and 1940s, which ranked him as one of the most prolific writers of all time. Coburn was so prolific that he wrote every lead story in *Western Story* from 1930 until the magazine folded. He even had two pulps with his name in the title, *Walt Coburn Western* and *Walt Coburn Action Novels*.

Faust published most of his serial westerns in *Western Story*, the Street & Smith pulp western magazine that stylized this new popular genre. His output was so high that, unknown to readers, several of his stories might appear in a single issue of a pulp under

In spite of the glamorous image of cowboys as Knights of the Range created by dime novel and pulp magazine authors, real cowboys were unskilled laborers who herded cattle, rounded them up and branded them, drove them to market, and did odd jobs around the ranch. This was not a life of glamour. The work, such as shown here at a cattle round-up in 1888, was hard, dirty, low-paying, and involved long hours in the saddle. (Library of Congress)

different pen names. On one occasion he wrote an entire issue of *Western Story* with different stories written under different names. Faust's style was arguably more polished and his wording not as extravagant as many of his other contemporary western authors. Some authorities have called his style, characterization, and plot superior to Grey's writings.[20]

Faust's first fiction story was "Convalescence," which appeared in *All Story* magazine in March 1917. His first western story was "The Untamed," written in 1917 and published as a serial in *All Story* in December 1918. His western stories were set in a violent frontier America. Many were based on ancient classical myths, often using almost super-human protagonists. His plots and writing reflected a growing interest among readers in violence in the western pulps and detective stories. An example of his rather brutal writing is, "Blood was bursting through the fingers of his hands and streaming down over his clothes. Blondy went to him and pulled the hands away from that frightful face. He had been shot through both cheeks. When he tried to speak, blood and shattered teeth spouted out and fell on the floor." Though this quote comes from one of Faust's western stories it could just as well been from a hard-boiled detective yarn of the times.[21]

As Max Brand, Faust discovered a popular formula for his westerns in the early 1920s and continued using it for the rest of his career. He said that his guiding principle for pulp stories and later B-western film scripts was, "Action, action, action is the thing. So long as you keep your hero jumping through fiery hoops on every page you're all right." He also added, "There has to be a woman, but not much of one. A good horse is much more important."[22] This view was echoed by best selling western author Elmore Leonard, who once commented that men don't read a western novel or go to see a western movie for women and sex scenes, but for the action.[23]

One of Faust's memorable stories was "Twelve Peers," which appeared as a serial in *Western Story* starting in February 1930. The story was reprinted as a book and then quickly made into a successful motion picture as *Destry Rides Again*. The book sold over a million copies and the film was so popular that it was filmed three times–in 1932 with Tom Mix, in 1939 with James Stewart and Marlene Dietrich, and in 1954 with Audie Murphy.

Faust grew up on a ranch in California, but always claimed that his stories didn't resemble real life as much as cowboy melodrama.[24] Faust once claimed that he wrote all his stories around a single basic plot. He felt that in order to create conflict, the good man had to become bad and the bad man had to become good. He claimed that a plot where the bad man stayed bad and the good man stayed good had no plot conflict. Faust did not follow the traditional plot line of a historical context, but used the idea of a violent frontier. This may have been historically inaccurate, but the concept as a plot device was phenomenally popular. Faust was not particularly proud of his pulp fiction, and continued to write fiction and poetry for the slick magazines, such as *Esquire, Cosmopolitan, McCall's, Ladies Home Journal*, and *The Saturday Evening Post*.

When World War II seemed inevitable, Faust returned to America to Hollywood early in 1938. He worked at Metro-Goldwyn-Mayer and Warner's studios for $1,500 a week, in the process cranking out 30 film scripts.[25] When World War II broke out, Faust became a war correspondent. In May of 1944 he was trapped by a heavy enemy artillery barrage while the troops he was attached to were charging a German artillery position at Santa Maria Infante in Italy. He was hit in the chest by German shell fragments and died on the battlefield at age 52.

Louis L'Amour

One of the more recent popular western writers was Louis L'Amour, one of the most famous and best-selling authors in the history of western fiction, and one of the top-selling authors of all times. He wrote 89 novels and many short stories that had sold 320 million copies as of 2010. More than thirty motion pictures have been made from his novels and stories. One of his most popular books was *Hondo* (1953), which was published after the appearance of the film of the same name. The film was developed from L'Amour's short story "The Gift of Cochise."

Louis L'Amour, whose real name was Louis Dearborn LaMoore, was born in Jamestown, South Dakota, in 1908. He grew up in South Dakota and Oklahoma not long after the days of the real Wild West. Before becoming a writer, he worked at various labor and factory jobs that later helped him with insight into developing his literary characters.

L'Amour served in World War II, then started writing boxing stories, detective stories, and adventure stories for the pulp magazines. He published dozens of adventure stories, mostly about the Far East. He even wrote three of the continuing Hopalong Cassidy stories under the pen name of Tex Burns.[26] In the late 1940s, he turned full-time to writing about the West. He knew first-hand the places he wrote about as he had traveled extensively in the West with his parents during his early years. Though the traditional western story faded in the 1960s and 1970s, his books continued to sell by the millions. He published two or three novels a year and his publisher could count on sales of at least a million for each new book.

L'Amour continued the tradition of lively, well-plotted adventure stories set in the West, writing about courageous heroes fighting villains and Indians. His protagonists lived by a code of honor and loyalty, showed mental and physical toughness, and overcame great odds with their frontier skills. L'Amour's storytelling talent turned him into a major author of western fiction with a huge readership, and he took over Zane Grey's best-selling status. His writing was honored with a Congressional Gold Medal and the medal of freedom.

Like Max Brand, Louis L'Amour said that stories had to keep moving along at a fast pace and he believed in a well-told tale with plenty of action. This formula worked well during the Depression years, as a reader could work vicariously through the hero's personal problems, many of which he could identify with in his real world. At the same time he could immerse himself in an action-packed yarn.

From Print to Film

In a further boost to the popularity of the western, American filmmakers adapted hundreds of thrilling short stories, novels, and magazine articles into motion pictures. Producers felt that audiences were more likely to go to see a movie when they had read and enjoyed the original book or story. "The Tin Star" by John W. Cunningham, for example, was published in *Collier's* in 1947. It was turned into the classic western *High Noon* (1952) with Gary Cooper as Marshal Will Kane and Grace Kelly, in her first starring role, as his Quaker bride.

Film-makers, however, tended to tinker with and revise book plots, adding and subtracting elements as they fancied, thinking they could "improve" the story. Unfortunately, the resulting movies were not always the same as the book. Plots were changed for the movie version either because the book was too long or too short to make a suitable movie, sometimes because the book did not translate well into a visual image, or because the outcome was too depressing. Most moviegoers wanted a happy ending, so changes were often made to a book to make the film ending more upbeat. Sometimes studios purchased the rights to a book but only wanted to use a popular title, in this way hoping to use it as a draw for the movie for marketing purposes.

The other major issue with movie versions of western books and stories, just like many of the pulp stories themselves, was that they were not always historically accurate, but tended to be fictionalized and romanticized even more for the movies. This trend started in the early days of motion pictures. For example, with the motion picture version of the story "Broncho Billy and the Baby" by Peter Kyne, published in 1910 in the *Saturday Evening Post*. The Bronco Billy character was played by an actor named Max Aronson. The film was such a success that Anderson continued to use the character as continuing one. Over next few years he made almost 500 one and two reel movies about the character and he himself became known as "Bronco Billy" Aronson. Though many of his pre–1920 movies claimed that they stressed realism, his version of the West was still romanticized and fictionalized. Broncho Billy's western realism was modified into what Anderson envisioned it to be from reading the pulp western magazines and dime novels of the day.[27] This trend was continued by later actors, each one interpreting in his movies what he felt was the "authentic" West.

After World War II the tastes of the movie-going public changed and swept in a new demand for realism in literature and films. This brought changes to the traditional western story. Though romanticized pulp magazine and B-western stories continued to be cranked out, plots started to move towards more realism. One example is when Jack Schaefer wrote "Rider from Nowhere" for *Argosy* in 1946. He later expanded the story into a short novel titled *Shane* (1949), which was filmed as the motion picture *Shane* (1953) with Alan Ladd in the title role.

Hollywood attracted many of the pulp writers. Writer Borden Chase (real name Frank Fowler), for example, wrote pulp stories and movie screenplays, but became famous as a screenwriter rather than a novelist. Chase reportedly came up with his pen name after he saw a Borden's truck drive by a Chase Manhattan Bank.[28] Borden's story "The Chisholm Trail" was serialized in *The Saturday Evening Post* in 1946. This was later published as a hardback book as *Blazing Guns on the Chisholm Trail*. The story became the iconic motion picture *Red River* (1948), starring John Wayne and Montgomery Clift. Some of Chase's other screen successes were the movies *Winchester '73* (1950), *Bend of the River* (1952), *Vera Cruz* (1954), and *The Far Country* (1955).

James Warner Bellah wrote several short stories that featured the cavalry in conflict with Indians on the frontier. Most of them appeared in *The Saturday Evening Post* and were later made into extremely popular motion pictures. Throughout the 1930s and 1940s *The Saturday Evening Post* had a long tradition of not portraying the American Indian point of view, and in Bellah's novels and short stories Indians were portrayed as savages who had to be subdued and chastised.[29] John Ford made the movie *Fort Apache* (1948) based on Bellah's short story "Massacre," which appeared in *The Saturday Evening Post* in 1946, and on "Big Hunt," which appeared in 1947. Bellah's "Command" (1946) was used as the basis of the screenplay for director John Ford's *She Wore a Yellow Ribbon* (1949), starring John Wayne.

Alan LeMay was another pulp writer who wrote westerns. Among his stories that ended up on the screen were *The Searchers* (1956) and *The Unforgiven* (1960). "The Searchers" was first serialized in *The Saturday Evening Post*, then became the motion picture *The Searchers* (1956), starring John Wayne and directed by John Ford. Unfortunately, the magazine's anti–Indian editorial policy at the time resulted in the depiction of the Comanches as a savage and cruel people.[30]

Ernest Haycox was a skilled author of western fiction who wrote original plots with engrossing and well-depicted characters. Haycox sold stories to the pulps in the 1920s when the most popular plots were limited primarily to external conflicts. He tried to make changes in this basic approach by writing into his stories heroes and heroines who had internal conflicts. Haycox changed his western heroes from characters who existed solely for action into ones that included some reflection on their circumstances. Haycox's editor at *Western Story* did not like this approach, so Haycox started to send his stories to *Short Stories* and *Frontier*.

Haycox understood that his readers preferred action to introspection, so he provided plenty of action in order to make his stories popular and acceptable to editors. Many of his heroes remained ominous figures of violence and death. But, at the same time, he modified his stories so that his hero reflected along the way and learned by his mistakes. But then Haycox concluded the story with plenty of action. This turned out to be a successful combination and these new stories allowed his western stories to advance from the pulps to the slicks, such as *Collier's* and *The Saturday Evening Post*. *Collier's*, in fact, published more Haycox stories between 1930 and 1945 than any other writer.[31] The success of this type of story was the inspiration for many other writers. After 1945 Haycox sold mostly to *The Saturday Evening Post*. His novel *Canyon Passage* was serialized in *The Saturday Evening Post* in 1945 and was made into the motion picture *Canyon Passage* in 1946.

Haycox's most famous short story was "Stage to Lordsburg," which appeared in *Collier's* in April 1937. It became the motion picture *Stagecoach* (1939) with John Wayne and directed by John Ford.[32] Another Haycox story was filmed by Cecil B. DeMille as *Union Pacific* in 1939.

Luke Short was another popular author who wrote many novels that were turned into films. Short wrote dozens of novels and hundreds of short stories about the Old West in pulp magazines such as *Ace High*, *Star Western*, and *Western Trails*, in the process becoming one of the great names in western fiction. His colorful fiction stories had an authentic flavor of the Old West.

Frederick Dilley Glidden had worked as a newspaper reporter, a logger, and a trapper in Canada before he took the pen name Luke Short in 1936 after the famous real-life gunman.[33] Short's first novel was *The Feud at Single Shot*, published in 1936. He wrote slam-bang, shoot-'em-up action stories about frontier justice and right triumphing over evil. His heroes were strangers on horseback who rescued heroines from villains against overwhelming odds. This popular formula created 50 stories that sold over 30 million copies. His stories were serialized in *The Saturday Evening Post*, *Collier's* and *Adventure*. Glidden was familiar with the West and the Rocky Mountains as he lived and worked in Aspen, Colorado.

Frank Gruber was another author who was able to master the transition from the pulps to the slicks. He wrote at least 50 western novels between 1934 and his death in 1969, about half of which were made into films. His first western novel was *Peace Marshal*, which was serialized in *Adventure* magazine in 1939. Most of his stories were action stories and did not focus on character development and the hero's inner conflicts.

Gruber felt that there were seven basic plots as opposed to Max Brand's single one. He grouped them as the cavalry vs. Indians, the railroad story, the ranch story with homesteaders and squatters in conflict with land barons, the dedicated lawman story, the outlaw story, the revenge story, and the empire building story.[34] Gruber admitted, though, that these basic plots weren't as important as what the author did with them. So he expected that each story line would be expanded, added to, reversed, and given new twists.

Because western motion pictures were very popular in the 1930s and 1940s, there was a short-lived attempt to link pulp western stories directly to the movies. The magazines *Movie Western* and *Cowboy Movie Thrillers* illustrated their stories with publicity stills from B-western cowboy movies. Unfortunately, there were two basic problems with the concept. First, and most important, was that black-and-white still photographs from the movies did not reproduce well on cheap pulp paper. The ink smeared and soaked into the paper, and thus made the reproductions very poor. The second problem was that most of the photos had nothing at all to do with the stories they were used to illustrate. This was done deliberately due to concerns over copyright infringement, and the magazines even printed a disclaimer to that effect to inform the reader. Sometimes writers were given photos from a movie and told to concoct a story around them. But they were also told to be sure that the stories had nothing to do with the movie that the photograph came from.[35]

13

Pulps for Everyone

Though pulp magazines continued to serialize stories up to the 1940s, by the early 1920s readers were not as enthusiastic with serial publication as they had been fifty years earlier. They did not like having to wait a week or a month to see how the next chapter of a story turned out, thus the publication of serialized stories started to decline. Typical of this trend was *Western Story*, which by 1945 boasted a slogan on the cover that said, "All Stories Complete." The magazine had found that its readers were less likely to read and persevere with a long serial story.

Various other factors also influenced serial publication. For example, serial novels were more difficult to write as authors had to be prepared to speed up or slow down, or lengthen or shorten the story as they were writing it, depending on what else was appearing in the same issue of the magazine. Even more serious was postal reform legislation proposed by Senator Eugene Loud in 1897 in an attempt to decrease the delivery of serial novels through the mail. As a result, the quality magazines shifted away from a serial novel format and published more stories in a complete short form. Even pulp magazines moved towards publishing a complete novel in a single issue, and by the 1940s serialization of novels was rare.

The sheer volume of pulps that were sold monthly obviously reflected the tastes of the mass market. Readers could chose from stories about war, pirates, romance, exotic adventures, the West, detectives, sports, science fiction, mysteries, horror, terror, aviation, sea stories, or a host of other topics. The magazines that crowded the newsstands and attracted millions of readers each month contained boundless creativity, often with few attempts at logic or believability or, in the case of the later pulp magazines, of particularly good taste. But they were a barometer of popular and social culture, even though many were full of misogyny, xenophobia, and racial and sexual stereotypes.[1]

Pulp fiction provided writers with a decent living while allowing their imaginations to run free as they explored the exotic in the pages of their stories. Most of the pulps were written to a publisher's formula, with standard plots and characters, and rudimentary prose, but they provided a happy conclusion to leave readers with an upbeat feeling at the end. Fighting against apparently insurmountable odds, the hero wins the girl and subdues the villain.

As the 1930s progressed, men could read magazine stories and novels about Nazi spies and the coming of war. In the 1940s, stories turned to the global conflict and stories of wounded men returning home. In the 1950s, during the Cold War, stories included Communist plots in Eastern Europe. Popular plots for women were stories about waitresses, jungle explorers, schoolteachers, artists, singers, secretaries, and divorcees.

Pulps magazines were an incredibly diverse lot. No matter how specialized a reader's interests, there was probably a pulp magazine to cater to him or her. Some of the self-explanatory titles were *Oriental Stories, Dr. Death, Railroad Stories, Railroad Magazine, Foreign Legion Adventures, Zeppelin Stories, Big Chief Western, Nickel Western, Speed Adventure, Strange Tales, Black Book Detective, Dime Mystery, Horror Stories, Thrilling Detective, Top Notch, Air Stories, Popular Magazine,* and *Action Stories.* Other specialized magazines whose focus was advertised in their titles were *Courtroom Stories, Fire Fighters, Speakeasy Stories, Racketeer Stories, Speed Stories, The Feds, Prison Stories, Scotland Yard, War Birds,* and *Public Enemy* (later renamed *Federal Agent*).

Among the adventure pulps were *Sea Stories, Golden Fleece* (historical adventure), *Mammoth Adventure, The Magic Carpet, Jungle Stories,* and *Pirate Stories.* Among the sports pulps were *Sport Story, Football Action, Fight Stories,* and *Baseball Stories.* Aviation and war pulps included *Dare-Devil Aces, Sky Birds, War Birds, War Stories, Navy Stories, RAF Aces, Over the Top* ("Front Line Fighting Stories"), and *Wings.* Popular detective pulps were *Clues Detective Stories, Detective Fiction Weekly, All Detective,* and *Spy Novels Magazine.* For the women, romance magazines included *Love Story, Ranch Romances, Popular Love,* and *Husbands* ("The Illustrated Monthly Magazine of Meeting and Winning"). The exploitation pulps included *Horror Stories, Spicy Adventure, Spicy Mystery, Spicy Detective, Dime Mystery Magazine,* and *Terror Tales.* Supernatural pulps included *The Thrill Book, Strange Tales, Ghost Stories,* and *Weird Tales.* Science fiction included *Startling Stories, Planet Stories, Marvel Science Stories,* and *Thrilling Wonder Stories.* Among the hero pulps were *Doc Savage Magazine, The Shadow, The Avenger, The Wizard, The Spider, Nick Carter, Secret Agent "X,"* and *The Phantom Detective.*

There were too many genres and titles of pulp magazines to list them all here, but several categories are worth looking at in a bit more detail.

Sports

Sports pulps were always popular, with representative titles being *Thrilling Sports, Baseball Stories, Exciting Football, Popular Sports,* and *Super Sports.* Street & Smith's *Sport Story* magazine had circulation of 150,000 a month in 1923.[2] Popular Publications competed with a sports magazine named *Dime Sports.* In the early 1930s a typical issue had a baseball story, a rowing story, a tennis story, and a boxing story, supported by other related features and columns. *Fight Stories* magazine from Fiction House was primarily limited to hard-boiled fiction about boxing, accompanied by factual articles about famous boxers. A typical cover showed a boxer in the ring reeling backwards after another one has just slugged him, with a buxom blonde on the sidelines cheering on the winner.

Pulp sports magazines specialized in every type of activity a reader could want. The December 15, 1913, issue of *Top Notch Magazine* even offered a story about the now-forgotten sport of automobile polo, where players standing on the running boards of open touring cars roaring and sliding around a grass-covered field hung on as best they could while trying to hit a ball with a polo mallet.

Aviation Stories and Flying Aces

Aviation stories started to appear soon after the Wright Brothers made their historic first flight in 1903. Their adventures generated a great interest in flying and readers eagerly followed American aviation for the next 50 years. Boys wanted to learn how to fly, with the long-range goal of perhaps becoming a military or commercial pilot.

Estimates are that there were probably over 60 pulp series about aviation, with more than 400 titles devoted to flying activities. The first series of books devoted to flying appeared in 1909 with the *Airship Boys* series. Early stories focused on the activities involved with the first flights. As the use of aircraft expanded human knowledge about the world, popular stories were those written about exploration of relatively unknown areas by airplane, such as South American jungles, islands in the Pacific, and adventures over the North Pole.[3]

Capitalizing on heroic images from World War I, the aviation magazines turned to stories about the thrills of aerial fighting. Combination aviation and war stories appeared, inspired by the real-life flying aces and their aerial battles, which were known in slang terms as "dogfights." The first of this type of series was *Air Stories* from Fiction House, which appeared in 1927. Another that appeared the same year was *War Birds* from Dell Publications. The war stimulated the publication of other pulps such as *Wings*, *Flying Aces*, *Sky Birds*, *Sky Raiders*, *Battle Aces*, *Battle Birds*, *Dare-Devil Aces*, *War Aces*, and *Sky Fighters*. Their stories featured heroic Allied airmen flying biplanes made from flimsy canvas and wood, locked in mortal combat with ruthless German battle aces, roaring through the clouds and the skies of France and Germany as they chased after each other with blazing machine guns.

Public interest in aviation increased after Charles Lindberg's solo flight from New York to Paris in 1927. As a result, for a time, aviation stories became one of the most popular pulp genres. There were also a few extremely specialized aviation magazines, such as the obscure *Zeppelin Stories*, which was devoted solely to stories about zeppelins.

These two excerpts from the story "The Flaming Arrow," published in *The Lone Eagle* in 1934, show the type of non-stop action writing used in these pulps. "His eyes followed a serried line of fresh bullet holes drilled through the right wing of his ship. They began close to the wing tip at the trailing edge, and ran up over the wing, towards the forward fuselage—toward the gas tank." Biplane cockpits were open at the time, so pilots were always zooming around at low altitude. The danger was obvious. "A jagged, chattering, crackling burst of Spandau slugs ripped above his head, cut the cockpit about him to ribbons, snapped a strut in front of his face."

Participating in these exploits was G-8, a hero with a World War I flying background who combined spying with aviation in the pulp magazine *G-8 and his Battle Aces*. G-8's flying background was fighting the German High Command under the Kaiser in World War I. One of the villains he encountered was *Stahlmaske* (Steelmask), a sinister German opponent who wore a steel mask with slits for his eyes to see through. One of this villain's bizarre schemes was to use a machine like an army tank to scoop up Allied soldiers and process them into canned meat to resolve the German food shortage. Stories often included xenophobic racial stereotypes, such as the Chinese Chu Lung, known as the Oriental Master of Death.

The cryptically-named G-8 was assisted by buddies Nippy Weston and Big Bull Martin, who were also expert pilots. They were all based in France out of a hangar at an airport at Le Bourget, north of Paris. The series was written by Robert Jasper Hogan, with input from Henry Steeger, the publisher of Popular Publications. The fantastic plots combined adventure and flying with science fantasy and horror. G-8 and his crew had to face perils such as giant bats with poison breath, invisible monsters, wolf-men, zombies,

Heroic images of real-life flying aces and the aerial battles of World War I spawned magazines that combined stories of aviation and air fighting during the war. One of these described the exploits of G-8, a hero with a World War I flying background who fought the Germans and German High Command. He combined spying with aviation as a flying secret agent in the pulp magazine *G-8 and His Battle Aces*.

a chemical that turned men into mummies, ray guns, and zombies. Other flying aces appeared in specialized aviation magazines, such as *The Lone Eagle*, *Bill Barnes Air Adventurer*, and *Terence X. O'Leary's War Birds*.

The interest in aviation pulps declined after the Great Depression, though a few magazines continued to describe flying activities between the two World Wars, and to a lesser extent, in World War II. The realities of war are never fun or glamorous. A particular war can only appear that way when distanced by time and memory. In the early and mid–1930s it was easy to romanticize the flying aces of World War I. They were distanced in time and space from the horror of the trenches and the battlefields below them as they flew in clear skies searching for German planes.[4] By 1940 the reality of a new war in Europe deflected the interest of readers and made them less interested in World War I.

Science Fiction and Space Stories

Science fiction was a genre that flourished in the 1920s and 1930s. Prior to the 1920s, there had been only a limited amount of science fiction published, such as the stories of Jules Verne and British author H.G. Wells.

Some earlier dime novel stories had featured steam-powered airships or vehicles, such as *The Huge Hunter* and *Electric Bob's Big Black Ostrich*, but these stories used inventions rooted in the technology of the day, and were not involved in scientific prediction. They were more in the genre of today's Steampunk adventures.

Another type of specialized fantasy fiction pulp, though not quite what we think of as science fiction today, contained Lost Race stories, about finding a race of people unknown to civilization in Central America, South America, or darkest Africa. One subgenre combined the two and used scientific inventions to find strange, out-of-the-way places on or under the earth, such as using steam-powered submarines to find lost cities at the bottom of the ocean or at the North Pole. Though the roots of this type of story can be traced back to Poe, Shelly, Verne, and Wells with their fantastic inventions and improbable adventures, stories about lost races and adventures on other planets had been previously scattered in different pulp magazines under various names, such as "science fantasy," "scientific romances," "fantasy," or "weird tales."

The specific genre of science fiction that combined speculation with a scientific basis to create fantasy stories first appeared in *Amazing Stories*, a pulp created by Hugo Gernsback, an immigrant from Luxembourg. Gernsback was an inventor and electronics tinkerer who came to the United States when he was twenty and started publishing the first radio magazine, titled *Modern Electronics*. In 1922 he had some space to fill in the magazine, so he wrote a story that was fiction interwoven with science. After experimenting with magazine names and the addition of more stories based on science, Gernsback launched the first periodical magazine devoted to science fiction, titled *Amazing Stories*, in April 1926. The magazine sold over 100,000 copies per issue.[5]

Gernsback originally created the name "scientifiction" to describe this new genre, but finally settled on the name "science fiction."[6] The term "science fiction" had actually been used as far back as 1851 for stories that combined fiction with instruction in the sciences, but Gernsback reinvented and popularized the term.[7]

Gernsback's vision was to create a magazine that was devoted to new stories based on science. Ironically, however, most of the early issues of *Amazing Stories* contained decades-old reprints of Jules Verne and H.G. Wells before progressing to feature newer unknown writers with a scientific bent. The cover of *Amazing Stories* for August 1927 shows Martians invaders in large metallic octopus-like robots, shooting out death rays that have turned the landscape into an inferno while helpless humans flee. Reprints like this of *War of the Worlds* by H.G. Wells helped to revolutionize the emerging genre of science fiction. Nevertheless, the contents of the magazine continued to be mixed. The cover of the March 1928 issue of *Amazing Stories* listed the contents as "Radio News, Science & Invention, French Humor, and Radio Listeners' Guide." The cover featured an illustration of a Chinese mastermind shining some sort of ray onto the face of a captive while a large group of hooded and masked men in black robes peer out through eye slits, watching them.

Gernsback's vision was that a science fiction story must be a tale of adventure (though often with a romantic component) modeled on accurate scientific knowledge and which predicted a likely course for technological advancement. The magazine contained attempts to predict future scientific developments, such as space travel and television, but they were unfortunately only occasionally accurate. Gernsback lost the magazine when he had to declare bankruptcy in 1929. But he kept trying and founded four more science fiction magazines, though none lasted longer than a year.

The name "science fiction" went on to serve as an umbrella for imaginative and speculative stories published in a variety of magazines and general adventure pulps. Stories covered a range that included hard science, pseudo-science, and even crackpot science, and often included the praises and warnings of advancing technology. Stories might involve other planets, the future here on Earth, or time travel. Some authors continued to write scientific romances that included only a smattering of science. The emphasis of the writers was on heroes and action, such as that provided by Edgar Rice Burroughs with his Mars and Venus series. Other ingredients might be spacemen and monstrous aliens, otherworld princesses, mad scientists, and dedicated researchers. Time travel and space adventures were popular and were used to combine the conflicts of modern man and more primitive worlds, as described in many of the stories of Edgar Rice Burroughs.

The pulp magazines of the 1920s and 1930s were considered to be disposable literature and had a reputation for low literary quality. Unfortunately, by association, science fiction appearing in these pulps was not perceived to be of a serious or literary type, but rather frivolous speculation and a juvenile commercial pursuit that was not really a suitable subject for serious writers. Some writers, however, did succeed. One of Gernsback's authors in the first issue of *Amazing Stories* was Curt Siodmak, who had been a journalist in Germany in the 1920s. Siodmak later went to Hollywood and Universal Pictures where he scripted *The Wolf Man* (1941), *Frankenstein meets the Wolf Man* (1943), *Son of Dracula* (1943), and *House of Frankenstein* (1944). Ray Bradbury, author of the acclaimed *The Martian Chronicles* that made him famous, made his start and flourished in the pulp science fiction magazines.

Another popular writer who succeeded was Leigh Brackett, who wrote science-fiction and fantasy sword-and-sorcery swashbucklers. She also wrote private detective novels in the hard-boiled style. She went on to success in Hollywood and worked on the movie adaptation of Raymond Chandler's *The Big Sleep* (1946). She continued to write science fiction and fantasy, but also the screenplays for movies such as *Rio Bravo* (1959), *Hatari!* (1962), *El Dorado* (1967), and *The Empire Strikes Back* (1980).

The 1930s were the boom years for science fiction pulps, starting with 3 in 1937, growing to 12 by 1939. Representative science fiction pulps that came and went were

Thrilling Wonder Stories, Amazing Stories, Comet Stories, Cosmic Stories, Wonder Stories, Astonishing Stories, Future Science Fiction, Planet Stories, Marvel Science Stories, Science Fiction, Future Fiction, Super Science Stories, Astounding Stories, and *Startling Stories*. The cover of the January 1942 issue of *Startling Stories* listed three fiction pieces along with several other departments, including "The Ether Vibrates" containing announcements and letters, "Science Question Box" which answered readers' queries, and a review of fan publications by a Sergeant Saturn.

The closest rival to *Amazing Stories* was *Astounding Stories*, which was founded in 1930. The magazine started with a mixture of stories featuring adventure, excitement, and eroticism, then later turned to disaster, catastrophe, and apocalypse stories. In 1938 a new editor, named John Campbell, was appointed. Campbell believed more in science than in fiction, and changed *Astounding Stories* to feature more science and technology-oriented types of writing than the original swashbuckling adventure stories. He changed the name of the magazine to

Science fiction stories for the masses often featured peculiar-looking beings known as "bug-eyed monsters," otherwise affectionately called BEMs for short, such as the odd creatures shown on this cover of *Astounding Stories* for June 1936.

Astounding Science-Fiction and moved to raise the overall quality of the publication. Notable writers that appeared under his editorship included Isaac Asimov, Robert Heinlein, Arthur C. Clarke, and Theodore Sturgeon. L. Ron (Lafayette Ronald) Hubbard was also a popular writer. Hubbard had previously written western and adventure fiction before turning to science fiction and fantasy.[8]

The new *Astounding Science-Fiction* offered adult-oriented science fiction that was aimed at intellectuals, as opposed to other publications that catered to a more juvenile audience who liked to read about rocket ships, ray guns, and bug-eyed monsters. Bug-eyed monsters, also referred to as BEMs, commonly appeared in the late 1930s as the villains of science fiction plots.

Science fiction tended to be categorized as either space opera or fiction that used hard science. Space opera was mostly not science oriented, but featured escapist plots

This is an example of the "brass brassiere" school of cover illustration that was popular in the science fantasy pulps, where women wore anatomically improbable metallic breastplates and abbreviated costumes in outer space. The invention of the brass bra in science-fiction magazines is commonly credited to artist Earle Kulp Bergey. This illustration includes the other staples of science fiction magazines, an alien monster threatening the girl and the complex controls of a complicated-looking spaceship, with an alien planet in the background.

and plenty of action. One of the most successful of the space opera genres used the interplanetary hero. Important elements were fiendish aliens, ray guns, and rocket chases. Others were sword wielding spacemen, bosomy blondes, and aliens firing ray guns. *Planet Stories* was a science fiction pulp that specialized in stories of interplanetary swashbuckling space adventure and only soft science. Similar was *Captain Future*, which debuted in 1940 and lasted four years. Each story had a super-villain, and in each story the hero was captured and escaped several times. It is easy to guess the theme of the plots as they often involved a super-scientist hero, a robot assistant, and a beautiful voluptuous female companion. A good example was the space opera comic strip Flash Gordon, who with his companion and love interest Dale Arden along with scientist Dr. Hans Zarkov, faces Ming the Merciless, the evil ruler of the planet Mongo.

As part of the imaginative fiction of unknown worlds, the science fiction and fantasy pulps became notorious for implausible, but memorable, cover illustrations showing women struggling against bug eyed monsters, robots, and mad scientists. In the grand pulp tradition, these heroines commonly wore tiny or translucent outfits. The cover of *Marvel Science Stories* for May 1951 for instance, shows two astronauts carrying an unconscious woman up a ladder into a spaceship, somewhere in outer space. Both the men are wearing space suits, sealed bubble helmets, breathing masks, and heavy space boots. The woman, on the other hand, is wearing only a diaphanous dress and flimsy slippers. A similar situation appeared on the cover of *Thrilling Wonder Stories* for June 1943. An astronaut is shown in a complex spacesuit complete with breathing helmet, facing an alien, bug-eyed-monster, while his female companion is wearing an abbreviated costume that looks like only a tight leotard top.

Women on the covers of the science fantasy pulps often wore skimpy outfits with anatomically-unlikely metallic breast coverings, in what became known as the "brass brassiere" form of cover illustration. The invention of the brass bra in science-fiction magazines, which depicted semi-naked women dressed in metallic underwear in outer space, is commonly credited to artist Earle Kulp Bergey.[9] A typical example was the cover of the March 1945 *Amazing Stories*, which showed a woman in a 1930s Buck Rogers–like space outfit, complete with a brass bra and headpiece, manipulating some complicated-looking science fiction machinery connected to a glass tank containing a devilish-looking green alien creature. Another example is the cover of *Thrilling Wonder Stories* for August 1950, which has a woman in an abbreviated outfit that looks like a metallic one-piece swimsuit with a brass bra, holding a smoking gun.

In the satirical article "Captain Future, Block That Kick," humorist S.J. Perelman wrote an appropriate commentary on Captain Future stories. His comments could also be applied to any of the science fiction and hard-boiled detective pulps when he said, "In pulp fiction it is a rigid convention that the hero's shoulders and the heroine's *balcon* constantly threatens to burst their bonds, a possibility which keeps the audience in a state of tense expectancy. Unfortunately for the fans, however, recent tests reveal that the wisp of chiffon which stands between the publisher and the postal laws has the tensile strength of drop-forged steel."[10]

Love and Romance

Popular women's pulps were movie and confession magazines aimed at the working masses. The modern love story magazine was invented by Street & Smith as a magazine version of their earlier romantic dime novels. In 1913 they tried to develop a market with *Women's Stories*, but the concept didn't catch on. They tried again in 1921 with *Love Story*. This was more successful, and by 1929 the circulation had climbed to 100,000. Daisy Bacon took over as editor in 1929 and pushed the circulation up to 600,000 by focusing on old-fashioned sentimental romance stories.

The publisher's perception of the market was astute. By the end of the 1920s, half of all single women in America were employed, and the romance pulps, such as *Cupid's Diary* and *All Story Love Stories*, were geared to schoolgirls, secretaries and other female office workers, serving girls in shops, and domestic servants. Another large part of the market was young married women.

Millions of women read the love pulps and confession magazines. The romance market became so popular that in the 1930s Street & Smith expanded their offerings with *Real Love*, *Romantic Range*, and *Pocket Love*. Their success spawned many imitators and other publishers followed with *All Story Love, Exciting Love, Gay Love, Ideal Love, New Love, Thrilling Love, True Love, Popular Love, Sweetheart Stories, True Confessions, True Story, True Romances, Cupid's Diary*, and *Modern Romance*.

Most of the stories were formula tales of flirtation, courtship, and eventual true love, and can be summed up as girl meets boy, girl marries boy. The titles of romance stories played on the theme of idealized love, such as the one titled "Miracle of Love" in one issue of *Thrilling Love*. Just as in the dime novels, one of the romance formulas focused on overcoming social barriers. A popular plot was the poor girl falling in love with a rich or aristocratic man. Another popular one was a heroine who overcomes the threat of casual romance and meaningless passion on the road to true love.

Many of these plots were essentially carried over from the dime novels. The lovers usually had temporary obstacles in the path of their relationship that had to be overcome, but all were resolved by the end of the story. The moral message of these romance stories was that love was triumphant and permanent, and able to overcome all obstacles and difficulties. The romance story affirmed the ideals of monogamous marriage and the domestic life of a wife, and the outcome was always a happy and romantic marriage. Men's adventure stories often contained a love interest, but romance was secondary to the hero's triumph over danger and physical obstacles. Conversely, women's romance stories often contained elements of adventure, but any danger was used as a story element to challenge and solidify the love relationship.

The plots of the romance magazines were written in what was considered at the time to be a sophisticated style that now seems quaint. There was no implication of sex or sleeping together. A plot might revolve around a single girl exposed to the wrong sort of men, such as underworld gangsters, or a wife who was tempted by the flirtations of single young men, but physical relations did not proceed beyond that.

Interestingly, the love and true confession pulps geared for the female audience were more popular than male-oriented magazines. One study showed that a combination of eighteen of these magazines sold 3,000,000 copies a month. In 1938 *Ranch Romances* sold almost double the copies and came out twice as often as *Black Mask*, which was published, distributed, and marketed by same parent company. *Ranch Romances*, actually outsold and outlived the male-oriented western magazines. *True Romances* had a circulation of 544,000 when that of *Black Mask* was only 66,000. Ironically, *Black Mask* in its early days had published romance stories in addition to men's adventures.[11]

Though some women read adventure stories and some men read romances, the story with the most appeal for men was the adventure tale. Men preferred a male protagonist. The western pulps for men, the so-called horse operas, were written from a completely male viewpoint and did not contain the entanglements of any personal and domestic problems. The female equivalent of the adventure story was the romance, and women preferred that it had a female central character who went through the development of a love relationship, usually between a man and a woman.

Many of the popular western love pulps were sentimental sexless soap operas in a Western setting. In them, the virtuous heroine is swept off her feet by a romantic suitor without a hint of violence or sex. They end with a chaste kiss and the offer to live happily ever after in wedded bliss. Representative love pulps that used a western background were *Rangeland Love Stories*, *Romantic Range*, *Ranch Romances* (subtitle "Love Stories of the Real West"), *Western Romances*, and *Thrilling Ranch Stories*. Popular Publications decided that because crime stories and romance stories were both doing well, they combined the two genres into *Underworld Romances*. It was not a good combination, however, and lasted only three issues due to a lack of coherent stories.[12]

Industrialization and urbanization of American society started to result in changes for women in the period between about 1912 and 1917. After World War I the country underwent a revolution in middle class morals at a time when women were questioning their roles in sexual freedom, birth control, divorce, and women's rights. Changes in divorce rates, crusades of muckrakers, and the efforts of birth control advocates challenged the mores of the day. The romance and true confession magazines, and later the erotic pulps, started to reflect these loosening morals as the country advanced from Edwardian propriety to the flapper-girl looseness of the 1920s.

The Spicy Pulps

There was another category of love pulp that did not refer to the romantic type of love, but catered to male readers. This was the type represented by *Saucy Stories*, started in 1915 by Mencken and Nathan, the creators of *Black Mask*.

Early sexy pulps were *Snappy Stories*, *Saucy Stories*, and *Snappy Magazine*. *Snappy Stories* was subtitled "A Magazine of Entertaining Fiction." These were the racy magazines of their day and were considered quite shocking at the time. The words "spicy," "snappy," and "peppy" in the titles were code words for "sexy." Other keywords meaning the same thing were "entertaining," "zippy," and "saucy." Other "hot" pulps included *Bedtime Stories*, *Scandals*, *Stolen Sweets*, *Cupid's Capers*, *New York Nights*, and *Breezy Stories*. Even racier were fringe sex magazines such as *Scarlet Adventures* and *Ginger Stories*. *Stolen Sweets* and *Tattle Tales* included tasteful paintings of nudes on their covers, which were considered to be the soft-core pornography of the time. As these were considered too sexy for open display on the newsstands, they were sold under-the-counter at cigar stores and other establishments that catered to men, and customers had to specifically ask for them.

The perception was that anything French was racy, thus French implications were prominent in the titles of magazines such as *Parisian Life*, *La Paree Stories*, *Gay Parisienne*, *Pa-ree*, *French Night Life*, *French Scandals*, *French Frolics*, and *Paris Nights*. *Paris Gayety* was subtitled "Snappy, Mirthful Stories of Worldly Pastimes."

These pulps came mostly from small independent publishers, rather than the mainstream publishers. Most of the authors of the stories wrote under pen names so that they would not be identified. Several well-known authors wrote for the spicy pulps as they were paid well for the time at 3¢ per word.

The covers of these magazines promised stories of premarital and extramarital sex, but everything on the pages inside was implied rather than being explicitly described. Stories were the likes of "She Couldn't Say Don't" and "All Undressed and Some Place to Go." The following appeared in "Hot Rompers" in *Parisian Life* in 1931. "Her red damask lips moved in ardent phrases, probably flattery; her passion-fueled eyes gleamed soft, melting, beseeching into Bert Hamlin's as he stroked her knee with insinuating privilege." Though perhaps mild for today, this was considered to be hot stuff in 1931.

One sub-genre of the racy magazines that deserves special mention was the spicy series of detective pulps. The reason they are interesting is that the stories that appeared in them eventually became almost parodies of the hard-boiled detective magazines. The trend started in April of 1934, when Harry Donnenfeld and Frank Armer at Culture Publications decided to put openly erotic material into genre fiction that featured cowboys, private eyes, and exotic adventurers. So they introduced what was called the spicy group of pulps, which consisted of *Spicy Detective*, *Spicy Western*, *Spicy Adventure*, and *Spicy Mystery*.

Culture Publications took conventional detective, mystery, and western stories and filled them with lust, lechery, violence, and a smattering of sadism.[13] *Spicy Detective* often had brutal and erotic mystery stories with sadistic themes that were mobster-dominated and featured blazing guns, beating up women, sex, and violence. The artwork was dramatized to match these themes. The publishers specialized in cover illustrations of women in lingerie, such as their underwear or see-through negligees, or with their clothing partially ripped away. Complete nudity was usually avoided, though it was often acceptable for female corpses. If female nudity was shown, it had to be portrayed delicately and tastefully. Males, on the other hand, had to remain fully clothed. If sex occurred between characters, it had to be treated delicately, more by implication and suggestion than direct description.

The violent stories published in the spicy line were mostly written by Culture's usual authors. Stories were similar to the previous conventional adventure and detective stories, but added racy descriptions of sex and seduction. These were basically tales of exploitation that featured attractive young women being stripped, tortured, beaten, or mutilated by gangsters or violent criminals. The morality of the story was preserved by having the hero arrive in the nick of time. While these stories might be considered relatively tame by today's standards, they provided erotic reading for the young men of the time, as they contained numerous references to white thighs, swelling bosoms, quivering breasts, and tight pants that clung to full hips.[14]

The covers of *Spicy Detective* usually featured scantily clad women in their underwear and the artwork inside contained similar lurid elements. The contents page of *Spicy Detective* for August 1936 for example, had five simple line sketches of semi-clad women, all of them with breasts exposed. The cover of *Spicy Detective* for October 1936 illustrated the basic elements of the spicy line, in this case a smoking gun held by a shadowy male figure with his arm around the shoulders of a buxom young redhead in flimsy lingerie, who is staring off to the side with look of horror on her face. These covers were often considered so racy that they were torn off before they were sold.

In *Spicy Adventure*, heroine Diana Daw was always losing her clothes for some tenuous reason during her adventures in exotic locations and other situations. Even *Spicy*

In April of 1934 Culture Publications took the conventional hard-boiled detective story and filled it with lust, lechery, violence, and a touch of sadism. *Spicy Detective* often had brutal and erotic mystery stories with sadistic themes that featured blazing guns, woman bashing, and sex. The covers were dramatized to match these themes. The publisher wanted more than a hint of bosom and stockings, and preferred illustrations of underdressed women threatened by violence.

Western had girls running around in their underwear and featured an undressed comic-strip heroine named Polly of the Plains.

One of the toughest of the private eyes in the spicy line was Dan Turner, created by Robert Leslie Bellem. Bellem wrote over 3,000 stories for the pulps, including 300 Dan Turner stories. Turner continually became involved with sexy women and often ended up in their bedrooms for some reason or other. Women were Dan's specialty and he was good at describing them in spicy's favorite terms of soft white breasts and creamy smoothness.

Bellem's writing became so outlandish that Turner became the stereotype of the private eye and Turner stories from the 1940s were so colorful that they were almost parodies of themselves. The continual references to racy women and Turner's hard-boiled attitude can be seen in the following quotes from Bellem's story "Death's Passport," which appeared in *Spicy Detective* in 1940. Instead of drinking whiskey: "I irrigated my jitters with a nip of the same medicine." On women: "I could see the sudden surge of her gorgeous watcha-callems under her fawn frock. I commenced shaking her until her thingumbobs jiggled like mounds of aspic in an earthquake." And the following quotes describe Dan Turner's hard-boiled toughness: "An attendant with a badge tried to halt me at the gate and I dished him up a helping of knuckles, sent him skidding on his pistol pockets." "The slugs had rendered him deader than the 1918 Armistice." These descriptions became so hilarious that humor writer S.J. Perelman took a gleeful satirical look at Dan Turner in "Somewhere a Roscoe..." in *New Yorker* for October 15, 1938, poking fun at the trend in underdressed dames and violence that was full of cliches.[15]

Dan Turner also appeared in comic-strip form in *Hollywood Detective* as part of the illustrated saucy antics of Queenie Starr. Starr, nicknamed the "Glamor Girl of Hollywood," was a Hollywood starlet who was always somehow losing her clothes and running around in her underwear, or undressing and changing into an outfit for a movie scene. These sort of antics were not restricted to the pulps. The English tabloid newspaper *The Daily Mirror* featured a comic strip named "Jane" from December 1932 to October 1959. During Jane's varied adventures she was continually—but accidentally—losing her outer clothing and running around in her lacy French underwear, garter belt, and stockings for no particular reason related to the plot.

As well as introducing over-endowed women, Bellem wrote stories about other tough characters, as in this quote from Bellem's "Labyrinth of Monsters" in *Spicy Mystery* in 1937. "Never in his wildest nightmare of hell-spawned horror could Travis imagine such creatures as menaced the girl who invaded his bungalow that night." He described the villain's assistant as having "Fang-like teeth jutted from between slavering, drooling lips; the eyes were oddly narrow, eerily gleaming with some demoniac and hell-born inner glow."

One of Bellem's other legacies to the detective story was his outlandish, dramatic descriptions of the noise of guns when they fired. Guns in Turner stories never went "bang." They went "ka-chow" or "chow." This type of sound-related description was used by other authors. Some guns simply went "blam" and machine guns gave out the symbolic sound of "rat-tat-tat-tat."

As happened with any successful pulp genre, imitators jumped on the bandwagon with their own erotic pulps, such as *Snappy Detective*, *Candid Detective*, *Private Detective Stories*, and *Romantic Detective*, though the latter did not have much to do with the romantic type of love. The lingerie-clad women who appeared on the covers of *Spicy Sto-*

ries, *Spicy Mystery*, and *Spicy Detectives*, inspired similar covers on *Dime Detective*, *Private Detective Stories*, and *True Gangster Stories*, all of which showed buxom young women with torn dresses and a bosom that threatened to fall out at any time. A similar trend could be seen in the movie and confession pulps. The attraction of Hollywood produced *Stage and Screen Stories*, *Saucy Movie Tales*, and *Film Fun*, which featured actresses and starlets who apparently spent their entire lives on and off the screen in the skimpiest of underwear.

In the end, the spicy pulps were threatened by the Post Office and opposed by the moral standards of many local governments. By the late 1930s the openly erotic detective magazines had either been suppressed or closed down. In response, Culture Publications stopped publishing the spicy line and replaced it with the tamer "Speed" line. In a similar move, Edmar Publishing changed "Spicy" to "Snappy" in its titles to produce *Snappy Detective Mysteries* and *Snappy Romances*.

14

Yellow Perils and Weird Menaces

One of the oldest and strongest emotions of mankind is fear. In spite of the often unpleasant stimulation of being frightened, people are fascinated with fear, thus literature that featured sensational tales of horror and the fantastic in order to frighten its readers has always been popular. Thus it is not surprising that specialized types of fiction that attempted to scare readers with grotesque stories appeared in the pulp literature. Three notable genres of this type of fiction were the yellow peril pulps, the horror pulps, and the weird menace pulps. Each had its own area of focus and each was equally peculiar.

The Yellow Peril

Xenophobic yellow menace or yellow peril stories had been popular since the turn of the twentieth century due to paranoid fears about foreigners. The so-called "Yellow Peril" stories promoted the fear that the British Empire and its white Christian civilization was in constant danger of being overthrown by villains who represented other races or racial mixes, typically yellow or brown ones. "Yellow" was an imaginary western designation that mostly encompassed those races now classified as East Asian. The prime example of this yellow threat literature was the evil Chinese doctor Fu-Manchu and his hordes of conspirators, who were constantly plotting against the safety and purity of English society. Anti-Chinese attitudes were common in the United States during the late 1880s and the 1890s, thus helping to popularize this type of yellow peril story.

In reality, most of the Chinese who initially came to the United States were innocuous low-cost laborers in the California gold rush of 1849. Many more came as construction workers to build the transcontinental railroad during the 1860s. Chinese workers were also important in West Coast wineries, dairies, vegetable fields, fruit orchards, and canneries, and often found employment as laundrymen, cooks, gardeners, or woodcutters.

Though the Chinese labor force was a success on the railroads and in the gold diggings and mining, the Chinese were probably the subject of more prejudice and hate than any other immigrant group to the American West in the second half of the nineteenth century. At the same time that the Central Pacific railroad was importing Chinese by the thousands as construction workers, the president of the railroad, Leland Stanford, was denouncing them as the "yellow menace."[1]

The Chinese were tolerated in the beginning, but their success as laborers and small businessmen was their undoing. The Chinese were at the bottom of the labor scale and were willing to work for very low wages, which created a white resentment of cheap Chinese labor. Prejudice and a fear of losing jobs were voiced among white workers as a fear of economic competition. Essentially white workers were angry that the Chinese were willing to work harder for less pay. In reality, these competitive economic fears were groundless. In mining areas of the West, the Chinese merely sifted through old worked-out mine dumps that the whites had abandoned as worthless. The shops that the Chinese operated usually sold only Chinese goods that whites didn't want. As cooks or in laundries, the Chinese worked for much lower wages than whites would accept.

The Chinese tendency to work, live, and socialize together also aroused suspicion. White Americans were offended by Chinese culture, eating habits, language, unusual clothing, dissonant music, religion, secret societies, and a generally different way of life.[2]

Some anti–Chinese agitators went further and translated their fears and racial prejudice into violence. Violence was aimed not only at individuals, but mob violence targeted the entire Chinese race. The Chinese were frequently cheated, beaten, and robbed. They were often run out of town, and were sometimes even murdered. Legal retribution for these events was either slow or non-existent.

Part of the anti–Chinese attitude was inspired by their use of opium, which was used at the time as an excuse for persecuting the Chinese. Opium dens were common in almost every large city in America. The sociable atmosphere of the surroundings, a pleasant interaction with fellow smokers, and a place to temporarily escape from worldly pressures made the drug attractive to smokers. But, though opium smoking was not as widespread as morphine injection among whites at the time, it was the subject of widespread horror. Smoking opium in sordid surroundings was considered to be a dreadful Chinese wickedness, and opium dens were considered to be perverters of morals. Associated whispered rumors of debauchery said that respectable white women were smoking opium and then engaging in wild orgies with Chinese men afterwards. This fear was created not so much out of a fear of addiction as it was from the racial hatred associated with the Chinese and their reputation as the Yellow Peril. As a result, opium houses were relegated to the parts of town that included the other major establishments of vice, such as low-class saloons, gambling houses, brothels, and dance halls.

In spite of this, morbid fascination with opium dens was high. Opium dens appeared in Victorian literature to provide the type of stories that fascinated readers at the same time that they found them repellant. *The Mystery of Edwin Drood* by Charles Dickens, published in 1870, uses opium smoking at several places in the plot. Dickens actually visited an opium den in Bluegate Fields in London, where he may have gained inspiration for the old woman who supplies the opium. Another popular Victorian novel that used opium as part of its theme was *The Picture of Dorian Gray* by Oscar Wilde, originally serialized in *Lippincott's Monthly Magazine* in 1890.

Thrill-seekers who were not content with mere newspaper accounts toured local Chinatowns, hoping to experience depraved opium dens, debauched white women in a state of undress, houses of Chinese prostitution, and shady gambling dens. To meet their expectations, they were often led by evil-looking guides through dimly lit passages and underground tunnels to visit bogus dens set up in dank and dreary cellars.

All this background helped to popularize the Yellow Peril stories. Prejudice was amplified by whispered lurid tales and rumors. But even before the popularity of such stories, Victorian journalists looking for sleaze and scandal to report to the reading public had sought out Chinese opium dens, looking for lurid stories of corruption, excitement, and vicarious danger. Their sinister descriptions of squalid, wretched opium dens appeared in melodramatic newspaper and magazine accounts, and opium dens became one of the staples of sensationalist Victorian literature. Even Arthur Conan Doyle added fuel to the fire with the Sherlock Holmes adventure, "The Man with the Twisted Lip," in which Dr. Watson goes to an opium den in London to search for his missing friend Isa Whitney.

Mark Twain (Samuel Clemens) visited a Chinese opium den while he was a reporter for The *Territorial Enterprise* of Virginia City, Nevada, in the early 1860s. He reported that the "stewing and frying of the drug and the gurgling of the juices in the stem would well-nigh turn the stomach of a statue."[3] The London *Daily News* in 1864 described an opium den in an area called Palmer's Folly. A headline in the *Denver Tribune* of October 12, 1880, was "The Deadly Drug: A Young Man of Denver Falls Victim to the Prevailing Chinese Vice." A reporter for The *Rocky Mountain News* of October 27, 1880, stated that the den he visited was full of white women stupefied by the drug.

As a result of lurid stories like this in books and newspaper articles, the public equated the Chinese with everything evil and saw them as the primary symbol of degeneracy and corruption. Thus the concept of the "Yellow Peril" entered the imagination of the people. This resulted in stories that pandered to the fear that Japanese and Chinese hordes were ready to spread all over western Europe, destroying western civilization in the process. This type of national fear was not new. The ancient Romans worried constantly about the "barbarian hordes" waiting to overwhelm them from outside, and American colonists worried about slave revolts and Indians attacking during the night. This new manufactured worry, however, was fear of "the yellow man."

The Yellow Peril fears of the late twentieth century were also the result of worries about the precarious condition of British imperialism and the threat to white global dominance by non-whites in the colonies. The paranoia was based partly on China's increasing military power, and fears that the Asian empires would sink the world into a sea of blood rather than carry on the orderly progression of civilization that was part of the concept of Manifest Destiny and Imperialism. Whites celebrated divine expansion and technological progress as being unique to Europeans.[4] These fears were amplified by people who should have known better. English historian Charles Pearson, for example, was one of the most influential promoters of the idea of the Yellow Peril. In his book, *National Life and Character*, published in 1893, he proposed that there was going to be a tremendous population explosion of Asians who would challenge white dominance and threaten the white establishment and supremacy.

Race paranoia was amplified in the wake of Imperial Britain's reaction to political events in China at turn of the century. In 1900 hundreds of British officials were killed in the Boxer Rebellion in China. In 1912 the Manchu dynasty, which had ruled China since the seventeenth century, was overthrown. These events fueled the fear that the subjects of the British Empire would revolt and attack the white world. The long tradition in Europe of Asia competing with the West was also perceived as a threat. The result of all this fear and paranoia was Dr. Fu-Manchu, the literary creation of Sax Rohmer. Fu-Manchu represented a world divided between East and West, and was the personification of deep-seated anxieties over global relations and the interaction of cultures.

Sax Rohmer was the pen name of a young writer named Arthur Henry Sarsfield Ward. Ward had at one time been a bank teller and was struggling to sell short stories as a journalist. He was fascinated with the exotic aspects of the East and the occult, and his lurid turn of mind invented Fu-Manchu while researching a newspaper story on London's Chinatown.[5] As Sax Rohmer, he took the anxieties of the public about the mysterious

East and combined them with urban legends of vice, crime, and opium addiction in the London slums to create a fantastic world of sinister thrills.

Between 1913 and 1917 Ward wrote a series of very popular novels about a mysterious Chinese scientist named Dr. Fu-Manchu, whom he portrayed as the personification of evil. The doctor was the fiendish embodiment of a mysterious invincible foreign power bent on world domination. In the manner of Sherlock Holmes and Dr. Watson, Rohmer's Fu-Manchu stories are narrated by a Dr. Petrie, who has no first name in the stories. Rohmer supposedly borrowed the name from Flinders Petrie, a well-known archeologist of the time who made exact measurements of the Egyptian pyramids.

Fu-Manchu's intent was to use his intellect and Eastern cunning to try to destroy the western world and surpass it in its goal of colonial development. Fu-Manchu planned to dominate the world, which in late Victorian times was perceived by Ward to be the British Empire. To achieve this ambition, Fu-Manchu was backed by undisclosed wealth and secret resources from his government. In reality, in spite of the fears of a Chinese take-over, the Chinese population of Britain was only 147 in 1861, increasing to 665 by the early 1880s.[6] But many of these Chinese lived in London's Limehouse district, which Ward featured in the stories as a place of danger and mystery.

"Tall, lean and feline, high-shouldered, with a brow like Shakespeare and a face like Satan, [and] a close-shaven skull" is how Sax Rohmer described his Oriental villain Dr. Fu-Manchu. The slave girl in the flimsy translucent outfit was typical of the sensationalist paperback covers of the 1950s, which were designed to catch the male eye on a bookrack and stimulate purchase of the book.

Sax Rohmer became the popular and prolific author of dozens of exotic thrillers and mysteries, rising rapidly from literary obscurity to a fame that lasted almost 50 years. Fu Manchu was the central figure in 13 Rohmer novels published between 1913 and 1959, which resulted in a massive readership in both England and America.

The start of the Fu-Manchu saga was composed of a series of interconnected short stories in a British fiction magazine, starting with "The Zayat Kiss" in October 1912. In 1913 the stories were reprinted in book form in London as *The Mystery of Dr. Fu-Manchu*.

This and the later novels revolved around melodramatic action-filled stories that included the doctor's deadly arsenal of rats, spiders, fungi, and centipedes, all of which were guaranteed to revolt—yet fascinate—staid literary audiences. Fu-Manchu's henchmen included Negroes, mulattos, Burmese thugs, Chinese martial artists, Malaysian dacoits (robbers), lascars (East Indian seaman), stranglers, and various other criminals and assassins.[7]

Rohmer's Oriental villain was given stereotyped turn-of-the-century racial characteristics associated with "all Chinamen" of being cruel, clever, and cunning. Fu-Manchu was portrayed as well educated, remote, and arrogant in his vision of Chinese superiority, and combined exotic ancient eastern knowledge with modern western scientific scholarship. Rohmer introduced Fu-Manchu in the first few pages of the book in this xenophobic, stereotyped description as evil personified. "Imagine a person, tall, lean and feline, high-shouldered, with a brow like Shakespeare and a face like Satan, a close-shaven skull, and long, magnetic eyes of the true cat-green. Invest him with all the cruel cunning of the entire Eastern race, accumulated in one giant intellect.... Imagine that awful being, and you have a mental picture of Dr. Fu-Manchu, the yellow peril incarnate in one man."[8]

The locations for these Victorian pot-boilers included, of course, opium dens. In Rohmer's first book, *The Mystery of Dr. Fu-Manchu*, the hero, crime fighter Police Commissioner Nayland Smith, and his faithful companion and chronicler Dr. Petrie go to an opium den by the River Thames in search of a missing undercover policeman. Smith has been recalled to England from Burma to combat Fu-Manchu, as Smith has uncovered forbidden knowledge about the impending Yellow Peril.

Unlike traditional villains or the Indians of the East Coast of the early dime novels, Fu-Manchu does not desire or pursue white women. He does, though, employ a beautiful Egyptian slave woman named Kâramanèh as a useful tool to assist him in his fiendish plots. She features in the stories as a puppet of Fu-Manchu, but in pulp novel tradition she is conveniently attracted to Dr. Petrie in her own way, and helps him to escape various predicaments because of this attraction.

Sax Rohmer was not the first to write Yellow Peril books, but he was certainly the most popular and the most copied, and his stories raised the level of paranoia about Asians to new heights. One early Yellow Peril novel was *The Yellow Danger* by M.P. Shiel, published in London in 1898. The protagonist, who is not unlike the later Fu-Manchu, is Yen How, a medical doctor of Chinese/Japanese descent studying in England. He vows to destroy the white race and conquer the world for Orientals after a woman rejects his romantic advances. The cover of one version of the book shows a giant evil-looking Chinese man with a pigtail clawing at a model of the world with his long fingernails, all outlined against a background of brilliant red and yellow rays of the sun.

Later Yellow Peril stories took their inspiration from Rohmer's Fu-Manchu tales. The emphasis of these stories was on simple plot structure and plenty of fast action, with a treatment of stereotyped Asian villains that would today be far from politically correct. From the 1920s to the 1940s, fantasies of Asian invasions was the raw material of the emerging genre of science fiction. Asians were used to play out the fantasies of race hate, revenge, and militaristic aggression that were rooted in mainstream American and European politics. Characters in the stories were portrayed in either black or white terms, either all good or all bad with no in-between personality development or complexities. As had happened in the earlier Indian and captivity stories, yellow or brown skin became a label for evil.

In the mid–1930s Popular Publications tried to re-invent the Yellow Peril literature with the introduction of two pulp magazines featuring sinister Oriental villains. The first was Wu Fang, created by Roland Daniel. Wu Fang first materialized in a pulp magazine titled *The Mysterious Wu Fang*. His appearance was very similar to Fu-Manchu, and the plots were much the same. Like the Fu-Manchu stories, the locations for the plots were often shrouded with mysterious fog that concealed deadly perils. Similar to Nayland Smith, who was forever chasing Fu-Manchu, Wu Fang had a pursuer named Val Kildare, who had previously been an investigator with the Secret Service. The magazine was discontinued soon after it appeared.

In 1936 Popular Publications tried again and introduced *Dr. Yen Sin*. To save money, the first issue featured an unused cover left over from *Wu Fang*. The villain of the stories, Yen Sin, who appeared to be just like Wu Fang and Fu-Manchu, was pursued by Michael Traile. Traile was also known as The Man Who Never Sleeps, as the result of an unsuccessful brain operation that was bungled by a Hindu surgeon. Admittedly, though, this lack of sleep allowed him plenty of time to pursue Wu Fang and other varied evil-doers, including stranglers, spies, and exotic women, as well as to indulge in his various other hobbies, such as reading.

Yellow Peril fears were still very much on people's minds just before the outbreak of World War II. The cover of the first issue of Street & Smith's *Unknown* magazine in March 1939 showed a giant, evil-looking Chinaman looming over a globe and clawing at the East Coast of America. The bottom quarter of the cover depicted a city in flaming ruins. Though the specific city was not named, it was obviously intended to be New York.

The May 27, 1939, issue of *Argosy* showed a fierce-looking Japanese soldier carrying a rifle with a bayonet attached, standing on a map of the United States that is being consumed by flames. The title of the story was "Tomorrow" by Arthur Leo Zagat, and the accompanying sensationalistic verbiage screamed, "Will your children walk in chains as slaves of the Yellow Horde?" This was the first in a series of xenophobic stories that had as their theme the invasion and occupation of America of the future by unnamed Yellow hordes.

Cover artwork for the Yellow Peril literature matched the writing with visual melodrama in order to provide the maximum in sensationalist appeal. A favorite theme was to imply some sort of Yellow menace to helpless women. For example, *Detective Story* magazine for October 5, 1916, contained the story "The Yellow Claw" by Sax Rohmer. The cover shows a woman with a fearful expression on her face looking over her shoulder at a partially open door. From the darkness behind the door a claw-like hand is reaching out to turn off the light in the room. The specific menace is unseen and unknown, but the implications are that she is threatened and terrified by some sort of Yellow Peril.

Another example of this type of lurid artwork was the cover of *The Master Detective* for January of 1930, which showed a villainous-looking Chinaman with a greenish face, long fingernails, and a claw-like hand, wearing a black skullcap. He is looming menacingly over a blonde white woman who is cowering wide-eyed below him. Her dress is pulled low at the front to show one shoulder and large expanse of bosom. The woman is scared, yet is obviously fascinated and transfixed. She is ready to scream, but nothing is coming out of her mouth because her Chinese assailant has mesmerized her with his steely gaze and a threatening claw-like hand. The titles of the stories on this melodramatic cover were "The Murdering Bride of Philadelphia," "Who was the Twin Cities Arch-Killer?" and "The Mad Doctor in the Third Floor Rear." Though the titles sound very grim, none of these inside stories involved an Asian villain or protagonist.

The concept of the Yellow Peril never totally went away and, even in the 1950s, paperback books showing a fear of Chinese villains were still appearing on the newsstands. In 1950 James Hadley Chase wrote a detective thriller titled *12 Chinamen and a Woman*. The essence of the plot was that a woman is seeking revenge against Cubans who are smuggling Chinese labor into Florida, and who have killed her Chinese lover. In true pulp fashion, the cover promised "a virile mixture of hard men, soft ladies, and shameless violence." The artwork emphasized a close-up of the face of a terrified woman surrounded by a group of evil-looking Oriental faces. The impression from the cover painting is that she is about to be raped by a group of sinister-looking Chinese. The story inside, however, does not include any situation like that.

Pulp Horror

The first pulp magazine that specifically featured tales of horror and the fantastic was *The Thrill Book*, published by Street & Smith in 1919. Only 48 pages long, the magazine specialized in stories of the strange, the bizarre, the occult, and the mysterious. Writers were encouraged to send in their oddest stories with the invitation from the editors, "If you have an idea which you have considered too bizarre to write, too weird or strange, let us see it." *The Thrill Book* apparently wasn't as thrilling as its name. It didn't find enough of an audience to survive and lasted for only 16 issues over seven months. *Ghost Stories* was another pulp magazine that featured "uncanny, spooky, and creepy tales."[9]

One of the oldest and undoubtedly the most successful of the pulp horror and fantasy magazines was *Weird Tales*, a Chicago-based pulp founded in 1923. When the magazine was first published, it specialized in science fiction, occult fiction, and mystery, and the best of haunting and horror stories. In the 1930s it was the premier market in the world for supernatural fiction. Even in the golden age of pulp writing and fantastic tales of the 1920s and 1930s, the unique stories in *Weird Tales* were bizarre, and adverse publicity has subsequently made it possibly the most famous (or infamous) of the pulp magazines. *Weird Tales* was a strange and often unpleasant magazine. It was considered tasteless and unhealthy even by some of the others in the mainstream of pulp publishing.[10]

Weird Tales magazine was created by Jacob Clark Henneberger, who was the publisher of *The Collegiate World* and *College Humor* magazine. The first issue of *Weird Tales* magazine appeared on the newsstands dated March 1923, with the featured cover story titled "Ooze" by Anthony M. Rud, about a giant amoeba terrorizing the deep South. The first issue contained 24 stories, 192 pages, and sold for 25¢. The concept of the magazine is best indicated by some of the other stories in the first issue, which included "The Grave," "The Place of Madness," and "The Ghoul and the Corpse." Though the magazine remained in business for 30 years and 279 consecutive issues, sales were seldom above

Opposite: *Weird Tales* **promoted itself as "a magazine of the bizarre and unusual," specializing in publishing traditional and unusual horror, fantasy, and weird menace. The stories in** *Weird Tales* **really were weird and the authors who wrote them cultivated the reputation for being a little offbeat themselves. Though sales were seldom above the break-even point and the magazine never made much of a profit, it remained in business for 30 years as the most influential magazine in the history of fantasy and horror publishing.**

14. Yellow Perils and Weird Menaces

the break-even point. The magazine never made much of a profit and always had financial difficulties. Finances were so shaky that authors were often paid late, well after publication date.

The first editor of *Weird Tales* was Edwin Baird. The early stories he selected featured a broad range of fiction. The magazine was edited in the 1920s and 1930s by his more famous successor, an ex-reporter named Farnsworth Wright, who increased the horror content, focusing on a variety of bizarre stories that featured vampires, voodoo, galactic science, and ghost stories.

Weird Tales was unique in its devotion to occult and fantastic fiction. It even promoted itself on the cover as "A Magazine of the Bizarre and Unusual." The magazine specialized in stories of traditional and unusual horrors, fantasy, and weird menace. The stories were grotesque, containing grinning ghouls, creepy mummies, haunted mansions, deformed mutants, creatures from graves and tombs, vampires, werewolves, witch doctors, wolfmen, spiders, graveyard rats, black masses, sorcery, and even necrophilia. The magazine also contained reprints of classic horror tales by authors such as Daniel Defoe, Edward Bulwer-Lytton, and Edgar Allan Poe.

The covers for *Weird Tales*, showing violent action and beautiful women nude or in various states of undress, often featured brilliant red and yellow colors to catch the eye of a potential purchaser. Many of the covers were painted by Margaret Brundage, a Chicago housewife. Brundage was well qualified. She had attended the Chicago Academy of Fine Arts and trained as a fashion artist, but soon found that work for an artist was hard to find during the Depression, so she approached *Weird Tales*, who liked her work. Usually Brundage did several sample sketches to illustrate a story then asked editor Farnsworth Wright pick one of them and she completed it. She later recalled that he usually chose the one with the least clothing. Wright felt that his choice was the best for the covers and would sell the most copies.[11] Publisher Henneberger also preferred artwork on the cover and inside to show women with little clothing on.[12]

Though this type of art, which was considered by some critics to border on the erotic, appealed to schoolboys, it was not really reading approved by parents. Admittedly, though, stories that featured breakneck action and kinky sexuality were among the readers' favorites. Typical of this trend was the April 1934 issue that featured "Satan's Garden" by E. Hoffman Price. It was described as "The story of a terrific adventure, two beautiful girls, occult evil and sudden death."

In spite of its focus on the grotesque, *Weird Tales* was the most influential magazine in the history of fantasy and horror publishing, and helped to launch the careers of such notable writers of horror as H.P. Lovecraft in 1923, Robert E. Howard in 1925, Clark Ashton Smith in 1928, Robert Bloch in 1935, Henry Kuttner in 1936, and Ray Bradbury in 1942. Among its other well-known authors were Otis Adelbert Kline, Seabury Quinn, August Derleth, C.L. Moore, and Fritz Leiber.

Three of the regular and very popular contributors to *Weird Tales* were Robert E. Howard, H.P. Lovecraft, and Clark Ashton Smith. Robert E. Howard wrote adventure, western stories, fantasy, boxing, swashbuckling, and detective fiction, but his most popular tales were sword-and-sorcery stories. His most famous and successful creation was Conan the Barbarian, a fierce warrior-hero who lived 12,000 years ago, in a time of magic and monsters in the supposed pre-historic Hyborian Age. Conan was one of *Weird Tales*' most popular characters. The Conan stories were packed with ruthless action and drenched in blood. The tales were full of magic, monsters, spectacular violence, and voluptuous women. Conan fought mostly against magicians, sorcery, and malevolent wizardry, and amused himself in his leisure time with beautiful underdressed women. As a thief, pirate, and mercenary, most of his time was spent in violent fights. Seventeen of the Conan stories were published in *Weird Tales*, mostly in the 1930s. Interest in Conan faded away after World War II, until a revival of the stories in paperback in the 1960s made him popular all over again. Conan in later violent sexy comic books probably made as much money for Marvel as Spiderman. Howard invented several other similar warrior-hero characters, such as Solomon Kane, a sixteenth century English adventurer, and King Kull from Atlantis, another barbarian whose adventures took place in the dark times of prehistory.

Another of the popular authors who appeared in *Weird Tales* was C.L. Moore, whose story "Black Thirst" was described in the magazine as, "Another weird and thrilling tale about Northwest Smith, by the author of 'Shambleau'—an amazing story of ultimate horror." C.L. Moore was in reality Catherine Lucille Moore. Another *Weird Tales* author, Henry Kuttner, wrote to her thinking from the initials that she was a male author. After an exchange of letters that helped to straighten out the misunderstanding, the two were eventually married.

Part of the reputation of *Weird Tales* was that its authors were weirder than those of the other pulps. One of the odder ones was H.P. Lovecraft, who wrote grim and disturbing stories of horror that included stark portrayals of evil. Howard Phillips Lovecraft's real family was touched by eccentricity to the point of actual insanity. His father was institutionalized and mother was neurotic. Even Lovecraft, when he wrote of himself as a child, admitted, "I was very peculiar."[13]

When he grew up, Lovecraft was an eccentric recluse, but was probably the best-known and most widely-published writer of weird pulp fiction at the time. His preoccupation with death and decay led to his famous story "Cool Air." His stories at the time did not have a large readership and he did not receive much recognition during his career, except by a group of enthusiastic fans. His real fame came after his death in 1937. Today everything he wrote is still in print. His stories have been translated into many other languages, and have been dramatized on radio, television, and film.

Lovecraft's stories were influenced by Edgar Allen Poe, Ambrose Bierce, Arthur Machen, and Lord Dunsany. Though Lovecraft's prose may not always be the best and some of his plotting is mechanical, his stories are genuinely gruesome and fantastic. Editor Edwin Baird did not like Lovecraft's stories and rejected them, but publisher Clark Henneberger did and overruled him. Lovecraft's stories were so popular with the publisher that when Baird left the magazine, Henneberger offered Lovecraft the editor's post to replace him.[14]

Lovecraft's first short story for *Weird Tales*, "Dagon" (written in 1917) appeared in the October 1923 issue. After this, Lovecraft's fiction found a ready market and in 1924 several of Lovecraft's stories were published in *Weird Tales*, where most of his work later appeared. Lovecraft wrote 53 stories. Some of his most well-known were "The Outsider," "Pickman's Model," and the horror tale "The Rats in the Walls," which appeared in *Weird Tales* in March 1924. Lovecraft was also a ghostwriter for other authors of horror stories. His best-known ghostwriting job was "Imprisoned with the Pharaohs," which was written for stage magician and escape artist Harry Houdini.

Lovecraft's main theme was stories of weird and terrible galactic outsiders, and he is most famous for a series of stories that have been called The Cthulhu Mythos. They are a series of loosely connected bizarre nightmare tales, starting with "The Call of Cthulhu," published in *Weird Tales* in February 1928 as a 13,000-word novelette. In succeeding stories, Lovecraft developed the theme that the world was originally inhabited by a race of beings that practiced black magic. The stories are about confrontations between good and evil, and the power of the evil extraterrestrial invaders to survive hidden in our world. They were expelled into outer darkness, but are always lurking in the background and keep reappearing because of the foolish actions of ignorant mortals.

The Cthulhu Mythos is a blending of supernatural horror and science fiction. Lovecraft never specifically gave it this name, but referred to the tales as "Yog-Sothothery," after one of his evil Ancient Ones. The name "Cthulhu Mythos" came from other writers. Lovecraft wrote thirteen of the Mythos stories, and encouraged his friends, many correspondents, and other writers to extend the legend. Writers such as August Derleth, Clark Ashton Smith, Frank Belknap Long, Robert E. Howard, and Henry Kuttner added almost a hundred more stories.

Lovecraft's Cthulhu Mythos is similar in many ways to the Christian Mythos, which describes the expulsion of Satan from the Garden of Eden. Lovecraft's forces of evil are represented by the Ancient Ones, or the Great Old Ones, who rebelled against the defenders of order, the Elder Gods. The leader of the Ancient Ones is a blind idiot god named Azathoth. Other unspeakable horrors included Yog-Sothoth, Nyarlathotep, Hastur the Unspeakable, the Great Cthulhu, and Shub-Niggurath, also known as "The Black Goat of the Woods with a Thousand Young." Cthulhu is a type of water creature, Shub-Niggurath is a fertility god, and Hastur is a primal force of the air.

Lovecraft's success was due to innovation in his horror stories. He did not rehash the old topics of ghosts, werewolves, vampires, haunted castles, and similar supernatural elements. Instead, he built his stories around conventional settings, frequently using almost a documentary reporting technique. His tales often use the literary device of presenting hints, and bits and pieces of fragmentary evidence, then leaving the reader to fit all the pieces together. This technique forces the reader to think for himself, and thereby often creates more horror in his imagination than is in the actual story. This same technique was used the vampire tale *Dracula* (1897), in which Bram Stoker used excerpts from characters' diaries to let the reader figure out the reality for himself.

Lovecraft believed that the premise of any successful story had to be based on a convincingly constructed background and set in familiar surroundings. His technique was to start with existing knowledge and then add new supposed "facts" on top of that base. He often created a very dry factual story background by referring to books and newspaper clippings. Another of his methods was to use a credible narrator for the story, such as a fictional renowned professor from a university, and to invent the proper credentials for him. Many of the tales were told by supposed academics from Lovecraft's fictional Miskatonic University. Thus the plots were constructed with an imaginative twist added to accepted reality. From there Lovecraft continued into the realm of the impossible.

To add convincing believability to the stories of his Cthulhu Mythos, Lovecraft invented a series of reference books of secret knowledge. The primary book he often mentioned was his fictional ancient volume, the *Necronomicon*, supposedly written by the mad Arab Abdul Alhazred. When referencing it, Lovecraft hinted that it contained dreadful and frightening hints of the Ancient Ones. He gave the arcane book a very believable history and background, including references to translations into Greek and

Latin versions. In fact he made it so believable that the book has been occasionally requested from libraries and rare book dealers.[15] Lovecraft also invented the similar fictional *Pnakotic Manuscripts*, the *Book of Dzyan*, and the *R'lyeh Text*. Lovecraft's friends and other writers of Cthulhu fiction contributed similar references. Clark Ashton Smith invented the *Book of Eibon*, and Robert E. Howard contributed the *Unaussprechlichen Kulten* of Von Junzt. As an inside joke, Robert Bloch, who was later to become famous as the writer of the spooky motion picture *Psycho* (1960), developed a play on words on the name and ancestry of August Derleth, a friend and correspondent of Lovecraft and founder of Arkham House which published revival editions of Lovecraft. The book he came up with was Comte d'Erlette's *Cultes des Goules*.[16]

Like some of the ghouls in its stories, *Weird Tales* went through four different incarnations. The initial *Weird Tales* was published in 1923 and the magazine lasted until 1954. The magazine was sold in 1938 and the offices moved from Chicago to New York. By the 1950s the magazine was still afloat though it was now struggling, and could not repeat the success of its early years. It managed to remain in business until September 1954 when it finally folded. In the 1970s a pulp revival of the magazine that primarily featured reprints lasted for only four issues. Two more issues of the magazine appeared in the mid–1980s, then in the late 1980s a fourth attempt to return was made by publishers George Scithers, Darrell Schweitzer, and John Betancourt, which lasted into the 1990s.

Trying to repeat his literary success with *Weird Tales*, former editor Farnsworth Wright later founded an adventure fantasy magazine named *Oriental Stories*. It lasted for only nine issues. He rapidly renamed it *The Magic Carpet* and specialized in exotic adventure stories. The change was no more successful and the magazine folded after five more issues.

In the early days, *Weird Tales* had essentially no competition. If a bizarre story did not sell to them, it usually did not sell at all, and went into the writers' reject files. By the 1940s other magazines that also published weird fantasy had appeared, such as *Astounding Stories*, *Amazing Stories*, *Fantastic Adventures*, and *Unknown*. Science fiction pulps, such as *Astounding*, *Thrilling Wonder Stories*, *Startling*, *Thrilling*, *Famous Fantastic Mysteries*, and *Planet Stories*, were on the newsstands. *Fantastic Novels* appeared from Munsey, though it consisted mostly of reprints from *Argosy* and *All-Story*.

Other publishing houses produced magazines to compete with *Weird Tales* that were less-successful, such as *Tales of Magic and Mystery* and *Ghost Stories*. *Strange Tales*, published by Clayton Magazines in September 1931, lasted for only seven issues. Another short-lived effort was *The Fantasy Fan*. Better Publications put out *Strange Stories*, but it was also short lived. Street & Smith started *Unknown* in 1939 as a companion to *Astounding Science Fiction* and a rival for *Weird Tales*. Its horror and fantasy stories were more modern and "logical." The publisher changed the title to *Unknown Worlds*, but it was not much more successful and only lasted for thirty-nine issues. Indeed, none of horror and fantasy pulps were financially successful—or even very stable—as the readership for these types of stories was too small.[17]

The Weird Menace Pulps

The weird menace pulps were the ultimate effort by publishers to frighten readers and provide them with even more sensational and grotesque horror stories. They played to a morbid fascination of readers for every form of horror.

The weird menace pulps originated in October of 1933 when Henry Steeger of Popular Publications reworked the failing *Dime Mystery* magazine and introduced a new style of terror fiction magazine that became dubbed "weird menace" stories, also known as the "shudder pulps." The stories were about horror without the supernatural elements, and featured elaborate scenes of sadistic and bizarre torture. The villains were crazed fiends who seemed bent only on inflicting violent forms of torture on the heroines. The cover of *Dime Mystery* magazine boasted "The Weirdest Stories Ever Told." One was "My Lady of Death," which was described as a "spine-tingling terror novelette." The magazine also featured stories with titles such as "Girls for Satan's Birdcage," "Lash of the Living Dead," and "Beware the Boneless Death."

Part of Steeger's inspiration for changing the magazine was the continued popularity of Gothic romances. But the other part of his inspiration reportedly came from attending a performance at the Grand Guignol theater in Paris, which featured an acting company that attracted enthusiastic audiences to packed houses with realistic depictions of scenes of torture, horror, and bloodshed.[18] The Grand Guignol was known as "The Theater of Fear and Terror." The audiences watched extreme performances of simulated on-stage whippings, eye-gougings, and other bloody scenes that appealed to morbid popular tastes. The theater had its heyday in the 1920s and 1930s with plays such as *Castle of Slow Death*, *The Coffin of Flesh*, and *The Merchant of Corpses*. A particularly grisly performance was *Crucified; or, The Night of the Twelfth of May*.

The popularity of horror stories as entertainment was also being fueled in the 1930s by a series of motion pictures from Universal Studios, such as *Dracula* (1931), *Frankenstein* (1931), *The Mummy* (1932), and *Bride of Frankenstein* (1935), all of which helped to spur an interest in macabre stories. The continuing popularity of the sensations produced by horror films as a form of entertainment can be judged by the fact that when a remake of *Frankenstein* (1931) by Hammer Films as *The Curse of Frankenstein* (1957) was shown in England, nurses were stationed in theaters as a publicity stunt, supposedly to revive those overcome by the horror story they were watching. Nevertheless, theatergoers flocked to see the movie in spite of the alleged risk.

The grotesque stories in the first shudder pulps proved to be such a success that in 1934 Popular Publications came out with two other weird menace pulps, titled *Horror Stories* and *Terror Tales*. These also contained elements of unprecedented savagery, including sadistic sexuality. Stories had unpleasant titles such as "Little Beasts of Death" and "Brides for Satan's Pupils." *Horror Stories* ran stories with titles such as "Death Calls From the Madhouse," "Dance of the Beast People," and "Scourge of the Faceless Men."

By the late 1930s the weird mystery pulps were nothing but perversions and sadism tinged with sexual overtones, featuring helpless women bound and tortured by merciless fiends. The shudder-pulps concept was very popular, however, and by the late 1930s, Popular Publications had a combined circulation of its terror magazines of 1,500,000 copies a month.[19]

Seeing the success of this type of story, other pulp houses started publishing similar magazines in the 1930s with titles such as *Thrilling Mystery*, *Ace Mysteries*, *Uncanny Tales*, *Mystery Tales*, *Strange Detective Mysteries*, *Eerie Stories*, *Sinister Stories*, *Spicy Mystery*, *Strange Detective Stories*, and *Uncanny Tales*. These also featured gruesome, sadistic tales with titles such as "Models for the Pain Sculpture," "White Flesh Must Rot," "Flesh for the Swamp Men," "Meat for Satan's Locker," "Hosts of the Leper Men," and "The Tongueless Horror." One of the last of the shudder pulps to debut was *Eerie Mysteries*, which was first published in 1938.

Grotesque and sensational horror literature continued to be popular, such as this 1962 pulp magazine, *Fantastic Monsters of the Films*, from Black Shield Publications. This and several other contemporary magazines like it published stories and photographs from the best and the worst of the horror films and Saturday sci-fi serials that delighted movie audiences. Readers could also purchase a secret skull ring, a fake hypodermic bloodsucker, or a giant rubber spider for further entertainment, or they join the Fantastic Monster Club.

The shudder pulps catered to every conceivable form of torture and perversity, specializing in sadistic and frightening tales with bloodthirsty and psychotic descriptions of deformities, maimings, and disemboweling. The main theme of the shudder pulps was the torture of beautiful, innocent young women who were subjected to lust, insanity, and mutilation by deformed, grotesque sadists. The victims were often kidnapped brides or honeymooners who had stumbled into the wrong eerie old house at the wrong time. Continuing the gothic tradition, the settings involved storm-lashed nights over ruined castles that contained secret passages and mysterious dungeons filled with prowling madmen. Black magic and diabolical rites were added to heighten the atmosphere of menace and terror. Other disgusting shock elements often involved bloated rotting corpses and decaying flesh.

These were horror stories certainly, but not stories that featured the supernatural. This new type of story featured depraved fiends, ghoulish vivisectionists, deformed maniacs, sideshow freaks, fiendish criminals, devilish cultists, mad doctors, and insane scientists consumed by blood-spilling, eye-gouging, limb-hacking lust. These madmen were often masked or disguised, or wore long robes and cowls like monks to project a sinister appearance and add to the terror. The mad scientists was usually helped by a deformed assistant, such as a dwarf, a mutant, a cripple, or a hunchback, to help him.[20] The villains had permanently cruel facial expressions with piercing eyes. The motivation for the behavior of these mad doctors and their experiments was often obscure or bizarre. Stories and plotting might be weak, but the descriptions were detailed and ghastly, with explicit descriptions of sexual exploitation, sadism, and perversity.

As well as being grisly, the covers of these magazines were tinged with eroticism. The theme of the covers was generally sadistic, but also sexual, in nature, with the illustrations featuring young women in only bras and panties at the mercy of slavering madmen, depraved villains in hooded robes operated ghastly-looking instruments of torture, and young women naked or in tattered underwear being tortured with branding irons, vats of molten metal, cauldrons of boiling oil, and buzz saws.

Due to the increased popularity of these horror tales, in February 1935 *All Detective* magazine was reworked and retitled *Doctor Death*. Doctor Death was an old and crazy man who lived in a gloomy cave with walls covered by fungus, from which he waged attacks on civilization. Apparently this premise was not appealing for readers and the magazine lasted for only three issues. Another short-lived weird and crazy character was The Octopus, another madman who attempted to destroy civilization for his own bizarre reasons.

Weird Tales tried to add its own touch to the weird menace fiction with a character named Doctor Satan. This peculiar character wore a devil's costume, complete with a scarlet cape, a scarlet mask with devil's horns, and matching red rubber gloves. He wielded a variety of fantastic weapons, including an atomic ray that realigned the molecular structure of human skin. The readers of *Weird Tales* apparently did not take to the character, so he quickly disappeared. He did, however, appear in a fifteen-part movie serial titled *Mysterious Dr. Satan* starring Eduardo Ciannelli in 1940.

At the start of the 1940s the shudder pulps came under attack from the public, moral watchdogs, and politicians. World War II took its toll on weird fiction in the early 1940s and the interest in reading horror fantasy declined as people realized that the real horrors of war were far worse than what could be imagined in a story. As a result, *Dime Mystery* and the other Popular Publications shudder pulps toned down the blatant themes of sex and sadism in their magazines. The result was that sales started to sink and the market for weird terror declined. Unable to sustain themselves, the horror magazines folded and disappeared for good in the early 1940s.

In an effort to revive itself but still retain a bizarre reputation, *Dime Mystery* changed focus with its October 1938 issue and started to publish stories about detective heroes who were handicapped by deformities or birth defects, or who had bizarre diseases and medical problems. This gave rise to the nickname of the "defective detective" story. One detective, for example, suffered from amnesia, and another had deformed legs and was forced to crawl across the floor. English author Ernest Bramah wrote stories about a blind detective named Max Carrados, a wealthy man who had been blinded in youth. To compensate for his blindness he developed his other senses and faculties to the point where he could solve crimes.

15

The Pulps Fade Away

As America entered the 1940s, the heyday of the sensationalistic pulps was coming to an end. The decline and fall of many of the pulp magazines, however, had started previously due to the poor economic conditions of the Great Depression in the 1930s. Some publishers and magazines went bankrupt, some merged with others, and some were bought out by competing publishers.

By 1950, only a relative few of the western, detective, and science fiction pulps remained. Crime pulps that survived longer than most were *Ten Detective Aces*, *FBI Detective Stories*, *Thrilling Detective*, *Black Mask*, *All Story Detective*, *G-Men Detective*, *Dime Mystery*, *Super Detective*, and *New Detective*. In 1950 *Dime Detective*, *Black Mask*, *Detective Tales*, *Hollywood Detective* and *Popular Detective* were still on sale, but three years later all of them were gone. Pulp cowboy magazines were gone by the late 1940s and early 1950s, though romance westerns continued into the 1960s.

Two factors during World War II put increasing pressure on the publishers. One was a diminishing supply and increasing cost of pulp paper due to wartime restrictions. The other was the rise of comic books.

Paper was heavily rationed during World War II. Wartime restrictions curtailed any expansion of the industry and lowered the quality of paper used. As a result, many of the marginally successful pulps were discontinued during the war so that publishers could make better use of their paper allocation for their titles that sold best. Thus many of the niche publications of the 1920s and 1930s disappeared. Even after the war was over, production costs continued to soar. Between the end of 1944 and mid–1947, production costs rose by 72 percent.[1] Thus the combination of continuing paper shortages and rising costs pushed many of the pulp magazines out of business. Though a few outlasted the shortages, most of the rest of these magazines disappeared in the 1950s as Americans found new sources of cheap entertainment and thrills in lurid paperback novels, comic books, and television.

The first magazines to fade away during the 1940s were the hero pulps, as wartime readers rejected heroic fantasy for a more realistic world. By 1949, the American public's taste in crime fiction had also changed, which led to a more violent approach to stories in paperback detective fiction. Though most of the pulps were already gone by the 1950s, the rising popularity of comic books, radio, television, and motion pictures further decreased the popularity of the pulp magazines as mass entertainment and helped to speed the disappearance of the remaining ones.

The decline of the magazines also affected pulp authors. As there were increasingly fewer magazines, fewer stories were purchased and thus fewer writers were required to provide them. Some writers and stories crossed over to the slick magazines, such as *Cosmopolitan*, *Colliers*, or *The Saturday Evening Post*, and others to hardback novels. Some writers moved to Hollywood and churned out screenplays, and some stopped writing altogether and went to other jobs. Much of the story content, however, and many of the authors and cover artists, crossed over into the new mass-market paperback format.

Television

The final rival that helped to finish off the pulp magazines was the rising popularity of television. Television was still a novelty at the end of World War II and was found in only one percent of American homes. By 1953 television sets had appeared in 50 percent of homes. By the end of the 1950s this figure rose to 90 percent, and much of America's leisure time was filled by watching television instead of by reading.[2] Television completely changed America's entertainment habits. TV dinners appeared in 1954, making it unnecessary to even spend time preparing food and serving it in the dining room. Now a family could quickly eat in front of the television on a TV tray without interrupting their favorite show.

As the popularity of television as a free entertainment medium increased, many readers felt that the new television shows offered more realistic private eyes, cops, and cowboys, and stopped reading pulps. Even the popularity of comic books declined in the 1950s as the popularity of television grew. Television became so ubiquitous that critics became concerned about the effects of too much viewing upon the nation's young. Television supposedly made children neglect their homework, read less, spend less time outdoors in play, and spend their time slack-jawed in front of a glowing screen. According to a 1954 Gallup poll, 74 percent of adults believed that violence on television was a major contributor to violent juvenile behavior and juvenile delinquency, and criminal behavior among the young. Whether or not it does create this type of behavior has never been conclusively proven, but the fear was there. The same can be said for the playing of today's violent video games by the young.[3]

Comic Books

The second major factor that hastened the decline of the pulps was a rising competition from comic books, which offered readers the same world of escape, adventure, and romance. In essence, many of the comics were pulp stories recycled, which in turn had been recycled dime novels. One contributing factor was that, after World War II, paperbacks and comic books competed with pulp magazines for space on magazine racks. And they won. Comic books outsold the pulps as they had compact stories and could be read quickly by young readers. This took away much of the pulp audience as juvenile readers in particular turned to comic books and science fiction magazines for entertainment. Like the pulps, the comics covered a wide range of genres, encompassing crime, humor, war, the American West, romance, teenagers, horror, and science fiction.

Experiments with four-color comic books as a type of cheap magazine were under way as early as 1929. The quiet origin of the comic books as regular publications occurred in 1933 when Maxwell Charles Gaines of Eastern Color Printing took the comics section

As well as stories about superheroes, comic books featuring cute talking animals became very popular, particularly with girl readers. This comic book, featuring cat-and-mouse characters from the MGM cartoons, is an example of the popularity of the literary form, as this story of Tom and Jerry in "Tom Finds a Rare Bird" has been published in a French version.

from the traditional Sunday newspaper and redesigned it into a smaller size, 7 inches by 10 inches, and published it as *Funnies on Parade*. These "comic books" quickly attracted young readers. Gaines followed this success in May of 1934 by reprinting comic strips from newspapers to create *Famous Funnies* with a cover price of 10¢. The first comics used text in a box under the illustration, then later changed to bubbles laid directly over the action. Among others, the company published comic books about the Bible and American history.

Other competitors quickly followed. In 1934 Maj. Malcolm Wheeler-Nicholson, a former cavalry officer and pulp adventure writer, founded National Allied Publications to publish comic books. The layout used pulp plots and action in a cartoon format.

In 1935 Nicholson published *New Fun*, subtitled *The Big Comic Magazine*. One of the cartoon strips used Oswald the Lucky Rabbit, a character that had been created by Walt Disney and Ub Iwerks as Walt Disney Studio's first animated character. *New Fun* lasted for only six issues, but Nicholson persevered with the concept and started *New Comics*, which became *New Adventure Comics*, then was retitled *Adventure Comics*. This did much better than *New Fun* and lasted for 45 years under these different names.[4] As part of an expansion plan, Nicholson brought in two financial partners in 1937 and the three founded Detective Comics, Inc., later better known as DC Comics. Nicholson unfortunately overextended himself financially and was forced out of the business within a few years.

DC Comics published *Adventure Comics*, *Detective Comics*, and *Action Comics*. *Adventure Comics* provided a mix of action heroes, humor, and sports features. The first issue featured action-mystery stories that used the stock Chinese villains and typical heroes of the pulps. Heroes included a federal agent nicknamed "Speed," a freelance police investigator, and secret agent Bart Regan. One of the stories was "The Claws of the Red Dragon." *Detective Comics* featured private detectives and superheroes, such as the Crimson Avenger, and published the first Batman comic strip in May of 1939.

One of the minor characters who debuted in 1938 in *Action Comics* was Superman, written by Jerry Siegel and Joe Schuster, who had previously published an amateur magazine called *Science Fiction* in Cleveland in 1932. To their surprise the character was an unanticipated hit and DC Comics launched *Superman* as a comic with a single hero. This new comic book idea, with a superhero who could leap tall buildings and had x-ray vision, was very popular. By the seventh issue it sold 500,000 a month. The average issue sold 1.3 million copies, three to six times the sales of the typical comic book.[5] Similar to the old dime novel and pulp magazines days, readers could join the Supermen of America club and receive a membership certificate and a secret decoder to receive messages directly from Superman.

The management of DC Comics soon made the decision that all the stories in a particular comic would revolve around a single theme or hero. Superman was representative of these new superheroes. He was so popular that many other superhero imitators soon followed. In these narratives, endangered submissive women were always in need of rescue by super-powered men. Lois Lane, for example, was always being rescued by Superman from some peril in the nick of time. The majority of superhero readers and fans were boys aged from 12 to 17. Girl readers typically preferred romance stories and tales of funny animals. Thus the direction of the superhero narratives was determined by the purchasing patterns of the male adolescent.[6]

Though most of the readers were male, women superheroes were not absent. Wonder Woman made her debut in *All Star Comics* in 1941 and on the cover of *Sensation Comics* in 1942. She was created in 1941 by psychologist William Moulton Marston as an action heroine and role model for young women. She was intended to be a female hero in a male-dominated world. Marston believed that antisocial violent tendencies in society were caused by undesirable masculine traits. He felt that society would be more peaceful if these traits could be subdued by the socializing and loving influence of a powerful feminine figure with women's values. Part of the Wonder Woman theme was that men were supposed to submit to females.[7]

Wonder Woman's adventures, however, were not without criticism. Psychologist Marston frequently directed DC Comics to show her restrained in chains, as he felt that bondage increased her allure. She was usually the one who submitted, not the villains, and appeared in various episodes tied up, chained, gagged, bound, or otherwise manacled.[8] Another complaint was that her costume was more revealing than the male superheroes, consisting of a red bustier, form-fitting blue shorts, red boots, and a golden tiara. This tantalizing outfit led to objections that she was underdressed.

During World War II, comic books showed solid patriotism with their leading heroes fighting Nazi spies and infiltrators as the popular culture of the 1940s reflected the reality of the global conflict. Plots often featured real axis villains, such as Hitler and Mussolini, and Japanese saboteurs. Superheroes, such as The Shield and Captain America, battled Hitler. Publishers were fast to provide competitive comics and other hero characters, such as Aquaman, appeared. Villains, such as Lex Luthor (in Superman), the Joker, the Penguin, Cat Woman, Clayface, and Two-Face (in Batman), were developed. Superheroes in costumes were popular, such as the Green Lantern, the Red Tornado, the Flash, the Green Arrow, the Atom, the Spectre, the Submariner, Captain Marvel, Captain America, and a host of others.

Captain America dressed in a red, white, and blue costume that symbolized the American flag and had a big "A" on the forehead of his outfit. Captain America battled the Germans in Europe, the Japanese in the Pacific, and spies in America. When he was not dressed to fight for his country, he was in reality Private Steve Rogers. The cover of the first issue of *Captain America Comics* showed the hero punching Hitler in the face. His goal was to defend the territorial integrity of the United States against aggression.

After the war was over there was a downturn in interest in these super-patriotic characters. Superheroes like Captain America didn't have much reason to continue their exploits because the war had been won and there was nobody left to fight. As a result, *Captain America Comics* went through several changes, and finally disappeared in 1949.

Some superheroes, however, battled on. The superhero comics were replaced by lurid crime comics, which contained increased graphic depictions of violence and sex themes. *The Phantom Stranger* for August-September 1952 had the following description on the cover, "Out of the swirling mists of nowhere looms a mysterious figure to shield the innocent from the dark forces of evil … and then to disappear again into the void!"

Other comic book themes were introduced. All American Publications created *All-American Comics*, which consisted mostly of newspaper reprints, along with puzzles and a few of their own characters. They also published *Movie Comics* and *Mutt & Jeff*. In the late 1940s other types were added, such as romance, western, teen humor, crime, and funny animals. A few comics, such as *Our Army at War, Our Fighting Forces*, and *Star-Spangled War Stories*, had post-war themes. Jungle stories recycled themes from the pulps, such as *Congo Bill*, about an intrepid explorer and his sidekick in a leopard skin costume.

In 1948 comics with a western theme became popular. DC Comics launched *Western Comics*, featuring Rodeo Rick, the Vigilante, and the Wyoming Kid, and *All-American Comics*, with Johnny Thunder and Minstrel Maverick, who used his guitar as his weapon. This eventually became *All-American Western*. Again, very similar to the pulps, western and crime titles grew. Hopalong Cassidy returned in 1954 in *Hopalong Cassidy* comics, based on William Boyd's films, with photographs of the actor on the cover to illustrate the story. By the beginning of the 1950s superheroes were in decline, but science fiction comics rose in popularity as this was the beginning of the Space Age.

The popularity of comic books was not without its dark side and criticism was soon leveled at them. By the early 1940s, sales of comic books were in the tens of millions. *Action Comics* and *Superman* sold over two million copies a month.[9] In 1943 alone 25,000,000 comic books were sold each month. During World War II studies showed that comic books outsold major magazines by ten-to-one and, by the end of the war, comic books were far outselling pulp magazines. The *New York Times* reported that 25 percent of all books sent overseas to soldiers were comic books.[10] Studies in the mid–1950s showed that 12 percent of the nation's teachers and 16 percent of college graduates were reading comic books.[11]

There may indeed have been legitimate concerns as teachers and parents realized that millions of young Americans were not reading newspapers or magazines, but were reading comic books instead. Another issue was that, in order to attract readers, comic books had been increasingly adding lurid and graphic representations of kidnapping, torture, sex, violence, and crime. Critics felt that these violent depictions of anti-social behavior could induce corresponding violent and aberrant behavior in children.

One particularly outspoken critic was psychologist Frederic Wertham, who wrote a book titled *Seduction of the Innocent* (1954), claiming that comic books were dangerous and that the effects of graphic and violent themes were corrupting children. Wertham particularly disliked Wonder Woman and its implications of masochism. Other critics were concerned about the homosexual implications of the themes of millionaire bachelors and their young wards, such as Batman and Robin, and even the lesbian implications of Wonder Woman adopting a young girl.[12] *Crime Detective* magazine (subtitled "Real Police Cases") tried to sidestep the issue of morals by saying on the cover, "This magazine is dedicated to the prevention of crime. We hope that within its pages the youth of America will learn to know crime for what it really is. A sad, black, dead-end road of fools and tears."

What sparked much of the furor were the gruesome excesses depicted in William Gaines's EC Comics. The initials EC originally stood for "Educational Comics," but came to mean "Entertaining Comics." Gaines son, William, took over the company in 1947, and in the 1950s produced an explosion of horror, fantasy, crime, science fiction, and war comics. Both the themes and the illustrations were grotesque and gruesome. EC's publications had titles such as *Vault of Horror, Tales from the Crypt, Weird Science*, and *Shock SuspenStories*. These magazines were legendary and notorious for themes that included incest, bondage, sadomasochism, cannabalism, necrophilia, dismemberment, disembowelment, and family murders.[13] For example, the cover of No. 22 of *Crime SuspenStories* (sub-titled "jolting tales of tension in the EC tradition") shows an axe descending onto the out-of-view body of a young woman, then a second panel shows a hairy male hand holding up a dismembered woman's head by the hair. Horror and occult themes also appeared in *Mystery in Space, Strange Adventures*, and *House of Mystery*, the latter with titles such as "Wanda was a Werewolf" and "I Fell in Love with a Witch."

The frenzy that was raised over the gruesome drawings and text in these comics became so great that it led to a congressional investigation in 1954 and hearings about the potential corrupting influences of comic books. Testimony was gathered by the Senate Sub-committee on Juvenile Delinquency, headed by Senator Estes Kefauver. The threat of federal intervention led to the Comics Code Authority, a self-regulating group that was established in 1954 to review the editorial content of comics. The self-imposed industry guidelines they created included the following. "Guidelines of the authority prohibit displays of corrupt authority, successful crimes, happy criminals, the triumph of evil over good, violence, concealed weapons, the death of a policeman, sensual females, divorce, illicit sexual relations, narcotics or drug addiction, physical afflictions, poor grammar, and the use of the words 'crime,' 'horror,' and 'terror' in the title of a magazine or story."[14] The Comics Code specifically stated that "all scenes of horror, excessive bloodshed, gory or gruesome crimes, depravity, lust, sadism, masochism shall not be permitted," and specified that "violent love scenes as well as sexual abnormalities are unacceptable."

The power behind the words of the code was that magazine wholesalers refused to distribute comics that were not approved by the Authority, so in effect the Comics Code Authority put a rapid end to the production of lurid comic books, and the horror and crime comics quickly disappeared. This effectively abolished nearly all of E.C. Comics' magazines, leaving behind only their *Mad Magazine*, a satirical magazine that published biting parodies of American media and social customs.

The result was a return of the costumed heroes. Old ones were revitalized and new ones were created. Comic book titles and sales expanded, reaching a peak in the mid–1950s, with over 600 titles and sales of 90 to 100 million each month.[15] Popular genres included *Classics Illustrated*, which published illustrated versions of the world's great literary works, stories from Walt Disney, and cartoon animal characters from the movies, such as Tom and Jerry, Droopy, Woody Woodpecker, and Heckle and Jeckle.

The Rise of Mass-Market Paperbacks

After World War II, the pulp market shrank abruptly as cheap magazines declined in quality. The decline of the pulps occurred over a period from the mid–1940s to about 1960, as sales slipped away in the late 1940s and early 1950s and the market was taken over by paperbacks. Paperback books evolved from the earlier yellowbacks, dime novels, and pulp magazines. Some of the early ones were even reprints of old pulp novels and some were authored by the same writers who had written pulp novels. One perspective, then, is that paperback books were simply a new format for packaging cheap reading material.

Publishers had introduced cheap mass-market paperbacks in a small format just before World War II, but shortages of paper during the conflict limited any kind of business growth. Paperback books did not find their place until after the war when they became wildly popular and successful. In the economic boom that came after the conflict was over, many people who had not previously been considered part of the traditional book market started to read.

In the 1930s, hardback books were expensive, many of them costing as much as $2.50.[16] A further inconvenience for rural readers was that books had to be mostly purchased in bookstores in large cities. To counteract this, Allen Lane in England launched

Penguin Books in 1935 as an inexpensive form of paperback book. Though inexpensive, these were quality books, but were distributed like magazines in newsstands, drugstores, and department stores. In 1939 Ian Ballantine brought Penguin Books to the United States for American customers.

In late 1938, following the success of Penguin in England, a creative individual at Simon & Schuster named Robert Fair de Graff thought that perhaps he too could change the way people bought books by making them cheaper and small enough to fit both the hand and the pocket. This was a similar concept to that which spurred the origin of dime novels. De Graff obtained backing from the publisher and test marketed 2,000 copies of a soft-cover pocket-sized book of Pearl Buck's *The Good Earth*. The books were placed at random in stories in Manhattan and nearly all of them sold the same day. On June 19, 1939, Simon & Schuster followed this success with the release of ten more titles, each printed in 10,000 copies. The books were heralded by full-page advertisement in The New York Times that screamed, "OUT TODAY—THE NEW POCKET BOOKS THAT MAY REVOLUTIONIZE AMERICA'S READING HABITS."

The first ten titles were a mixture of culture and entertainment, including Shakespeare, Agatha Christie's *The Murder of Roger Ackroyd*, and James Hilton's *Lost Horizon*. The size was four inches by six inches, small enough to be tucked into a pocket or purse, and the cost was only 35¢. Using the business title of Pocket Books, with a kangaroo logo, this was the first American company to publish paperbacks on a large scale. There had been previous efforts by publishers, such as Street & Smith, to devise a form of mass-market paperback format for cheap reprints and books bound in paper for American readers during the early part of the twentieth century, but none had been successful or lasted long.

Like the earlier pulp magazines, paperback books were designed to be printed on roll-fed, rotary presses that were used to print pulp magazines and newspaper inserts. The original business intent for paperback books was to provide a cheap format in which to reprint of works of fiction and non-fiction. They were so popular, however, that they quickly became part of every publisher's product line.

The new paperback books were small enough to fit in the hand, yet the paper and binding were of good quality, and the books were easy to read, unlike other discount reprints of the day that had cheap bindings and tiny crammed type in two columns. As opposed to Penguin, who used sedate, uniform, non-illustrated covers, Pocket Books relied on full-color glossy covers like the pulp magazines to catch the eye of potential purchasers.

Looking for any potentially profitable market, de Graff put these small books where they hadn't been previously sold, such as in grocery stores, soda fountains, candy stores, drug stores, and in vending machines. Soon these cheap 25¢ books could be found in bus stations, train stations, and newspaper kiosks, aimed at working men and commuters on trolleys, trains, and subways. Many were sold in vending machines in airports and in train and bus stations, thus providing travelers with cheap reading material to take on their trips. Another target was stay-at-home mothers.[17] These novels of escapist literature allowed all of them to mentally escape temporarily from their conventional middle-class homes and lives.

Cheap paperback novels started to become a dominant form of entertainment for the masses, and within two years Pocket Books had sold 17 million copies. The business model was such a financial success that it attracted other major publishers, and by the mid–1940s many other companies had entered the paperback market. Printings of a million copies of a book were not unusual. Bantam Books, for example, sold 25 million books with western titles between 1947 and 1951.[18]

The competition among publishers became fierce. In 1941, when Avon Books was founded and published twelve reprints, Pocket Books sued Avon for infringement of their format. The courts, however, decided against them and ruled that not all small books could be called "pocket" books. The name "pocket book" became generic for paperbacks from Pocket Books, Avon, Popular Library, Dell, and Bantam, who were all publishing paperbacks and replacing the pulp magazines on the newsstands. After this decision, other publishers came out with their own versions of pocket books, though the war and paper shortages put a crimp in these new ventures. Pocket Library started in 1942, Dell in 1943, Bantam in 1945, and New American Library in 1949. New American Library had been publishing since 1939 as the American branch of Penguin Books.[19] The majority of the new paperback publishers were former or existing pulp houses that already had distribution channels in place and the resources to switch to paperback publishing and distribution.

Paperbacks originally concentrated on inexpensive (25¢ to 75¢) reprints of hardback originals, seeking their marketplace with working people who did not have a lot of money to spend on entertainment. These books were intended to bring quality authors to a large audience as inexpensive reading matter. The majority of the new paperbacks were reprints of hardbacks from trade publishers, covering a range of fiction, non-fiction, serious literature and "how-to" manuals. In 1945 there were 112 paperbacks in print. By 1946 there were 350 softcover titles in print, more than three times as many as in 1945. By 1946 the number was 353 and by 1951 it was 866, cranked out in cheap editions from Avon, Fawcett, Dell, Ace, Medallion, Gold Medal, Bantam, Cardinal,

Simon & Schuster started to publish their Pocket Book line of paperbacks in 1939, in a new format that was small enough to fit in the pocket and hand, yet were of good quality and easy to read. They were sold in airports, train stations, bus terminals, grocery stores, soda fountains, candy stores, drug stores, and vending machines. The first offerings from Pocket Books (with the kangaroo logo) were reprints of popular authors and books, such as P.G. Wodehouse and this 1939 paperback edition of *Jeeves*.

and Signet paperbacks.[20] Hardcover books were primarily sold in bookstores, but the new paperbacks were sold on newsstands and in drugstores alongside pulps, comics, and movie magazines, and depended on their lurid covers to attract readers. The paperbacks eventually crowded out the pulps.

Similar to the earlier dime novels and pulp magazines, the largest number of titles in the new paperback format were mysteries and lurid crime stories. Pocket Books started the trend in 1939 when it issued 34 reprints, of which four were mysteries. In 1940 it issued 53 reprints of which 19 were mysteries. Popular Library was founded in 1943 by Ned Pines and Leo Margulies of the Thrilling group of pulps. They reprinted 70 titles in their first three years, all of them mysteries. When Dell started in 1943, they published nearly all mysteries.[21]

Westerns were still popular in the 1950s and the pocket paperback book carried on the tradition of the dime novel cowboy with plots that included black-and-white morality, escapism, and nationalism. During one twelve-month period in the 1950s, of the 300 million paperbacks sold, 100 million were westerns.[22] Another indication of this popularity is that Bantam Books sold 25 million western paperback novels between 1947 and 1951.[23]

American filmmakers adapted many of these thrilling western novels into movies, which added a further boost to the popularity of the books. Conversely, the novels had a built-in audience of readers that were likely to go to see the movie when they had read and enjoyed the book. Almost any paperback novel (or film) about the Old West was all but guaranteed to make a profit, whereas many serious literary novels failed to recoup their expenses.

As paperbacks spread, they were not restricted to just westerns, mysteries, and lurid detective stories, but added titles that would appeal to a wider audience. Pocket Books exposed many readers to modern literature. Avon used paper covers of a heavy weight and had lurid covers like the pulp magazines; however, they also published popular and genre fiction books by literary authors, such as William Faulkner, Raymond Chandler, Noel Coward, and John O'Hara. Mentor published serious nonfiction works, such as the scientific text *The Birth and Death of the Sun* (1945) by Professor of Physics George Gamow, and James Coleman's *Relativity for the Layman* (1958). Of course, as well as quality nonfiction, Americans read millions of lowbrow paperbacks, crime stories, romances, mysteries, westerns, and steamy potboilers like *Peyton Place* (1956).

The new paperback boom was also good for authors. When Erskine Caldwell's book, *God's Little Acre*, was first published by Viking in 1933 it sold 8,300 copies. A later edition published by Modern Library sold 66,000 copies. But when it was released as a Signet paperback, the book sold three-and-a-half million copies in a year and a half.[24] More than 25 million paperback reprints of Caldwell's books were sold between 1945 and 1951.

Publishers of the first paperbacks mostly reprinted hardback stories. Soon, however, the popularity of the new format was so great that it forced them to find original manuscripts to supply enough material. In the 1950s publishers started to print more original titles and produce higher quality paperbacks in the $1.50 to $2 range. Paperback sales soared to 350 million by 1958. By early 1960s paperbacks were providing inexpensive reading matter for millions of readers and made up 30 percent of all titles published. The major markets were same outlets that pulp magazines had used for years, drugstores, newsstands, bus stations, supermarkets, army posts, and airports. But now paperbacks started to move into bookstores and college bookstores.[25]

Paperbacks and the Military

The paperback book concept that emerged before World War II was so successful that a group named the Council on Books in Wartime worked with the Office of War Information and the army and navy to develop the Armed Services Editions of paperbound books. During and immediately after World War II, these books, printed on cheap paper like that of pulp magazines, provided inexpensive editions of hardcover reprints and paperback originals in a compact paperback form for servicemen. These books were distributed free of charge to armed services personnel around the world between 1943 and 1947. The size and format made them convenient for soldiers and sailors, as they were designed to fit into the breast or hip pocket of a uniform. Similar to the Civil War and their mass distribution of dime novels to soldiers, paperbacks served as entertainment for World War II servicemen spending long and boring hours waiting for wartime action. The Council selected a wide range of books that were geared to all levels of literacy. They hoped that this exposure to books would create an attachment to reading in members of the military and raise the literacy level of those with a limited education.

The books were very popular with servicemen overseas as they were often the only reading easily available, and families were encouraged to send them to troops at the front. Several organizations sponsored book drives to send paperbacks to the soldiers. Publishers cited patriotic motives for buying their books and even the lowest escapist books were promoted in the name of morale and national loyalty. Pocket Books proclaimed, "Books are weapons in the war of ideas." Penguin Books and the *Infantry Journal* cooperated to produce Fighting Forces Penguin Specials.

The Council worked to distribute and deliver an estimated more than 123 million paperbacks to overseas servicemen in a cooperative effort with the army and navy, and private publishers and printers. Mysteries, westerns, classics, history, poetry, and best sellers, from popular to highbrow, made up most of the 1,322 titles distributed.[26]

This program was partly responsible for the phenomenal growth of mass-market paperback publishing in American following the end of World War II. Its success showed that mass-produced paperbacks were economically viable and technologically possible.

Paperback Cover Art

In an effort to boost sales, publishers soon turned to lurid artwork on the covers of paperbacks to attract purchasers, just as their pulp magazine and dime novel ancestors had done earlier. The covers of paperbacks became gaudier, the colors brighter, and the women's clothing became scantier and more revealing.

When paperbacks made their debut in 1939, crime stories were popular and early paperbacks were reprints of previously-published mild mystery stories by authors such as Agatha Christie. With time, however, the stories became more hard-boiled like Dashiell Hammett. In response, in the late 1940s, paperback book designers turned to the pulp magazines for inspiration for their covers. The result was sex, sadism, and the smoking gun. Like the earlier pulps, the tough and sordid realism of the stories produced lurid cover illustrations that used bold colors and dramatic illustrations. Many covers were in bad taste, often did not reflect the content of the book, and were merely designed to promote a book through sensationalism. Like the pulps, many covers depicted a moment of violence, illustrating a menace (usually to underdressed women) or some sort of erotic suggestion. Each cover was designed to illustrate an entire moment of drama—often more than the text it was suppose to portray—such as a hero grimacing at his opponent during an act of violence or a beautiful woman clutching a smoking revolver. Paperback covers flourished with an utter disregard for good taste and moral uplift, the covers were voyeuristic rather than decorative, and their illustrations became a fantasy rather than the real world.

This new style of cover was designed by art directors to hopefully stand out over the competition with gaudy colors and flagrant lasciviousness for someone passing a newsstand or drugstore bookrack. Many of the covers were lurid and colorful, steamy with hints of sex and violence. A common image was a woman in semi-transparent lingerie holding a cigarette, which implied a "bad" woman whose story would be further described inside the book. Another prevalent image was a woman in a bedroom, usually only half-dressed. Other popular cover topics were flying fists, corpses, and violence against women. A frequent image was a woman holding a gun, often threatening a man. The men's faces on these lurid covers were often contorted and grimacing. Publishers competed with each other to display the maximum amount of eroticism and violence from a limited set of circumstances. One example of a paperback that met these criteria in a single cover was a paperback from Popular Library, *Bodies are Where You Find Them* (1949) by Brett Halliday, which showed a woman with a lot of leg showing and wearing a see-through negligee, holding a revolver and struggling with a poorly-shaven man who is trying to overpower her. Another was the cover for *Case of the Red Box* (1937), a Nero Wolfe novel by Rex Stout, which shows a woman lying on the floor with her skirt hiked up to the tops of her legs, revealing stocking tops and an expanse of white thigh.

Imitating the method used by dime novels and pulp magazines, many paperbacks were repackaged with lurid covers on the front, and back covers written in terms to attract the reader. Books by popular authors, such as Zane Grey, for example, were republished in paperback form, year after year, with tantalizing pictures on the front covers and thrilling descriptions on the back covers to entice the reader to buy the book. One paperback version of *Forlorn River* shows a granite-faced cowboy shooting his gun, against the background of a wild eyed, rearing horse, with the description, "Forlorn River is a story of the Old West—of the lawless days of cattle-stealing and the thrilling pursuit and capture of wild horses. It is full of the intensity and dash which made up life then and which Zane Grey brings vividly to life in print."[27]

In the early 1950s there were many cries of indignation that paperbacks were becoming too blatant, and pressure was applied by the government to tone them down. But the trend continued through the 1950s. The cover for *Kiss Tomorrow Goodbye* (1949) by Horace McCoy from Signet Books, for example, has "Love as Hot as a Blow Torch.... Crime as Vicious as the Jungle" emblazoned across the top. The cover illustration shows a woman dressed in a black bra and tight black skirt taking off her blouse in front of a man sitting on the bed. Even nonfiction paperbacks were subject to this type of sensationalization.[28]

Magazines and Sensationalized Masculinity

Magazines, such as *True*, *Argosy*, and *Stag*, which were intended to appeal to male escapist fantasies and make the reader believe that he was a rough, tough he-man, dominated the pulp magazine market for men after World War II. Publishers used the same approach and appeal as the dime novels that made the reader yearn to be a cowboy or a circus star or a seafaring adventurer. These macho magazines focused on male bonding, with an emphasis on the outdoors and adventure.

One example of how a magazine succeeded by catering to these psychological needs and subconscious masculine desires was *True*. It grew to a circulation of two million by offering its readers a reassurance of their masculinity. Most of its readers were sedentary suburban dwellers, but the magazine catered to their desire to be all man by slanting its articles to make the readers feel as if he was a hairy-chested he-man who lived in the woods and participated in outdoor adventures every day. It catered to the male ego and desires.[29]

In spite of a lurid cover to attract buyers, this Signet paperback book was a serious history book of Denver's sporting ladies. A friend of the author's purchased it and was so disappointed that the interior text did not live up to the cover's promise that he was going to throw it away, but gave it to the author instead. This example from 1962 illustrates how the front and back covers of early paperbacks were designed to catch a casual browser's eye and sell a book with lurid pictures and lush descriptions (though not necessarily totally accurate) of the contents, just as the earlier dime novels and pulp magazines had done.

As the other pulps declined, so did the macho men's magazines. Though a few of these magazines were still around in the 1950s and 1960s, they were the very end of the pulp magazines. The few that remained emphasized he-man stories, and used the techniques of the pulps to promote themselves with lurid covers in sensational colors to attract passing buyers and boost sales. *Man's Magazine* for October 1961, for example, featured a huge leering face of German Field Marshal Kesselring that dominated the cover. The titles heralded him as "The Nazi Butcher of Rome." In the background a Nazi storm trooper is gunning down a shirtless man while other prisoners are forced to watch. Other lurid story titles on the cover were "10 Italians Must Die for Every German," "I Crashed an Insane Asylum," and "How Your Personality Affects Your Love Life."

When the macho male pulps vanished away, they were replaced by magazines with a quieter and more urban approach, but they still catered to male fantasies. They reflected the male need for escapist entertainment that started in the dime novels and appeared in the pulp magazines, only brought up to date for the modern urban male. The first of these was *Esquire*, which began as a men's fashion magazine aimed at the suburban male. It was first published in October 1933 in Chicago, becoming a monthly magazine with the second issue in January 1934. Pin-up drawings by George Petty, and later by Alberto Vargas, made it the most daring men's magazine in America during the 1940s. Petty's pin-up girls started in 1933 with their final appearance in 1956. The Vargas girls, created and drawn by Alberto Vargas, first appeared in October 1940 and continued until March 1946.[30] Vargas began his career in the 1920s as a poster artist for Flo Ziegfield and the Ziegfield Follies. When the Follies closed in the 1930s, Vargas switched to Hollywood and painted movie-studio posters. Blacklisted for union activity, in World War II he turned to painting pinups of long-legged dream girls for *Esquire* that made him world famous. The innocuous girlie paintings in *Esquire* by Vargas and Petty were given greater prominence during Work War II, so that the magazine could qualify for a bigger paper allocation. The claim was that these pin-ups boosted the morale of the soldiers and so contributed to the war effort.[31]

One of the young men hired by *Esquire* who worked as a promotional copywriter at $60 a week was Hugh Hefner. Before that he had worked as an advertising copywriter at a department store in Chicago, and then as a copywriter at two advertising agencies. At the same time he wrote, published, and promoted a paperback book of cartoons titled *That Toddlin' Town*. In 1951 *Esquire* moved its offices to New York and Hefner decided not to go, and went to work as promotion manager for Publisher's Development Corporation, a small magazine group that included some girlie magazines.[32]

Hefner considered *Esquire* to be the primary beacon of male tastes, fashion, and sophistication. He decided to start his own rival magazine, and *Playboy* magazine was born. The first issue appeared in November of 1953. *Playboy* brought the dime novels and pulp magazines full circle and up to date. *Playboy* was a young man's vision of escapist fantasy and romance (read sex) in the 1950s. The concept was to create an escapist guide to the ultimate good life for sophisticated young men, or those who wanted to be. Again just like the pulps, only repackaged for the 1950s male urban office worker. The idea was based on the male fantasy that each reader was a suave, worldly young man-about-town who lived in a penthouse, drove an imported sports car, dressed in the latest fashions, was knowledgeable about wine and song, and who was successful with women. Dreams and yearnings for action and risk were epitomized by the fictional James Bond, created by best-selling author Ian Fleming. Every reader fantasized that he was a jet-setting superhero enmeshed in bold adventures, beautiful women, fast cars, and sophisticated gadgetry. To complete the circle, Vargas girls first appeared in *Playboy* in March 1957, then appeared as monthly pinups from 1960 to 1978, which may have reflected nostalgia for Hefner's prior days at *Esquire*. The combination of escapism, adventure, and women was an unbeatable formula. In January 1957 *Playboy* sold 687,593 copies, as compared to 778,190 for *Esquire*.[33]

Escapism was still what readers wanted and publishers supplied.

Postscript

Dime novels and pulp magazines are no more. Just as the pulp magazines supplanted the dime novels, comic books and radio killed the pulp magazines, and finally television took over from all of them. However, the plots and characters in today's lurid and sensationalistic books and magazines have stayed much the same, though updated to modern times with specific situations, genres, and methods of presentation changing to match the updated tastes of the reading public. Sensationalized crimes, assaults, killings, thievery, kidnapping, murders, and associated criminals still flood our reading material and appear nightly on the television news. And new genres have been added with drug addiction, juvenile delinquency, racism, and homosexuality.

Victorian morbid fears and concerns of being buried alive were transformed in the 1950s to fears about the atomic age and the possibility of nuclear annihilation by bombs and radioactive fallout. This morbid fear was updated to gloom-and-doom science fiction stories of insect and human monsters created by nuclear war and radiation accidents. Movies reflected these fears in *The Beast from 20,000 Fathoms* (1953), *The Creature from the Black Lagoon* (1954), *The Blob* (1958), *Godzilla* (1954), *Crack in the World* (1965), and a host of giant spiders, scorpions, and other mutant monsters terrorizing the Earth. Later fears were reflected during the space race to danger from other worlds with titles such as *The Invasion of the Body Snatchers* (1956), and *The Thing from Another World* (1951), based on a 1938 story by John Campbell in *Astounding Science Fiction*.

Though the fear and fascination of the morbid and sensational seem like affectations of the past, they have not gone away, as revealed by a casual look at the checkout stands in grocery stores. Sensational tabloid newspapers continue to crank out stories that cater to the morbid, lurid, and sensationalistic tastes of the reading public. In the 1990s, the concept was extended to the newsmagazines on television, which feature sex, murder, and mayhem in the reporting of titillating sex crimes, bloody murder scenes, and real-life gory incidents. The television networks added sensationalized real-life quasi-documentary crime investigations to their program schedules because they are relatively cheap and easy to produce, and the viewing audiences love them.

Nostalgia for the vanished western frontier continues in paperbacks as a pulp fantasy vision of the West where problems are easily and simplistically solved. The image of the rugged Westerner, with his simple and free lifestyle, has been kept alive in advertising for whiskey, beer, cars, clothing, and many other products.

As censorship crumbed in the 1960s, sensational eroticism only hinted at in the pulp magazines of the 1930s became mainstream, and erotic fiction in paperbacks was increased in terms of graphic descriptions by a host of small paperback publishers. Topics such as gay and lesbian pulp fiction from mainstream publishers like Cleis Press and Kensington Publishing became acceptable and were sold by respectable bookstores. The earlier chaste romance novels morphed into the lusty sub-genre of paperbacks known as "bodice rippers," where romantic fiction added rape and threatened rape for the reader's titillation.

Similarly, detective and mystery fiction has become more graphic. Violence, revenge, and retribution, and graphic descriptions of all three are still part of popular literature today. Consider these passages from 2004 from *Persuader* by Lee Child, one of the leading and best-selling authors of thrillers today. "I pulled my head back and hooked one hand under his jaw and put the other flat against the side of his head. Wrenched his jaw hard to the right and smashed his head downward to the left and broke his neck."[1] And from the same book in another equally violent passage to rival Mike Hammer. "I shot him in the head. Just jerked the muzzle out of his ear and fired once left-handed into his right temple. The sound was shattering in the dark. Blood and brain and bone chips hit the far wall. The muzzle flash burned his hair."[2] Lee Child's books regularly make the top of the *New York Times* bestseller list and there are no complaints about the content and level of violence from enthusiastic readers.

Echoing the feeling of the public in the 1930s who saw gangsterism taking over their streets, many urban Americans in larger cities believe that there is too much crime, that their persons or property are in danger, and that regular law enforcement is not coping with the problem. Hence the continued popularity of violent revenge motion pictures such as the *Dirty Harry* movies with Clint Eastwood, the *Death Wish* series with Charles Bronson, and the *Die Hard* movies with Bruce Willis, where the hero takes the law into his own hands, just like various earlier masked avengers.

As author Lee Mitchell put it, "Genres must regularly transform themselves, imaginatively manipulating classic givens, if they are to maintain a compelling hold over their audiences."[3]

They are constantly doing that.

One wonders what is next.

Chapter Notes

Preface

1. Goulart, *The Dime Detectives*, 5.
2. W.H. Hutchinson, "Virgins, Villains and Varmints," in James K. Folsom (ed.), *The Western: A Collection of Critical Essays* (Englewood Cliffs: Prentice-Hall, 1979), 36.
3. Edward J. Whetmore, *Mediamerica: Form, Content and Consequences* (Belmont: Wadsworth, 1995), 10–12, 170–171.
4. Carey McWilliams, "Myths of the West," *North American Review* 232 (November 1931), 428.
5. Earle, *Re-Covering Modernism*, 77.

Chapter 1

1. Edgar R. Burroughs, *Swords of Mars* (New York: Ballantine, 1963), 9
2. This fascination with fear can be seen in the popularity of tourist horror attractions such as *The Chamber of Horrors* at Madame Tussauds Wax Museum in London, where Marie Tussaud started scaring visitors in 1843, though it closed permanently in 2016 due to complaints from families with young children. The popular *London Dungeon* tourist amusement attraction is full of scenes of gory and macabre horror. This type of attraction exists as far away as New Zealand, where the brochure from *Spookers Scream Park* in Auckland reports, "Spine chilling, blood spilling, thrilling, terrifying horror will grab hold of you from start to finish. Come and experience pure horror." Spookers also offers catered birthday parties along with a school and tour group package.
3. Haining, *The Art of Mystery and Detective Stories*, 15.
4. Wald and Elliott, *The American Novel 1870–1940*, 276.
5. Wilson and Wilson, *Mass Media/Mass Culture*, 26.
6. *Ibid.*, 132.
7. Wald and Elliott, *The American Novel 1870–1940*, 293.
8. It is difficult to calculate the equivalent purchasing power of money from the past, due to contemporary currency conversion, inflation, and other factors, but the pound may be equivalent to perhaps about $35 today, making the former British penny worth about 15¢.
9. Goodstone, *The Pulps*, ix.
10. Haining, *The Classic Era of American Pulp Magazines*, 17.
11. Correctly speaking, "Victorian" refers to the time period between 1837 and 1901 when the English monarch Victoria was on the throne; however, the term "Victorian" is also used here in a wider sense to designate the characteristic moral and social climate that existed during the later years of Queen Victoria's reign.
12. Harvey Green, *The Light of the Home* (New York: Pantheon Books, 1983), 166.
13. Nathan Belofsky, *Strange Medicine: A Shocking History of Real Medical Practices Through the Ages* (New York: Perigee/Penguin, 2013), 156.
14. *Ibid.*, 157.
15. *Ibid.*
16. Paul Begg, *Jack the Ripper: The Uncensored Facts* (London: Robson Books, 1988), 29.
17. Adam Hart-Davis, *What the Victorians Did for Us* (London: Headline, 2001), 213.
18. During a similar scare in 1981, experts with no statistics to back them up claimed that 50,000 children were vanishing every year due to the effects of pornography. Even the Federal Bureau of Investigation questioned the size of these figures and the paranoia eventually subsided. (James R. Peterson, *The Century of Sex: Playboy's History of the Sexual Revolution* [New York: Grove Press, 1999], 422–423.)
19. Goulart, *Cheap Thrills*, 178.
20. The word "vampire" was later used as a name for a beautiful, but unscrupulous, woman who beguiled or seduced a man. This name, which was later shortened to "vamp," was used as both a noun and a verb.
21. The popularity of the *Police Gazette* was given a nod of recognition in the motion picture *Cat Ballou* (1965), which used colored paper and vintage period woodcuts similar to the magazine as illustrations for the titles.
22. Mark Gabor, *The Pin-up: A Modest History* (Köln: Benedikt Taschen Verlag GmbH, 1996), 41–43.
23. Sullivan and Schurman, *Pioneers, Passionate Ladies, and Private Eyes*, 106.
24. Kim Todd, "Those Magnificent Women and Their Typing Machines." *Smithsonian*, November 2016, 60–67.
25. Bongco, *Reading Comics*, 121.
26. David Nassaw, *The Chief: The Life of William Randolph Hearst* (New York: Houghton Mifflin, 2000), 79.

Chapter 2

1. Wilson and Wilson, *Mass Media/Mass Culture*, 106.

2. Harvey Green, *The Light of the Home* (New York: Pantheon Books, 1983), 7.
3. Paul Begg, *Jack the Ripper: The Uncensored Facts* (London: Robson Books, 1988), 13.
4. Steinbach, *Women in England*, 79.
5. David H. Murdoch, *The American West: The Invention of a Myth* (Reno: University of Nevada Press, 2001), 34.
6. Wilson and Wilson, *Mass Media/Mass Culture*, 25.
7. Paul Begg, *Jack the Ripper: The Uncensored Facts* (London: Robson Books, 1988), 14.
8. *Ibid.*
9. In a similar manner the expression "tit for tat" came originally from "tip for tat" which meant an exchange of gossip, or retaliation in kind, as "tat" is a name for gossip and "tittle-tattle" is one name for gossip revealing other people's secrets.
10. Kellow Chesney, *The Victorian Underworld* (London: Penguin, 1970), 408.
11. Paul Begg, *Jack the Ripper: The Uncensored Facts* (London: Robson Books, 1988), 14.
12. See Jeremy Agnew, *Crime, Justice and Retribution in the American West: 1850–1900* (Jefferson: McFarland, 2017), 18–23, for further comments about the reality of the Code of the West.
13. It should be noted that some psychologists have argued that there is a pornography of violence that arouses strong erotic feelings in some individuals. However, links are controversial, unclear, and outside the scope of this book.
14. Cawelti, *Adventure, Mystery, and Romance*, 6.
15. Wilson and Wilson, *Mass Media/Mass Culture*, 159.
16. Earle, *Re-Covering Modernism*, 60.
17. Theodore Peterson, *Magazines in the Twentieth Century* (Urbana: University of Illinois Press, 1956), 41, 53
18. Wald and Elliott, *The American Novel 1870–1940*, 356.
19. Steinbach, *Women in England*, 49–50.
20. Anderson, *When Passion Reigned*, 28.
21. As a point of curiosity, in 1868 Britain produced three million corsets and imported two million more from France and Germany.
22. Anderson, *When Passion Reigned*, 26.
23. *Ibid.*, 51.
24. Earle, *Re-Covering Modernism*, 136.
25. Wister, *The Virginian*, 4.
26. John S. Haller and Robin M. Haller, *The Physician and Sexuality in Victorian America* (Urbana: University of Illinois Press, 1974), 193.
27. *Ibid.*, 202–203.
28. Steinbach, *Women in England*, 178.
29. Orson S. Fowler, *Creative and Sexual Science: Or Manhood, Womanhood, and their Mutual Interrelations* (New York: Physical Culture Publishing, 1870), 891.
30. Mary Wood-Allen, *What a Young Woman Ought to Know* (Philadelphia: Vir Publishing, 1905), 123–124.
31. Neurasthenia and hysteria were common diagnoses for Victorian men and women. "Hysteria" in women was an ethereal diagnosis that was used to describe nebulous symptoms related to almost every disease in women. The corresponding nebulous mental "disease" said to be peculiar to Victorian men was neurasthenia, a combination of fatigue, weakness, irritability, and an inability to concentrate that was thought to be brought on by the stresses of contemporary life. In the view of Victorian "enlightened" thinking, hysteria was theorized to be due to factors such as bad physical or moral education, living in a city, overindulgence in coffee and tea, and a bad constitution. After about 1895, the disease faded from the medical scene as a specific ailment.
32. John H. Kellogg, *Ladies' Guide in Health and Disease: Girlhood, Maidenhood, Wifehood, Motherhood* (Des Moines: W.D. Condit, 1883), 214.
33. John S. Haller and Robin M. Haller, *The Physician and Sexuality in Victorian America* (Urbana: University of Illinois Press, 1974), 105.

Chapter 3

1. Sullivan and Schurman, *Pioneers, Passionate Ladies, and Private Eyes*, 60.
2. Cox, *The Dime Novel Companion*, 80.
3. Murdoch, *The American West*, 35.
4. Goulart, *Cheap Thrills*, 28.
5. Sullivan and Schurman, *Pioneers, Passionate Ladies, and Private Eyes*, 62.
6. Cox, *The Dime Novel Companion*, xiv.
7. Wald and Elliott, *The American Novel 1870–1940*, 280.
8. Cox, *The Dime Novel Companion*, 60.
9. Dinan, *The Pulp Western*, 5.
10. This was very important as Victorian standards placed a very high value on pre-nuptial virginity for respectable women. A woman who strayed before marriage was considered to be a fallen woman who would never find a husband.
11. Wald and Elliott, *The American Novel 1870–1940*, 26.
12. *Ibid.*, 286.
13. Pearson, *Dime Novels*, 83.
14. Sullivan and Schurman, *Pioneers, Passionate Ladies, and Private Eyes*, 14.
15. Murdoch, *The American West*, 62; Sullivan and Schurman, *Pioneers, Passionate Ladies, and Private Eyes*, 18.
16. Sullivan and Schurman, *Pioneers, Passionate Ladies, and Private Eyes*, 19.
17. Goulart, *Cheap Thrills*, 25.
18. Cox, *The Dime Novel Companion*, 178.
19. Wald and Elliott, *The American Novel 1870–1940*, 26.
20. Cox, *The Dime Novel Companion*, 179.
21. *Ibid.*, 181.
22. *Ibid.*, 266.
23. Pearson, *Dime Novels*, 46.
24. Sullivan and Schurman, *Pioneers, Passionate Ladies, and Private Eyes*, 18.
25. Cox, *The Dime Novel Companion*, 100–101.
26. *Ibid.*, 182.
27. Don Russell, "The Cowboy: From Black Hat to White," in Charles W. Harris and Buck Rainey (eds.), *The Cowboy: Six-Shooters, Songs, and Sex* (Norman: University of Oklahoma Press, 1976), 11.
28. Cox, *The Dime Novel Companion*, xv.
29. *Ibid.*, xxi.
30. Pearson, *Dime Novels*, 212.
31. *Ibid.*, 68.
32. *Ibid.*, 110.

Chapter 4

1. Murdoch, *The American West*, viii.
2. Though perhaps not considered totally appro-

priate in today's world, I have chosen for the purposes of this book to retain the convention of the dime novels of using the generic name of "Indians" for Native American tribes. I intend no disrespect by the use of this name. I also wish to remain consistent with the historical record. The dime novels' conception of "Indians" was a nameless, faceless caricature of Native American peoples that existed primarily to attack white settlers, cowboys, or soldiers, and be shot down in large numbers. Their actions and culture were not necessarily consistent with any specific Native American tribes. Similarly I have used the term "white" men (or women) to generically designate the Caucasian ethnic division of the human race.

3. David C. King, *First People* (New York: DK Publishing, 2008), 121.
4. Robert V. Hine and John M. Faragher, *The American West: A New Interpretive History* (New Haven: Yale University Press, 2000), 66.
5. Jeff Guinn, *The Last Gunfight: The Real Story of the Shootout at the O.K. Corral—And How It Changed the American West* (New York: Simon & Schuster, 2011), 11.
6. James F. Cooper, *The Last of the Mohicans* (New York: A.L. Burt, 1920), 112.
7. Sullivan and Schurman, *Pioneers, Passionate Ladies, and Private Eyes*, 200.
8. Pearson, *Dime Novels*, 33.
9. Cox, *The Dime Novel Companion*, 96.
10. Cawelti, *Adventure, Mystery, and Romance*, 211.
11. "Manifest Destiny" was the concept that white Americans had the obligation to displace existing Native American cultures and settle the vast empty areas between the Mississippi and the Pacific Coast. The term was coined in 1845 by John L. O'Sullivan, editor of the *New York Morning News*.
12. Sides, *Blood and Thunder*, 251.
13. *Ibid.*
14. *Ibid.*, 392.
15. *Ibid.*, 257–259.
16. *Ibid.*, 285.
17. Much of what we know about Cody comes from his autobiography, *The Life of Hon. William F. Cody, Known as Buffalo Bill*, first published by Frank E. Bliss in 1879 in Hartford, Connecticut. Experts feel that much of what is contained in it must be regarded as suspect and this particular story may have evolved out of his later re-invented show-business persona. Cody claimed that he had been the first rider for the Pony Express in 1859; however, the Pony Express did not start until 1860 and none of the stops he listed as stations were correct. Statements by his sister, his former teacher, and Cody himself, place him in school in Leavenworth, Kansas, at the time.
18. Buffalo Bill referred to his *Wild West* extravaganza as an "equestrian drama," as Cody didn't like the name "show." He felt that the participants were not entertainers, but were re-creating authentic history and a realistic portrayal of life in the Old West.
19. Cox, *The Dime Novel Companion*, 149.
20. Rita Parks, *The Western Hero in Film and Television: Mass Media Mythology* (Ann Arbor: UMI Research Press, 1982), 65.
21. Ned Buntline (ed. Clay Reynolds), *The Hero of a Hundred Fights: Collected Stories From the Dime Novel King* (New York: Union Square, 2011), 424.
22. *Ibid.*, 5.
23. Pearson, *Dime Novels*, 107.
24. Charles W. Harris and Buck Rainey, *The Cowboy: Six-Shooters, Songs, and Sex* (Norman: University of Oklahoma Press, 1976), 10.
25. Cox, *The Dime Novel Companion*, 185.
26. Wayne M. Sarf, *God Bless You, Buffalo Bill: A Layman's Guide to History and the Western Film* (East Brunswick: Associated University Presses and Cornwall Books, 1983), 43.

Chapter 5

1. Murdoch, *The American West*, 64.
2. Etulain and Marsden, *The Popular Western*, 16.
3. Edward L. Wheeler, *Deadwood Dick, the Prince of the Road; or, The Black Rider of the Black Hills* (Cleveland: Arthur Westbrook Co., 1877), 31.
4. Watson Parker, *Deadwood: The Golden Years* (Lincoln: University of Nebraska Press, 1981), 136.
5. Murdoch, *The American West*, 52.
6. Etulain and Marsden, *The Popular Western*, 14.
7. Marshall Sprague, *Money Mountain* (Boston: Little, Brown, 1953), 252.
8. Authorities claim that there are only 33 original Deadwood Dick stories, though the title of this last one would imply 35, unless the last two were written posthumously by another author using a pen-name.
9. Cox, *The Dime Novel Companion*, 75.
10. *Ibid.*
11. Etulain and Marsden, *The Popular Western*, 10.
12. Rita Parks, *The Western Hero in Film and Television: Mass Media Mythology* (Ann Arbor: UMI Research Press, 1982), 41.
13. Cox, *The Dime Novel Companion*, 154–155.
14. Murdoch, *The American West*, 52.
15. Cox, *The Dime Novel Companion*, 77.
16. Richard Slotkin, *Gunfighter Nation: The Myth of the Frontier in Twentieth-Century America* (New York: Atheneum, 1992), 137.
17. *Ibid.*, 147.
18. Murdoch, *The American West*, 92.
19. William Keleher, *The Fabulous Frontier* (Santa Fe: The Rydal Press, 1945), 125.

Chapter 6

1. Haining, *The Art of Mystery and Detective Stories*, 49.
2. Pearson, *Dime Novels*, 140.
3. *Ibid.*
4. Cox, *The Dime Novel Companion*, 295.
5. Pearson, *Dime Novels*, 213.
6. *Ibid.*
7. Ruehlmann, *Saint With a Gun*, 50.
8. *Ibid.*
9. Wilkie Collins, *The Moonstone* (New York: Random House, 1937), 81.
10. The Hansom cab, named after its New York inventor, Joseph Hansom, was a small two-wheeled carriage for two passengers, drawn by a single horse, with the driver standing outside, above and behind the cab. Holmes and Watson sometimes traveled in a Brougham, also named after its Scottish inventor, a larger four-wheeled carriage with the driver sitting up front behind four horses.
11. This figure is always held up as an excessively low payment for this first Sherlock Holmes story, but remember that Conan Doyle could not place it with a publisher and even considered throwing it away, in which case the world would never have had Sherlock and Watson. Plus it was perhaps equivalent about $4,000 in today's dollars.

12. Haining, *The Art of Mystery and Detective Stories*, 158–159.

Chapter 7

1. Jack Nachbar, *Focus on the Western* (Englewood Cliffs: Prentice-Hall, 1974), 21.
2. Bleiler, *Eight Dime Novels*, ix; Sullivan and Schurman, *Pioneers, Passionate Ladies, and Private Eyes*, 67–69.
3. Earle, *Re-Covering Modernism*, 9.
4. Goodstone, *The Pulps*, xiv.
5. Earle, *Re-Covering Modernism*, 9.
6. Rabinowitz, *American Pulp*, 32.
7. Nolan, *The Black Mask Boys*, 267.
8. Dinan, *The Pulp Western*, 76.
9. Goulart, *Cheap Thrills*, 180.
10. Earle, *Re-Covering Modernism*, 63.
11. Richard W. Etulain, *Telling Western Stories: From Buffalo Bill to Larry McMurtry* (Albuquerque: University of New Mexico Press, 1999), 151–152.
12. William T. Pilkington, *Critical Essays on the Western Novel* (Boston: G.K. Hall, 1980), 27.
13. Theodore Peterson, *Magazines in the Twentieth Century* (Urbana: University of Illinois Press, 1956) 41, 53.
14. Server, *Danger Is My Business*, 50.
15. Goulart, *Cheap Thrills*, 31.
16. Server, *Danger Is My Business*, 13.
17. Ibid., 92.
18. Goulart, *Cheap Thrills*, 34.
19. Dinan, *The Pulp Western*, 43.
20. Server, *Encyclopedia of Pulp Fiction Writers*, 230
21. Earle, *Re-Covering Modernism, 100*; Server, *Encyclopedia of Pulp Fiction Writers*, 36.
22. Dinan, *The Pulp Western*, 100.
23. Goulart, *Cheap Thrills*, 15.

Chapter 8

1. Hutchison, *The Great Pulp Heroes*, 102.
2. Server, *Encyclopedia of Pulp Fiction Writers*, 45.
3. This was not true of the popular motion pictures made from the books in the 1930s, which were toned down for family audiences.
4. Hutchison, *The Great Pulp Heroes*, 253.
5. Edgar R. Burroughs, *The Warlord of Mars* (New York: Ballantine, 1963), 48.
6. Burroughs' Martians are human-like, but are oviparous and hatch from eggs laid by the women. See *A Princess of Mars* for further details.
7. Edgar R. Burroughs, *The Warlord of Mars* (New York: Ballantine, 1963), 29.
8. Edgar R. Burroughs, *The Chessmen of Mars* (New York: Dover Publications, 1962), 145.
9. Server, *Encyclopedia of Pulp Fiction Writers*, 45.
10. Hutchison, *The Great Pulp Heroes*, 254–258.
11. Server, *Danger Is My Business*, 49–50.
12. Jim Hitt, *The American West from Fiction (1823–1976) into Film (1909–1986)* (Jefferson: McFarland & Company, 1990), 21.
13. Goulart, *The Dime Detectives*, 181.
14. Server, *Danger Is My Business*, 94.
15. Ibid., 94.
16. Goulart, *Cheap Thrills*, 73.
17. Ibid., 66.
18. Nolan, *The Black Mask Boys*, 29.
19. Goulart, *Cheap Thrills*, 58.

Chapter 9

1. Athanasourelis, *Raymond Chandler's Philip Marlowe*, 14.
2. Ibid., 13.
3. Hare, *Pulp Fiction to Film Noir*, 8.
4. Goulart, *The Dime Detectives*, 96.
5. Nolan, *The Black Mask Boys*, 20.
6. Ibid., 26.
7. Wald and Elliott, *The American Novel 1870–1940*, 339.
8. This theme was later used in several motion pictures, including *Yojimbo* (1961), a Japanese Samuri film; *Fistful of Dollars* (1964), a revenge western with Clint Eastwood; and *Last Man Standing* (1996) with Bruce Willis, about a 1930s Chicago gang war in a small Texas town.
9. Breu, *Hard-Boiled Masculinities*, 9.
10. Nolan, *The Black Mask Boys*, 32.
11. "Gat" is a slang gangster term for a semi-automatic pistol, derived from the last name of Dr. Richard Gatling, the inventor of the Gatling gun, an early type of machine gun.
12. Carroll John Daly, "Three Gun Terry," *Black Mask*, May 15, 1923.
13. Nolan, *The Black Mask Boys*, 39.
14. Erle Stanley Gardner, "Getting Away with Murder," *Atlantic*, January 1965, 72.
15. Nolan, *The Black Mask Boys*, 35.
16. Ibid., 27.
17. Popular silent-film comedian Roscoe "Fatty" Arbuckle was charged with rape and murder after a minor film starlet named Virginia Rappe died following a drinking party in San Francisco. The tabloid press had a field day. Arbuckle was finally exonerated after three jury trials, but his career as a film star was already ruined. Hammett called the whole affair "a newspaper frame-up." (Ruehlmann, *Saint With a Gun*, 59).
18. Cline, *Dashiell Hammett*, 11.
19. Hare, *Pulp Fiction to Film Noir*, 30.
20. Wald and Elliott, *The American Novel 1870–1940*, 342.
21. Nolan, *The Black Mask Boys*, 91–92.
22. Ibid., 77.
23. Cline, *Dashiell Hammett*, 17.
24. Dashiell Hammett, *Red Harvest* (New York: Vintage, 1992), 7.
25. Ibid., 52.
26. Ibid., 213.
27. Ibid., 57.
28. Ibid., 72.
29. Ibid., 203.
30. Ibid., 215.
31. Ibid., 216.
32. Hare, *Pulp Fiction to Film Noir*, 26.
33. Robert L. Chapman and Barbara A. Kipfer, *American Slang* (New York: Collins, 2007).

Chapter 10

1. Skinner, *The Hard-Boiled Explicator*, 13.
2. Ibid.
3. Hare, *Pulp Fiction to Film Noir*, 87.
4. Raymond Chandler, *Farewell, My Lovely* (New York: Pocket Books, 1943), 135.

5. Ruehlmann, *Saint with a Gun*, 91.
6. O'Brien, *Hardboiled America*, 94.
7. Mickey Spillane, *I, the Jury* (New York: Signet Books, 1968), 7.
8. *Ibid.*, 174.
9. Cawelti, *Adventure, Mystery, and Romance*, 183.
10. Earle, *Re-Covering Modernism*, 209.
11. Mickey Spillane, *Kiss Me, Deadly* (Thorndike, ME: G.K. Hall, 1993) 197.
12. *Ibid.*, 215–216.
13. Mickey Spillane, *The Big Kill* (New York: Signet Books, 1951), 150.
14. Server, *Encyclopedia of Pulp Fiction Writers*, 60.
15. Earle, *Re-Covering Modernism*, 112.
16. Server, *Encyclopedia of Pulp Fiction Writers*, 70–71.
17. Goulart, *The Dime Detectives*, 186.
18. *Ibid.*, 198.
19. *Ibid.*, 135.
20. Server, *Encyclopedia of Pulp Fiction Writers*, xiv.
21. Frank Scarpetta, *Mafia Wipe-Out* (New York: Belmont Tower, 1973), 48.
22. Donald Hamilton, *The Silencers* (New York: Fawcett, 1962), 34.
23. *Ibid.*, 37.

Chapter 11

1. Helena Huntington Smith, "Sam Bass and the Myth Machine," *The American West* 7, no. 1 (January 1970), 32.
2. Quoted in the epigraph of Mitchell, *Westerns*.
3. Paul O'Neil, *The End and the Myth* (Alexandria: Time-Life Books, 1979), 32.
4. Etulain and Marsden, *The Popular Western*, 10.
5. Owen Wister, *The Virginian* (New York: Macmillan, 1902), 448.
6. Murdoch, *The American West*, 89.
7. *Ibid.*, 65.
8. Rita Parks, *The Western Hero in Film and Television: Mass Media Mythology* (Ann Arbor: UMI Research Press, 1982), 69.
9. Ramon F. Adams, *Old Time Cowhand* (New York: Macmillan, 1961), 5.
10. Owen Wister, *The Virginian* (New York: Macmillan, 1902), 160.
11. Etulain, *Telling Western Stories*, 18.
12. Dinan, *The Pulp Western*, 96–97.
13. Frantz and Choate, *The American Cowboy*, 156.
14. Rita Parks, *The Western Hero in Film and Television*, 1.
15. Dinan, *The Pulp Western*, 59.

Chapter 12

1. Harris and Rainey, *The Cowboy*, 17.
2. Dinan, *The Pulp Western*, 39.
3. *Ibid.*, 37.
4. Goodstone, *The Pulps*, 86.
5. Readers interested in the titles of the many pulp magazines devoted to the western may wish to consult Dinan, *The Pulp Western*, pages i–v for a more comprehensive listing. Estimates are that there were probably more than 165 titles.
6. Hutchison, *The Great Pulp Heroes*, 270.
7. William T. Pilkington, *Critical Essays on the Western Novel* (Boston: G.K. Hall, 1980), 28.

8. Hitt, *The American West From Fiction (1823–1976) into Film (1909–1986)*, 131.
9. Mitchell, *Westerns*, 129.
10. Etulain and Marsden, *The Popular Western*, 40.
11. Hitt, *The American West From Fiction (1823–1976) into Film (1909–1986)*, 126.
12. Zane Grey, *Riders of the Purple Sage* (London: Hamish Hamilton, 1952), 45.
13. Hitt, *The American West From Fiction (1823–1976) into Film (1909–1986)*, 162.
14. *Ibid.*, 137.
15. Murdoch, *The American West*, 82.
16. Harris and Rainey, *The Cowboy*, 14.
17. Champlin, *The Wild West of Louis L'Amour*, 141.
18. Server, *Danger Is My Business*, 26.
19. Server, *Encyclopedia of Pulp Fiction Writers*, 35–36.
20. Etulain and Marsden, *The Popular Western*, 78.
21. Dinan, *The Pulp Western*, 86.
22. Goulart, *Cheap Thrills*, 134.
23. Dinan, *The Pulp Western*, 44.
24. Goulart, *Cheap Thrills*, 138.
25. Dinan, *The Pulp Western*, 85.
26. Server, *Encyclopedia of Pulp Fiction Writers*, 174.
27. Harris and Rainey, *The Cowboy: Six-Shooters, Songs, and Sex*, 26.
28. Goulart, *Cheap Thrills*, 136.
29. Hitt, *The American West From Fiction (1823–1976) into Film (1909–1986)*.
30. *Ibid.*, 74.
31. Etulain and Marsden, *The Popular Western*, 80.
32. This is the movie that made Monument Valley on the Arizona/Utah border famous and Ford returned to it as a location for the rest of his directing career. Interestingly, in spite of the film's reputation, location shots of the valley itself only appear on the screen in *Stagecoach* for a total of about ninety seconds. The rest of the "Monument Valley" footage was actually back projection used in the studio in Hollywood.
33. The real Luke Short was a gambler and saloon keeper in the West in the late 1800s who was involved in several notorious gunfights and shooting scrapes. He was a dapper dresser and kept his revolver in his pants in a pocket specially lined with leather for a fast draw.
34. Parks, *The Western Hero in Film and Television*, 30.
35. Dinan, *The Pulp Western*, 52.

Chapter 13

1. Earle, *Re-Covering Modernism*, 103.
2. Goulart, *Cheap Thrills*, 180.
3. Sullivan and Schurman, *Pioneers, Passionate Ladies, and Private Eyes*, 134.
4. Another example from television is the popular series *M*A*S*H* in the 1970s and early 1980s, about an army field hospital during the Korean War and how they dealt with horrific battle casualties. This could not be made until long after the real conflict was over.
5. Server, *Danger Is My Business*, 118.
6. *Ibid.*
7. Wald and Elliott, *The American Novel 1870–1940*, 382.

8. In 1950 Hubbard published a guide to self-help psychology that he named Dianetics (from Greek words meaning "through the mind") in *Astounding Science Fiction* magazine. Eventually, in 1953, Hubbard's movement turned into a religious organization named the Church of Scientology.
9. Haining, *The Classic Era of American Pulp Magazines*, 29.
10. S.J. Perelman, *The Best of S.J. Perelman* (New York: The Modern Library, 1947), 212.
11. Earle, *Re-Covering Modernism*, 78.
12. Server, *Danger Is My Business*, 82.
13. Haining, *The Classic Era of American Pulp Magazines*, 81.
14. Dinan, *The Pulp Western*, 43.
15. Another humor piece by Perelman is "Farewell My Lovely Appetizer," a delightful parody of the private detective stories of the 1930s. These two enjoyable pieces of writing have been collected in many places, but both appear in S.J. Perelman, *The Best of S.J. Perelman* (New York: The Modern Library, 1947), 9 and 291.

Chapter 14

1. Lucius Beebe and Charles Clegg, *The American West* (New York: E.P. Dutton, 1955), 319.
2. Larry Barsness, *Gold Camp: Alder Gulch and Virginia City, Montana* (New York: Hastings House, 1962), 233.
3. Mark Twain, *Roughing It* (New York: Harper & Brothers, 1913), vol. II, 110.
4. Tchen and Yeats, *Yellow Peril!*, 124.
5. Server, *Encyclopedia of Pulp Fiction Writers*, 225.
6. Martin Booth, *Opium: A History* (New York: St. Martin's Press, 1996), 211.
7. An enjoyable tongue-in-cheek analysis by humorist S.J. Perelman of the extremes in *The Mystery of Dr. Fu-Manchu* can be found in "Why, Doctor, What Big Green Eyes You Have!" (S.J. Perelman, *The Most of S.J. Perelman* [New York: Simon & Schuster, 1962], 453–459.)
8. Sax Rohmer, *The Mystery of Dr. Fu-Manchu* (London: Guild Books, 1953), 18–19.
9. Server, *Danger Is My Business*, 33.
10. Server, *Encyclopedia of Pulp Fiction Writers*, 180.
11. Haining, *The Classic Era of American Pulp Magazines*, 108.
12. Server, *Danger Is My Business*, 35.
13. Server, *Encyclopedia of Pulp Fiction Writers*, 178.
14. Carter, *Lovecraft*, 37.
15. Modern author Michael Crichton used a similar technique in his novel *Eaters of the Dead* (made into a motion picture as *The 13th Warrior* [1999]), which he wrote in the form of a scholarly monograph. The novel was purportedly based on a manuscript written by a real Arab traveler in the tenth century who was one of the earliest scholars to describe the Vikings. One of the translators in the scholarly-looking bibliography is listed as Per Fraus-Dolus of Oslo. This expands the joke because the name when literally translated from the Latin means "by trickery-deceit." The imaginative bibliography even lists as a source the *Necronomicon* as edited by H.P. Lovecraft. Readers wrote to rare book dealers and universities trying to obtain copies of the original references and pursuing the imaginary footnotes. They were reportedly somewhat irritated when they were unable to find them. Crichton eventually acknowledged that the text, scholarly footnotes, and the bibliography "should be properly viewed as fiction." (Michael Crichton, *Eaters of the Dead*. New York: HarperCollins, 2009.)
16. Lovecraft, *The Dunwich Horror and Others*, 13.
17. Server, *Danger Is My Business*, 46.
18. Haining, *The Classic Era of American Pulp Magazines*, 132.
19. Server, *Danger Is My Business*, 31.
20. Movie audiences will remember the genuine menace projected by the hooded Jedi Master in *The Empire Strikes Back* (1980) in the *Star Wars* series of motion pictures, and the hooded villain in *The Last Action Hero* (1993).

Chapter 15

1. Goulart, *Cheap Thrills*, 183.
2. Goulart, *The Dime Detectives*, 233.
3. Oakley, *God's Country*, 107.
4. Cowsill et al., *DC Comics*, 12.
5. Wandtke, *The Amazing Transforming Superhero!*, 39.
6. Bongco, *Reading Comics*, 126.
7. Wandtke, *The Amazing Transforming Superhero!*, 151–152.
8. Jill Lepore, "The Origin Story of Wonder Woman," *Smithsonian*, October 2014, 56–65.
9. Server, *Danger Is My Business*, 135.
10. Wandtke, *The Amazing Transforming Superhero!*, 115.
11. "Comic Strips Down," *Time*, 65, March 14, 1955, 86.
12. Wandtke, *The Amazing Transforming Superhero!*, 115.
13. Witek, *Comic Books as History*, 14–15.
14. M. Thomas Inge. *Handbook of American Popular Literature* (New York: Greenwood Press, 1988), 79.
15. Oakley, *God's Country*, 258.
16. Perhaps about $34 in today's dollars.
17. Rabinowitz, *American Pulp*, 33.
18. Joe B. Frantz and Julian E. Choate, Jr., *The American Cowboy: The Myth and the Reality* (Norman: University of Oklahoma Press, 2001), 5.
19. O'Brien, *Hardboiled America*, 35.
20. Ibid., 38.
21. Goulart, *The Dime Detectives*, 232.
22. Jake Page, "Writer of the Purple Prose," *Smithsonian*, December 2001, 84–89.
23. Frantz and Choate, *The American Cowboy*, 5.
24. Frank L. Schick, *The Paperbound Book in America; the History of Paperbacks and Their European Background* (New York: Bowker, 1958), 142.
25. Oakley, *God's Country*, 257.
26. Earle, *Re-Covering Modernism*, 168.
27. Zane Grey, *Forlorn River* (London: Pan Books, 1951).
28. A comic look at this type of lurid repackaging was satirized in George Axelrod's 1952 play *The Seven Year Itch*. Richard Sherman works for Brady Publishing who wants him to make up a provocative titles and sexy covers to sell 25¢ paperback versions of *The Portrait of Dorian Gray* and Louisa May Alcott's *Little Women* in drugstores. A serious book written by Sherman's psychotherapist, titled *Of Man and the Unconscious*, becomes *Of Sex and Violence* to make it sell, with a lurid

cover depicting another respectable and learned therapist as the "Mad Lover of Leipzig" terrorizing a victim.

29. Vance Packard, *The Hidden Persuaders* (New York: Pocket Books, 1969), 76.

30. Mark Gabor, *The Pin-up: A Modest History* (Köln: Benedikt Taschen Verlag GmbH, 1996), 77.

31. Russell Miller, *Bunny: The Real Story of Playboy* (New York: Holt, Rinehart and Winston, 1984), 53.

32. *Ibid.*, 26–29.

33. *Ibid.*, 53.

Postscript

1. Lee Child, *Persuader* (New York: Bantam Dell, 2004), 129.

2. *Ibid.*, 207.

3. Lee C. Mitchell, *Westerns: Making the Man in Fiction and Film* (Chicago: University of Chicago Press, 1996), 259.

Bibliography

Agnew, Jeremy. *The Creation of the Cowboy Hero: Fiction, Film and Fact.* Jefferson, NC: McFarland, 2015.

Agnew, Jeremy. *Entertainment in the Old West: Theater, Music, Circuses, Medicine Shows, Prizefighting and Other Popular Amusements.* Jefferson, NC: McFarland, 2011.

Agnew, Jeremy. *The Old West in Fact and Fiction: History Versus Hollywood.* Jefferson, NC: McFarland, 2012.

Anderson, Patricia. *When Passion Reigned: Sex and the Victorians.* New York: Basic Books, 1995.

Athanasourelis, John P. *Raymond Chandler's Philip Marlowe: The Hard-Boiled Detective Transformed.* Jefferson, NC: McFarland, 2012.

Bleiler Everett F. *Eight Dime Novels.* New York: Dover Publications, 1974.

Bold, Christine. *Selling the Wild West: Popular Western Fiction 1860–1960.* Bloomington: Indiana University Press, 1987.

Bongco, Mila. *Reading Comics: Language, Culture, and the Concept of the Superhero in Comic Books.* New York: Garland Publishing, 2000.

Breu, Christopher. *Hard-Boiled Masculinities.* Minneapolis: University of Minnesota Press, 2005.

Calder, Jenni. *There Must Be a Lone Ranger: The American West in Film and in Reality.* New York: Taplinger Publishing, 1974.

Carter, Lin. *Lovecraft: A Look Behind the Cthulhu Mythos.* New York: Ballantine, 1972.

Cawelti, John G. *Adventure, Mystery, and Romance: Formula Stories as Art and Popular Culture.* Chicago: University of Chicago Press, 1976.

Champlin, Tim. *The Wild West of Louis L'Amour.* Minneapolis: Voyageur Press, 2015.

Cline, Sally. *Dashiell Hammett: Man of Mystery.* New York: Arcade Publishing, 2014.

Cowsill, Alan, and Axle Irvine, Matthew K. Manning, et al. *DC Comics: A Visual History.* New York: DK Publishing, 2014.

Cox, J. Randolph. *The Dime Novel Companion: A Source Book.* Westport: Greenwood Press, 2000.

Denning, Michael J. *Mechanic Accents: Dime Novels and Working Class Culture in America.* New York: Verso, 1987.

Derleth, August. *The Cthulhu Mythos.* New York: Barnes & Noble Books, 1997.

Dinan, John A. *the Pulp Western: A Popular History of the Western Fiction Magazine in America.* Boalsburg, PA: BearManor Media, 2003.

Earle, David M. *Re-Covering Modernism: Pulps, Paperbacks, and the Prejudice of Form.* Farnham: Ashgate Publishing, 2009.

Etulain, Richard W. *Telling Western Stories: From Buffalo Bill to Larry McMurtry.* Albuquerque: University of New Mexico Press, 1999.

Etulain, Richard W., and Michael T. Marsden. *The Popular Western: Essays Towards a Definition.* Bowling Green: Bowling Green University Popular Press, 1974.

Franz, Joe B., and Julian E. Choate, Jr. *The American Cowboy: The Myth and the Reality.* Norman: University of Oklahoma Press, 1955.

Gabor, Mark. *The Pin-Up: A Modest History.* Köln: Benedikt Taschen Verlag GmbH, 1996.

Geherin, David. *The American Private Eye: The Image in Fiction.* New York: F. Ungar, 1985.

Goodstone, Tony. *The Pulps: Fifty Years of American Pop Culture.* New York: Bonanza Books, 1970.

Goulart, Ron. *Cheap Thrills: An Informal History of the Pulp Magazines.* New Rochelle: Arlington House, 1972.

Goulart, Ron. *The Dime Detectives.* New York: The Mysterious Press, 1988.

Griffin, Scott T. *The Centennial Celebration Tarzan.* London: Titan Books, 2012.

Haining Peter. *The Art of Mystery and Detective Stories.* Secaucus: Chartwell Books, 1986.

Haining, Peter. *The Classic Era of American Pulp Magazines.* Chicago: Chicago Review Press, 2000.

Haining, Peter. *The Penny Dreadful.* London: Gollancz, 1975.

Hammett, Dashiell. *Red Harvest.* New York: Vintage, 1992.

Hare, William. *Pulp Fiction to Film Noir: The Great Depression and the Development of a Genre.* Jefferson, NC: McFarland, 2012.

Harris, Charles W., and Buck Rainey. *The Cowboy: Six-Shooters, Songs, and Sex.* Norman: University of Oklahoma Press, 1976.

Hart-Davis, Adam. *What the Victorians Did for Us*. London: Headline, 2001.

Hitt, Jim. *The American West from Fiction (1823–1976) into Film (1909–1986)*. Jefferson, NC: McFarland, 1990.

Hulse, Ed. *The Blood 'n' Thunder Guide to Pulp Fiction*. Morris Plains: Murania Press, 2007.

Hutchison, Don. *The Great Pulp Heroes*. Oakville, Ontario: Mosaic Press, 1996.

Jones, Robert K. *The Shudder Pulps: A History of the Weird Menace Magazines of the 1930s*. West Linn, OR: Fax Collector's Editions, 1975.

Lovecraft, Howard P. *The Dunwich Horror and Others*. New York: Lancer Books, 1963.

Lovecraft, Howard P. *Supernatural Horror in Literature*. New York: Dover Publications, 1973.

McCann, Sean. *Gumshoe America: Hard-Boiled Crime Fiction and the Rise and Fall of New Deal Liberalism*. Durham: Duke University Press, 2000.

Mitchell, Lee C. *Westerns: Making the Man in Fiction and Film*. Chicago: University of Chicago Press, 1996.

Murdoch, David H. *The American West: The Invention of a Myth*. Reno: University of Nevada Press, 2001.

Nolan, William F. *The Black Mask Boys: Masters in the Hard-Boiled School of Detective Fiction*. New York: William Morrow, 1985.

Oakley, J. Ronald. *God's Country: America in the Fifties*. New York: Dembner Books, 1986.

O'Brien, Geoffrey. *Hardboiled America: The Lurid Years of Paperbacks*. New York: Van Nostrand Reinhold, 1981.

O'Neil, Paul. *The End and the Myth*. Alexandria: Time-Life Books, 1979.

Parks, Rita. *The Western Hero in Film and Television: Mass Media Mythology*. Ann Arbor: UMI Research Press, 1982.

Pearson, Edmund. *Dime Novels; Or, Following an Old Trail in Popular Literature*. Boston: Little, Brown, 1929.

Rabinowitz, Paula. *American Pulp: How Paperbacks Brought Modernism to Main Street*. Princeton: Princeton University Press, 2014.

Reynolds, Quentin. *The Fiction Factory, or from Pulp Row to Quality Street: The Story of 100 Years of Publishing at Street and Smith*. New York: Random House, 1955.

Ruehlmann, William. *Saint with a Gun: The Unlawful American Private Eye*. New York: New York University Press, 1984.

Sarf, Wayne M. *God Bless You, Buffalo Bill: A Layman's Guide to History and the Western Film*. East Brunswick: Associated University Presses, 1983.

Server, Lee. *Danger Is My Business: An Illustrated History of the Fabulous Pulp Magazines*. San Francisco: Chronicle Books, 1993.

Server, Lee. *Encyclopedia of Pulp Fiction Writers*. New York: Checkmark Books, 2002.

Sides, Hampton. *Blood and Thunder: An Epic of the American West*. New York: Doubleday, 2006.

Skinner, Robert E. *The Hard-Boiled Explicator: A Guide to the Study of Dashiell Hammett, Raymond Chandler and Ross MacDonald*. Metuchen: Scarecrow Press, 1985.

Smith, Erin A. *Hard Boiled: Working Class Readers and Pulp Magazines*. Philadelphia: Temple University Press, 2000.

Steinbach, Susie. *Women in England, 1760–1914*. London: Weidenfeld & Nicholson, 2004.

Sullivan, Larry E., and Lydia C. Schurman (eds.). *Pioneers, Passionate Ladies, and Private Eyes: Dime Novels, Series Books, and Paperbacks*. New York: Haworth Press, 1996.

Tchen, John K, and Dylan Yeats (eds.). *Yellow Peril!: An Archive of Anti-Asian Fear*. London: Verso, 2014.

Thompson, Richard A. *The Yellow Peril: 1890–1924*. New York: Arno Press, 1978.

Wald, Priscilla, and Michael A. Elliott (eds.). *The American Novel 1870–1940*. Oxford: Oxford University Press, 2014.

Wandtke, Terence R. (ed.). *The Amazing Transforming Superhero!: Essays on the Revision of Characters in Comic Books, Film and Television*. Jefferson, NC: McFarland, 2007.

Wilson, James R., and Stan L. Wilson. *Mass Media/Mass Culture*. New York: McGraw-Hill, 1998.

Wister, Owen. *The Virginian*. New York: Macmillan, 1902.

Witek, Joseph. *Comic Books as History*. Jackson: University Press of Mississippi, 1989.

Index

Numbers in ***bold italics*** indicate pages with illustrations

Aarons, Edward S. 143
advertising 98, ***99***, 100
American News Company 94, 97
anatomical museums 8
Argosy 28, 45, ***95***, 96
artwork, cover *see* cover art
Association for the Prevention of Premature Burial 9
Atlantic Monthly 28, 29, 158
authors, dime novel 3, 36, 37, 40, 47, 55
authors, pulp 101-102, 104, 204-205
aviation pulps 174-177

Beadle, Erastus Flavel 38-41, 54
Beadle & Adams 33-35, 38-41, ***39***, 55, 67
Bell, Ernest A. 14
Bellem, Robert Leslie 186
Bennett, James Gordon 7
Bergey, Earle Kulp 180-181
Billy the Kid 77-78, ***77***
Black Mask 124-130, ***128***, 131, 134-135, 183
blood-and-thunder novels 3, 33
Boone, Daniel 52, 56
Boyd, William 150, 209
Brand, Max 166-168
brass bra ***180***, 181
broadsheets 5-6, 12, 142
Broncho Billy 169
Brundage, Margaret 196
bug-eyed monsters (BEMs) 179
Bulldog Drummond 141
Buntline, Ned 60-61
burial, premature 10-11
Burroughs, Edgar Rice 5, 105-109, 178
Butterick Company 97

Calamity Jane 68-69, 71-72, 74
Canary, Martha Jane *see* Calamity Jane
Cap Collier 79-80
captivity narrative 14, 51-52, ***53***
Carson, Kit 51, 56-58
Chandler, Raymond 135-136, 138
chapbooks 8
Child, Lee 220
Chinese 188-190

circulation figures 4, 7, 28, 55, 73, 92, 93, 94, 96, 126, 138, 150, 163
Clay, Bertha M. 82
Clayton Magazines 97, 160, 199
cliffhangers 27, 46, 58, 69, 107
Code of the West 27, 151, 222
Cody, "Buffalo Bill" 58-63, ***59***, 148, 223
coffins 9-11
Collins, Wilkie 87
comic books 205-210, ***206***
Comics Code Authority 210
Conan Doyle, Arthur 87-90, ***89***, 190
Conan the Barbarian 196-197
cone effect 3
Constructed Mediated Reality (CMR) 3, 14
Continental Op 131-133
Cooper, James Fenimore 1, 46, 52-54, 55, 147, 164
copyright 37, 172
Council on Books in Wartime 214
cover art 37-38, 92, 102-104, ***103***, 157, 214-215, ***216***
cowboys, fictional image 145, ***146***, 147, ***149***, 153, 155-157, 162, 163
cowboys, real ***149***, 152-154, ***167***
Cranston, Lamont 115
Cream, Neill 12
Crockett, Davy 56
crossdressing 38, 40, 46, 69, 82, 165
Cthulhu mythos 197-199
Culture Publications 184, ***185***, 187

Daily Mail 26
Daly, Carroll John 127-130
Dan Turner 186
Day, Benjamin 7
DC Comics 207-208, 209
Deadwood Dick 8, 47, 51, 66-73, ***67***, 112, 137, 223
death and dying 8-11
Dent, Lester *see* Robeson, Kenneth
Denver Dan 73
Denver Doll 73, 79
detective, hard-boiled *see* hard-boiled detective
detectives, thinking 121, 126
DeWitt, Robert M. 34
Diamond Dick 73-74
Dime Mystery 15, 97, 174, 200, 202, 203, 204

dime novel collections 4
Dime pulps 97
distribution companies 46, 94, 97
Doc Savage 101, 118–120
Dracula 15–16, *15*, 87, 198
Duval, Claude 8, 34

EC Comics 205–206, 209
Edwards, John Newman 76
Ellis, Edward Sylvester 55–56
escapism *see* literary escapism
Esquire 217

fan clubs 100–101, 117–118
Faust, Frederick Schiller *see* Brand, Max
fear 5, 10–11, 27, 188, 219, 221
Fighting the Traffic in Young Girls 14
films, Western 169–172
Fowler, Orson 32
Fox, Richard Kyle 17, 19
Frank Leslie's Illustrated Weekly 20, 29, 158
Frankenstein 16
Fu Manchu 85, 190–193, *191*

G8 175–177, *176*
Gaines, Maxell Charles 205, 207
Gaines, William 209
gangsterism 121–122, 124, 126
Gardner, Erle Stanley 134–135, 142
Gernsback, Hugo 177–178
Golden Argosy see Argosy
Grand Guignol theater 200
Grant, Maxwell 115
Grey, Zane 162–166, *163*
Grimm's Fairy Tales 5, 15

Haggard, H. Rider 110–112
Hamilton, Donald S. 144
Hamlet 5
Hammett, Dashiell 130–133, 138
hard-boiled detective 98, 122–144, *123*
Harmsworth, Alfred 26
Harper's 1, 20, 28, 29, 63, 77, 151, 164, 158
Hawkeye 1, 52
Haycox, Ernest 170–171
Hearst, William Randolph 21
Hickok, "Wild Bill" 63
High Noon 169
hoaxes, newspaper 7
Hogan's Alley 21
homosexuals 133
Hopalong Cassidy 150, 168, 209
Hornung, E.W. 90, 126
horror 14–15; *see also* fear
horror pulps 194–203, *201*
Hull, Edith Maude 16
Hutchinson, W.H. 1

I, the Jury 136–140
Illustrated London News 20
Ingraham, Prentiss *59*, 61–62

Jack the Ripper 11–13
Jackson, William 5
Jane 186

Jesse James 74–77, *75*
Jewett, Helen 7
John Carter 106–108, *108*
Judson, Edward Carroll Zane *see* Buntline, Ned
jungle adventures 105–112, *111*

King, Charles 148
King Brady 80, *81*, 82
King Philip's war 51–52
King Solomon's Mines 111–112

labor wars 70–71, *70*
Lambeth Poisoner 12
L'Amour, Louis 168–169
Language, "bad" 36, 48
language, dime novel *see* language, "bad"
Last of the Mohicans 52–54, *53*
Leatherstocking 52–54, 61, 156
Leroux, Gaston 16
Leslie, Frank 20
Lew Archer 136, *137*
literacy rates 22
literary escapism 27, 64, 93, 124, 155, 215–218
Lloyd, Edward 8
locked room mystery 85
lost race adventures 110–112, 177
Lovecraft, Howard Phillips 196–199
Lowndes, Mrs. Belloc 13
Ludlow Massacre 71

Macbeth 5
Macdonald, Ross 136, *137*
Mack Bolan 143
magazines 28
Malaeska 54–55
Manifest Destiny 56, 223
Mann Act 14
Marston, William Moulton 208
Martian novels 106–109, *108*
Martin, Dean 144
masked avengers 112–117, *123*, 160–161
Matt Helm 144
McCulley, Johnston 112–113
McWilliams, Carey 3
Mencken, H.L. 124, 131
Merriwell, Frank 36, 42, 45, 91
Mike Hammer 136–140, *139*, 220
Monsieur Lecoq 79
The Moonstone 87
Morrison, Frank *see* Spillane, Mickey
Mulford, Clarence E. 152
Munro, George 33, 42–43, 80
Munro, Norman 33, 43
Munsey, Frank 19, 33, 45–46, 96, 97, 106
Muscular Christianity 30–31

Nathan, George Jean 124, 131
National Police Gazette 17–20, *18*, 28, 113, 153, 221
Natty Bumppo 52; *see also* Leatherstocking
Necronomicon 198, 226
New York Herald 7, *25*
New York Journal 21
New York Sun 7
New York Tribune 7, 54
New York World 7, 20–21

Newgate prison stories 5
Newnes, George 26
Nick Carter 82–84, 87, 91, 92
novels, romance 29–32
novels, Western 147–152

obsessions, morbid 8–11
Operator #5 117, **119**
opium den 19, 189–190
Outcault, Richard F. 21

Pall Mall Gazette 13, 26
paper rationing 204
paperback books 210–213, **212**
Patten, Gilbert 36, 42
payment rates 37, 88, 101–102, 104, 106, 184, 223
penny awfuls, bloods, horribles 8
penny dreadful 3, 7
penny papers 5–7
Perelman, S.J. 181, 186, 226
Perry Mason 134–135
Phantom of the Opera 16
Philip Marlowe 135–136
Pinkerton Detective Agency 86–87, 130
Poe, Edgar Allen 9, 85, 86, 177, 197
Police Gazette see *National Police Gazette*
Popular Publications 15, 93, 97, 104, 115, 127, 141, 160, 174, 175, 183, 193, 200, 202
postal rates 24, 34, 91, 173
printing press 23–25, **23**
private eye 86
Prohibition 121–122
pseudonyms 55, 62, 63, 84, 102, 166, 183–184
Pulitzer, Joseph 7, 21
pulp literature defined 92–94
pulp reader profile 93
pulps, leading 97
pulps, opinions of 1, 3
pulps, specialized 97–98

Race Williams 128–130, **128**, 136
Raffles 90, 126
Raine, William Macleod 152
rape 12, 13–14, 16, 17, 30, 37, 46, 52, 53, 109, 147, 164, 220
Red Harvest 132
reporting, sensationalized 2–3, 6–8, 11–14, 20–21
Reynolds, George W. 30
Robeson, Kenneth 101, 118–120, 142
Robin Hood 8, 65, 66
Roe, Clifford G. 13
Rohmer, Sax 190–192
romance novels see novels, romance
romance pulps 161, 181–183
Rowlandson, Mary 51–52

The Saint 141, **141**
sales figures see circulation figures
Sally the Sleuth 143, 144
Sam Spade 133
science fiction 48–49
science fiction pulps 177–181
sensation fiction 30–31
sensationalized reporting see reporting, sensationalized

serial novels 100, 106, 112, 113, 173
Seth Jones 55
The Shadow 114–116
Shane 170
Shaw, Joseph Thompson 125–127
The Sheik 16
Shell Scott 143
Shelley, Mary Wollenstonecraft 16
Sheppard, Jack 8
Sherlock Holmes 85, 87–90, 121, 122, 190
shilling shocker 3, 7
shudder pulps see weird menace pulps
slick magazines 28, 92, 96, 98, 102, 168, 171, 205
The Smart Set 125, 131
Smith, Francis Schubael 41–42
spicy pulps 125, 143, 161, 183–187, **185**
Spillane, Mickey 136–140
sports pulps 174
Stagecoach 171
Standard Publications 97
Standish, Burt L. 42
Stead, W.T. 26
steam literature 24
Steeger, Henry 127, 175, 200
Stevens, Ann Sophia 54
Stoker, Bram 15–16, 198
story papers 25–26, 33, 43
Street, Francis Scott 41–42
Street & Smith 34–35, 41–42, 97
superheroes, pulp 117–118
swashbuckling 2, 29, 93, 112–113, 196
symbolism, phallic 30

Tarzan 106–107, 109–110
Taylor, Buck 62
television 205
Terrill, Roger 15
terror 14–15; see also fear
Terry Mack 127–129
Texas Ripper 12
The Thin Man 133
thrilling pulps 97, 117
Tousey, Frank 33, 43–45, **44**, 80
Turpin Dick 8, 65, 112
Twain, Mark 11, 190

Valentino, Rudolph 16
Varney the Vampire 8, 16, 30
Vidocq, Eugéne 86
Villette, John 5
The Virginian 148–152, **151**, 153

Ward, Arthur Henry see Rohmer, Sax
weird menace pulps 199–203
Weird Tales 194–199, **195**, 202
Wertham, William 209
Western frontier 50–51
Western novels see novels, Western
Western pulps 158–162, **159**
Westerns see films, Western
Wheeler, Edward Lytton 66–70, 72–73
Whetmore, Edward Jay 3
white slavery 13–14, 164, 165
Wilkinson, George 5
Williams, Tennessee 93

Wister, Owen 148–152
women detectives 142–143
Wonder Woman 207–208
Wright, Farnsworth 196, 199

yellow journalism 20–21
Yellow Kid 21
Yellow Peril literature 98, 188–194

Zorro 112–113, 114, 160

www.ingramcontent.com/pod-product-compliance
Lightning Source LLC
Chambersburg PA
CBHW081551300426
44116CB00015B/2845